THIS . . . IS
CBS

A CHRONICLE OF 60 YEARS

THE
PRENTICE HALL
CORPORATE LIBRARY

THIS . . . IS
CBS
A CHRONICLE OF 60 YEARS

ROBERT SLATER

Prentice Hall
Englewood Cliffs, New Jersey 07632

Library of Congress Cataloging-in-Publication Data

Slater, Robert. (date)
    This—is CBS: a chronicle of sixty years / by Robert Slater.
        p.   cm.
    Bibliography: p.
    Includes index.
    ISBN 0-13-919234-4
    1. CBS Inc.—History.   I. Title.
PN1992.92.C38S57   1988
384.54'0973—dc19

Editorial/production supervision
  and interior design: SOPHIE PAPANIKOLAOU
Senior acquisitions editor: JEFFREY A. KRAMES, III
Cover design: LUNDGREN GRAPHICS, LTD.
Manufacturing buyer: MARY ANN GLORIANDE

©1988 by Prentice-Hall, Inc.
A Division of Simon & Schuster
Englewood Cliffs, New Jersey 07632

The publisher offers discounts on this book when ordered
in bulk quantities. For more information, write:

Special Sales/College Marketing
Prentice-Hall, Inc.
College Technical and Reference Division
Englewood Cliffs, NJ 07632

Printed in the United States of America
10 9 8 7 6 5 4 3 2 1

ISBN   0-13-919234-4

Prentice-Hall International (UK) Limited, *London*
Prentice-Hall of Australia Pty. Limited, *Sydney*
Prentice-Hall Canada Inc., *Toronto*
Prentice-Hall Hispanoamericana, S.A., *Mexico*
Prentice-Hall of India Private Limited, *New Delhi*
Prentice-Hall of Japan, Inc., *Tokyo*
Simon & Schuster Asia Pte. Ltd., *Singapore*
Editora Prentice-Hall do Brasil, Ltda., *Rio de Janeiro*

CONTENTS

AUTHOR'S NOTE

The idea for this book jelled in my mind soon after I had completed *The Titans of Takeover,* a series of portraits of the major players in the business takeover game. One chapter in that book, also published by Prentice Hall in the winter of 1987, focused on the 1985 takeover threat undertaken by Ted Turner against CBS. As *Titans* was nearing publication, CBS passed through a headline-grabbing crisis (in the fall of 1986) brought about by CBS President Thomas Wyman's proposal to sell the company to Coca-Cola. It occurred to me that this episode was but one of many, many colorful vignettes in the sixty-year life of CBS and that there was a wonderfully rich story to tell—from beginning to end, or at least to 1988, a fitting date as it marked the network's sixtieth anniversary.

A vast literature exists on the subject of American broadcasting. My task, in setting out to write a historical narrative of CBS, was to probe that literature—in books and magazines and newspaper articles—and glean the most significant and colorful material. I sought to buttress that search with interviews. I wanted to speak to those individuals who, by virtue of their many years of experience and/or their particular jobs, could offer their own insights into CBS.

I am grateful to all those who agreed to be interviewed, some of whom I saw more than once. In the order of my meetings with them, they are Ann Luzatto, Daniel Schorr, Bruno Wassertheil, Ze'ev Chafets, Michael Elkins, Bob Simon, Alan Alter, George Schweitzer, Av Westin, Mike Dann, Frank Stanton, Burton "Bud" Benjamin, Sam Roberts, Roger Colloff, Douglas Edwards, David Buksbaum, Ernest Leiser, Robert "Shad" Northshield, David Boies, Fred Friendly, Tom Wyman, Phyllis Dubrow and Dallas Townsend. There were others whom I saw, who asked not to be identified.

I especially want to thank Alan Alter, the deputy foreign editor at CBS. Alan gave of his time in showing me through the back corridors of the CBS Broadcast Center, a fascinating experience and one that helped me understand the subject that much more.

I made it clear to CBS's officials that I was not interested in writing an "official" version of events, but that I would appreciate help in collecting information. I am happy to note that I received good cooperation from those officials, and I was permitted to talk with many of the people whom I wished to see save for a few. My requests to see Bill Paley and Laurence Tisch were turned down: Paley declined on the grounds that he was engaged in the writing of his second set of memoirs; Tisch passed word through a spokesman that he simply did not want to meet with writers at the time (the summer of 1987).

I wish also to thank others who provided support for this project. Martin Silverstein of the CBS Photo Archives was of great help in allowing me to look through the large photo collection and choose a number of photographs for this book. Andrea Sachs of *Time* magazine was of enormous technical assistance, aiding me in transcribing numerous interviews. Leslie Dickstein served as an invaluable research aide, locating books and articles about CBS, and suggesting a number of interesting research paths for me to pursue.

In each of my book projects, my editors and colleagues in the Jerusalem Time-Life Bureau have been encouraging and helpful, and I have benefited from their insights and their assistance. I thank them one and all. I especially thank Jean Max who provided important technical assistance.

From the moment I mentioned to Jeff Krames, my editor at Prentice Hall, that I wanted to do a historical narrative of CBS, I received only encouragement, the kind that ought to make any author happy and grateful. Throughout the period of research and writing, Jeff displayed an unwavering enthusiasm for what I was doing. I express my gratitude to him as well as to Sophie Papanikolaou, who served as production editor, and Sally Ann Bailey, who was the copyeditor.

I reserve the last word for my family. As with my previous books, they have functioned virtually as a collective "co-author," my wife reading early drafts and commenting on them, the children peppering me with questions about CBS. Glued as they are to the television set nightly, my immediate family needed no indoctrination in the subject of my book. Still, they exhibited great interest in what I was doing, leading me to believe that, given their own excitement about the personalities and programs that are part of the CBS story, many others would be curious about Bill Paley's child as well. To my collective "co-author," I dedicate this book—to my wife Elinor and to my children, Miriam, Adam, and Rachel.

Robert Slater
January 1988

CREDIT LIST

The author is grateful to the following for granting permission to quote from:

"America Inside Out," by David Schoenbrun, McGraw-Hill Book Co. Copyright © 1984 by David Schoenbrun. Reprinted by permission of the author and the author's agents, Scott Meredith Literary Agency, Inc., 845 Third Avenue, New York, New York 10022.

"The Reason-Why Man" (March 13, 1964) and "The Most Intimate Medium" (October 14, 1966); reprinted by permission from *Time* magazine.

"Sign Off: The Last Days of Television," by Edwin Diamond. The MIT Press. Copyright © 1982 by Edwin Diamond.

"Look Now, Pay Later: The Rise of Network Broadcasting," by Laurence Bergreen. Doubleday & Co., Inc.

"The Media In America," by John Tebbel. Thomas Y. Crowell Co.

People magazine, for using excerpts from an interview with William S. Paley in the April 8, 1979 edition.

"The Electric Mirror: Politics in an Age of Television," by Sig Mickelson. Dodd, Mead and Company, Inc.

Columbia University Oral History Research Office: The Reminiscences of Arthur Judson, Hans V. Kaltenborn, Howard Barlow, and Fred Friendly.

"Takeover: The New Wall Street Warriors: The Men, The Money, The Impact," by Moira Johnston, Arbor House.

From an article published July 18, 1948 by *The New York Times.* Copyright © 1948 by The New York Times Company. Reprinted by permission.

"American History, American Television: Interpreting the Video Past," John E. O'Connor. Frederick Ungar Publishing Co., Copyright © 1983 John E. O'Connor (ed.).

"Due to Circumstances Beyond Our Control," by Fred Friendly. Random House. Copyright © 1967, 1968 by Fred Friendly.

"Minute by Minute . . . ," by Don Hewitt. Random House. Copyright © 1985 by Don Hewitt and CBS, Inc.

"Forever Lucy: The Life of Lucille Ball," Joe Morell and Edward Z. Epstein. Lyle Stuart Inc.

"The Powers That Be," by David Halberstam. Alfred A. Knopf, Inc. Copyright © 1975, 1976, 1979 by David Halberstam.

INTRODUCTION

There was a time, far back in the distant past, when the human species passed each 24-hour period without listening to a radio or without gazing into a television screen. There was a time. Tell that to a youngster of the 1980s who spends 4 to 6 hours each day absorbed in the latest adventure series, cartoon, or miniseries, and you will get an odd stare, as if you had raised the subject of the dinosaurs or something even more prehistoric.

Yes, there was a time. Alas, it has long gone, and will probably never return. This century has become both the age of radio and the age of television. Life began to revolve around the radio in the 1930s. The nation stopped for whatever it was doing to listen to "Amos 'n' Andy." That included the president of the United States. Nothing seemed nearly as important than to tune in to the antics of this highly entertaining pair.

Then, in the early 1950s, life began to focus on television, and it proved even more addictive than radio. In that decade, viewers watched "I Love Lucy"; in the 1960s, "Beverly Hillbillies"; in the 1970s, "All in the Family"; and more recently, "Dallas." A nation held its breath in the early 1950s in expectation of when Lucy would deliver her baby. Thirty years later, it waited with growing impatience to find out "Who Shot JR?" We had all become, in that wonderful phrase, couch potatoes, mesmerized, riveted to the television screen. From radio, and even more from television, several generations of Americans acquired their values, their life-styles, and their modes of behavior.

The broadcasting industry, therefore, has become a dominant part of our lives. It comprises the men and women who choose what entertainment programs to air each season, who decide how the news will be presented to us. Within that broadcasting industry, one institution stands above the rest, the giant of the radio networks and later television networks, the Columbia Broadcasting System, or, as it is more commonly known, CBS.

This is the story of CBS, one of America's most renowned enterprises, the network which in so many ways set standards in both entertainment and news. It is the story of the people of CBS, entertainers like Jack Benny, Bing Crosby, Arthur Godfrey, and Ed Sullivan, and broadcast journalists like Ed Murrow, William Shirer, Walter Cronkite, and Dan Rather. It is the story of the builders of CBS as well, first and foremost Bill Paley, the founder and shaper of the institution who, sixty years later, remained the captain of the ship; of Paul Kesten, Frank Stanton, and others. It is the story of an enterprise which grew and grew and grew so that by the 1980s its sales approached the $5 billion mark.

For its first four decades, little attention was paid to the network, little was written about it. Its stars, of course, basked in the glare of publicity. But not CBS. That changed in the 1970s and the 1980s. The public's interests changed. In later years, the public wanted to know about other people connected with the network, the news personalities as well as the business executives behind the scenes. At the same time, curiosity was increasingly aroused about the media. Who were these people with so much power? How did they make decisions about what to put on the air? By the 1970s and 1980s, that curiosity had proved nearly insatiable about the broadcasting industry in general—and CBS in particular.

Few companies have aroused so much public interest as CBS in the past few years. Newspaper stories about the network invariably get first-page treatment. CBS news executives have found publishers for their memoirs. The publishers invariably ask them to spice the text up with as much inside gossip and infighting as possible. Ed Murrow has had a pair of biographers as has Bill Paley. Personalities at the network have been the subjects of books, from Burns and Allen to Ed Sullivan, from Amos 'n' Andy to Jackie Gleason. Some have written their own memoirs, Harry Reasoner, Eric Sevareid, Dan Rather, and Mike Wallace. Bill Paley has written his memoirs and is, at this writing, working on a second volume. There have been books on aspects of the company, most notably one focusing on CBS News. When someone—Sally Quinn—tried to make a splash on CBS as a co-anchor of the morning program, and couldn't, she even wrote a book about her experiences. And there are several books just about CBS's most successful program of the 1980s, "60 Minutes."

Why all the public attention? In a sense, the answer is self-evident. Newspaper editors, magazine writers, and publishers alike fill the news-stands and bookstores with folklore about CBS—because, quite simply, the public is interested. But it is more than that. Image is very important at CBS, or more properly self-image. That is perfectly understandable, given the public exposure of the company. CBS is like the movie actress who wakes up in the morning and wants to make sure that she looks as beautiful as possible for her public. But it is a task made difficult, nearly impossible, some would say, by the fact that CBS is not just one movie actress, but hundreds, if not thousands of different, sometimes contradic-tory voices.

CBS is not the CIA. People talk. Correction. People talk a great deal. In few American institutions do the employees of a company spend so much time explaining, defending, promoting, arguing about the place as at CBS. Members of the CBS community, many of them at least, are in love with the place. Many have come to believe, and quite rightly, that there is something special about the air, the atmosphere. And, not sur-prisingly, they want to shout about it from the rooftops. Pride in the net-work is deep and significant. The pride explains the excessive verbiage, and it explains the pain that so many have felt in the last few years when the company had to recast itself into a tighter ship.

With all that overflowing pride, and with all the attention showered on CBS, it is no wonder that so many aspects of the CBS story have been sketched in public. Yet, to my delight, as I contemplated how to sum up this incredible institution in a book, no one had yet chronicled the net-work throughout its entire sixty-year period. What the public has thus far are bits and pieces of the most exciting media institution in the world. It does not yet have the story fashioned from start to finish, news and entertainment, personalities in front of the cameras and behind the scenes, the shaky early days of pioneering, and the later days of conglom-eration and setback. *This . . . Is CBS* is offered as a coherent look at the network.

It is, what I call, a narrative history, not a comprehensive history, not an account of everything that went on at CBS. I have selected those people, those facts, those episodes that struck me in my research as sig-nificant and pulled them together into a chronological whole. The reader who is a careful follower of CBS will spot the lacunae. I do not mention every entertainment program, every news documentary. Rather, I have sought to take those aspects of the company that played a meaningful part in the development of radio and television—and of CBS itself.

There might be a temptation to look at the network's sixty years in "rise and fall" terms. But we are lacking sufficient perspective to do that.

We can chronicle the rise—indeed CBS began its climb in the late 1920s and early 1930s and continued into the late 1970s, even early 1980s. But, while the last few years have been grave for the network, as takeover artists have taken their toll, it would be a mistake to conjure up an image of a network that is going under. This is still a multibillion-dollar operation, and while it had become in 1987 a very different place from the one just five years before, it was still CBS. No greater symbol of that continuity was the fact that the man who founded the company in 1928 was still around in the winter of 1987, holding on to the title of chairman, trying to reinvigorate the child from whom he could not separate himself.

Our story begins in the 1920s.

one

"That Miserable Radio Adventure, That Mere Shoestring."

This might have been the story of a cigar-maker, or no story at all, had a young American of Russian ancestry not veered from the family cigar business in order to enter the intriguing, burgeoning world of broadcasting after World War I. He veered, so it appears, because he believed that radio might prove a useful medium for advertising cigars. That tells us a great deal about William S. Paley. As a young man, he had, as far as one can tell, no grand or singular vision, no long-range goal to build a vast communications empire. That was not surprising. No one in those days knew the commercial boundaries of the magical little box called radio. No one could have forecast its incredible popularity nor could anyone have imagined that within three decades, radio would give way to television as the nation's most important source of home entertainment. In time, the broadcasting industry—comprising radio and then television—would revolutionize the daily habits of Americans and the rest of the world.

At the beginning of our story is a young man of Russian Jewish ancestry, born to a family used to wealth. The men in the family would find themselves torn over what to do with that wealth. At times, they dreamed,

---

as did Bill Paley, of retiring early to a life of leisure and quiet. But these were only dreams. Their hearts were in their work.

Bill Paley was born in Chicago on September 28, 1901. His sister Blanche was born four years later. She received more attention from their mother, Goldie, than did her older brother. Convinced that his mother did not find him attractive, Bill developed an inferiority complex: he actually believed he was unappealing in some way. At the same time, Bill developed a strong, positive relationship with his father, Sam Paley. Listening to his father talk about his cigar business, young Bill was eager to please him; going to work in the cigar business was one obvious way. Spending his summers working for his father in the Congress Cigar factory, young Bill swept the floors, ran errands, and absorbed everything about the business that he could. He made a special point of learning how to put the bands around the cigars and how to mix tobaccos in the "kitchen." Each day Bill ran off to the post office to purchase federal bonding stamps that went on each cigar box.

Despite a mixed record at school, he displayed an enthusiasm for reading, though school itself was not very pleasurable for him. Perhaps significantly for his future career as a broadcasting executive, he had a good ear for music. After he attended a Mischa Elman concert, young Bill decided to become a violinist. That career goal was quickly crushed by a violin teacher who refused to teach him, because, the teacher claimed, Bill could not sing on pitch. Undeterred, the youngster learned how to play piano, became adept at it, and even toyed with becoming a pianist. But he soon tired of the instrument.

Whether it was a sense of mischief in the young man or his father's belief in the virtues of a military education, young Bill, at age 16, was sent off to complete his high school education at the Western Military Academy in Alton, Illinois. By now, he did well academically, earning two years of high school credit in a single year. Thus, in 1918, he was admitted to the University of Chicago when he was only 17 years old. With the United States in the war, Bill was eager to enlist, but his father talked him out of such a step. Workers struck the Paley family's cigar factory in Chicago, and though such strikes had happened frequently, this new turmoil led Bill's father to investigate the prospects of opening a factory in the East.

A year later the family moved to Philadelphia. Forced to rush back to Chicago when his father Isaac died, Sam left Bill to establish the new factory. A month later, Sam arrived in Philadelphia and Bill entered the University of Pennsylvania's Wharton School of Business. Unlike many other college students, Bill had already decided on a career. Accordingly, getting good grades seemed beside the point. Bill concentrated on the school's social life. He joined a fraternity, Zeta Beta Tau, and during his senior year became its president. During his summers he worked for his father. After graduation in the spring of 1922, he worked full time in the cigar factory. Sam tended to the cigar manufacturing and Uncle Jake Paley handled the books and sales. The cigar business did well, and soon the Paley's Congress Cigar Company operated twelve factories in Pennsylvania, Delaware, and New Jersey. Bill became vice president and advertising manager; Sam and Jake were grooming him to take over the business one day.

In that post–World War I period, the temporary end to international violence enabled the earth's peoples to do far more than supply cigars and earn pots of money. The previous century's enormous progress in connecting distant parts of the world, whether by railroad, telegraph, or telephone, had been briefly interrupted by the war. But once the fighting stopped, those same impulses to draw humankind closer together were again racing. What seemed like magic to many, a communications revolution was taking root at the same time that young Mr. Paley was learning the cigar trade. It was a revolution, because in one more way, the world was getting smaller. The building of highways, the laying of railroad track, and the charting of the skies had diminished the time it took to travel great distances. And now, the new media of mass communications—radio and, later, television—would connect all sorts of people, once too remote to communicate with one another.

Beginning in the 1920s, radio became the dominant piece of furniture in the American home. And why not? Nothing was quite like it. Until radio came along, one could only listen to a Mozart or Brahms concert by purchasing tickets and then journeying to the concert hall. Until radio was invented, it was unimaginable that someone living in the United States might hear the brilliant oratory of a Winston Churchill unless he traveled overseas and was in London's House of Commons at just the right time. Yet, this tiny box could provide the concert and the Churchill oratory without the listener having to venture out of his living room!

The first radio broadcast came in 1920 and, though the first radios were simple (they sold for the grand price of $10), Americans greeted the new gadgets enthusiastically. One who did so was William S. Paley. Undeniably, the arrival of radio had a profound impact upon the young man, then in his midtwenties. Although the crystal set that a friend showed him, in retrospect, seemed primitive, Bill was immediately entranced. The friend adjusted the earphones and, suddenly and magically, music appeared to come out of thin air. Recalling the enthralling moment fifty years later, Paley wrote that he had been "dumbfounded." (1) The next step was to obtain a crystal set for himself but the stores didn't have them yet. So he asked someone to build a radio for him. Once that was done, he frequently stayed up nights taking in the sounds of voices and music from the enchanting little instrument.

Hundreds of thousands of Americans were doing the same thing. In 1921, only 50,000 radios existed, but just a year later, the figure had leaped to 600,000! Accommodating the growing listening audience, the number of radio stations increased from only 30 in 1922 to 556 the next year. When Calvin Coolidge triumphed in the 1924 presidential election, 10 million Americans listened to the results over 3 million radios as radio sales rose by 250 percent, a record gain at that time. But other than the quadrennial hoopla of an American election, radio focused little on politics, devoting most of its energies and time to entertainment. Radio and later television addressed the question constantly: were the airwaves best used for entertainment or for disseminating information? The rationale for entertainment was based on the premise that listeners and viewers enjoyed being entertained and were therefore more likely to purchase the advertisers' products. To become enterprises that were considered serious, however, radio and television should, the alternative argument ran, focus on public affairs and news. Although the debate continued for years, radio and television were dominated by entertainment programs as they were deemed essentially advertising media. Public affairs and news programs, incapable of reaching large audiences for the most part, were grudgingly offered in small doses.

Even if radio stations had been interested in reporting politics and other news on a regular basis, they wouldn't have done so because newspapers were considered the proper vehicle for getting such information across to the public. Indeed, in 1924 the Associated Press insisted that its presidential election returns be available to newspapers only. A radio station that broadcast AP election results did so at the risk of being fined by the wire service! If the vast potential for transmitting news over radio had not yet been realized, the little box did possess an unquestionable capacity for encouraging consumer demand. Radio listeners, by some strange alchemy, could be turned into customers for all sorts of products. Advertising in newspapers ($800 million in 1929) was still far greater than on radio, but between 1927 and 1929, the years when Bill Paley was getting acquainted with radio, advertising revenue on this new medium grew from $4 million to $40 million. The natural appeal of radio as a means of luring listeners to buy products was becoming increasingly obvious to many. None would sense it more than did Bill Paley.

It was in the summer of 1925 that the young man decided to test radio as an advertising medium. Left in charge of the cigar business during the absence of his father Sam and Uncle Jake, who were in Europe, Bill took advantage of his temporary authority to arrange for La Palina cigars, the pride and joy of the Paley business, to be advertised over WCAU, the local Philadelphia radio station, on a one-hour program called the "La Palina Hour." Although each broadcast cost the Paley family only $50, Uncle Jake's frugality led him upon his return to explode at his extravagant nephew, ordering this "foolishness" ceased at once. Jake had no time for this new playtoy called radio. Reluctantly, Bill obeyed. Then, a funny thing happened. Over lunch a few weeks later, Sam Paley was forced to acknowledge to his son that people had been stopping him on the street to ask why the "La Palina Hour" had left the airwaves so abruptly. Until that crucial luncheon, crucial because it was about to launch Bill Paley on a career in broadcasting, the young man had sought in vain to convince Uncle Jake that radio possessed a mysterious capacity for getting people to buy a product. Grudgingly, Jake confessed to Sam that Bill had all along been thinking soundly: some of Jake's friends, Jake noted in further confession, had also been wondering what had happened to the program. Owning up to his misjudgment, Bill's uncle saw to it that the "La Palina Hour" was quickly restored to the airwaves.

There then arose the question of just how deeply committed to radio Congress Cigar should become. Radio stations larger than WCAU soon turned to the cigar firm, enjoying as it did a reputation of being a thriving enterprise, to seek its advertising dollar. The elder Paleys needed little coaxing. Thanks to Bill, they had been witness to a plain and simple truth: radio had the capacity to reach audiences far larger than any single newspaper. Although they had invested half a million dollars in print advertising, the Paleys quickly realized that the "La Palina Hour," costing only $50 a broadcast, had a more substantial impact on Congress Cigar sales than did newspaper advertisements. So when his close friend, Philadelphia building contractor Jerome Louchheim, asked Sam if Congress Cigar would advertise the La Palina cigar on a radio network over which Louchheim had just won control, Sam was willing to consider the idea seriously.

At first Sam had mixed feelings. He was only too aware that commercial radio was still in its infancy and had not yet attracted large businesses such as Congress Cigar as advertisers. Questions arose: would the advertising really pay? Who was out there listening? What proof was there that radio was indeed a moneymaking machine? That year's sagging cigar sales eased some doubts, permitting Sam Paley to feel that there wasn't much to lose. Presented with a contract that called for Congress Cigar to pay $50,000 for thirteen weeks of radio advertising, Jake grimaced, parsimonious as ever. Still, the contract was signed. Asked to organize a 30-minute radio program that would become the vehicle for the advertisements, Bill put together "The La Palina Smoker," which featured an orchestra, a female vocalist ("Miss La Palina"), and a comedian who doubled as master of ceremonies.

The network on which the program would be broadcast was called the United Independent Broadcasters. UIB had come to life in the wake of a personal disappointment suffered by impressario and concert master Arthur Judson. Upon learning that RCA czar David Sarnoff had planned to begin his own radio network, Judson approached him with a proposal. Until then, radio stations had been using artists free of charge, creating fear among concert impressarios like Judson that concerts would gradually lose their audiences. Seeking to rescue performers from eventual penury, Judson asked Sarnoff to let him organize a bureau that would provide to the new network leading performers who would be paid for their radio performances. Rather than sell a client to just one radio station, Judson realized that it would be far more profitable to place the artist with an entire network of radio stations such as Sarnoff was creating. Seemingly approving of the idea, Sarnoff asked Judson to prepare something in writing for him. Judson did so. He also formed his own firm, the Judson Radio Program Corporation, in anticipation of placing his musical artist-clients with radio stations. After Judson submitted his plan to Sarnoff in early 1926, Sarnoff read it with apparently great interest. If it was within his power once he organized his network, Sarnoff assured, he would certainly put Judson in charge of the programs and of supplying the artists.

Naturally, when Sarnoff had actually organized the National Broadcasting Company later that year, Judson sought him out, asking what he planned to do about his proposal. Nothing, Sarnoff said curtly, leaving Judson livid. Recovering from the blow only slightly, Judson fumed that he would set up his own network. That induced Sarnoff to lean back in his chair and laugh hilariously. "You can't do it," he insisted. "I have just signed a contract to take one million dollars' worth of long lines from the telephone company. In any event, you couldn't get any wires even if you had a broadcasting station. It can't be done." (2)

But Arthur Judson decided that it could be done, and that he would do it. With three partners and an initial investment of $75,000, he founded the United Independent Broadcasters network. It was no accident that the word "independent" was chosen; Judson and his colleagues wanted to send a loud and clear signal that they were protesting RCA's monopoly of the airwaves. Because UIB eventually became CBS, and because NBC's David Sarnoff had given Arthur Judson the brush-off, it has become part of the folklore of the broadcast industry that Sarnoff inadvertently set in motion the creation of CBS! Had Sarnoff reacted more warmly toward Judson's proposal, there might not have been a Columbia Broadcasting System.

Despite overwhelming odds, Judson and two associates, Major J. Andrew White and George Coats, undertook the rather formidable task of breathing life into UIB. One of the true pioneers of radio, White had organized the first commercial broadcast, the Dempsey-Carpentier fight on July 2, 1921. Having taken a vow to become abstinent, White always wore a white carnation as a symbol of that vow. Coats had been a promoter and salesman of paving machinery.

Soon after the network was incorporated on January 27, 1927, Coats convinced Leon Levy, who along with his brother Ike, ran WCAU, to sign up the Philadelphia radio station as UIB's first affiliate. During the network's first year, Coats signed up sixteen affiliate stations. Each station was to supply ten hours of air time a week—in return for which it would be paid $50 an hour, or $500 a week per station, at an annual cost to UIB of $416,000. In addition, Judson & Co. bought a moribund low-power station owned by the Atlantic Broadcasting Company (hence, for many years, the call letters of this key CBS station, ironically, were WABC!). Considering that UIB had little prospect of securing advertising to sponsor the time or of obtaining the needed phone lines to pipe the broadcasts to the affiliates, the $416,000 commitment posed considerable risk.

The most pressing problem, however, was the lack of telephone lines. Applying to the telephone company, Judson and his associates were told that all the lines were in use and it would take another three years before new ones could be furnished to UIB. Fortunately for the UIB management, that seemingly overwhelming problem was overcome by some astute lobbying in Washington and, within a matter of hours, the lines were made available to UIB.

With little hope of raising the $100,000 a month it would cost to operate the network, Judson and his colleagues sought, in today's parlance, a "white knight," a company that would buy UIB out and would do so in a friendly manner by leaving the management intact. During the summer of 1927, Judson turned to the well-heeled Columbia Phonograph Company, which, as luck would have it, was interested in founding its own radio network. For a number of years Columbia had led the field in record pressing, but radio, which could broadcast the sounds of music far more effectively than could those scratchy, tinny records, had fast become a competitor. Louis B. Sterling, Columbia's owner, had watched as Sarnoff's RCA had absorbed the Victor Talking Machine Company. To meet the threat of this now-larger rival, Sterling thought of purchasing a radio network. Judson's UIB happened to be eager for such a white knight, and so for $163,000, Columbia purchased the network's operating rights. In return, Judson agreed to change the name of the network to the Columbia Phonograph Broadcasting System. The $163,000 was an incredibly high price, considering that UIB was still very much a paper operation.

The network debuted on September 18, a Sunday that counts among the major milestones of CBS history, or more precisely, prehistory. Four days later, Leon Levy married Sam Paley's daughter Blanche, forming a family connection between UIB and the Congress Cigar Company. The previous eight months had been most troublesome for Arthur Judson and his team. But the opening program that evening gave a sudden new impetus to assure the network's survival. Judson's colleague Major White gleefully sent word to the affiliates how they would know when to switch from local to network programming: "You will hear the orchestra or musical instrument melt into the strains of 'Hail, Columbia'—then the announcer's voice saying something to this effect: 'This is the . . . hour on the Columbia Chain, a program which is coming to you from the New York studio.'"

On that gala premiere the network's own 22-piece orchestra played with Howard Barlow conducting. Showing a certain amount of nerve, Barlow asked to be paid $15,000 a year to direct the orchestra, and was pleasantly shocked to learn that the network had agreed to that generous sum. Informed that the Berkey and Gay furniture company had agreed to sponsor the program, Barlow chose a woodsy theme for his musical selections, including "Tales of the Vienna Woods" and "To a Wild Rose," the latter tune a reference to rosewood. Barlow had looked for an exotic piece with which to open the program. Originally, he had chosen the ballet music from the "Ballet Egyptienne," Egypt being the home of ivory and ebony. But just 15 or 20 minutes before airtime, Berkey and Gay backed out, too late for Barlow to drop the woodsy music. The network chose artists from the Metropolitan Opera Company to perform the Deems Taylor–Edna St. Vincent Millay opera, "The King's Henchman," a signal that UIB planned to maintain high musical standards. Parts of the broadcast were decidedly makeshift. Employees from the flagship station WOR realized to their chagrin at the last moment that the control room would not be ready in time. They were forced to monitor the broadcast from the only soundproofed space available—WOR's men's room!

The debut came off smoothly save for one unexpected glitch—a thunderstorm broke some wires, delaying the start of the broadcast for 15 minutes. When the program did begin, thousands within listening range of sixteen cities heard their first radio opera. Not perfectly, though. At times, due to heavy static, the broadcast came through only faintly. That led John Wallace, the correspondent for *Radio Broadcast,* to write that the evening of September 18, "witnessed your humble correspondent, tear-stained and disillusioned, vowing to abandon for all time radio and all its work and pomps. We have since recovered and will go on with our story." (3)

As remarkable an achievement as the gala premiere was, it proved incredibly costly, plunging UIB to the brink of bankruptcy. Sterling had understood that there would be losses during his first few months at the helm but nothing as large as occurred. As of the debut, UIB had sold only one program hour to an advertiser. All that it could do was to fall back on Columbia's $163,000, but that disappeared quickly. Advertisers experimented with UIB but then quickly shifted over to NBC. Without an alternative, Arthur Judson and Major White approached Betty Fleischmann Holmes, who was an old friend of Judson's, a board member of the New York Philharmonic, and, most important, heiress to the Fleischmann yeast fortune, only to discover that she was aboard ship in mid-Atlantic. No matter. The kindly woman provided $45,000, which went to pay AT&T for its long-line service.

Then in December the Columbia Phonograph Company, which had retained the right to cancel on a month's notice, opted out, having invested $300,000 altogether. It sold the operating rights back to UIB for a cash payment of $10,000 plus thirty hours of free broadcasting. UIB was permitted to keep the name Columbia, a decision that at the time held little significance. The word "Phonograph" was deleted, and so the new on-the-air name of the network became, as we know it today, the Columbia Broadcasting System—CBS!

When the payroll could not be met, Arthur Judson poured his heart out to WCAU owners Leon and Isaac Levy, who appealed to their friend, Philadelphia builder Jerome Louchheim, finally convincing him to buy an interest in the network. Louchheim had constructed all the subways in Philadelphia. While he saw commercial prospects in radio, colleagues sought to warn him against investing in the small network. "Now, Mr. Louchheim," his lawyer said to him, "you are putting half a million dollars in this thing. Next month, you put another half million, a month after that another half million, and it is just a bottomless barrel, I warn you." Louchheim apparently had his own reasons for investing, viewing the purchase of UIB as a political asset as much as a business gamble. It seemed that Senator William Scott Vare of Louchheim's home state of Pennsylvania was influential in letting subway contracts. Consequently, Judson and Coats had sold Louchheim on the benefits of owning a radio network that could be used to help reelect Vare. To his despondent lawyer, Louchheim roared: "Whose money is it? Give me the pen." (4)

On November 7, Louchheim was elected chairman of the board of directors. The Levys purchased a smaller amount of shares in UIB at the same time. Altogether the three men invested $135,000. Immediately thereafter, they sent a $100,000 check to AT&T to assure that the long-line service would continue. Louchheim had no luck in turning the network around. During UIB's first full year, it had net sales of $176,737, but expenses adding up to $396,803—a net loss of $220,066.

In an act born as much out of desperation as nerve, Leon Levy and Major White marched off to the sixteen affiliates with a new plan to save the network. Until now, the affiliates were receiving $500 a week in network guarantees, a sum Columbia simply could no longer afford. Levy and White wanted the affiliates to agree to drop these guarantees. In new contracts that Levy and White asked the affiliates to sign, they would receive payment only for sponsored network programs which they aired. Sensing that UIB's survival and their fates were inextricably linked, the affiliates bowed to the network's request.

But, with no sponsors clamoring at UIB's door, its situation remained grim. So much so that the network's hapless leadership no longer wondered whether survival was possible, but merely when the best time would be to abandon the obviously sinking ship. The network was still $1 million in the hole, leading Louchheim to ask Ike Levy rather forlornly in August 1928 at which point they should call it quits. Despondently, as if he knew that the patient was soon going to die but could not bring himself to pull the plug, Ike answered that they should keep the network going for ten more days. It all seemed so irrelevant. No one appeared to want the comatose network, not even Leon Levy, who when asked, gave the rather lame excuse that he was not prepared to move away from Philadelphia. However, when seven of the final ten days had passed, an event occurred that surely qualified as a miracle. Arriving in the mail that day was an advertising contract worth $750,000 from Vitaphone, a subsidiary of Warner Brothers. Had that contract reached UIB just three days later, the network would have gone out of business.

Even with this last-minute influx of treasure, the network did not seem worth saving. So it was time for Jerome Louchheim, weary of his sagging investment, to look for someone with deep pockets. Through Leon Levy, he turned to the Paley family, approaching Sam during the fall.

Perhaps it was not the best sales technique, but Louchheim acknowledged that the network's books were in a mess and all that he wanted to do was to get this lemon of a network off his hands. "You at least have a cigar to advertise," Louchheim said to Sam, "and you can make some use out of it. I can't use it. I have nothing even to try to sell over it." (5) Sam would have none of the deal. But another Paley expressed interest, someone who had a million dollars burning a hole in his pocket, a restless young man who could cavalierly dismiss the financial hardships of UIB, sensing as he did radio's great potential.

Young Bill Paley was prepared to risk the entire fortune, acquired by selling his Congress Cigar stock, on acquiring Louchheim's interest in the network. But what if it would take more than his fortune to pull the network out of its doldrums? Just what was involved? Bill had no way of knowing. Nor did he know whether Louchheim would even consider selling the network to someone so inexperienced. Still, he planned to find out.

He went directly to Louchheim, notifying the Philadelphia builder that he wanted an option to purchase a good part of his UIB stock. Bill asked for just over 50 percent; he wanted to gain absolute control of the company. Before coming to an acceptable price, the two men agreed that 50.3 percent would be transferred to Paley. However, Louchheim demanded $200 a share, or $503,000. Paley breathed a sigh of relief at having to shell out only part of his funds. He was under no illusions that his investment would be confined to that sum. And indeed he had to agree, as part of the buyout of Louchheim's stock, to put another $100,000 in acceptable securities with AT&T—to replace the similar-sized bond Louchheim had put up for its wire services. Before he signed the papers with Louchheim, Paley won agreement from the builder to place Louchheim's remaining shares in a voting trust for five years. One key provision of the deal was that the voting trustee would have to support Paley-nominated board members, assuring that Bill Paley, in taking over the company's presidency, would encounter no board opposition to his policies. Louchheim and Paley signed an option contract on September 19 by which Paley agreed to pay $45,000 at once: the option was to last ten days, and Paley would lose the sum if he did not go ahead with the rest of the arrangement. The history of CBS effectively began with the September 19, 1928 date.

It was a most incredible bargain that Mr. Paley, just eight days away from his twenty-seventh birthday, had struck. He had just won the right to purchase a company that within the next two decades would grow into a major force in the communications industry and that in the period of the 1950s and 1960s would become the predominant broadcasting institution of its age. But, at the time, all that achievement was light years away, unbenownst to this young man who was about to make a huge gamble.

He had one more obstacle to overcome—his father. Bill regarded his $1 million as "sacrosanct" (his own word) and as such would only consider using it if his father, as the family's business patron, acquiesced. It would not be easy. As thrilling as the purchase of UIB would be, young Paley worried that his bold deed might cause his father anguish. "Our relationship," he wrote in his memoirs, "was then a crucial thing in my life." (6) Had Sam and Jake not sold Congress Cigar in 1927 to the Porto Rican–American Tobacco Company for nearly $30 million, Bill might have felt guilty about appearing to abandon the family business. However, after the sale, Congress Cigar was no longer the family business. Sam and Jake were under contract to the new owners, but Bill was not. Beyond that, he had tired of the cigar business. It lacked glamor, and it lacked the opportunity to meet important people. Bill wanted both the glamor and the connections and hanging around a tobacco factory was not the best way to obtain them. Still, he could not sunder himself from the to-bacco business that quickly; he envisioned taking a leave of absence for a few months, putting UIB into shape, and then turning it over to profes-sional managers, enabling him to return to Philadelphia and the cigar business. Now, approaching his father, Bill felt nervous, as well he should have: Sam believed in the tangible side of life: land, factories, physical products. UIB was none of those, just an office with furniture, a concept that had not even been implemented. The network—what was a network anyway?—didn't even own any radio stations in its own right.

At first Sam hesitated. He asked for 24 hours to think about the proposition. Bill must have tossed and turned that night trying to fall asleep. True, his father had consistently advocated Bill taking on some responsibility of his own. But buying a radio network? A totally unproven one at that? Sam sensed after a while that the investment was a reason-able risk: if Bill failed, he would at least gain some valuable experience; and if he succeeded, he would have a foothold in something far more exciting than the world of cigars. Informing Bill that he and Jake would give their blessing, Sam added that the Paley family would not sit around while young Bill went off and gambled his fortune on an unknown quan-tity: it would help him purchase some of the Louchheim stock. Hence, Bill bought $400,000 worth, and the Paley family was in for $100,000. What Sam did not say to his son, indeed could not say, was that, should Bill turn UIB around, he would likely not return to Congress Cigars. Bill couldn't think that far ahead, or didn't want to.

At first, Bill Paley regarded his new acquisition as a sideline. He was con-vinced that he could get away with spending a few days in New York and then, once UIB's mess was straightened out, return to Philadelphia and Congress Cigars. On September 26, he had purchased the Louchheim interest in the company—51 percent, worth some $500,000. He kept 2,085 shares and gave the other 510 to family members. Now, the newly installed president of the twenty-two station network of United Indepen-dent Broadcasters knew that it was not clear at all that he would be able to do much about the mess. The title of president sounded impressive, but in fact he had acquired nothing more than what an article in *Fortune* mag-azine called "that miserable radio adventure, that mere shoestring." (7)

In time, Paley would turn that "mere shoestring" into the single most important broadcasting institution in the country. Along the way, he would become one of the most accomplished and publicized business leaders. Those who were with him at the beginning recall no empire-building instinct within the man; nor do they remember that he was especially interested in the art and practice of broadcasting. Thus it was that Peter Goldmark, the brilliant CBS inventor, wrote, "A man who is voted from time to time the richest man in show business, Bill Paley has never publicly seen himself as a communications executive; he has seldom given a talk on communications or seemed fully to understand how communications technology was changing the modern world and what to do about it." (8) Radio, and later television, was, for the new UIB president, but a means to an end. The end, of course, was creating a business that was as profitable as possible.

Personally, Paley wanted to make a good first impression on the dozen or so employees who peopled the offices on a single floor of New York City's Paramount Tower. But that was made difficult by his youth and the fact that no one seemed to know who he was. When he arrived at UIB's door for the first time, Albert Bryant, a new office boy, gave Paley a hard time, assuming he was someone of no real importance. Before the new president could get to see anyone, Bryant insisted that he produce identification. Paley was determined never to be taken as a nonserious youth. To try to get around the stigma of his youth, Paley decided he would quite simply have to age—overnight! So he ordered lots of high-collared shirts and conservative suits from a newly engaged tailor. He definitely looked older, but, forgetting to vary the color of the suits, Paley solved one problem by creating another: his employees became persuaded that he owned only one suit! What was more, the UIB staff still insisted on calling him "Young man . . . ."

Soon thereafter, the "young man" touched base with the major figures of the advertising world. Armed with a conviction that radio was potentially a goldmine for advertisers, he decided to conduct his own survey within the advertising community—to find out whether the insiders' opinions matched his own. They did not. Most of the answers were discouraging. Only the people at Young & Rubicam offered a glimmer of hope. Despite ominous forecasts that radio advertising was a nonstarter, Paley doubted that the new medium could be brushed off so lightly. One day he was walking among the marquees of Broadway. He spotted the Capitol Theater, then the most resplendent of the New York movie palaces. The movie it was presenting was a second-rate feature. Gazing across the street to another, far smaller, less ornate theater, he noted that it was offering a first-rate motion picture that he wanted to see. The thought comforted him immensely. UIB, as far as he was concerned, was the small theater. It still had no stations, no sponsors, no studio, just a small office inside a cavernous building. NBC, of course, was the Capitol Theater. But what counted, Paley told himself, was what the "theater" had to sell. In the case of the two theaters, it was a movie; with NBC and CBS, only programming would matter, not the ornate exteriors. It was a lesson he would never forget.

He learned some valuable lessons from his parents as well. His father told him to hire bright people and make sure to listen to them. He took his advice at once. He hired the top public relations specialist, Edward L. Bernays. To Paley, there was great status in having a PR man: it meant that he was important enough to need someone to "handle" his dealings with the public. His mother had suggested that he only do what he couldn't delegate others to do, especially as they might do it better. Bill's mother may have lacked confidence in her son, or she may have thought he would need all the help he could get: at any rate, she provided a man-servant for him, an appendage that he seemed to accept happily enough. He may have suffered some embarrassment at dinner parties when his hosts wondered why a guest would require such accompaniment.

Unlike the people at NBC, Bill Paley quickly saw the commercial prospects of creating a chain of stations that would broadcast the same program at the same time to an audience around the country. For its part, NBC at first thought the very idea of putting commercial messages on radio somehow vulgar; it was only when CBS began to make headway in building a commercial network that NBC discarded its disdainful attitude toward using the new medium for profit making. Meanwhile, Paley was moving forward with his plans.

The problem before Paley was how to assure that the entire network could be available to an advertising client. Under UIB's original contract with the affiliates, the network had to purchase ten hours a week from each affiliate at $50 an hour. That meant that the UIB had to shell out $8,000 a week regardless of whether it covered the expense by selling time to sponsors. Upon taking over, Jerome Louchheim had altered the arrangement somewhat. Under his new contract, UIB still had to pay the affiliates for the time the network utilized for commercial programs; how-ever, the stations were now obligated to pay the network for whatever "sustaining" programs UIB originated. They were called "sustaining pro-grams" because their costs were "sustained" by the network instead of the sponsor. Even after nearly a year's trial, this new system did not dent UIB's huge costs, largely because sponsors remained scarce and the sta-tions did not purchase a sufficient number of sustaining programs.

Paley saw a better way of doing things. He proposed giving the affili-ates "sustaining programs" for free but with the proviso that UIB would have the right to preempt local time; in this way, national sponsors could reach the entire United States. Paley paid the affiliates for the preempted hours only after a certain quota of network preemptions had been reached. The greater the number of network shows an affiliate took, the more the affiliate earned. If Paley couldn't do much about the high cost of those long-line telephone wires, he could certainly utilize them to their fullest, which, thanks to this neat strategy toward the affiliates, he managed to do. To implement his new plan, Paley gathered a selected number of Southern unaffiliated stations together at the Ambassador Hotel in New York City in November. Twelve showed up. Paley talked about his new concept of sharing sustaining and commercial time over the air. At the conclusion of the session, every station agreed to sign up. "Suddenly," noted Paley with obvious satisfaction, "in one day, we had a Southern leg to our network." (9)

To his delight, Paley went on the air for the first time on January 8, 1929 to announce that CBS had become the largest radio network, owing to its forty-nine stations in forty-two cities. Technically this was true, as NBC was divided into the "Red" and the "Blue" networks; but if taken together, the combined NBC networks were larger than CBS. When Paley had taken over in September 1928, UIB was operating on a shoestring, in danger of closing, with only sixteen stations in eleven states. But now, only four months later, it was king. NBC had become the first to have coast-to-coast broadcasting, beating CBS by two weeks, but even that wasn't enough to dampen the enthusiasm at CBS. Much of what the young network was doing was experimental, the staff was still groping. Only twenty-one hours of broadcasting went out every week. But it was a start.

The key fact of life during this early phase of broadcast history was the rivalry between NBC and CBS, the two main radio networks. The rivalry would last for years and carry through to the present (in later years, ABC became a serious competitor to the two networks). Ironically, in those early years, the two networks needed one another in some intriguing ways: CBS required NBC for RCA-manufactured or RCA-licensed equipment; NBC, for its part, required CBS to point to as a competitor whenever attacked as a monopoly. Yet, even as certain parts of the relationship were symbiotic, the two networks developed from different motivations, different backgrounds. The Radio Corporation of America, parent of NBC, had started the network as a public service—and as a way to lure potential listeners into purchasing RCA-made radios. Consistent with his company's approach, NBC founder David Sarnoff was always the technical man, always giving preference to equipment rather than the substance of what went over the airwaves. At CBS, the emphasis was different. The CBS radio network stood on its own; it had no connection with the manufacturing of radio equipment. Bill Paley and his associates could concentrate on the network, on giving it an identity, on making sure that what it produced was of high quality. If equipment was the anchor at NBC, at Bill Paley's CBS, it was programming.

Programming, originally, focused on culture and education. Over the Red and Blue (NBC) networks, one could listen to Shakespeare, opera stars, clergymen, and well-known journalists. NBC's strategy of putting an emphasis on the high-brow cultural side appeared to be paying off as the public bought radios at a faster rate than cars or electrical equipment. Stimulating radio sales as well was NBC's coverage of the 1928 presidential election between Republican Herbert Hoover and Democrat Alfred E. Smith. By the summer of 1929, NBC was demonstrating that light entertainment was more welcome to listeners than heavy cultural and educational programs. It was a lesson that CBS would learn and exploit. The proof came with the debut of NBC's "Amos 'n' Andy" on August 19. No radio program would have a greater effect on the industry. Thanks to its immense popularity, "Amos" spawned a whole genre of serials, including "The Rise of the Goldbergs" (later shortened to "The Goldbergs") and "Clara, Lu, and Em." "Amos" was so popular that sales of Pepsodent, the show's sponsor, tripled within a few weeks of the program's debut. Derived in part from the world of comic strips and in part from the burnt-cork minstrel shows, "Amos 'n' Andy" has been credited with boosting radio sales to $842 million. Millions of people planned their day around the show for fear of missing it. The stars of the show were two white actors (Freeman Fisher Gosden as Amos and Charles J. Correll as Andy). They played a pair of simpleminded blacks from Atlanta who came to Chicago where they began the "Fresh Air Taxicab Company of America, Incorpulated." The company's main asset was a broken-down topless car. Ever the unsophisticated one, Amos uttered, "Ain't dat sumpin?" Given the dreary atmosphere created by the Depression, the escapism offered a welcome relief to the audience. The message for CBS was clear. Americans had indicated that what they really wanted from radio was light entertainment. CBS was prepared to provide it. Bill Paley would have to attract popular entertainers to the airwaves. It would not be easy. Some would be reluctant to sing or talk into a microphone—without a live audience! But Paley would go at it undeterred, knowing, as he did, that these entertainers would become the bread and butter for the network. They would bring in larger and larger audiences, and in turn those audiences would bring in increasing revenues to CBS. In December, eager to purchase a flagship station that could serve as the site of CBS's network programming, Paley had bought up WABC in New York City for $390,000. The price was right, and it included a programming studio in Steinway Hall on West 57th Street near Sixth Avenue. Concerts were broadcast from the Steinway Concert Hall downstairs. But space was needed for programming studios, and so in July 1929 Paley moved the network out of the four rooms in the Paramount Tower to six floors in a new building on Madison Avenue and 52nd Street, signing a one-year lease for $1.5 million. Six studios were built on the three upper floors along with broadcasting equipment rooms and programming offices. When the new CBS headquarters was ready, there was Paley, looking formal in his stiff high collar, cutting the ribbon along with Olive Shea, Miss Radio of 1929. Adding to the festivities, President Herbert Hoover spoke from the White House over the CBS network. Eventually, CBS would take over most of the building and occupy it for the next thirty-five years.

Word got around that William Paley and CBS were on the move. Advertisers were streaming in—sales were $4.1 million a year. Outsiders grew interested in looking over the new, fast-growing enterprise to check whether it was possible to buy into it. William Fox was the most serious. But Fox, of Twentieth Century Fox, had no idea how tough and inflexible Bill Paley would be. He had no desire to sell CBS, part or whole. Still, it was not every day that the young and inexperienced Paley had a caller like Bill Fox. Concealing his reverence for the movie mogul, Paley thought no harm could come from the two men talking. For Fox's part, he asserted boastfully to Paley that with his financing and knowledge of show business, "We'll make you into something." (10) Spending a few weeks looking over CBS's books, Fox finally made Paley an offer: he was prepared to buy half of the company. Seemingly pleased, Paley asked just what those terms were. Fox replied without missing a beat that he would purchase the half interest at the same rate that Paley had paid for his share of CBS. Astounded, livid, his intelligence insulted, he would later say, Paley went for his hat on Fox's desk, shook hands with him, and told Fox it was nice to have known him. Lots of phone calls were made, but Paley refused to talk to Fox anymore. That was that.

Although funds from the Paley family and other stockholders had helped CBS to combat its early financial problems, more cash was needed if proper programs were going to be developed, and if more affiliates were to be wooed into joining the network. For that reason, Bill Paley was not displeased in the spring of 1929 when the 56-year-old Adolph Zukor, dean of the American movie industry, came knocking on CBS's door. Zukor, head of Paramount, the man who introduced the feature film, who had created the star system in Hollywood, was also interested in purchasing CBS. Radio appeared to be increasingly serious competition for the movies, and Zukor thought it a shrewd move to obtain an interest in one of the bigger radio networks. Back in 1927, he had tried to purchase an interest in UIB, but ran afoul when Arthur Judson demurred, disliking Zukor's plan to rename the network Paramount Broadcasting. Zukor didn't go to Paley himself; he sent a messenger. It was a short trip. All the messenger had to do was go upstairs from Zukor's office to Paley's in the Paramount building at Times Square. Even getting an emissary from such a giant in the field was heady stuff for Paley, like receiving a message from a legend, he would later write. But, fresh from his experience with William Fox, Paley was ready.

The messenger asked right off whether Paley would sell CBS, part of it or all. Paley said CBS needed a well-heeled angel, but the price had to be right. Paramount was acceptable because it was in a related business. But the bottom line was this: Paramount had to meet Paley's price, $5 million for 50 percent of the company, take it or leave it. That represented ten times what Paley and his family had paid for half of UIB. The messenger, who had been planning for a negotiation, began to do just that—negotiate. He denigrated the price. Paley couldn't possibly mean it. Yes, he did, Paley said quietly. Returning a day later, the messenger thought he would have no trouble wrapping up a deal for $4 million. Paley would almost certainly be thrilled at Zukor's generous price. But Zukor and the messenger had misunderstood. Paley wanted $5 million, no negotiation, no lower price, $5 million. A day later, the messenger returned, this time to offer $4.5 million. And again Bill Paley just stood there stonefaced, asking the man to stop wasting Paley's time.

Now, the Paley family got into the act. Uncle Jake called to voice his astonishment that Bill could turn down $4.5 million from Adolph Zukor. Success, he told his nephew, had obviously gone to his head. Paley told Jake what he had told the messenger, $5 million or no deal. As parting words, Jake said that he spoke for Sam Paley as well in insisting that Bill pick up the phone and hope that Zukor had not retracted the marvelous offer by now. But times had changed. Bill Paley no longer felt a moral obligation to lean on his father or uncle for advice. He was his own man now. And young Mr. Paley was not budging from his stance. A few hours later, Sam called, said much the same thing as Jake, but ran into the same brick wall. The next day, Zukor, through the messenger, asked to see Paley in person over lunch. Paley agreed, showing up at the lunch on his own. Adolph Zukor, accompanied by a dozen colleagues, wanted to get right down to business. Zukor began with flattery, he wanted Paley aboard. Fine, said Paley, but first they had to agree on price. Never, said Zukor, had he ever met someone who stuck to his opening price. Always there was give and take. Zukor simply asked why Paley was being so stubborn. The price, said Paley calmly, was based on his evaluation of CBS in two years time, on his conviction that after two years CBS would be making the kind of money that would attract many people. Lunch broke up and there was still no deal. But at 5 o'clock that afternoon the messenger descended on Paley again, this time to say that Zukor had caved in; Paley would get his $5 million for a half interest.

The deal with Zukor meant that the young network might just survive. In fact, due to that bargain, CBS's credit rating was strengthened, a significant event in its early history. On June 13, 1929, the contracts were signed. With the Paramount deal, CBS was now valued at $10 million. To appreciate what Paley had done, it is worth recalling that only nine months earlier he had purchased half the company's shares from Jerome Louchheim for a half million dollars! In other words, the company was then valued at only $1 million. Paley's business acumen had improved its standing tenfold in less than a year. Paramount now owned 50 percent of CBS, and fifteen other shareholders owned the other 50 percent. But that did not mean that Paramount could gain complete control simply by acquiring another share from one of those shareholders. Paley was too shrewd to let that happen. By virtue of the agreement with Paramount, the total number of CBS shares was raised to 100,000, half called "Class A," which went to Paramount and half, "Class B," which went to the fifteen shareholders. Each class elected its own directors; this meant that neither side could acquire formal voting control. Although a majority of shareholder votes on each side elected that side's directors, to truly gain control, one side would have to acquire over half of the stock on the other. That was impossible to do with the Class B stock since the Paley family controlled a majority of it.

Paley and Zukor disputed whether Paramount would pay in cash or with Paramount stock. Paley insisted on cash, but Zukor argued that Paramount's stock, then at $65 a share, would be more than double that price within a year, so why shouldn't Paley take it and get rich? This time in a compromising mood, Paley agreed but on one condition: should CBS earn $2 million by March 1, 1932, Paley and the other CBS shareholders had the right to insist that Paramount buy its stock back at $85 a share. In other words, Paley was saying: if I can put CBS on a profitable path, I will demand that Paramount drop out of its half-ownership. Zukor thought that a good deal and readily accepted. So CBS stockholders were given 58,823 shares of Paramount stock that was worth $3.8 million altogether; they also had the right to have Paramount buy back those shares two years later for $5 million, but only on the condition that CBS had made $2 million in profits in the interim. The papers were signed on June 13, 1929.

Paley seemed rather relaxed about the whole Paramount deal. The fact that he was entwined with another company which had 50 percent of CBS was of little consequence to him. He could always buy the CBS stock held by Paramount back; a "first-refusal" clause allowed CBS to match any price which was bid for the stock by someone else. Most important, by virtue of the Paramount deal, he had turned CBS into a far larger company than before, one that was now ready to stand on its own feet and move forward. Talk of survival would, it was hoped, be a thing of the past. Still, there was the present with which to contend. Should he wish to jettison Paramount in the future, he would first have to make sure that CBS had sufficient revenue; indeed, given the network's financial shakiness in 1929, Paley could not be sure he would be able to keep Paramount from taking over CBS. The year before, the network had lost $380,000 with a gross revenue of over $1,500,000; and in 1929, it had earned only $474,000.

Clearly impressed with Paley as a result of their deal, Zukor hoped that the CBS founder would help him run his expanding entertainment empire which included firms that manufactured radios, pool tables, and bowling equipment. Even though Zukor was prepared to pay Paley $600,000 a year, Paley said no, preferring to stay in broadcasting exclusively. Zukor insisted that Paley could run CBS with his left hand and manage Zukor's empire with his right, but Paley knew better.

Part of William Paley's scheme for CBS was to grow as quickly as possible. As the Paramount deal was concluding, CBS was making strong advances in attracting new affiliates around the country, particularly in the South, East, and Midwest. Optimistic that the network would eventually penetrate the West, CBS had assumed some AT&T radio line leases there, making it imperative that it attain a foothold on the West Coast. The search was on for new affiliates. One regional network there belonged to a wealthy man who doubled as the franchise dealer for Cadillac cars in California. Don Lee owned KFRC in San Francisco and KHJ in Los Angeles and he was about to expand northward to Seattle and Spokane. Paley hoped to persuade Lee to join the CBS network. On the phone with him, Paley must have come off sounding like a young man in a hurry. (11) Lee told him that his proposal was far too serious for a telephone conversation and that Paley ought to take the train out to California. That meant devoting an entire week to travel to California and return, a whole week away from the office. Paley thought the time worth it.

Arriving in Los Angeles, Paley was put up at the Ambassador Hotel by Lee and then whisked away for several days' leisure on the *Invader*, Lee's luxurious yacht. Impatient to discuss business, Paley was forced to wait until after the first night aboard. Finally, in the morning he broached the subject. Lee, who was dead serious, told Paley that one of his rules was never to discuss business while aboard the *Invader*. Flabbergasted, Paley insisted that he had to go back to New York. Unperturbed, Lee said simply that their business would have to await their return to Los Angeles. Deciding it was far easier to join than to fight, Paley got into the swing of things, and for four days relaxed, read, and ate good meals, all the while socializing with Lee's array of interesting guests.

Back in Los Angeles, Paley showed up at Lee's office ready to do business only to have Lee say that he would discuss the subject with Paley but only after Paley returned to the *Invader* for another three or four days. "You still look tired," said Lee. Paley argued that his business in New York required his presence. Lee was adamant. Paley wondered if he had Don Lee cornered. "In other words, if I do agree to go back on the boat, we do have something to discuss?" Yes, said Lee. All Paley could do was call his office, deal with a few items, and return for another four days on the *Invader,* without business ever being raised.

Finally, the two men were back in Lee's office. To Paley's surprise, the deal was completed without negotiations. Calling in his secretary, Lee said tersely that she should take down Paley's terms for affiliating Lee's stations with CBS—and then write those terms into the contract. Paley asked Lee what terms he had in mind, and Lee responded, as if he had more important matters pressing, "Whatever you dictate and whatever you think is fair, I'll sign." After they signed the contract on July 16, 1929, and Lee became the CBS Western representative, Paley walked away thinking that, in his attempt to be fair, he had probably been more generous with Lee than had they actually negotiated. Nonetheless, CBS now had a genuine coast-to-coast network.

The new success encouraged Paley to engage in some nearly-disasterous self-promotion. In January 1930 he held a press reception at home, providing a generously-supplied bar which, despite Prohibition, was freely-used by reporters. The next morning, a perturbed Paley phoned his public relations man Bernays to report that the *Chicago Tribune* was about to write that Paley was a bootlegger, a news story that, if written, would devastate CBS. The quick-witted Bernays phoned the *Tribune's* city desk and pleaded for the story to be spiked: "Paley," said Bernays, "was just entering corporate life and he would be destroyed if word got out that he had been serving liquor at home." Precisely why the *Tribune* agreed to Bernays' request is unknown. But the story was killed. Nearly burned by exposing himself to the public that one time, Paley vowed that he would be more cautious and would weave a cocoon of privacy around himself.

Paley had by this time accomplished a great deal. He didn't seem to mind the ups and downs. At one point, he was not sure he wanted to work so hard. He gave serious thought to the hardships his father and uncle had to endure in building up the cigar business, and he had felt sorry for them, sorry that they had not had a chance to enjoy life. He toyed with the idea that, if ever given the same chance, he would not become ensnared in his job, he would retire early—perhaps at the age of 35. He took the vow seriously too. "I imagined it a personal deal that I had made with God, or some superior being, which meant, logically, that if I did not live up to my oath, I would be punished." (12) But as he became increasingly immersed in his work and excited over radio's prospects, Paley decided that he would take his chances, hope that he wouldn't be punished, and skip early retirement. He had a network to build.

two

"HOW ARE ALL YOU DEAR OLD BOOBS?"

Wherever it looked, whatever it did, CBS confronted the immovable mountain that was the National Broadcasting Company. As it had started earlier than CBS, Sarnoff's NBC had the better facilities. The affiliates it had garnered were the cream of the crop: the high-powered stations that embraced large listening audiences and hence offered advertisers a larger potential clientele. Not only that, by virtue of its head start, NBC had signed up the biggest concert stars for its programs. Indeed, network radio for a while was virtually synonymous with NBC.

And then along came CBS, the new kid on the block, a struggling dwarf, eager to make its mark. To his credit, Bill Paley understood that there was little point in trying to outdo the fancy exterior NBC had built. Indeed, he sensed quite correctly that facilities would not matter in the end; what went over the airwaves would. The key then was in developing the best programming. He would concentrate his efforts on trying to sense what the public wanted to hear, and then give it to them. Like that small theater he had noticed as a young man, he and his burgeoning network would be judged not on their exterior, but by what was going on inside.

Gradually, CBS began to pick up steam. By 1931 Paley had built it

---

into the world's largest radio broadcasting system with five stations owned outright and over ninety affiliates; it had a gross that year of $11 million. By March 1932, CBS had $3 million in profits—not merely the $2 million Paley had hoped for—and so Adolf Zukor was obligated to pay Paley and the others $85 a share for their Paramount stock ($5 million in all). Zukor tried to secure a delay in paying the $5 million. Reluctantly, Paley agreed, principally because he knew that Paramount did not have the $5 million in hand. He offered Zukor a new proposal. Paley and the CBS stockholders would repurchase CBS stock held by Paramount for $4 million. Paramount, with little choice, went along. Paley quickly converted some of the acquired CBS stock into cash; he and the other stockholders shared a $2 million check, making him a wealthy man.

The early 1930s were good years for CBS, largely because radio was becoming so popular. Almost 14 million radios were in use in 1930, which meant a potential listening audience of over 50 million. Incredibly, even though a depression was on, CBS's net sales went from $4,172,000 in 1929 to $12,984,000 in 1934. And net profits went up more than five-fold in that same period, from $474,000 to $2,274,000. Revenue in 1935 would rise to $15.4 million, and profits would jump to $2.8 million. As Paley's network prospered, affiliates began to defect to CBS so that there were ninety-seven in 1935.

A major reason for CBS's success was Paley's effort at luring major advertisers over to the new network. His first step was to hire the right leadership. As head of his promotion department he selected Paul Kesten, a man of great intelligence and a rich enthusiasm for life. Kesten had a grasp of words, both written and oral, and could pull off a clever promotional scheme. Only 30 years old, the Milwaukee-bred Kesten had ventured to New York, becoming a copyeditor for an advertising agency. Ed Klauber, another of Paley's chief lieutenants, had brought Kesten to CBS in early 1930 and, although Kesten had not completed college, he was deemed the right man to handle CBS's promotion needs. Small and thin, with large eyes and a receding hairline, he was a careful dresser and a fast thinker. Kesten's great achievement was to push the company into market research. He had understood that it was not enough simply to come up with ideas that sounded cute and snappy. It was crucial to sense what the public thought, what programs did they want to hear, and what programs did they dislike? How could those listeners be continuously attracted to CBS? Armed with that knowledge, it would be possible to lure the listeners into buying the products of advertisers. To get at those answers, Kesten later hired Frank Stanton, one of his shrewdest moves. Paley took a quick liking to Kesten, sensing the man's genius for turning out the right kind of promotional copy, sensing that Kesten had a knack for bringing listeners into the network.

Paley was quick to spot that programming and advertising were two sides of the same coin. However, just as it had grabbed the top talent for its programming, NBC had developed a monopoly over the best advertisers. One was the American Tobacco Company, makers of Lucky Strike cigarettes. It had been advertising over nine NBC stations, denying to CBS both needed revenue and a stamp of legitimization. Paley wanted to lure American Tobacco over to CBS. The man to approach was George Washington Hill. The head of American Tobacco, he was something of a legend in broadcast advertising. He had originated the successful practice of repeating slogans, specifically L.S.–M.F.T. (Lucky Strike Means Fine Tobacco); he had also pioneered the art of catch phrases. Remember "So round, so firm, so fully packed. So free and easy on the draw"? George Washington Hill again. To get Hill to switch to CBS would indeed be a significant breakthrough. But it was not to be easy.

In late 1930 or early 1931 (Paley's recollection is faulty on the point), Paley arranged a meeting with Hill. The tobacco man appeared to like Paley's ideas but stopped short of signing on with CBS. Finally, Paley proposed to Hill that American Tobacco should sponsor martial music five times a week for 15 minutes on CBS. Hill thought about the idea and decided that he liked it. Winning over American Tobacco was an important moment for CBS even though the cantankerous Hill would prove a thorn in Paley's side through the years. Once, the ill-tempered Hill insisted that Paley compensate him when the CBS comedy team of Stoopnagle and Budd mispronounced Lucky Strikes, calling it Lucky Strokes. Mispronouncing the name of the cigarette was, to Hill, tantamount to not advertising, as listeners would not understand that the brand's real name was Lucky Strike. Hill demanded that Paley pay $50,000 "to get over the principle." In defense, Paley tried to explain that most advertisers had been dying to get their products mentioned on the comedy show—however strangely they were pronounced. But Hill stood his ground, and only when Paley actually sent the $50,000 to Hill did the advertiser relent.

CBS was hardly in a position to diversify at this early stage. The network's major steps in diversification would only come later. But, when Paley was approached by the head of the Music Producing Managers Association, Milton Diamond, in December 1930 with an urgent request for help, Paley acceded. He helped merge seven of the leading concert bureaus in the United States into what was called the Columbia Concerts Corporation. It was a deal that would prove of great benefit to CBS. For, all at once, the network now represented 125 of the leading concert singers, soloists, and musicians, among whom were Yasha Heifetz, Ezio Pinza, Lily Pons, Yehudi Menuhin, Vladimir Horowitz, Paul Robeson, and Lotte Lehmann.

Not officially part of CBS, Columbia Concerts had as its chief operating officer Arthur Judson, who headed two of those seven concert bureaus. With CBS owning most of the stock, Paley was chairman and president. Close to that time, CBS also formed the largely unprofitable Columbia Artists Bureau, a talent management agency aimed at arranging theater and movie house bookings for some of the network's radio performers such as Bing Crosby and the Mills Brothers. (In 1941, the Federal Communications Commission, arguing that the network was both buying and selling talent, deemed this as a conflict of interest, leading CBS in that year to sell its share of Columbia Concerts as well as Columbia Artists. The latter firm was sold to Music Corporation of America, which went on to become the largest talent agency in the world.)

In the same spirit of diversification, Paley would have much better luck later that decade when he paid a mere $535,000 in 1938 for the American Record Corporation. ARC's chief asset was the Columbia Phonograph Company, in 1927 the largest stockholder in UIB. Purchasing ARC "turned out to be the best deal I ever made, except for buying CBS itself," Paley would say years later. (1) The man from whom he bought ARC thought it was a lemon, but Paley sensed that the record industry, though devastated by the Depression, would recover and flourish: radio would help by broadening the number of people who appreciated listening to music. Paley renamed the company Columbia Recording Corporation, and later it became Columbia Records, the same Columbia Records that would be home for Frank Sinatra, Doris Day, Pearl Bailey, Dinah Shore, Bob Dylan, Aretha Franklin, Michael Jackson, and Bruce Springsteen. In that first year, the firm lost $73,000. It went on to become one of the largest record companies and CBS's most significant nonbroadcasting activity.

During Columbia Records' first year, CBS hired a composer, young and struggling at the time, named Goddard Lieberson, as the assistant to the director of the Masterworks Division. He was paid $50 a week. He would become the president of Columbia Records in 1956 and remain at the helm until 1971 when he became a senior vice president at CBS. The record company began to grow dramatically once Paley got the ingenious idea of dropping the price of classical records from $2, the price of RCA records, to $1 apiece. RCA's initial fury turned into gratitude when it became apparent that both CBS and RCA were selling far more records at the lower price. (By 1947 Columbia Records was doing $25.4 million worth of business—up from $7.7 million in 1944. After it introduced the long-playing record in June 1948, the entire industry was revolutionized. Within eight months nearly 600,000 new record players were sold as well as over 2 million long-playing records.)

It soon became apparent to Paley that the way to attract advertisers was to find compelling programs through which the advertisers' products could be publicized. Once the advertiser was interested in sponsoring a certain program starring an entertainer, Paley would then approach that entertainer and begin the bargaining. Then sponsor and entertainer would be brought for a live audition. If Bill Paley had done his homework, the sponsor would quickly agree to advertise on the new program. As Paley prepared to line up his winter radio schedule for 1929, he decided to try out this approach on prospective advertisers.

He began by focusing on Paul Whiteman, conductor of the most popular orchestra in the United States. Like many other artists, Whiteman was ambivalent toward entertaining on radio. But Paley decided that it was worth a try. He offered Lennen & Mitchell, the advertising agency for P. Lorillard Company, makers of Old Gold cigarettes, the opportunity to sponsor a radio show built around Whiteman. Yes, came the reply, Lorillard was interested: if Paley could snare Paul Whiteman, there would be a deal. With that, Paley rushed to Chicago's Drake Hotel where the famous bandleader was playing. Paley knew that Whiteman had done some spot appearances on radio; during the break he introduced himself and asked Whiteman if he would consider doing a weekly radio program over the CBS radio network.

"Young man," the roundish, but charming Whiteman asked, "you don't think I'm going to do a regular program on radio, do you?" (2) He pronounced the word "radio" as if it were a dangerous piece of equipment that would explode upon touching. With a patronizing air, the bandleader explained to his intruder that radio would likely ruin his reputation. Paley was nothing if not perseverent. This was the same man who had wiled away days on the *Invader* to secure a deal, who had turned down $4.5 million from George Zukor to get his asking price. He was not about to give up on Paul Whiteman. Between turns at leading the band, Whiteman continued grudgingly to converse with Paley. By now it was long after midnight and young Mr. Paley searched for something that would entice Whiteman to take a chance with radio. Finally, an idea struck him. True, Whiteman enjoyed a wonderful reputation. But he had rarely performed before more than a few hundred people. Paley held out the promise to Whiteman that radio would give him a vastly larger audience. Dawn was nearing, and Whiteman's armor was cracking.

"By God," he finally said to Paley. "You've sold me. I'll try it." (3)

Whiteman signed a contract with CBS, and on Tuesday, February 5, 1929, at 9 P.M. the weekly "Old Gold Program" debuted. George Gershwin's familiar "Rhapsody in Blue" became Whiteman's theme. Appearing with him regularly were the blues singer Mildred Baily and a young comedian named Eddie Cantor. There would be many hours and many negotiations between Paley and other stars, but few would have the impact or significance of his signing Whiteman. For he was the first, and he was a major entertainment figure. For Whiteman to enter the CBS embrace was a major step forward for the young network.

But it had a long way to go as exhibited in its apparently disastrous showing when the first of the Crossley ratings appeared in 1930: nearly every winner belonged to NBC. "Amos 'n' Andy" logged a 53.4 rating; "Rudy Vallee Varieties," 36.5; and "The Lucky Strike Dance Orchestra," 27.8. Only two CBS programs managed to earn decent ratings. All the others were 3.3 or below. The reaction at CBS was shock, anger, disbelief. Fear was expressed that advertisers would fall by the wayside. Fortunately, Paul Kesten had a brainstorm. Disliking the message, he decided to kill the messenger. Who, in fact, could guarantee that the Crossley ratings were accurate? Why not seek another messenger? Who knows? The new messenger might find out a different set of "facts."

And so CBS hired Price, Waterhouse and Co., the highly respected accounting firm, and asked it to conduct a survey that would examine the popularity of certain radio programs within range of CBS affiliates. This survey produced remarkable results. In the ten largest American cities, CBS programs were more popular than NBC's by respectable margins. Of the fifty-seven cities covered in the Price, Waterhouse survey, CBS triumphed 34 to 31 over the first NBC network, and 32 to 21 over the second. Kesten's effort proved effective: the second set of ratings attained a high degree of credibility, and as a result CBS's advertisers remained faithful.

Armed with those ratings, Paley sought to secure more talent for CBS. He was fascinated by entertainment and programming, and no one was better at deciding what would sell. Nonetheless, luring the artists to radio remained a challenge. Paley sensed that a radio audience would want to hear the comedian Will Rogers. But Rogers was in no mood to go before a cold mike. He wanted an audience present. He wanted the audience to react, laugh, cheer him on. Getting in front of a microphone without an audience, no matter how many listeners were supposed to be tuned in, seemed bizarre. In a stroke of luck, Paley ran into Rogers at a Mexican gambling casino. He stopped him at the door as Rogers was leaving. Rogers was reluctant at first. The very thought of trying to be funny when there was no live audience to laugh at his jokes seemed reprehensible. Paley solved the problem: he promised Rogers there would be a live studio audience. Rogers softened and on Sunday evening, April 6, 1930, the comedian began a thirteen-week series out of the CBS affiliate, KHJ, in Los Angeles. Paley was true to his word, rounding up forty employees from the office and studio to laugh at the appropriate places.

Besides Will Rogers, Paley brought other stars to CBS: in 1932 Fred Allen, and George Burns and Gracie Allen, Goodman Ace with Jane, and

Jack Benny with Mary Livingstone. Not everyone signed on. Paley had spotted and liked Rudy Vallee when he was an unknown nightclub singer. He wanted him for CBS. But Vallee went over to NBC. Paley fought energetically to woo the Metropolitan Opera, only to lose that prized institution to NBC. Along the way he discovered Morton Downey, the Irish tenor, and the Boswell Sisters. And Bing Crosby.

Sailing on a business trip to Europe on the *S.S. Europa* in June 1931, Paley took long walks on the deck, and each time he did he heard the song, "I Surrender, Dear." The singer caught his attention. He finally looked at the record on which was written, "Chorus by Bing Crosby." Paley had never heard of him. He cabled CBS: SIGN UP SINGER NAMED BING CROSBY." Upon Paley's return, Ed Klauber delicately informed the CBS boss that no action had been taken to put Crosby under contract after picking up reports that he was an unreliable artist who didn't show up for performances and was in trouble with his union. Furious, Paley said he didn't care about any of that, he wanted the singer under contract to CBS. Paley had an instinct about Crosby, about the attractiveness of his singing voice. He was sure he had a winner in him. If Crosby were an unreliable performer, Paley would make him reliable. But first there was the matter of the contract.

Ordinarily, Crosby would have been entitled to CBS's going rate for new talent: a weekly salary of between $100 to $500. Once a sponsor was found for the performer, the contract could be renegotiated. Making sure that NBC knew that CBS was interested in his client, Crosby's attorney insisted on $1,500 a week, with a jump to $3,000 once a sponsor was found. Paley thought the price absurd, but, eager to have the singer, he paid it.

At first Crosby was given the 7 to 7:15 P.M. spot five nights a week, pitted against NBC's "Amos 'n' Andy." Realizing that it was senseless to employ heavier artillery against "Amos," CBS used that time slot to introduce new singing talent. With such overpowering competition, Bing seemed less popular than he really was. Paley only found out just how popular the young crooner was when he read a newspaper story that told of youngsters mobbing Bing after a nightclub stint; they yelled, kicked, and screamed and tore his clothing. Bing was breaking records at New York's Paramount Theater, but despite that, Paley was unable to find a sponsor for his radio program as long as it was pitted against the clout of "Amos 'n' Andy."

Paley tried other talent in that spot. Asked to listen to four black singers just in from Cincinnati, Paley declared himself too busy. Someone had the sense to urge him to delay his luncheon appointment so that he could hear one song. Putting off his lunch, Paley liked the sound of these four men and soon thereafter put the Mills Brothers in Crosby's spot. Kate Smith followed, carefree, plump Kate with her booming voice, Kate who would turn "God Bless America" into something as famous as the national anthem. When he wrote the song in 1918, Irving Berlin called it "sticky" and put it away in a trunk, but two decades later Berlin permitted Kate to sing it over Bill Paley's network, and the song entered American legend. Crosby, the Mills Brothers, Kate Smith—the Paley instinct for talent was growing. Although the Price, Waterhouse ratings back in 1930 had given CBS self-confidence in its struggle with NBC, Paley knew that he would have to bring as many of the big-name entertainers as possible into the CBS tent if his network was going to remain competitive.

Radio, of course, was more than a means of entertainment. It had, in some eyes, a loftier, more noble purpose—covering the news. Yet, during its early years, few understood or appreciated just how it would be possible to replicate what the daily newspapers were doing. If radio news was no more than reading wire copy, then the task of broadcast journalists was simple. But, if radio was going to take upon itself the responsibility of actually covering the news, the task of the broadcast journalist would be considerably more complicated. What news would he be expected to cover? How much time would the network give over to the enterprising feats of its own reporters? No less important, just how would the news be presented? With straightforward objectivity? Salted with opinion? There were no rules, no standards at the time.

Still, the fledgling news staff displayed a noticeable zeal. On election night 1928, CBS carried the first news broadcast—as contrasted with the presentation of a live event. At that time Ted Husing, a sportscaster, sat in the newsroom of the *New York World* and passed on election results fresh from the wires to CBS listeners; Husing sandwiched his reports between live musical selections. Like later broadcasters, he was keenly interested in "beating" the opposition, in this case the newspapers, and beat them he did. He announced hours before the printed press that Herbert Hoover had won the presidential election. Husing was originally hired to be the CBS office manager, but he drove Paley crazy, giving him wrong answers to everything. Then one day Major J. Andrew White, whose duties included broadcasting football games, called in sick; Husing got Paley's approval to substitute for White, and thus began the career of one of the most famous sportscaster in the nation.

Somehow, no one is quite sure how, Bill Paley developed an appreciation for news almost from the start. One theory has it that Ed Klauber was in fact hired for the express purpose of instructing Paley in the art of news broadcasting. And so when news was happening, he wanted CBS to be the network that would be covering it. As an illustration, when Prime Minister Ramsey MacDonald of England visited the United States and made a special address to the American people, it was broadcast through an exclusive arrangement with NBC. Paley was irate and protested loudly. He would have been more than willing to give up his entertainment schedule for that time period so that he too could broadcast MacDonald's remarks. But he would not get his way. By way of dramatizing his protest, he ordered the CBS network to go silent and remain off the air for the duration of MacDonald's speech. In those days no one bothered to calculate how much advertising revenue had been lost when news was given preference over entertainment programs. (During the 1930s, Paley would not hesitate to interrupt the radio network entertainment schedule for special programs from Europe. Such a preference for the news would remain CBS policy and would only become the subject of a controversial dispute between programming and news executives in later years.)

Conventional wisdom has it that Edward R. Murrow set the standards for radio news coverage, and there is a measure of truth in that statement. Yet, in 1929, quite some time before Murrow had a firm foothold in CBS, Bill Paley hired an assistant to the president who deserves the true credit as the father of broadcast journalism. His name was Ed Klauber. Broadcast journalism owes much to this rather unpleasant fellow, for it was he who established many of the standards which the networks adopted, standards of restraint, integrity, professionalism. In short, he took radio news seriously and in so doing influenced others to do the same. Klauber, by all accounts, was not an easy man to be around, "a dour, difficult man, inclined to be autocratic and even tyrannical," according to William Shirer, who was a CBS correspondent in Europe in the late 1930s and early 1940s. (4) Although Klauber appeared to feel compassionately toward his employees, he had a tough exterior and little of that compassion came through routinely. Physically, he was short and heavy, and he wore an incongruous pince-nez. While everyone else preferred casual, shirtsleeve dress, Klauber looked stuffy and formal in his coat and firmly knotted tie. As a youngster he had wanted to be a doctor but gave that up to go into journalism, becoming the night city editor for *The New York Times*. As such, by the time Klauber arrived at CBS, he was a polished journalist who believed firmly that news should be presented without the reporter personalizing or rendering his own opinion. That may sound rather commonplace today, but few had bothered at the time of radio's founding to give much thought to how radio news should be conveyed. Had it not been for Klauber, radio might have followed the lead of the sensationalist printed press. Had it not been for him, radio might have indulged in noisy, bombastic, opinionated reports that would inaccurately be called news coverage. But it did not. Klauber was uniformly acclaimed as a masterful editor, "always insisting," in Ed Murrow's words, "that it had to be right, before it was written. He was sparing with praise, and penetrating with his criticism." (5)

Within a year after joining the network, Klauber became executive vice president. He was in fact one of the handful of people at CBS who were indispensable to Paley during those early years. Klauber had a philosophy about the news. That philosophy has survived because of its compelling nature. Assuring its survival was a simple, but meaningful act carried out by Fred W. Friendly, who appears in our tale later on. Friendly presents each of his journalism students at Columbia University as well as visitors to his office with a calling card on which the Klauber creed appears. On the card it says: "What news analysts are entitled to do and should do is elucidate and illuminate the news out of common knowledge or special knowledge possessed by them or made available to them by this organization through its sources. They should point out the facts on both sides, show contradictions with the known record and so forth. They should bear in mind that in a democracy it is important that people not only should know but should understand, and it is the analysts' function to help the listener to understand, to weigh and to judge, but not to do the judging for him." Because of Klauber's principles, the men and women who were hired at CBS news in the 1930s and thereafter lived and breathed the words of this creed. Klauber set a tone, created an atmosphere in which an Ed Murrow and many others could work and flourish. By impressing upon Bill Paley the importance of covering the news aggressively and conscientiously, Klauber was responsible for giving an air of seriousness to radio news that it otherwise would not have had.

(One frequently mentioned example of Klauber's insistence on maintaining high standards in news coverage occurred in 1940 when Wendell Wilkie was running for president. After Wilkie concluded a major speech, CBS's commentator Hans von Kaltenborn prepared his radio commentary to read: "I listened to Wendell Wilkie's speech last night. It was wholly admirable." As he wrote those words, however, Kaltenborn realized that Ed Klauber would simply not accept such personalizing or editorializing, so, scribbling them out, he wrote instead, "Millions of Americans of both parties listened to Wendell Wilkie's speech last night. Most of them agreed it was wholly admirable.")

The CBS news operation of the early 1930s got a big boost when Paley hired Lowell Thomas. Although hired as an entertainer, Thomas would become the preeminent newscaster of his day. In 1930 the only daily news broadcast on the air was done over NBC by a hard-drinking, colorful war correspondent named Floyd Gibbons; it was sponsored by the sober *Literary Digest.* In truth, Gibbons had attained a certain popularity partly because his 15-minute newscast preceded "Amos 'n' Andy." His rat-tat-tat, machine-gun approach to reading the news coupled with a certain irreverence won listeners as well. Gibbons, however, liked to drink, and after the night he pounded on the door of R. J. Cuddihy, president of Funk and Wagnalls, parent company of the *Literary Digest,* asking for some liquid refreshment, his days were numbered. It was around this time that Bill Paley grew determined to grab Gibbons's program away from NBC. With Gibbons no longer a likely candidate for moving over to CBS with the program, Paley had to find a replacement: Paley sensed that Lowell Thomas might be the vehicle.

One August afternoon in 1930 Lowell Thomas, who was known for his personal adventure books and lectures on travel, was summoned to the Madison Avenue and 52nd Street building of CBS. He was introduced to Paley who whisked him to a studio on the twentieth floor, put him in front of a microphone, and said, "When you hear the buzzer, start talking. Talk fifteen minutes—I don't care what about. Then stop." (6) Thomas spotted three musicians standing nearby. Would they be good enough, he asked them, to play something Oriental when he started talking? The buzzer sounded. From the musicians came the sounds of "In a Persian Garden." Thomas began talking, about India, his experiences in the Khyber Pass, T. E. Lawrence, Afghanistan, whatever came to mind. Only later was Thomas told that R. J. Cuddihy and eighteen editors and executives of the *Literary Digest* had been listening to his voice. Apparently interested but not quite convinced, the *Digest's* delegation asked Thomas to do a summary of the day's news a few days hence as a further trial. Hustling Thomas off, Paley said, "We mustn't fail. We'll get you the best brains in the business to prepare this broadcast. It has to be a masterpiece." (7)

Paley asked three CBS executives to help; Thomas called upon three acquaintances, but hours passed and no one could come up with anything worth writing down. Finally, Thomas sought help from another acquaintance, and eventually put together a respectable script. Thomas proceeded to CBS, walked up to the microphone and said, "Good evening, everybody." He then somehow told the news and after 15 minutes said "Good night." Thomas was given the job. On his final broadcast, Gibbons sneeringly referred to his successor as a professor, overlooking Thomas's impressive credentials. Thomas was in the rather unusual situation of reporting the news for both CBS and NBC; Cuddihy chose to keep NBC for the eastern half of the United States, with CBS taking the West. At 6:45 P.M. on September 29, 1930, NBC and CBS announcers introduced Thomas on the air as "the *Literary Digest's* new radio voice, informing and entertaining you with the latest news of the day." On that first broadcast, Thomas spoke about the new Fascist leader in Germany. "There are now two Mussolinis in the world which seems to promise a rousing time. Adolf (Hitler) has written a book (*Mein Kampf*) in which this belligerent gentleman states that a cardinal policy of his now powerful Germany is the conquest of Russia. That's a tall assignment, Adolf. You just ask Napoleon." The only other person engaged in news at the time was Hans von Kaltenborn, but he was on CBS only twice a week and did commentary. Thomas, the heir to Gibbons's huge audience, had many more listeners.

Six months after Thomas began, Cuddihy decided to move the program back to NBC totally, because of the lure of "Amos 'n' Andy." (Lowell Thomas remained with NBC until 1947, at which point he returned to CBS and stayed with Paley's network until his final night of broadcasting, May 14, 1975. Thomas's forty-six years on the air were one of the longest stints in the history of broadcasting. Thomas claimed to be the first to broadcast from a mountaintop, a coal mine, an airplane, a helicopter, a ship, and a submarine.)

The presence of an Ed Klauber in the newsroom and a Lowell Thomas at the mike made it clear that Bill Paley was paying attention to news. Much more so than NBC's David Sarnoff, who had little interest in broadcast journalism; he preferred concentrating on cultural programs. Paley thought differently. He sensed early on that putting his resources behind the news operation would help put CBS on the map. After all, NBC had enticed the major entertainment stars even before CBS had gotten under way. Paley needed a field to make his own niche, and news provided that. And within the news field, the area of greatest prestige, Paley sensed, lay in overseas news broadcasting.

The first news broadcast from overseas occurred in 1930 from the London Naval Disarmament Conference. In January of that year, an American delegation sailed to the conference on the ocean liner *S.S. George Washington* hoping to return home with a naval limitation treaty that would cut down armaments. Two radio newsmen, CBS's Frederick William Wile and NBC's William Hard, were also on board the *George Washington.* During the next two months the newsmen asked delegates to describe the event, knowing full well that their versions would be larded with excesses of chauvinism and subjectivity. CBS managed to provide twenty-three broadcasts from the conference, but few were listening. The reason: CBS's policy of insisting that such broadcasts be live. Because of the time difference between London and New York, the American audience was sleeping during the live broadcasts. Had the network allowed its reporter to use a tape recorder, he could have sent taped reports for broadcast at a time when there would be more listeners. CBS, however, had a rule against its newsmen using such machines, tape recordings of news events being considered a fraud on the listener.

Wile recruited Cesar Saerchinger, the 40-year-old London-based reporter for the Philadelphia *Public Ledger* and the *New York Post.* After

Wile returned to the United States, Saerchinger was appointed "European Director, Columbia Broadcasting System." He thus became CBS's first foreign correspondent. "Just getting into my stride," Saerchinger cabled CBS. "Have plan to submit." He wanted to bring such luminaries as George Bernard Shaw, John Masefield, and the Prince of Wales to the network's microphones. Saerchinger sought approval from Sir John Reith, the director-general of the BBC, to have CBS use BBC studios and other facilities. To Reith, a broadcasting network had an obligation to shape public tastes. Commercials were taboo. "What I'd like to know," he asked Saerchinger, "is how you Americans can successfully worship God and Mammon at the same time." (8) The question, apparently rhetorical, didn't elicit a response.

Without much enthusiasm, Reith agreed to the CBS request. So Saerchinger could proceed. Using BBC facilities, he organized numerous programs, relaying them by telephone cable or shortwave; in all, thirty writers and statesmen appeared. CBS asked Saerchinger to line up Pope Pius XI for a broadcast ("Contact old gentlemen direct" were his marching orders). One guest was the American Secretary of State, Henry L. Stimson. In 1932, Saerchinger tried to arrange for that rising German politician, Adolf Hitler, to give a 15-minute talk for which Hitler would be paid $1,500, but CBS cabled back in that now-famous phrase, "Unwant Hitler at any price." John Masefield put in a plug for radio during his appearance. He bemoaned that the printing press had become "a detriment to poetical art. . . . It has had this result—it has put away the power from his public." But perhaps, he conjectured, radio could return poetry to its rightful place so that it could "compete once again with the delights of the marketplace."

The Masefield broadcast produced little reaction compared to the one by George Bernard Shaw. Pursuing Shaw for months, Saerchinger had assured the British playwright that he would have complete freedom to say what he wished over the airwaves. Still Shaw was dubious. Shaw tested the broadcaster. What would happen if he chose to talk about Russia? No problem, said Saerchinger. Still, Shaw wondered. Finally, after a nine-day journey to the Soviet Union, Shaw informed Saerchinger he was ready to go on the air. He did so on October 11, 1931, greeting his American listening audience with these words: "Hello America! Hello, all my friends in America! How are all you dear old boobs who have been telling one another for a month that I have gone dotty about Russia? . . . Russia has the laugh on us. She has us fooled, beaten, shamed, shown up, out-pointed, and all but knocked out. We have lectured her from the heights of our modern superiority and now we are calling on the mountains to hide our blushes in her presence. . . . Our agriculture is ruined and our industries collapsing under the weight of our own productiveness because we have not found out how to distribute our wealth as well as to produce it." So outraged were some over the Shaw broadcast that CBS felt it had to allow Rev. Edmund A. Walsh, vice president of Georgetown University, to reply. He called Shaw "the licensed charlatan of English letters."

This was a major moment for radio, and for CBS. Controversial remarks had been aired, there had been revulsion at what had been said, and the right of reply had been invoked. Radio had, in a sense, passed the test of dealing fairly with strong views.

If radio had been in its early childhood in the early 1930s, television was still in swaddling clothes. Although some had been advocating its introduction commercially as early as 1923, little had been done during the 1920s to launch the new medium. But then, although the dawning of the television age was still nearly two decades off, experiments were getting under way in the early 1930s. On July 21, 1931 CBS started its television experimentation with the birth of W2XAB (later WCBS). New York Mayor Jimmy Walker presided at the opening ceremony, and Kate Smith and George Gershwin provided the music. Kate sang the tune that would become most associated with her, "When the Moon Comes Over the Mountain," the Boswell sisters sang "Heebie Jeebie Blues," and Gershwin played his own song "Liza" on the piano. W2XAB began a schedule of entertainment and discussion programs in the evening; it covered the 1932 presidential election as well. But it was all terribly experimental. Two weeks before Franklin Roosevelt was inaugurated as president, W2XAB, financially strapped due to the Depression, suspended its broadcasts. The 18-month experiment had led CBS to believe that prospects for early commercialization were thin. Even though CBS was in better financial shape than were other segments of the nation's economy, investing too heavily in television appeared unwise.

Later in the 1930s, CBS renewed its interest in television. This time its efforts revolved around a young man named Peter Carl Goldmark. Born on December 2, 1906 in Budapest, he was a member of that small fraternity of brilliant twentieth-century Hungarian scientists (others were John von Neumann, Edward Teller, and Eugene Paul Wigner). Goldmark gave CBS—and America—the long-playing record and color television, and much, much more. Part of an accomplished family, he had a great uncle, Karl Goldmark, who was a leading nineteenth-century opera composer. Another great uncle, Joseph Goldmark, discovered red phosphorus, which was essential for the manufacture of kitchen matches. As a child, Peter was precocious, taking over the family bathroom for his experiments, assembling a huge motion picture projector. Keen on fiddling with technology, he put together a primitive television set, describing it this way: "The picture came through in postage-stamp size. You could hardly make it out, it flickers so. It was also in color—all red. But it was the most exciting thing in my life." (9)

Throughout school in Hungary and later in Austria, Goldmark appears to have been uncertain about what to do professionally. Music appealed to him more than physics; he played both the piano and cello. Yet he did take an engineering degree at the Berliner Technische Hochschule and earned a doctorate in physics at the University of Vienna. His dissertation, "A new method for determining the velocity of ions," paved the way for television projection. Although his faculty advisers encouraged him to become a physicist, he decided against further academic work. A chance encounter in Vienna during the summer of 1933 with Hans von Kaltenborn, the well-known CBS commentator, introduced him to the world of American broadcasting. Kaltenborn listened patiently to the young scientist's ideas about television. Sufficiently impressed, Kaltenborn gave Goldmark a letter of introduction to CBS. Sailing for England, Goldmark returned to inventing. Hired by Pye Radio Ltd. in Cambridge, he built a mechanical television transmitter. Two years later, in 1935, Goldmark set out for New York, seeking American citizenship and employment. He never used Kaltenborn's letter of introduction, perhaps forgetting its existence. Within four days of his arrival, and with only $150 in his pocket, Peter trudged off to fourteen firms, including RCA, which was first on the list, and CBS, only to be turned down by all of them on the first try. RCA's rejection of Goldmark would haunt David Sarnoff for years. Eventually, after hearing about an article Goldmark had written about television, Paul Kesten, then a senior CBS executive, phoned Goldmark and offered him work at $100 a week. It seems that Bill Paley was interested in exploring the possibilities of television and here was an opportunity. Goldmark began work on January 1, 1936.

Since the early 1930s, NBC had been telecasting from the top of the Empire State Building. Shortly before Goldmark arrived at CBS, David Sarnoff had announced that he would increase his investment in television to $1 million. Realizing that the costs would be high, Bill Paley could not allow Sarnoff to race ahead in the television field; he decided to build a competing transmitter, larger and better than NBC's. He enlisted Goldmark in the project. Could he do it, Paul Kesten asked him? Goldmark wondered whether he was being asked to climb higher than the Empire State Building. Still, Peter said, yes. "I was learning fast the importance of positive thinking." Paley ordered a transmitter for the Chrysler Tower; a studio was organized in nearby Grand Central Station. CBS had invested $1 million in the project, a huge amount for a corporation worth $30 million. A thirty-person team was set up to move television along at CBS. Competition was fierce. Just as CBS was preparing to televise its first show, RCA showed President Roosevelt opening the New York World's Fair. There was a chagrined Peter Goldmark watching the show at home on one of the two hundred experimental sets in existence. With so few sets, few gave much thought to television's potential. Some at CBS thought it a waste of effort with little prospect for making money; others wondered whether it would be possible to fill up all that time with decent programming. There were more immediate challenges: a chunk of ice had fallen from CBS's transmitting tower and had almost struck a passerby. The next day the newspapers assailed television as a danger to humankind. CBS was warned that if it wanted to remain in the Chrysler Building, it would have to assure that no more ice fell from its tower. That problem was solved, removing one major obstacle on the path to commercial television. But the real progress in bringing television to the nation was still far away.

Meanwhile, another young man was getting a sense of the joy and potential of public affairs broadcasting. He was largely unknown in the early 1930s. His main connection to radio and CBS was through an educational program series, "The University of the Air." In time, the young man would like the program so well that he would take over its operation entirely, arrange the broadcasts, and invite the guest speakers. That program would be where many would hear the name Ed Murrow for the first time. Eventually, it would become a household word.

Starting in 1929 CBS had provided airtime for the National Student Federation of America during the daytime hours when little revenue could be generated. In return, the students did CBS the favor of attracting major figures who would appear as speakers at no cost over the network's "University" program. The presence of these famous guests on the network program added a luster to CBS. On September 15, 1930 at 3:30 P.M. in one of broadcasting history's most important moments, Ed Murrow, who was the Federation president, debuted as host. His guest was the executive secretary of the Association of American Colleges, Robert L. Kelly. Not exactly the kind of prestigious world figure with whom Murrow would later rub shoulders, Kelly spoke that afternoon on the rather general and innocuous subject of "Looking Forward with Students." Soon, Murrow came to value the power and immediacy of radio. He arranged overseas broadcasts, an experience that would prove important for his later work. Meanwhile, he was able to attract such international stars as the Indian leader Mahatma Gandhi; British Prime Minister Ramsey MacDonald, speaking from London; and the German President Paul von Hindenburg from Berlin. When Albert Einstein and Rabindranath Tagore, the Indian poet, visited the United States for the first time, Murrow managed to snare them as guests as well.

"HOW ARE ALL YOU DEAR OLD BOOBS?"

Although still a fledgling network, CBS made important strides in its news coverage during the early 1930s. By the spring of 1931, it was touting itself as the number one news network. The main reason for such a claim: CBS interrupted its regular commercial programs with news bulletins far more than did NBC. For instance, CBS virtually canceled its regular program schedule to provide complete coverage of the dramatic story of the Lindbergh kidnapping in March 1932. Insisting that the story was too sensational, NBC refused to send out a bulletin when the news broke. As a matter of policy CBS had its announcers interrupt programs with bulletins ripped off the United Press teletype machine. The CBS news department conveyed to United Press that it preferred national bulletins over local ones, and it preferred to have bulletins filed during the daytime rather than the evening. During this early period of news broadcasting, CBS broadcast three news programs a day, one at 11:55 A.M., a second at 4:30 P.M., and the final one, a 15-minute program, at 11 P.M.

It was also in 1931 that one of the better known radio news programs of the period made its debut: "The March of Time." As different from today's "The CBS Evening News" with Dan Rather as day is from night, "March" used actors to portray the main figures in the news. Aired on Fridays at 8:30 P.M., it began with Howard Barlow's concert orchestra and faded to the Voice of Time: "On a thousand fronts the history of the world moves swiftly forward." The music ended and the voice continued: "Tonight the Editors of *Time,* the weekly news magazine, attempt a new kind of reporting of the news—the reenactment as clearly and dramatically as the medium of radio will permit, of some memorable scenes from the news of the week—from the March of Time!" The public would come to associate Westbrook van Voorhis, the third Voice of Time announcer after Ted Husing and Harry Von Zell, as the most famous voice of doom around America. Jack Smart played Huey Long; Ted de Corsi played Mussolini; Jeannette Noland did her imitation of Eleanor Roosevelt; Bill Adams played Franklin Roosevelt. Examined from the perspective of CBS's sixty years, it seems incredible that the network would have permitted such a program to be aired. In later years, CBS news executives would ridicule any attempt to portray the news artificially through such contrivances as actors. "The March of Time," so popular in the 1930s, would have never gotten off the ground in later decades. (Once, CBS correspondents were chosen to "play" delegates to a Paris-based 1970s Vietnam peace conference. They conducted a fictionalized dialogue that was supposed to approximate what would soon go on in the actual conference. Shown the tape just before airtime, CBS News President Richard Salant blew up at the program's producer, Ernest Leiser: "You can't put this on my air. You guys are cheating. I will not have my correspondents play the roles of actors in something that is a legitimate political story." Only because there was too little time did Salant allow the program to be shown. (10)

If news coverage still lacked a certain authenticity, that did not mean that radio men were uninterested in getting access to news events and sources. Indeed, the years 1932 and 1933 were a great turning point in radio's coverage of the news: It became a more mobile tool, one that brought newsmakers directly into the living rooms of America. CBS played a leading role in these developments. The first occurred on election night in November 1932. Although presidential elections had been covered by radio since 1928, for the first time commercial considerations were being abandoned—and the event given the widest possible exposure. CBS discarded all its usual programs and devoted the prime time of the evening to the reporting of the election returns. As a result, it became standard practice to preempt commercial programming for events of national political importance. Over the years, CBS news and programming executives would quarrel over when it was proper to preempt. Despite the continuous tensions, the news division usually got its way.

Another event of great significance occurred on March 12, 1933 when CBS (along with NBC and the Mutual Broadcasting System) arrived at the White House and set up equipment in front of a fireplace in the Diplomatic Reception Room. The fireplace setting had been Franklin Delano Roosevelt's idea. He hoped to conjure up an image of a man sitting in his living room talking informally to neighbors over for a chat. Harry C. Butcher, manager of the CBS Washington office, thought that what Roosevelt had in mind was a "fireside chat" and the name stuck. In simple language, the president spoke about the complexities of the American banking system, and his pleasant, unpatronizing style caught on. Radio, for the first time, had proven its utility as an instrument in American politics.

The news department received a shot in the arm when Ed Klauber hired Paul White, a tall, tough editor from the United Press. He was taken on in 1930, as a staff member in the publicity department. White would become one of the major forces in news broadcasting. As Hans von Kaltenborn has noted, White was "outstanding in his prompt realization that radio was a medium which does things that the newspaper never could do. He sensed radio's great opportunity of reaching more people more directly than through the press. He was always eager for new adventures in radio broadcasting. He had a great sense of competition—loved the idea of beating the other networks or of doing something original." (11)

White had been born in Kansas and was a graduate of the Columbia School of Journalism. By the time he had joined CBS, he had been both an editor and reporter for the United Press for six years. He had covered major trials, trans-Atlantic flights, and strikes and had one of the best known bylines in the country. At CBS, he would eventually develop the first network news staff of 500 correspondents and stringers when United Press began to withhold its services from radio under pressure from the newspapers. The experience would prove that it was possible for radio to gather its own news.

Until White came along, the news had been presented without the smooth, conversational delivery that has become part and parcel of every modern-day broadcast. Instead, readers—and that was all they were—spoke in stilted, awkward styles, tearing off the wire service copy and reading the material straight into the microphone without editing or rewriting. White introduced a new style in the delivery of radio news, one that was adapted to the new medium. Still, news broadcasts were very different from those we hear in the 1980s; news was then offered either as "talks" or "special events," with little distinction being made between the two types of programs. It was White who decided that a single person should read the news to avoid confusing the listener, paving the way for the news anchorperson that has become a pivotal and permanent part of broadcasting. White also brought the competitive style of the wire services to the radio network. He spoke fast, drank hard, mixed easily with his news colleagues, and above all, loved gadgets. (During World War II, he would arrange the nightly roundups of shortwave reports from overseas on what he called his "piano," the telephone console that hooked his correspondents into the network.)

Even though radio news was still not polished, its presence was being felt, especially by the newspapers whose editors sensed that unless some restraints were placed on the new medium, radio would quickly overcome the printed page as the chief source of news. Sensing the competition, newspaper editors saw no reason to help radio acquire a news-gathering capability. Competition existed not only for news, but also for advertising. Newspaper publishers were growing concerned over the increased competition from radio. Hollywood also worried because diminishing box office revenues suggested the growing power of radio. By the end of 1932, most of the major studios had adopted a policy forbidding their contract stars to go on radio. To provide its election night coverage in 1932, CBS made a deal with United Press editors who promised to supply election results for $1,000. But, a few days before the election, United Press president Karl A. Bickel phoned Paul White to say that, under pressure from UP subscribing newspapers, the wire agency had to break its contract to supply CBS with election results. Coming to the rescue was the Associated Press, which offered CBS (and NBC) election results free of charge. The AP was unaware that United Press had canceled its contract with CBS at the last minute. Oddly enough, United Press tickers did in fact run in the CBS newsroom that election night. No one seems to recall why. In any event, never before had radio covered a news event so comprehensively as it did that election night.

But the insecurity felt by the wire services did not vanish. By the spring of 1933 all the competing wire services took protective steps against radio, deciding that their product would not be available to the networks. That, in effect, left radio without sufficient news for its broadcasts. Meanwhile, Ed Klauber was trying to build up a group of CBS newsmen. Several months after hiring Paul White, Klauber sent a memo to Paley that was a rallying cry for the network to develop its own news resources and to apply its own standards to the coverage of news. The memo called for "consistent training" of all personnel so that broadcasts could attain a definite CBS standard of excellence. It also noted that CBS was to "proceed on the principle that the primary purpose of a news broadcast is to convey information and that the time has gone by when excited, fevered, hysterical outbursts of words are an adequate technique." Broadcasters were directed to avoid "colloquialism generally and familiarity in particular . . . along with thanks, backscratching and praise by one participant in a broadcast for another . . . ." (12) Had the newspapers not groused, had the wire services not railed against the growing power of radio news, CBS news might have not have followed Ed Klauber's clarion call to develop its own operation. Radio news might have remained a kind of secondary, catch-as-catch can operation, with too little resources available and too little enthusiasm shown to give it any prominence. But events were forcing CBS to give careful thought to building up its own news operation.

The major turning point was the arrival of an advertiser prepared to back the concept of an independent, CBS-run news service. During the summer of 1933 General Mills proposed to Paul White that if CBS could develop its own news service for under $3,000, it would pay half. Thus in September CBS formed the Columbia News Service. White was given responsibility for it. This step was the beginning of what would become the CBS news-gathering operation that stretched across the oceans, employing thousands of people, creating many of the standards and modus operandi of the broadcasting industry. Eager to outdo NBC, White set up a CBS news organization, replete with correspondents in all major cities, many of them "stringers" (reporters paid only for material actually used). Bureaus were opened in New York, Washington, Chicago, and Los Angeles, with correspondents paid higher rates than those offered by newspapers. CBS gave the Columbia News Service three program slots: 5 minutes every weekday at 12 noon and at 4:30 P.M. and 15 minutes every night at 11 P.M.

The News Service was bound for trouble almost immediately. In reaction to its establishment, newspapers threatened not to list CBS programs in their pages; sponsors of CBS shows considered canceling or shifting over to NBC. The worst insult came when CBS applied for access to the Congressional press galleries. It was denied, informed that those

"How Are All You Dear Old Boobs?"

galleries were reserved only for newspapers and news services. Clearly, some compromise was needed, and when it was achieved by the end of the year, the network welcomed it. Meeting at the Hotel Biltmore in New York City in December were representatives of NBC, CBS, and the National Association of Broadcasters, as well as the AP, UP, INS, and the American Newspaper Publishers Association. They worked out what came to be called the "Biltmore program," designed to keep the networks from interfering with the newspapers, but, at the same time, to offer a way for radio to get the news it required. CBS agreed to drop its news service and NBC agreed not to build one of its own. A Press-Radio Bureau was to be organized with the networks footing the bill. The whole thrust of the accord was meant to protect the newspapers. The bureau would supply the broadcasters with bulletins from the AP, UP, and INS, but those bulletins would always refer listeners to the newspapers for further information. Moreover, no broadcast news item could be more than thirty words. The morning news would have to be aired after 9:30 A.M. and the evening news after 9, hours that would be the least competitive for newspapers. Radio news would be confined to two 5-minute periods each day—a total of 10 minutes every 24 hours. Most astonishing was the restriction that radio could only broadcast news that was 12 hours old. In effect, the large networks had agreed not to produce the news and to provide only the barest of news coverage.

One wonders how radio executives could have agreed to such restrictive terms. One wonders, given the enthusiastic response among the public to radio, how even newspaper executives could have imagined that such an agreement would prove workable. It, of course, did not. The Press-Radio Bureau opened for business on March 1, 1934. But, soon, it became apparent how foolish it had been to expect radio's management to let newspapers dictate its early burial as a conveyer of news. The system quickly became inoperative as an increasing number of radio stations objected to the Biltmore program's terms. The refusal to go along with those terms was one more small step in the development of broadcast journalism.

CBS was forced to deal with the question of what people could or could not say on the air during this period. No one wanted to let the government decide such matters. Yet, until confronted with Father Charles E. Coughlin and his extremist preaching over CBS, the network had not involved itself in whether to censor those who used its airwaves. In 1930, Father Coughlin, then a 45-year-old Canadian preacher, was broadcasting his "Golden Hour of the Little Flower" over seventeen CBS stations between 6 and 7 P.M. on Sundays. Seeking contributions, he promised to send a donor in return a souvenir crucifix which had touched a relic of the True Cross. Within three months of his joining CBS, 80,000 letters and $20,000 had been received. The mail kept increasing until 150 clerks were required; by 1934, when some broadcasts would elicit more than 1 million letters, he was getting more mail than anyone, including the President of the United States. His listening audience was larger than most of the comedy and variety programs of the day. When his shows exhibited an increasing amount of anti-Semitic venom, Ed Klauber demanded that he submit his radio scripts to CBS in advance. Coughlin's reaction was unbending. In his next sermon, he railed at CBS for attempting to censor him. He suggested that those who supported him write to the network expressing their anger. One million listeners penned letters.

Here was evidence of the drawing power of this new medium, of its potential for stirring emotion. But here was evidence as well of the need for broadcast leaders to think carefully about how to assure that the power of radio to stir emotion should not be abused. After conferring with Paley, Klauber eliminated Father Coughlin's airtime. The CBS executives felt they had to demonstrate that they were not censoring religious comment as such, and so they planned, beginning in April 1931, to broadcast a regular Sunday church hour that would make airtime available to religious leaders of all denominations. The Father Coughlin controversy had an important effect on CBS's attitude toward the way in which opinion should be aired over the radio. "Broadcasting," Paley would say, "must forever be wholly, honestly, and militantly non-partisan. This is true not only in politics but in the whole realm of arguable ideas. We must never have an editorial page . . . we must never try to further either side of any debatable question." (13) To understand Bill Paley's later disgruntlement with some of the broadcasts of Ed Murrow and other CBS personalities, it is worth remembering the CBS boss's dictum: no editorial pages at CBS, no partisanship. Paley would try to enforce that dictum. As we shall see, he did not always succeed.

CBS needed to improve its programming. David Sarnoff had decided to put his main effort in developing new technology. Television was forever on his mind. But Bill Paley had little interest in pursuing the technical side of the broadcasting industry. He chose to push programming instead. Experimentation was possible, given the fact that only one-third of CBS's radio schedule was sponsored. Clearly, these hours provided an opportunity, and Bill Paley finally decided to exploit it. He put an advertisement in the newspapers that said, "Wanted—a big man for an important creative and executive post in radio broadcasting. This man will head a large department in one of the biggest organizations creating radio programs today. His job will be to create new radio programs for some of the most important advertisers on the air." Six hundred replies were received.

Oddly enough, the man who landed the job was William B. Lewis. He got it purely by accident. He had written a letter to Paley's home which somehow had become mixed up in the finalists' pile for the programming job. While his credentials were not perfect, something about him appealed to the CBS brass. So, early in 1936, Lewis was appointed CBS vice president for programming. He was immediately given a mandate to experiment, to open new frontiers in radio programming. Lewis resurrected an idea proposed earlier by Irving Reis, a studio engineer, and in July 1936 the "Columbia Workshop" was born, a laboratory for experiments in radio, with sound effects, filters, microphones, and echo chambers. Salaries were low. Writers received $100 for a produced script; actors were paid $18.50 for a half-hour performance, including rehearsal time. But getting on the air was what counted.

That fall Reis received a half-hour script in the mail called "The Fall of the City," a verse play written by Archibald MacLeish. MacLeish had been a football and water polo player at Yale; later, he had become a lawyer and was now a poet. The play took place in a crowded city square. For unexplained reasons, the crowds anticipate and seem to welcome a conqueror, accepting enslavement. The play was meant to depict the evils of totalitarianism, similar to that sweeping through Europe. In the MacLeish parable, the people prefer the enslavement of the conqueror to a free, democratic society and the burden it imposes on an individual. Irving Reis obtained approval to broadcast the program from New York City's Seventh Regiment Armory on March 4, 1937. Extras were recruited from City College of New York. A young actor named Orson Welles played the radio announcer's role. Rehearsals were beset with problems: one day men with tennis racquets showed up, insisting that they had reserved the armory for their match; on another day National Guard trucks rolled in; no one had bothered to cancel maneuvers. Aired opposite NBC's Jack Benny program, "The Fall of the City" made Orson Welles a star. But "Fall" was significant for other reasons. Other poets quickly realized that this new medium could be hospitable for their work. Through radio, the poets sensed, they could reach millions, a bright alternative to writing poetry books that would only grow dusty on bookshelves. The publicity surrounding "Fall" drew artists to radio, among them Stephen Vincent Benét, W. H. Auden, Maxwell Anderson, and Edna St. Vincent Millay. With their participation, radio moved to a new level of acceptability. As for CBS, it gained a fresh self-assurance in producing the works of MacLeish, Norman Corwin, and others. "Columbia Workshop" had become the flagship of CBS radio programming. Now, for the first time, CBS was a major source for programming.

The 1930s had turned CBS into a vital force. It had taken time. At first few thought the network would survive its birth pangs. Talk of bankruptcy was always in the air. It was the upstart network, it was the grass-roots phenomenon fighting the established NBC. Slowly, a CBS identity would be formed, in programming, in its coverage of the news. The network, during the 1930s, would learn to take itself seriously, and when it did, the public reacted positively. Bill Paley did not do it alone; he relied upon others. Some of those he chose, such as Ed Klauber and Paul Kesten would set their mark on the organization by virtue of their own, distinctive personalities. But, above all, it was Paley's instinct for what the public wanted that accounted for CBS's rising to the heights. Few have managed to probe deeply into his personality largely because of Paley himself. He tells us in the early pages of his memoirs that "I don't think I am a very easy person to know." (14) He is right about that. And then later on, perhaps inadvertently, he tells us why his personality remains so closed to the public. "I have had very few intimates . . . I do not like the idea of depending on others. I don't feel safe. When I find myself becoming dependent on one particular person I start to worry about what would happen if he or she were no longer there, and about who could take his or her place . . . I always keep my reserve." (15) Indeed, he has. (He did marry—twice. The first time in May 1932, to Dorothy Hearst, the daughter of a Los Angeles insurance executive. Then, after divorcing her in July 1947, he married Barbara "Babe" Cushing the same month.) So reserved has Bill Paley been, that whenever anyone who knew him tries to describe him, they generally fail to come up with anything beyond bland generalities.

Despite that Paley reserve, or perhaps because of it, he enjoyed a good press at this time. The writer of a June 1935 *Fortune* magazine article wrote about the CBS founder in words Paley could have dictated himself. "Mr. Paley as a businessman is a theme that practically brings tears to the eyes of his directors—never in all their lives, they say, have they been associated with anybody as clever at business. Not only is he a master advertiser and feeler of the public pulse, but these gentlemen say he is the greatest organizer, the best executive, the quickest thinker, the coolest negotiator they have ever seen." Then elsewhere it noted: "Perhaps his most outstanding characteristic is enthusiasm—for radio, for his friends, for his hobbies, for anything he does."

three

"I'd Like to Forget . . . the Thud of Hobnail Boots."

The two worlds of entertainment and public affairs would wage a constant silent war in the minds of CBS executives. Should one be pursued over the other? Should equal attention be paid to both? Intuitively, Bill Paley realized that the entertainment battle with NBC was like a war of attrition, and like such wars, years might pass before a winner was declared. But public affairs was different. As the mid-1930s approached, neither company had staked out a solid position. The potential of news broadcasting was still not clear. So much was experimental. The public's desire to be informed, to have radio cover world events as immediately after they occurred as was technically possible, was clear. So the "arms race" in radio in the 1930s was waged over the issue of who could bring the news to the listener more quickly.

Before 1935, broadcasting from overseas was minimal. Sometimes the reason was technical, sometimes political. Static frequently interfered with broadcasts. Moreover, there were few high-powered shortwave stations that could be employed for trans-Atlantic transmissions. Still, it was becoming increasingly obvious that American listeners wanted to know what was going on in Europe. Yet, given the political leanings of some European countries, it became evident quickly that bringing world events to CBS's listeners was going to be far more difficult than was piping in the sounds of a famous orchestra from a New York sound studio.

One event brought all this into sharp focus, pointing to the potential and the power of radio. On October 2, 1935, the Italian leader Benito Mussolini sent his soldiers across the Eritrean border into East Africa. A young Ed Murrow, who was director of talks at CBS, had decided it would be good "radio journalism" to have the views of the Ethiopian delegation broadcast as well as the Italians from Geneva. It was arranged that Edgar Ansel Mowrer, the Paris correspondent for the *Chicago Daily News*, would interview the official spokesman of Italy. On October 9, the chief Ethiopian delegate, Beirond Tecle Hawariate, explained his country's views, and the following night it was to be the Italian spokesman's turn. Baron Pompeo Aloisi, the head of the Italian delegation, sat at the microphone with newsman Mowrer by his side. Just as they were about to start, a phone call came in from London with the message that there would be no broadcast: the British Post Office was refusing to relay the talk along the London–New York circuit. The reason: League of Nations sanctions against Italy which had been voted that very day. Murrow, needless to say, was fuming. In the headlines the next day the news of British sanctions against Italy was combined with the British cutoff of the Geneva transmission. Sensing the harm that radio could bring—to themselves, in this case—the British had acted to stave off the damage that would be inflicted should the Italian spokesman talk over radio. In time, Baron Aloisi would get on the air, using the Rome transmitter. What had infuriated Murrow was the simple fact that he couldn't bring the story home to his listeners. His instincts were that of a journalist, pure and simple.

No one knew how Ed Murrow had acquired those instincts. Something of Ed Klauber's purity must have have rubbed off on Ed; something of Paul White's enthusiasm for the trade must have also. Unquestionably, Murrow was a product of the Klauber-White school. Yet Murrow would take what he had learned farther than his mentors. He would give journalism a high moral purpose, and, in using radio to achieve that purpose, he would turn the new medium into a permanent and irrevocable force. Of all the personalities in the CBS story, none has engaged the public as much as this man.

He had been a speech major in college during the 1920s and had played the lead in several campus productions. He had a furrowed brow, dark eyes, and a cigarette in his fingers that became a trademark of sorts. He graduated from Washington State in June 1930 and went on to become president of the National Student Federation of America. For the next few years he worked both at home and overseas with student and educational groups. Then in late 1934, Stephen Duggan, who was a retired professor of political science and one of the earliest commentators on radio, aired a network commentary series over radio. Duggan had been asked to run "Last Week Abroad," a commentary program on that week's foreign news affecting American policy. It was broadcast for twenty-five weeks on Friday afternoons over the "American School of the Air," the CBS educational series, quickly attracting an audience. Duggan received $50 a broadcast. Murrow, as Duggan's second-in-command, arranged the programs and learned much about radio and current issues in American foreign policy. He also managed to impress Fred Willis, right-hand man to William Paley.

When a new job opened up, director of talks to coordinate broadcasts on current issues, Murrow seemed an ideal candidate. Fred Willis suggested that Murrow call on Ed Klauber, the CBS executive vice president. Klauber, however, had in mind broadcaster Raymond Swing for the job. But Swing realized that he would not be doing any broadcasting, an anathema to him. He had won his reputation as a radio commentator in England where he had worked for a long time as an American newspaper correspondent. After returning to the United States, Swing appeared on a weekly trans-Atlantic program exchange and did a weekly talk on foreign affairs for the "American School of the Air." Ed Klauber, however, didn't like his voice for some reason, and so Murrow was finally asked to become director of talks.

Murrow scheduled speakers on all sorts of subjects. The appeal of radio was becoming obvious, and Murrow contributed much to the idea that radio could serve a unique purpose as a national public forum. Appearing on the program were Secretary of State Cordell Hull, Senator William Borah, New York Governor Al Smith, and Socialist leader Norman Thomas, as well as Minnesota Governor Floyd B. Olson. Murrow got into some hot water—it never seemed to bother him—when he invited Earl Browder, the Secretary of the Communist Party, onto the program. Browder was his party's next presidential nominee. This marked the first time that a radio network had granted free time to a Communist. Murrow was unruffled by critics who suggested that he should not have given the Communist leader such a broad forum. Murrow countered by noting that the Communist Party was registered in thirty-nine states and because of that, fairness dictated that he allow it on the air. But there were pickets, and six New England stations decided not to run the show. Hearst editorials made some unpleasant remarks about CBS and Congressman John McClellan of Arkansas accused the network of treason. In 1936 Murrow arranged 311 broadcasts from twenty-seven foreign countries, double the number from the previous year.

Murrow was never intimidated in front of the microphone. Robert Trout, the main CBS announcer at the time, is credited with teaching Ed the tricks of the trade, the most important of which was to stay cool on the air. Once, Murrow and Trout were at a Christmas Eve party at which Ed persuaded the announcer to give him a chance to read the evening news. Trout doubted Murrow would manage it, but he read the news flawlessly. It was a sign of what lay in store.

In the mid-1930s, little was known about why people chose certain products over others. Some at CBS had an interest in finding out. They hoped to woo advertisers away from the newspapers. Anyone who had fresh ideas about how to discover what we know today as merchandising would be welcome. Thus, Frank Stanton came to CBS in 1935. He remained there for nearly four decades, rising steadily into positions of leadership, effectively running the organization at times, and, perhaps most important, becoming a highly respected industry spokesman.

Thirty-six years old, he had started in CBS's audience research department in the fall of 1935 and eventually became its director. From his days in graduate school at Ohio State, Stanton, fascinated with radio, wanted to look into the question of why people reacted positively to certain radio shows but negatively to others. The sophisticated ratings systems that were developed later on did not exist. Stanton thought there was room for a research project that would try to gauge audience reaction to radio programs. He went to the dean of the Graduate School of Business at Ohio State, seeking approval to undertake this project as part of his own studies, but was quickly rebuffed. Radio, said the dean, was a passing fad that would amount to nothing. What was the point of wasting his time on it. Stanton could not be knocked down so easily. He took his idea to the Psychology Department and won its approval for the project. Thus, Frank Stanton, who would become one of the leaders of the broadcasting industry, earned a doctorate in industrial psychology, not communications, not advertising, not even business. His doctorate examined why and how people perceive various stimuli. He had done research on audio and visual effectiveness for the conveyance of information and established test procedures for making rough measurements of the effectiveness of the two approaches in moving and retaining information. His 1935 doctorate thesis was titled, "A Critique of Present Methods and a New Plan for Studying Radio Listening Behavior." Stanton sent several copies to CBS and NBC. NBC showed little interest. Another study of his, called "Memory for Advertising Copy Presented Visually vs. Orally," attracted attention at CBS. His thesis: people recalled facts that they had heard far more than those they had read. CBS was most receptive to such an idea, hoping to lure new advertisers all the time. Looking over Stanton's ideas, Paul Kesten was impressed. He wrote him: "I don't know of any other organization where your background and experience would count so heavily in your favor or where your talent would find so enthusiastic a reception." The letter worked. Stanton agreed to work, starting at $50 a week in CBS's small Research Department. From the beginning, many viewed Stanton as a workaholic, but one with little self-confidence.

In 1937, working with Dr. Paul Lazarsfeld of Princeton University, Stanton devised a program analysis system that was called "Little Annie." While Stanton tends to downplay the machine as significant, others have credited it with being the first qualitative measurement device. It was meant to determine the probable appeal of a radio program by suggesting how large an audience that program would be likely to draw. Knowing such information, CBS would be able to gauge whether the program would be able to attract a sponsor.

"Little Annie" required a small listening room with twelve seats spaced in front of a long table. At each location was a pair of push buttons, which was wired to a central recording device. CBS personnel would go out into the streets of New York and Los Angeles and find people moving around tourist centers, asking them if they would be willing to aid in selecting shows that the country would hear on the network. Those who agreed would place their left hands on the red buttons and their right hands on the green ones. Watching pilot shows on the screen, they would be asked to give their reactions by pushing the buttons, the red button for anything the viewer didn't like, the green for anything he did like. The answers were then graphed on a controlroom board. The viewer then was asked to fill out a written questionnaire, again seeking to discover whether he liked or disliked the show. For each pilot, CBS would get eighty opinions. Stanton's standing was not hurt by the fact that "Little Annie's" statistics successfully predicted a program's popularity quite accurately.

It was only in 1936 that radio began to tap the potential for international coverage of events. CBS was the decided leader. But not everything went smoothly. It was not that there wasn't big news from Europe. There was certainly a great deal of that: the death of King George V, the fall of Ethiopia, civil war in Spain, German troops moving into the formerly demilitarized Rhineland in defiance of the Versailles Treaty. CBS did its best to cover those events. Yet the news was still taking a backseat to entertainment. For all the growing importance of overseas news, American radio still believed that programs from across the ocean should entertain, rather than inform. This led to the incongruous reality of American radio carrying foreign vaudeville acts and Toscanini playing at Salzburg while there was civil strife in Austria, upheaval in Germany, and rising tension throughout the rest of Europe.

The pace of overseas news did impress some at CBS. Every Sunday at 12 noon, Cesar Saerchinger, who had set up CBS's first London office, would come on the air. Ed Murrow was busy lining up commentators from Paris and London, but until then, no one had tried to bring the same day's news to the listening audience. And for good reason. Live broadcasts to the United States lacked sophistication. American network radio refused to use recordings—CBS and NBC argued that what they were selling was live shows, that any half-baked studio could put on a recorded show. Yet the news from Europe was increasingly frightening; despite the difficulties, broadcasting directly from Europe seemed more and more to be a necessity.

CBS's news division's first tests would be the coverage of war-related stories. Past wars had been covered by newspapers, though battles had been described over radio. But no reporter had taken his microphone into the thick of battle, described what he saw, risked his life in doing it, giving the listener a "you are there" sensation. No one until Hans von Kaltenborn in 1936 did his famous radio reporting from the battlefield. Kaltenborn, then 50 years old, was a newspaper veteran and part-time radio commentator. He had not been sent to cover the Spanish Civil War by CBS. He traveled to Europe paying his own expenses. He had been broadcasting on CBS for six years, always unsponsored except for three months under Cunard Line auspices. Although he was not considered commercial material, CBS still felt there was a place for him on the air. Kaltenborn did two broadcasts a week and earned $50 for each broadcast. Often it was felt that Kaltenborn injected himself intrusively into his reports. But at least he was prepared to go outside the newsroom and look at the news up front. That made him different. Not everyone was willing to venture so far, or, as in Kaltenborn's case, so close to the dangers that outside coverage might bring.

Born in the United States to German parents, the Harvard-educated Kaltenborn had worked for the *Brooklyn Eagle* before becoming a commentator for AT&T's radio station WEAF in the mid-1920s. He had hoped to have as much freedom to say what he wanted as he had at the newspaper, but he did not. After criticizing a judge who was trying a case involving AT&T, Kaltenborn was warned that he was endangering the case. The warning hardly impressed him; in the end, AT&T fired him, and his next radio job was as a CBS news analyst. He was known as someone who could talk freely about almost anything, and often did. He had strong principles about the role of a commentator and one was that sponsors could not interfere with his broadcasts. Once, when Eddie Cantor invited him to appear on his show to do a skit—on the NBC Red network—Kaltenborn said no. The reason: the skit led into a commercial.

As is so often the case with newsmen, luck played a role in Kaltenborn's precedent-setting war coverage in 1936. The CBS network, still more interested in the coverage of "events" than hard news, had sent Cesar Saerchinger to Berlin to organize coverage of the Olympic Games. Then events in Spain became dramatic, and Kaltenborn, who was traveling in Europe, began broadcasting and did so every day for five weeks. Situating himself in Hendaye, France, just across the Spanish border, he provided the first running commentary on the war largely by interviewing battle-weary participants who had crossed over from Spain. Without their own men, the networks had to rely on newspaper correspondents in Spain to do the broadcasting. To make matters worse, those correspondents were operating under major censorship handicaps. At one stage, when the Spanish rebels engaged the Spanish Loyalists in Irun, a frontier city, CBS had a man on the spot, Hans von Kaltenborn, or nearly so. The fighting had spread into farmlands outside the Spanish city, and Kaltenborn, coming upon an abandoned farmhouse, figured out how to get a microphone and transmitting equipment in a haystack—a comparatively safe place. Kaltenborn's French engineer found a piece of French land which projected into Spain within a bend of the Bidou River. This small river marked the boundary line between France and Spain. The main highway followed the bend of the river on the Spanish side. Kaltenborn recalled: "As the battle seemed likely to follow along the highway, we figured that if we were lucky enough to establish a microphone on this French piece of soil we might be able to broadcast an actual battle between the advancing Franco forces on one side of the river bend and the retreating Republican forces on the other. Of course we had to establish our microphone in France since all telephone connections stopped at the border." (1)

The engineer discovered that the few French farmers living on the neck of land had already been evacuated in advance of the battle. One phone existed in one of the farmhouses. Finding the telephone connection workable, the engineer fixed Kaltenborn up with a long cable. That cable enabled the broadcaster to carry a mike into the field toward the bank of the river where at a later stage of the battle of Irun he would be located between the two armies. "It turned out just as we had anticipated," Kaltenborn recalled. "The battle developed in such a way that this particular piece of French land was a no-man's land between the two armies." (2) The advancing army's objective was the city of Irun. Neither side wanted to trespass into France as both sought favors from the French; they knew too that France would retaliate for any violation of French soil. French planes loaded with bombs flew over the area regularly, ready to drop bombs on any Spanish contingent trespassing; the French engineer had taken pains to apprise the authorities of what he and Kaltenborn were doing. "I felt reasonably safe hiding behind a haystack

in the French field," said Kaltenborn. "Bullets and shells whipped overhead but only an occasional spent rifle bullet dropped in the field." (3)

Next, Kaltenborn had to assure that the connection was indeed
good. Bayonne was difficult. But getting through to Paris was the hard
part. Again, Kaltenborn: "I remember Bayonne particularly because on
one occasion when I was ready to broadcast the battle, and we had our
connections established—CBS had given us the go ahead—we found that
the Bayonne engineer had gone out for an aperitif and consequently we
couldn't get by Bayonne." (4) After getting through that first time, CBS
advised Kaltenborn, hugging the haystack for dear life, that a number of
commercials had already been scheduled, and the battle broadcast would
simply have to wait. Stand by, please, he was instructed. Several times
later trouble occurred at some relay point. All Kaltenborn could do was
be patient while his engineer worked double-time trying to keep the line
open and repairing the wire, cut several times by bullets. "I watched the
battle, listened to the whistle of the bullets, and hoped for the best," Kaltenborn said. (5) It was an early example of another kind of battle the
news department would wage in earnest with its more powerful colleagues in the entertainment division—the battle for air. Eventually, Kaltenborn was able to describe the battle in progress, picking up the live
sounds of bullets and shells and transmitting it to his radio listeners.
There was lots of static over the radio, but the war was live. And, most
important of all, CBS had a war correspondent in place. For his work
during the Spanish Civil War, Kaltenborn received an award from the
Headliners Club of Atlantic City for the best broadcast of 1936. And,
more important, he was made a regular commentator for CBS.

The Kaltenborn broadcast from the Spanish Civil War was a breakthrough. By proving that such live broadcasts were indeed possible, it
anticipated the coverage from war-torn Europe during World War II. Just
as CBS and radio had demonstrated that it could cover a battle, the network was about to prove that it could provide the same on-the-spot coverage for a fast-breaking political crisis in Europe. In December 1936, few
noticed the tiny story in the *Chicago Daily News* mentioning that in the
English town of Ipswich a Mrs. E. A. Simpson had filed for divorce against
a Mr. Simpson. This story was taking British understatement a bit too far.
For the real story, between the lines, was the romance between the king
of England and an American socialite, Mrs. Wallis Simpson, who soon
would be divorced for the second time. A constitutional crisis was at

---

hand, but the British press weren't allowed to tell the story—which gave American radio a marvelous advantage in covering it.

The tale of the beleaguered couple was tailor-made for radio: it was fast moving, dramatic, and colorful. A news-hungry audience, unable to get enough juicy details about Buckingham Palace's most famous romance, would rush to their radios for every mouth-watering fact.

One man understood all this need as few others would. Ed Murrow. First, he had a deeply rooted sense of respect, tempered with amusement, for the English. He quickly sensed that radio—and specifically CBS—could capitalize on what some would call "the love story of the century." If the British wanted to censor this story, silly as that might be, it wasn't going to hamper Ed Murrow's judgment. Censorship was meant to protect lives, not reputations. Paul White was away, and so Murrow went to Ed Klauber. He then put Murrow in touch with Paley's chief assistant, Fred Willis. The decision was made. CBS should go after the story and not spare the resources. And so Murrow and the others worked 24 hours a day to put the story on the air, on the phone with Cesar Saerchinger in London, getting English broadcasters to give commentary on the air, putting out news bulletins. Leading figures in law, sociology, Parliament, and academic life from Britain appeared on CBS during the ten days of the palace crisis. CBS presented thirty-nine 15-minute broadcasts. Ironically, CBS offered more in the way of commentary and news to its audience than did British radio. It was a foreshadowing of the Murrow broadcasts during World War II.

With all that hard work, it was not surprising that the biggest scoop in the Windsor-Simpson romance went to CBS. Saerchinger was on the London–New York circuit, and he wanted airtime at once. Without thinking twice, Murrow cut into a program, and there followed the CBS London man's announcement, broadcasting directly from the House of Commons, telling the American audience even before British MPs had heard the news, that Edward VIII had declared he was abdicating. "The king has abdicated," Saerchinger said. "Here is Sir Frederick Whyte to speak to you about this momentous event." American listeners had learned of the abdication even before the British prime minister had read out the royal message. Later in the day, through the crackling shortwave came the emotion-filled voice of the former Edward VIII, stating that he was leaving the throne for "the woman I love."

As he had demonstrated in the abdication crisis, Ed Murrow had always had the right instincts, the nose for news, the ability to be in the right place at the right time. This time, February 1937, when Ed Klauber asked Murrow to become European director for CBS there was no hesitation, no self-doubt. This, despite the fact that Ed was not yet 30 years old. Murrow was sure that Europe was a political cauldron, that this month, next month, next year, the Germans would wreak even more havoc. He had no idea what form the violence would take, only that it would occur, and he knew that he wanted to be there. And in doing so he began the story of CBS in Europe, of CBS in wartime. He could not know that his efforts would be regarded as a significant and heroic chapter in the early history of broadcasting. Each step that he took, each decision that he made was part of the legend that would take form. When Klauber had asked him about the new job, Murrow had been attending the annual meeting of the National Education Association in New Orleans. Murrow said yes immediately. He knew that the new job was likely to do harm to his prospects for rising through the administrative ranks at CBS. But that counted not at all with him; what did count was the chance to become a witness to history. Some would say that Murrow was sent to Europe because CBS could not find a niche for him in New York, that in fact the new assignment was a kind of consolation prize. Even if that were the case, Murrow appeared enthusiastic. Going to Europe, he would say afterward, "gave me an opportunity to watch Europe tearing up its maps, to see and hear the last peacetime performance at Salzburg; Vienna cheering the arrival of the oppressors; dismemberment of Czechoslovakia by her sworn friends; then the full tide of war sweeping across Europe like a brown stain. It gave me the opportunity to know Britain in her darkest, and finest, hour." (6) It was pure Murrow, and it was said from his heart. Somehow, when he said it, it didn't sound corny or artificial.

Although the decision to send Ed Murrow to cover the "walk-up" to World War II now looks prescient, the truth lay elsewhere. Newspapers and news agencies were beefing up their staffs for the war that seemed inevitable. But CBS was not. It was still a popular notion that radio was unsuited to cover the news. CBS network officials actually believed that piping music from Europe back home to the United States was the best thing the network could do to promote peace. One said that CBS had performed the greatest service to international understanding by broadcasting the "Song of a Nightingale"; originating from Kent, England, "Nightingale" had been voted "the most interesting broadcast of the year" in 1932 by American radio editors. (7) As far as the network was concerned, covering overseas news meant having an editor in New York rip off news copy as the paper spewed from the clacking wire service machine.

Although there were foreign correspondents, none worked full time for an American radio network. The voices of European and American newspaper journalists were heard on American radio, as were those of authors and politicians. They were the experts, and their opinions were sought. No one thought it necessary to send an American radio reporter overseas to do nothing but report the news. Radio was still too experimental. Indeed, reporting from abroad for radio was not a recognized profession. Ed Murrow went to Europe not as a reporter, but rather as a person in charge of arranging "talks" and supervising "events." He was paid $8,000 a year. When he applied for membership in the correspondents' association in London, he was rejected. He was not even allowed to attend its meetings. Radio, it seemed, had no status at all. (Seven years later, in a neat turnabout, Murrow would become president of the association.)

And so, at the age of 29, Ed Murrow sailed for England where he took over CBS's European Bureau, not yet a reporter, but deeply aware that he was sitting on a powder keg. He made it clear at the outset that he would make changes. Soon after his arrival, Murrow told the tall, bushy-browed director of the BBC, Sir John Reith, that he [Murrow] planned to make broadcasting down to earth by taking his microphone into country villages, to let the people speak. Murrow interviewed a philosophical London cabby, Herbert Hodge, as one of his first "down to earth" people. Hodge was so popular that he became a CBS feature, commenting on affairs from a pub on Saturday nights. Thinking the pub broadcasts something of a slap at the BBC, the British press reported them widely. Here was an American broadcaster reaching out to the public, to the average man, in a way that no BBC reporter had done, or was likely to do.

Not everything would go as smoothly. When Murrow asked the CBS secretary to phone Winston Churchill, at home if necessary, for an appointment, he was told by secretary Kay Campbell that one didn't behave that way in England. The custom was to write a note and wait for a reply a few days later. Murrow was not about to change his American working habits. He ordered the secretary to pick up the phone. Realizing how valuable a contact Murrow would be, Winston Churchill answered his unconventional overture positively.

Not all efforts of Murrow's would reap such quick results. Before he had arrived on the scene, NBC had gained a great advantage in parts of Europe by allowing others to believe that it was just like the other state-run radios in Europe. It had a "national" in its name, didn't it? Thus, NBC deserved primary attention among the American radio networks. Moreover, NBC had signed contracts as far back as the 1920s, with certain state radios, particularly the Austrian and the German, granting NBC an exclusive relationship with those state radio networks. Murrow's first task was to break NBC's monopoly. Slightly easing his task was the paroxysm of fright that coursed through NBC upon its staff's learning that CBS had assigned Murrow to London. Max Jordan, NBC's representative in Europe, raced off to the continent to strengthen the network's already solid links with the various European state radios.

∽∿∽∿∽∿

CBS had to expand its news-gathering role in Europe to cover the news seriously. Ed Murrow realized that he needed someone to provide first-hand coverage on the continent. In the summer of 1937 he found him— an American foreign correspondent who had been plying his trade for a number of years in Asia as well as in Europe. His name was William Shirer. They got along from their first meeting although they were different in personal appearance and style. Murrow, the suave, handsome figure, perfectly groomed, perfectly tailored, was a study in contrast with the short, stocky newspaperman in rumpled clothes, metal-rimmed glasses hanging casually on his nose. Shirer considered the telegram from Murrow inviting him to meet for dinner at the Adlon Hotel in Berlin on August 27, 1937 as the opportunity for a free meal. In exchange for the dinner, the local man was expected to give his analysis of the political situation. Shirer thought too little of radio to want to get involved full time with such people. The previous May he had actually done a broadcast for CBS providing reaction from Berlin to the Hindenburg disaster; the experience was so nerve-wracking—he had trouble speaking—that he vowed to steer clear of radio.

But, as he prepared to meet Murrow for dinner, Shirer knew that his job with INS (International News Service) in Berlin had just ended that week; he had high hopes of a job offer from *The New York Times*. Soon after they began dinner, Murrow started to pick his brain, confirming Shirer's view of what the meeting was all about. But then, suddenly, Murrow asked how committed Shirer was to the *Times*. Not very committed at all, was the reply—a truthful one, though Shirer would have wanted the facts to be different. Why had Murrow asked? Well, he explained, the story was getting too large, and he was looking for an experienced foreign correspondent, someone who could open an office for CBS on the continent. Was Shirer interested, Murrow asked? Shirer said yes, still excited even after he learned that CBS would not pay him more than the $125 a week he had been making recently. Murrow did not have the authority to wrap up the deal with Shirer. The CBS bureaucracy would have to be broached. But Murrow thought that a mere formality. Is it a deal, Murrow asked? Still taken aback, Shirer said yes, it was a deal. He forgot about his disenchantment with radio. Shirer wanted work, and here was someone offering it to him.

Following dinner, Murrow apologetically noted that Shirer would have to pass a voice test before CBS would give the final nod. It was as if the bottom had fallen out for Shirer—knowing how nervous he had been the last time, he doubted he would pass muster. In his diary, Shirer wrote that "I have a job. I am to go to work for the Columbia Broadcasting System. That is if . . . I have a job if my voice is all right. . . . Who ever heard of an adult with no pretenses to being a singer or any other kind of artist being dependent for a good, interesting job on his voice. And mine is terrible." (8) Murrow thought it largely unimportant whether the correspondent had a good broadcasting voice. What counted was whether the man was a good correspondent. If he was, the public would accept him as an authority, whether his voice was too high pitched or too nasal. Because Murrow was able to convince the New York brass of his view, CBS would emphasize the correspondent's reporting and writing abilities over his broadcasting skills. It was a principle which Murrow and those who followed him at CBS would develop, creating the greatest news-gathering operation in broadcasting. Believing that he would have little trouble convincing his superiors to hire Shirer, no matter how he sounded on the air, Murrow sought to lift Shirer's spirits, to tell him that it would be all right. Still, Shirer had his doubts.

The trial broadcast was held on Sunday, September 5, in the early evening. The CBS staff did little to put Shirer at ease before the momentous event. Claire Trask, the local CBS representative, had inadvertently left her written introduction behind, and so she had to scurry to a nearby cafe to retrieve it. To make matters worse, the lone microphone was stuck at a height of seven feet, making it all but impossible for Shirer to use it. Inventively, Shirer had himself and Claire boosted atop a piano packing case so that their mouths were level with the mike. Ten seconds later they were on the air. Shirer worried, not about his voice cracking, but whether he would be able to refrain from convulsing in laughter over his standing on a piano case. Murrow had advised him to avoid the impression that he was reading from a script. He had tried to remember that.

After it was all over, Shirer believed he had sounded plodding and fainthearted, yet he had done his best to speak with conviction and a sense of authenticity. With the trial completed, it was as if he had awakened from a nightmare; he recalled in sorrow that his voice had seemingly soared an octave and that he had trouble speaking because his lips were so dry. Shirer was convinced he had been a disaster.

Murrow had promised a final answer within two days, but when there was no word from him during that period Shirer had all but given up hope. Finally, a few days later, Murrow phoned Shirer person to person from London with the good news. They think you are terrific, Murrow said with great enthusiasm. That, of course, was stretching the truth. In fact, when the brass heard Shirer, they told Murrow, "Forget about him. His accent is Midwestern. He's not for radio." But Ed Murrow fought for his principles; he needed reporters like Bill Shirer. Such was Murrow's clout even in those early days that he made it clear he would not take no for an answer, and the ploy worked. New York relented and a shocked Shirer agreed to start October 1. That evening, at a stadium in Nuremberg, Shirer happened to sit next to Frederick T. Birchall, the chief foreign correspondent for *The New York Times*, who had strung him along about the *Times* job. Shirer couldn't wait to tell the *Times* man his good news. Birchall sounded incredulous that Shirer could even think of taking a job with radio. How could such a serious newsman contemplate so superficial a medium as radio? Why, within a few years, said Birchall, Shirer would be eager to return to newspaper work.

But for now, he was a radio reporter—and for CBS. Well, not quite a reporter. "One disappointing thing about the job . . . ," he confided to his diary after a week of chatting with Murrow in London in early October, "Murrow and I are not supposed to do any talking on the radio ourselves." (9) Rather, he and Murrow were required to hire newspaper correspondents to do the broadcasting. The system was all wrong to Shirer: he, with his foreign languages and years of experience, knew far more about the political story in Europe than did most of the newspaper correspondents. Why should he not get on the air? The CBS explanation, as conveyed by Murrow, made no sense whatsoever: were he and Murrow to report directly on the air, that would commit CBS editorially. Shirer's disappointment notwithstanding, the practical matter of needing a regular paycheck left him little choice but to hang on to the CBS job until he could land one again with a newspaper. Meanwhile, choosing Vienna over Geneva as his European headquarters, he bore the impressive title of "Continental Representative of CBS."

Bill Shirer's first assignment was to weaken the hold NBC had on broadcasting from Europe. He had to try to break the monopoly NBC had over using German and Vatican broadcasting facilities. Germany proved easier to change than did the Vatican. Nazi Propaganda Minister Joseph Goebbels personally gave Shirer the approval to broadcast, understanding the value of having another large American radio network broadcasting from Berlin. The Vatican may have understood that point as well, but its officials insisted upon several hundred dollars payment at once as well as a modest annual contribution. Unhappy at being forced to pay someone what he considered a bribe, Bill Paley at first objected. He finally relented after Shirer explained that there were no alternatives. Shirer's first news assignment was to accompany the Duke and Duchess of Windsor on a planned trip to New York where they were to do a broadcast for CBS as part of their American tour aimed at studying the labor situation. But the American visit was scrapped after the couple was heavily criticized in the United States for adding Nazi Germany to their itinerary.

While doing these assignments, Shirer could not forget that he was first and foremost a newspaperman. He wanted to report, to get on the air. Bill Paley wouldn't budge on the point, and so Shirer was left with the frustrating chore of hiring newspaper correspondents for broadcasts he would have preferred to do himself.

He was still perplexed by CBS's policy when he arrived in Vienna on a Friday morning in the spring of 1938. The date was March 11. The Austrian government, led by Chancellor Kurt von Schuschnigg, was deteriorating, due both to internal pressure caused by Nazis in his cabinet and external pressure caused by Adolf Hitler himself. Schuschnigg planned a plebescite for that Sunday. Cabling Paul White in New York, Shirer begged to be permitted to broadcast the plebescite results that evening. He was the spot. What was more, he was an eyewitness to monumental events. CBS would have the story alone. NBC's Max Jordan wasn't even in the country. What a golden opportunity for the network to show it was on the ball. Shirer would certainly have enough to broadcast. In the next hours, demonstrating Austrian Nazis forced the plebescite to be called off. Shirer thought of contacting Murrow to enlist his help in getting on the air. Murrow was in Poland where he was organizing the CBS "School of the Air" program. Shirer tried to reach him but had no luck. Schuschnigg came on the radio to announce that the Germans, threatening to invade Austria, had ordered him to step down in favor of a German-appointed figurehead, or else the German army would march. As it turned out, Dr. Arthur Seyss-Inquart, Schuschnigg's successor, made it clear that the Germans would invade—despite the Austrian capitulation.

Shirer knew that he had the greatest scoop of his career; he was the only American radio man around. But would CBS put him on the air? When Murrow finally called him, Shirer said cryptically, "The opposing team has just crossed the goal line." (10) To which Murrow replied, "Are you sure?" Shirer answered, "I'm paid to be sure." Dispirited, Shirer conveyed the sad fact that he couldn't put the story on the air. Ed Murrow had an idea. Shirer should fly to London the next day. He could then give the first uncensored eyewitness account of the depressing events in Austria. Shirer knew the journey could be a complete waste of time: Murrow, after all, could not guarantee that CBS would acquiesce in allowing him on the air. But he would do it. He had nothing to lose—and a lot to gain.

Arriving in London, Bill Shirer was thrilled to learn that for the first time CBS was actually going to permit one of its own staff to broadcast the news. "Neither of them (Murrow and Shirer) at the time was really a broadcast newsman," Paley wrote in his memoirs. (11) Shirer noted bitingly in his own memoirs that it was more accurate to say that neither he nor Murrow were permitted to be broadcast newsmen.

Meanwhile, Murrow was itching to get on the air as well. He decided to go to Vienna. Flying to Berlin first, he chartered a 27-seat Lufthansa transport for $1,000, the one plane he could get. He was the only passenger. He arrived in Vienna just in time for the arrival of the Nazi soldiers. Getting on the air from Vienna would prove troublesome. NBC had an obvious advantage over CBS because of its contract with RAVAG, the Austrian state radio: NBC had access to broadcasting facilities while CBS did not. Although ill, Bill Paley called the head of RAVAG, an old acquaintance. It was no use. The official confessed that he was no longer in control. Paley listened to a grown man weep through the receiver.

In London, Bill Shirer was about to make broadcasting history in a BBC studio. At 11:30 P.M., the CBS New York announcer introduced Shirer with great flare: "A little more than 24 hours ago, Nazi troops passed over the border into Austria. . . . At the time of the invasion yesterday, William L. Shirer, Columbia's Central European Director, was in Vienna. This afternoon he flew to London to bring you an uncensored, eyewitness account of the move. . . . We take you now to London." Shirer made his first newscast. This blockbuster broadcast acquired quick recognition for CBS. Later, everyone at CBS would claim credit for the Shirer breakthrough. Bill Paley and Bob Trout, the New York newscaster, each thought he might have been the originator of the idea. The Shirer broadcast, as it turned out, was but a foretaste of greater things to come.

The next day, March 13, Murrow and Shirer arranged to do CBS's first world news roundup. Paul White had phoned that Sunday afternoon to ask the two men to arrange a news roundup from the major European capitals. CBS was planning on airing the show at 1 A.M., London time, eight hours later. Shirer said yes, but admitted later: "The truth was I didn't have the faintest idea how to do it." (12) Getting the foreign correspondents lined up was the easy part; Shirer knew them all, and the only potential difficulty was locating them on a Sunday evening. Shirer and Murrow by now were friendly with the directors and chief engineers of the European broadcasting systems. And Shirer could speak French, German, and Italian to the engineers. New York telephoned each capital with the cues. Shirer wondered whether the engineers would be able to understand the cues in English!

The show lasted 30 minutes. CBS wanted Shirer and a Parliament member from London, Murrow in Vienna, and three American newspa permen, one each in Berlin, Rome, and Paris. Murrow and Shirer chose Edgar Ansel Mowrer of the *Chicago Daily News* in Paris (he and Shirer had known each other in Berlin); Frank Gervasi of INS in Rome; Ellen Wilkinson, a Labor member of Parliament from London; and Pierre Huss of INS in Berlin. Technically, the major problem was getting Gervasi's copy out of Italy. Unable to "landline" Gervasi's voice to the large transmitter in Geneva, Italian engineers employed a radiophone to get him through to London. Shirer planned to reread Gervasi's account to New York.

Shirer wrote his own broadcast, enticed Edgar Mowrer and Ellen Wilkinson to cut short their weekend, and arranged with Frank Gervasi in Rome to phone his remarks into London if all other transmission efforts failed (which they did). Fifteen minutes before the 1 A.M. roundup was to begin, Shirer raced to the BBC broadcasting house to find that Ellen Wilkinson had just arrived. Through his earphones, he was amused to hear the calm voice of CBS announcer Bob Trout in New York: "The program 'St. Louis Blues' will not be heard tonight." Instead there would be a special broadcast "which will include pickups direct from London, Paris, and such other European capitals as at this late hour abroad have communications channels." (Even as they went on the air it was not clear how much of the program would get through) ". . . Columbia begins its radio tour of Europe's capitals with a transoceanic pickup from London. We take you now to London."

Shirer knew that the next 30 minutes might produce a piece of history for radio. No one had yet tried such daring logistics. Each correspondent would report live, each one thousands of miles from the others. The planning had to be perfect as each of their reports would have to be scheduled down to the second. The first world news roundup. Shirer opened by doubting the British would do anything more than protest Hitler's aggressive acts. Parliament member Wilkinson echoed him, adding that, while the British were annoyed at Hitler, no one wanted actually to get involved in a war. She described the British as exhibiting only "interested curiosity."

In Paris, Edgar Mowrer doubted whether anyone realized just how menacing Hitler was. He recalled that the French had watched Germany invade France twice before in the past 70 years, implying that they might roll over once again. Still, he noted that the French people had "felt an electric shock" when they saw Hitler's troops moving across the German border. Ed Murrow described a Vienna that had lost a great deal with the arrival of the Nazis. He began in that confident, quiet voice, "This is Edward Murrow speaking from Vienna. It's now nearly 2:30 in the morning and Herr Hitler has not yet arrived. No one seems to know just when he will get here, but most people expect him sometime after 10 o'clock tomorrow morning." He described the change he had found in Vienna. "They lift the right arm a little higher here than in Berlin and the 'Heil Hitler' is said a little more loudly . . . ." A censor sat next to Murrow to make sure he kept to his script. This was the first of the more than 5,000 broadcasts Murrow made in his lifetime. In Berlin, Pierre Huss of the INS sounded a theme that was too pro-Nazi for Shirer's taste, and he instantly regretted not selecting someone more objective.

Still, technically and otherwise, the show was a sensational success—and it made history. Shirer did an incredible juggling act that evening. It set the stage for CBS's twenty-day coverage of the Czech crisis the following September. Radio had not only presented the news, but it had also looked at events almost immediately after they had occurred. To do that, it had turned to specialists located where the action was occurring—and those specialists had delivered news and insights that ordinarily would have taken days to show up in a newspaper. No other medium could match radio's swiftness. News broadcasting, in a sense, came of age that evening in those different capitals in Europe. It was as if the executives and the reporters at CBS had issued a public statement: no more tearing off the wire copy and reading it; no more relying upon others for the news and analysis; now, CBS itself would be responsible for putting together an account of what happened and why it happened.

The word was passed from Paul White soon after the broadcast that the CBS brass, including Bill Paley, were thrilled. Shirer and Murrow were on their way to becoming regular CBS broadcast stars. CBS had pioneered a news format that would last down through the years. Others who came later could not improve on the format CBS had used that evening. But no one was in a mood to rest on laurels. In passing on his congratulations, Paul White wondered whether Shirer and Murrow could do it again, say, tomorrow night. "No problem," said an exhausted, delighted Bill Shirer. He could not disguise his pleasure at noticing the entirely new attitude at CBS. Whereas before he was not permitted to broadcast, now his superiors in New York did not seem to be able to get enough from him! By the time Shirer got around to that second news roundup, again with pickups from London, Berlin, Paris, Vienna, and Rome, the technical side was somewhat easier. The broadcast was aired at 3:30 A.M. London time Tuesday. Shirer now found that radio's immediacy fascinated him. His reports were getting to listeners as quickly as the wire services were reporting the news. Shirer was now bitten by the radio bug.

On Monday, March 14, Hitler finally entered Vienna almost at the same time that Prime Minister Chamberlain was acknowledging sadly to the House of Commons that the Anschluss was a blow to his policy of appeasement. Once again, Murrow was on the air from Vienna that afternoon. "Hello, America . . . Herr Hitler is now at the Imperial Hotel. Tomorrow there is to be a big parade, and at that time he will probably make his major speech. . . . Please don't think that everyone in Vienna was out to greet Herr Hitler today. There is a tragedy as well as rejoicing in this city tonight."

A marvelous footnote can be attached to that action-packed weekend, and it concerns, of all people, William S. Paley and Winston Churchill. The latter had made a little-noticed speech that Monday, March 14, noting in pain and shock what the dimensions of Hitler's strategic victory had been in conquering Austria. Sensing how eloquent Churchill had been and how important his comments were, Shirer raised with Bill Paley the idea of having Churchill repeat those words over CBS. Paley leaped at the idea, proposing to Shirer that he offer Churchill 15 minutes of airtime. When Shirer asked what Churchill was to be paid, Paley said $50. Shirer grimaced: he doubted Churchill would accept at that price. Without pausing, Paley told Shirer that Churchill would be doing a "sustaining program," one without commercials, and that was the pay. Shirer urged that Churchill be paid $500 or, if not that much, at least $250. Paley stuck to his guns. With little choice and little hope, Shirer phoned Churchill over at the House of Commons, put the offer to him, and was hardly surprised when he was told, yes he would love to do the broadcast, but not for $50. Unperturbed, Shirer explained that this was to be a "sustainer," and surely Churchill would not want to be sponsored under any circumstances. Apparently failing to understand all these nuances, Churchill said abruptly he would do the program for $500 and that was that. And thus CBS lost the opportunity to put Winston Churchill on the air.

Following his stay in Vienna, Murrow arrived in London and reported what he could not say in Austria: "It was called a bloodless conquest, and in some ways it was, but I'd like to be able to forget the haunted look on the faces of those long lines of people outside the banks and travel offices. People trying to get away. I'd like to forget the tired futile look of the Austrian army officers and the thud of hobnail boots and the crash of the light tanks in the early morning of the Ringstrasse, and the pitiful uncertainty and bewilderment of those forced to lift the right hand and shout 'Heil Hitler' for the first time. I'd like to forget the sound of the smashing glass as the Jewish shop streets were raided; the hoots and jeers aimed at those forced to scrub the sidewalk . . . ." That was pure Murrow, and broadcasts like that would make him a superstar.

Broadcasts like that—and there would be many more in the next few years—were the means by which Murrow set a new tone in broadcast journalism, quietly describing and analyzing events that he had seen, had felt, had been in a real sense, a part of. His talents and insights and use of a medium that was so widespread in America gave Murrow a legendary reputation; he became larger than life, leaving ambassadors and other journalists behind. He would become even more important, some would say, than CBS. Other journalists would follow in his path, many of them print journalists willing to make the switch to radio. If it was good enough for Ed Murrow, they would say, it was good enough for them.

Now, Shirer had to endure situations that were partly amusing, partly bewildering. One occurred during the evening of May 2. He was in Rome to cover the expected arrival of the king of Italy and Adolf Hitler at the Quirinale Palace. CBS wanted him to report from the roof of the royal stables which overlooked the palace entrance. Shirer was hesitant, but if that was what CBS wanted, he would do his best. Shirer had to do the broadcast live in keeping with CBS policy. To Shirer's chagrin, the Italian king and Hitler arrived 6 minutes ahead of schedule. By the time Shirer was live on the air, the host and guest had arrived in their carriage, gone into the palace, moved over to a balcony where they waved to the crowds, and then headed on. CBS's policy prevented Shirer from emulating the European broadcasters who were recording the event for later broadcast feeds. To Shirer, the policy seemed self-defeating, not to mention impractical. A policy of live coverage only meant relying upon shortwave radio transmissions which were sensitive to atmospheric conditions, including sunspots and magnetic currents from the North Pole. Because of that policy, many broadcasts did not get through. Murrow and Shirer felt frustration: the ban kept CBS radio correspondents from covering the news in depth around Europe. It was bad enough now. But what if war came? Unless the live-only policy were scuttled, it would be all but impossible to cover the war properly. No broadcast reporter could run after the news and capture the sights and sounds of war unless he could employ a tape recorder. But CBS was not moved.

Such questions were technical. Others were more substantive. Was war indeed coming? Should CBS act as if fighting was inevitable? Some would say that the fact that the network gave so much attention to the Anschluss crisis (and later Munich) reflected the network's conviction that the continent would soon be in flames. But it also appeared to reflect CBS's conviction that the United States should prepare itself for taking part in the coming war. Americans who had no interest in becoming involved in European problems thought ill of CBS for "promoting" the war. CBS executives appeared not to worry about such criticisms. Their correspondents were covering the news. If their reports, however subtly, underlined the Nazis' evils and in that way pushed the United States into war, the correspondents were not to blame. They were merely the messengers. CBS had little to worry about as a consensus formed within the United States against the Nazis: the more CBS did to cover the European crisis, the more applause it won. (There was one notable exception, when German-Americans, angry over Hans von Kaltenborn's anti-Nazi commentary early in 1939, threatened to boycott his sponsor, General Mill's Gold Medal flour.)

Some, however, were adamantly against America entering a European war. CBS tapped this sentiment when, in 1938, Ed Murrow received permission from French Premier Daladier to visit the Maginot Line to make the first broadcast from that strategic and highly secret fortification. Murrow was not permitted to give the names of towns or to identify regiments, but he could describe the possibility of war, which he did eloquently. NBC felt that Murrow had erred in making such a broadcast, believing that he had glorified the military prowess of one country over another and, hence, had compromised American neutrality. An antiwar outlook had emerged within the NBC inner sanctum, and Ed Murrow and CBS were offering a contrary opinion. As it turned out, NBC benefited from playing down the chances for war. After Murrow's Maginot Line broadcast, the German broadcast authorities responded by improving their relations with NBC.

four

"DRESSING UP IN A SHEET . . . AND SAYING BOO!"

No one was striving to make news more "authentic" than Ed Murrow. By shifting the network's newscasts from the studio to the field, he was giving a whole new dimension to broadcast journalism. Many would say later that broadcast journalism did not exist until Murrow and his "boys," the other correspondents whom he chose to report for CBS around the world, began to file from overseas. The Murrow team was now prepared to cover Europe's most severe crisis during this fall of 1938. Backstopping the overseas correspondents was Hans von Kaltenborn whose knowledge of Germany and the German language coupled with his indefatigability made him an ideal "anchor."

CBS was in a far better position to broadcast the September 1938 crisis than it was the earlier March one. CBS engineers had helped the Czech government set up a shortwave radio station that enabled direct communication with the United States; this avoided Prague having to go through Berlin, as CBS had been forced to do during the Austrian crisis. (1)

By early September it was clear that Czechoslovakia was next on Adolf Hitler's agenda. Murrow and Shirer, sensing that the news would soon concentrate on Prague, proposed a then revolutionary idea—that

Shirer be allowed to broadcast 5 minutes a day from there. CBS could not rid itself of the notion that the network was an instrument of entertainment. The previous March, the Anschluss—and CBS's coverage of it—had elevated the work of the news division to a new importance. Americans were growing concerned about the rumblings from Europe; there were some who even suggested that the United States might be forced to get involved. It became imperative to know—and to know immediately—just what was happening on the other side of the ocean. In the end, a compromise was reached. On September 11, CBS agreed to let Shirer begin broadcasting for five minutes each day from Prague, but he had to cable beforehand when he thought the news did not warrant a broadcast. Shirer's preference would have been for a 100 percent commitment from the network. Europe was most certainly on the brink of war, and Prague was inevitably going to be the next troublespot. Why act as if reality lay elsewhere? Still, considering that earlier in the year the network had not even been prepared to allow him and Murrow to do news broadcasts, Shirer felt that he had come a long way. And he did have a promise from CBS that he could get something out every day as long as the news justified it.

CBS's coverage of the Munich crisis began impressively on September 12. Seeking to play down the European tensions, NBC gave little advance publicity to Hitler's address to the annual Nazi rally in Nuremberg. For its part, CBS chose to dramatize it, believing that the speech was of major significance. That Monday morning listeners heard a CBS announcer declare that "the entire civilized world is anxiously awaiting the speech of Adolf Hitler, whose single word may plunge all of Europe into another world war." At 2:15 P.M. a voice cut into the network to say that CBS was interrupting the Enoch Light program to bring listeners Hitler's "world-awaited talk." Relayed by the shortwave station in Berlin, the Chancellor's speech was broadcast clearly. CBS had a translator at work as Hitler spoke. NCB offered no editorial comment, but CBS's Hans von Kaltenborn offered analysis as soon as Hitler concluded over an hour later. "Adolf Hitler has spoken," he said in melodramatic tones, "and the world has listened . . . ." He noted the threatening nature of Hitler's remarks, that Czechoslovakia would have to reach a settlement with the Sudeten Germans "or the Germans would see to it that a settlement was reached." Kaltenborn's listeners were hearing Hitler for the first time.

CBS realized that the situation provided an opportunity to outdo NBC. It was as if CBS itself had declared war and its general was sitting in New York: Hans von Kaltenborn. He was the hero of the day, translating

Hitler's fiery speeches and explaining and predicting what the next diplomatic steps would be. For Kaltenborn, the next eighteen days—between September 12 and 30, when Chamberlain returned from Munich with the promise of "peace in our time"—would prove exhilarating if exhausting. He did 102 extemporaneous broadcasts out of Studio Nine on the 17th floor of the CBS building in New York City; some would be "two-way" broadcasts with Murrow and the other reporters in Europe, some would be news roundups. Between stints he would catch a quick nap on a nearby couch. When there was a news break, Paul White rushed in to say, "A flash, Hans." Kaltenborn would rise slowly, and White would press the button to turn on Hans's microphone. An attendant rushed in with the bulletin. Kaltenborn read it and then commented on it. This happened so often that some in the newsroom began to joke about bulletins interrupting bulletins.

But the CBS effort was in fact no joking matter. The network had decided that the news from Europe was what people wanted to hear, and they would hear it, even if it meant scrapping commercials, even if it meant scrapping entertainment. At times, it was trying for Kaltenborn. He would have to keep in touch with the control room, looking for signs when he was about to go off the air. On occasion he would just begin to launch into an analysis of a foreign leader's speech when the signal would come that he must get off the air in 1 minute!

CBS news department officials found that they were forced to make continuing judgments about whether the story in Europe was more or less important than local American stories. Sometimes their judgments got them into hot water. For example, a huge storm struck New England when the Munich crisis was at its height. Recalled Kaltenborn: "Here we were in the midst of two outstanding news stories, both ideal for radio coverage, one overseas and one domestic. I believe it is the first time when a foreign crisis got the preferred coverage over a domestic disaster." (2) In this case it was a no-win situation for CBS. Protests came in from New England and Long Island, complaining about the paucity of storm coverage. How could a radio network give preference to an event 3,000 miles away when such a major news story was happening locally? Still others would register their horror that the network could devote attention to a mere storm when the world was on the verge of war.

Despite the criticism and the fatigue, Kaltenborn relished every moment of the Munich coverage; he came to feel that he had been preparing all his life for this one series of broadcasts. Kaltenborn had an incredible background for these broadcasts: he had interviewed the foreign personalities involved; he could translate from French or from German instantaneously. But it was his gift of extemporaneous speaking that made him supreme. A bulletin would be handed to him, and after he read it, he would explain its significance at once, giving his work an unsurpassed immediacy. He did have one problem which he eventually solved. The problem was his name. It sounded German. Given the growing American disdain for Germany, Kaltenborn decided on the nineteenth day of the Munich crisis that he would be wise to change his name. And so he became H. V. Kaltenborn.

With Kaltenborn's superb, steady hand in New York and the unprecedented on-the-spot coverage in the field, it was only natural that the listening audience would keep their radios tuned to CBS. When the crisis was a week old, NBC was rushing around trying to find a commentator who could compete with Kaltenborn. They tried a few people but none measured up. Each one lacked Kaltenborn's depth and his ability to extemporize. A few months later NBC acquired Kaltenborn's services. James Roty, a frequent critic of radio, wrote in *The Nation* on October 15, 1938, in an article entitled "Radio Comes Through" that Kaltenborn was "brilliantly illuminating. . . . For the first time, history has been made in the hearing of its pawns." Kaltenborn had become so luminescent a star that he was invited to appear on an Eddie Cantor program for a large fee on November 21, 1938. He was introduced as "the greatest news commentator of our time, Columbia's gem of the ozone." In retrospect, one can now say that Kaltenborn was one of the broadcasting industry's earliest anchormen. In his tireless demeanor and the expertise which he brought to his subject, he seemed a forerunner of Walter Cronkite or Dan Rather. In those early days of radio, the news broadcaster's appeal to his listening audience counted far less than it would later on. Yet, Kaltenborn clearly had stirred those listening.

While Kaltenborn's star was shining in New York, Murrow, Shirer, and the rest of the CBS European staff had gained the reputation as the most hard-working and colorful of those broadcasting from the scene. CBS did 471 broadcasts during the crisis, 135 of which were bulletin interruptions. NBC had slightly fewer programs (443) but it had more airtime (59 hours to CBS's 48 hours). Still, CBS was clearly perceived as the winner during Munich. Munich would have its place in broadcasting history: during the Anschluss crisis, first the European, then the "world news roundup" came to the fore, with separate reports from several cities around the world. During Munich, the news roundtable began, with correspondents in four or more cities, tied together by shortwave circuits as well as landlines, carrying out a spontaneous, ongoing conversation rather than reading their separate scripts. The first such roundtable discussion linked New York with Washington, London, and Paris. Such events are considered commonplace now; in 1938, they were an innovation.

In the field, Ed Murrow was the star. "By his clear voice, crisp tones and authoritative manner," wrote his biographer Alexander Kendrick, "the young man became a household name and personality. As was to be the case through his entire career, people who heard him felt they knew him." (3) To his colleagues, Ed Murrow was always something of a miracle-worker. Had he come out of a newspaper background, his superb reporting and his sharply honed instincts would have seemed understandable. But Murrow came from a completely different background. He had never studied journalism, never practiced it. So his colleagues wondered how it was that someone could report so professionally.

"Calling Ed Murrow! Calling Ed Murrow!" Thus would H. V. Kaltenborn call out over the airwaves. The phrase became famous, signifying both the bold, new experiment in broadcasting and the courage and daring of this individual reporting from the field. In truth it was rare that Kaltenborn would have to search pleadingly over the airwaves for young Mr. Murrow. Murrow was able to do 35 broadcasts during that September Munich crisis; he also arranged 116 others from eighteen European cities. Listeners got into the act as well once CBS distributed maps of the territory Murrow, Shirer, Kaltenborn, and Trout were covering. At times, however, it was technically impossible to reach the reporters in the field. For instance, on September 15, the fourth day of the crisis, bad weather adversely affected shortwave transmission, making CBS frequencies inaudible. Murrow was unreachable. All Kaltenborn could do was to turn to cabled news. To the chagrin of CBS, NBC relayed its shortwave broadcasts to New York via a Capetown–Buenos Aires circuit (even though the distance was three times greater, the delay was a mere few seconds).

Still, despite the technical difficulties, CBS stretched the possibilities of broadcasting. On September 20 at 6 P.M., Paul White phoned Bill Shirer in Germany and suggested he do a broadcast from the train he was about to take with other newsmen to cover the Chamberlain-Hitler meeting. Shirer would conduct interviews with the correspondents about the prospects for war or peace. The problem was that no facilities existed on the train for such a broadcast. Then Shirer had the bright idea of doing the broadcast from the train station before the train pulled out. So he lined up American and British correspondents for the 10 P.M. show. Then he had to figure out what he could say over the air. Were he to tell the truth, the Nazis might cut off the transmission. All he could do was hope for the best. One by one, the correspondents spoke. An Italian journalist spoke in halting English. A French newsman started spouting French, and so Shirer provided an on-the-spot translation into English. Just then Shirer noticed that the train was pulling away. Cutting the Frenchman off in midsentence, he dashed for the train. Soon thereafter he jotted in his diary that he was afraid that the show was something of a failure. To his shock, a cable arrived for him the next day from New York: "Friedrichstrassebahnhof show last night a knockout!" That was how much he understood about American radio.

The coverage of the Munich crisis made it clear that radio could serve another purpose besides its original one—entertainment. As television would in a later age, radio had become a national resource during the Munich crisis, informing the entire nation and doing it with great immediacy. At the time of Munich, 27.5 million American households (out of 32 million) had radios. Munich also provided valuable lessons. In the past, radio had always relied upon others, actors, speakers and orchestras when it came to entertainment and newspapermen when it came to news. But Murrow and his "boys" had shown that radio could develop its own team which could stand on its own two feet. Not only that, the reports which they had sent from Europe demonstrated the great advantage radio had over newspapers: it was faster, it could reach many more people, and it could present the players in person, alive. No one was happier than Bill Paley. He could not have imagined that in taking over a radio network, he would be creating a whole new medium that would have such a vast impact. His excitement was evident in the cable he sent to Murrow and Shirer: "Columbia's coverage of the European crisis is superior to its competitors' and is probably the best job of its kind ever done in radio broadcasting." (4) The CBS reporting of the Munich crisis appeared so extraordinary that the network issued a statement congratulating itself on its achievement. In that statement, CBS pledged to continue the kind of news broadcasting which has provided "comprehension" as well as information. And it hailed the arrival of radio "not merely as a disseminator of the news, but as a social power." Thousands of listeners had sent messages praising CBS for its coverage.

The Munich Pact may have fooled some, in the United States and in Europe, into believing that war had been averted, but it did not fool Ed Murrow or Bill Shirer. Both felt that fighting would eventually break out. Poland, they agreed, would be the next victim, and CBS would need its own staff of radio reporters to cover the hostilities. They would have to be Americans, so they could move from one side to the other. NBC, they had heard, was planning to use big guns like Churchill in London and former Foreign Minister Flandin in Paris. Clearly, Murrow, Shirer, and the others knew, a general war would prove a far more daunting test of their skills as radio journalists than Munich. It was time to get prepared.

While the CBS news-gathering team in Europe was just beginning to flex its muscles, others in the network were about to engage in some bold experimentation that would illustrate the power, some would say the frightening potential, of the new medium. At that time, many rules of the game which are taken for granted today had not yet been written. Enough latitude existed to allow radio to reach the point of absurdity on a certain Halloween eve in 1938. The man at the center of the fuss was 23-year-old Orson Welles, Broadway star and impressario and radio's "The Shadow," alias Lamont Cranston. Because of his rising fame, CBS had invited Welles to broadcast 1-hour dramas in the Sunday 8 P.M. time slot, and he happily agreed.The program was called the "Mercury Theater."

The rival NBC show in that time period, the "Chase and Sanborn Hour," was so popular, thanks to, among others, Edgar Bergen and his wooden dummy Charlie McCarthy, singer Dorothy Lamour, and master of ceremonies Don Ameche, that no sponsor could be found for "Mercury." The week before Halloween, its rating was a mere 3.6 percent compared to a whopping 34.7 percent for the Chase and Sanborn show.

As they would throughout the years, ratings affected people's judgment about what to put on the air. It most likely affected Orson Welles's judgment when he planned to dramatize "War of the Worlds" by H. G. Wells. Wells had written a classic pseudoscientific thriller about men from Mars invading earth in a flying cylinder (at first thought to be a meteorite) in 1898. When Welles mentioned the play to his writer, Howard Koch, he thought little of it. Insisting that science fiction could not be made into decent drama over the radio, Koch actually had almost convinced John Houseman, the "Mercury Theater" editor, to consider substituting "Lorna Doone," but Welles remained adamant. And with his forceful personality, Welles managed to convince him on October 25, five days before the show. At one stage the idea was broached—no one now recalls just who made the suggestion—to do the show as a simulated news broadcast so that the arrival of the Martians sounded as authentic as possible. Suddenly, the naysayers began to respond to the idea. In the high echelons of CBS, however, there was fear that the program would seem too realistic. So the CBS brass asked for thirty-eight script changes. The Museum of Natural History was changed to the "National History Museum," the National Guard became the "Militia," and the U.S. Weather Bureau became the "Government Weather Bureau."

Despite such changes, the atmosphere at the time made the program seem realistic. So unsettling were the Depression and the war scare in Europe that people seemed ready to believe almost anything. Was it all that unlikely that an Armageddon might be just around the corner?

Moreover, since the Munich crisis, radio had become the accepted means for learning about major news quickly—via bulletins conveyed in a dramatic voice, suddenly interrupting one's favorite radio program. Americans had grown increasingly confident about radio, believing that the words coming from it carried a high degree of reliability, more so even than daily newspapers. The Welles cast did its part to create an air of authenticity as well. The actor who played the first network announcer,

---

Carl Phillips, had made a point of listening repeatedly to the hysterical tones of the radio announcer who described the Hindenburg blowing up at Lakehurst in May 1937.

Perhaps out of a genuine fear that the program would be taken seriously, or out of a certain sense of responsibility, Orson Welles sought to provide ample warning to his listeners that the whole program was "just a play." He warned them at the beginning and he warned them at the end—and he even inserted more warnings during the four CBS station breaks. But he overlooked the possibility that listeners would tune in at different times during the program without having heard any of the admonitions. Many radio listeners did in fact join too late to hear the opening words of caution, and many were too busy twisting their radio dials at the station breaks to detect the truth.

What they heard, and what would stick in their minds as terrifyingly real, was the usual opening of the Mercury Theater," the Tchaikovsky theme, a weather report that was truthful, and then an announcer declaring, "We now take you to the Meridian Room in the Hotel Park Plaza in downtown New York, where you will be entertained by the music of Ramón Raquello and his orchestra." Then, just like a horror movie which starts out slowly and then gets increasingly petrifying, the script took listeners to the New Jersey town of Grovers Mill, 22 miles from Trenton. It was 8:12 P.M. The time was significant, for Edgar Bergen and Charlie McCarthy had just completed their opening skit and a commercial followed for Chase and Sanborn coffee.

Millions of listeners quickly switched their dials—to CBS where an announcer was saying, over the sounds of sirens and crowd noises, ". . . I'll move the microphone nearer. Here (Pause). Now we're not more than 25 feet away. Can you hear it? Oh, Professor Pierson!" "Professor Pierson" was none other than Orson Welles, and he was reading his lines with great equanimity. The announcer asked him if he could tell the audience the meaning of "that scraping noise inside the thing?"

"Possibly the unequal cooling of its surface," Pierson noted calmly. Did he still believe it was a meteor, he was asked? "I don't know what to think," came the professor's matter-of-fact reply. Then, although the subject of invaders from space had not even been raised yet, he volunteered some startling information. "The metal casing is definitely extraterrestrial . . . not found on this earth. Friction with the earth's atmosphere usually tears holes in a meteorite. The thing is smooth and, as you can see, of cylindrical shape."

Just than announcer Phillips interrupted to note that "Something's happening!" Suggesting that "this is terrific," he excitedly noted that the end of the "thing" had begun to flake off and that the top was starting to rotate like a screw. The crowd around grew excited. An announcer came on to say that this was the most shocking thing he had ever witnessed.

"Wait a minute! Someone's crawling out of the hollow top. Someone or . . . something. I can see peering out of that black hole two luminous discs . . . are they eyes? It might be a face. It might be . . . ." The crowd by now was shouting and the announcer sobbing. He described in even more graphic terms what he saw, something wriggling out of the shadow like a gray snake, and another and another. Then he saw what appeared to be tentacles followed by the "thing's" body, and he described it as large as a bear and glistening like wet leather. The face had him spellbound. "I can hardly force myself to keep looking at it. The eyes are black and gleam like a serpent's. The mouth is V-shaped with saliva dripping from its rimless lips that seem to quiver and pulsate . . . ."

A terrifying fear seemed to grip everyone, including the announcer who by now was forced to give way to a second one. The replacement quietly observed that "We are bringing you an eyewitness account of what's happening on the Wilmuth farm, Grovers Mill, New Jersey." After a brief musical interlude, the announcer returned to the air to say that they were going back to Carl Phillips at Grovers Mill. By this time, policemen were trying to move closer to the Martians, but the extraterrestrials shot out a sheet of flame to keep the officers back. The crowd wailed, a barn blew up, and then all was quiet on the air. A new announcer declared disappointedly that circumstances beyond their control prevented the station from continuing the broadcast from Grovers Mill. As perplexing as it must have been to listen to the broadcast, one can imagine how panic-stricken the true believers must have felt when suddenly the direct news reports from the farm ceased.

Just as suddenly, the reports were resumed, but they were now worse, much worse. At Grovers Mill, state police were being burned to a crisp; the commander of the state militia in Trenton, Brigadier General Montgomery Smith, announced that the government had placed Mercer and Middlesex counties and the environs under martial law. Pierson, who somehow broke away from the Martians, now told listeners that the visitors were definitely armed with what he described tentatively as a heat ray. The second announcer confessed that he had reached "the unescapable conclusion" that a vanguard of an invading Martian army had indeed landed in the Jersey farmlands. No friendly ETs, these little "things." This was clearly an encounter of a different kind. The announcer added in a near state of shock that the New Jersey National Guard had been rubbed out as had the Army Air Corps even as martial law was decreed over a wider region, throughout New Jersey and eastern Pennsylvania.

All that the President of the United States could do was to declare a national emergency. A man described as the Secretary of the Interior but sounding strikingly like Franklin Roosevelt merely prayed to God for help. An "end of the world" hysteria appeared to grip a telephone operator who proclaimed from Newark, New Jersey, that poisonous black smoke was billowing in from the Jersey marshes. The operator urged the population to move into open spaces inasmuch as gas masks were now useless. Cars were told which routes to take. But where could one safely go?

Only one announcer was still alive, a fellow named Ray Collins who stood on a rooftop in New York City and spoke as bells chimed in the background to warn residents that they should evacuate the city. He advised listeners to take the Hutchinson River Parkway and to avoid the bridges to Long Island which were already saturated. A choir was singing in the background while Ray Collins delivered a bulletin that spoke of "Martian cylinders" dropping around the nation, one outside Buffalo, another in Chicago, yet another in St. Louis. Oblivious to what was actually going on in the real world, Collins tossed out descriptions of the Martians even though the gas had obviously affected his voice. A massive tragedy was played out before his eyes, black smoke drifting over Manhattan, the metal hands of the Martians rising up, thousands of citizens running in vain toward the East River as the gas rendered them lifeless. The gas reached Times Square, crossed Sixth Avenue, Fifth Avenue, all the while people were dropping. Collins began to fade out as he frantically noted that the gas was only 100 yards away, then 50 feet. An operator appeared on the air to ask where everyone in New York City was.

Finally, there was a station break.

Moments before—at 8:32 P.M. precisely—a CBS program supervisor named Davidson Taylor was called away from his control panel in Studio One to take a phone call which notified him that nearly two out of every three local stations had interrupted the broadcast to calm listeners and to stress that the program was pure fantasy. During the program a phone call came from a police station to the CBS control. "What's going on up there?" asked an officer. One policeman peered through a porthole window at CBS to find out for himself, but when he tried to enter, an actor pushed him out. What the phone call and the peeping cop indicated were that the Welles broadcast was mushrooming into something beyond what the "Mercury Theater" players had imagined.

Either to protect the CBS staff from frantic citizens outside the building or, perhaps more likely, to cage the staff in while some tough questions could be asked, a knot of policemen surrounded the building. Meanwhile during the station break CBS was again informing its audience that Orson Welles and his "Mercury Theater" were in fact pulling a fast one on them. And for some time thereafter, CBS made sure to announce hourly that the Welles broadcast was total fabrication. But that had no effect on the hundreds of thousands of people who took the show seriously, took to the streets, and acted very much as if the end of the world were at hand. So many hysterical people crowded Riverside Drive that it became impassable to traffic. Worse affected was northern New Jersey—

that, after all, was the region where the little "men" had been located. The threat of asphyxiation and death by flames sent people to their cars, to train and bus stations. The end of the world was in progress, and a ticket to anywhere was in great demand. While governors insisted that martial law had not been declared, the disbelieving crowds were pouring into churches in tears; their aim was to seek absolution prior to the inevitable arrival of the extraterrestrials. The slightly less fearful made sure to call local stations and police to get a firsthand reading of the planetary crisis. Howard Barlow, the CBS conductor, was driving with his wife back from the country that night and noticed that nobody was going into New York. Yet there were thousands of cars streaking out of New York as fast as they could. "We wondered what in the world was the matter." (5)

"Goodbye, everybody," Orson Welles said to his listeners in parting as the show wound down to a close. "And remember, please, for the next day or two the terrible lesson you learned tonight . . . and if your doorbell rings and nobody's there, that was no Martian! It's Halloween." Welles concluded the broadcast by saying that it was "the Mercury Theater's own version of dressing up in a sheet . . . and saying Boo!" But that was not the end of it. A mayor from the Midwest phoned John Houseman in the control room to say that the residents of his city were running amok in the streets. Woe to CBS if, as Welles had just insisted over the air, the whole program was one big put-on! No sooner had Houseman put the phone down than blue-uniformed New York City police penetrated the inner sanctum of CBS to report the latest news in their angriest tones: because of the program there had been numerous suicides and deaths on the road. A crowd in a New Jersey building tried to vacate the premises, resulting in a mass tragedy.

Around the United States phone calls came into newspapers. Some 875 calls were registered at *The New York Times*. People were asking what to do. The Associated Press sent out an explanatory bulletin to member newspapers. Calls flooded police stations. Priests were sought by many seeking confession. Others simply headed for the highways between New York and Philadelphia. A few people found old gas masks in closets. Sailors were summoned back to ships from their shore leave. When an Indianapolis woman screamed at church congregants that the world had come to an end according to the radio, the church service broke up. Residents in the State of Washington thought they had ample proof when a power failure occurred in their town.

It was not clear how many reports of deaths and tragedy were true, but CBS and Welles clearly had a problem. Although, as it would eventually become apparent, no one was actually killed, John Houseman said later, "We thought we were mass murderers for a while." (6) For Welles and Houseman, there was little consolation in the fact that, having broken no law, they would not have to go to jail. Listening to the reports of how people reacted to the program, Welles might have thought prison a pleasant holiday compared to what might be in store for him. Still, although many citizens wanted to wring Orson Welles's neck, some were amused. One was Franklin Roosevelt. The day after the program the President sent Welles a cable, saying, "This only goes to show all intelligent people were listening to Charlie McCarthy."

The press was less amused. The morning after the program it headlined: "Radio War Terrorizes U.S., Panic Grips Nation as Radio Announces 'Mars Attacks World.'" There was not much anyone could do against Welles, but the Federal Communications Commission, promising that it would think of establishing a new radio code, described the program as "regrettable." For CBS's part, little could be done. Davidson Taylor, the CBS program supervisor, had been summoned the morning after the program to Ed Klauber, for what he assumed would be announcement of his dismissal. Instead, Klauber said simply, "I've read the script. Not knowing what we now know, I'd have cleared it, too." (7)

Afterward, some analyzed why so many had panicked. A Princeton University survey said that 6 million heard the program, and of those 1 million believed it and were frightened. Writer Dorothy Thompson thought it the news story of the century. She asked not so much why large numbers had panicked, but what it meant in political terms. What emerged from the program, in her view, was a new awareness of just how dangerous the actual "Martians" of everyday life could be. What Welles had pointed out with great poignancy, she observed, was the frightening manner in which the true "terrors" of this century, Mussolini, Stalin, and Hitler, played to the crowds, appealed to their emotions, and sought to win them over. This analysis may have been true, but few were soothed by it. There was general belief that Welles still should not have been permitted to toy with everyone's emotions so cavalierly. Thus, broadcast officials decreed that there would be no more interruptions for fictional news bulletins on radio dramas. Those fictionalized bulletins were all too realistic. Another question was raised by the famous "Martian" broadcast: before the "War" program, "Mercury Theater's" ratings had been low. Yet the furor caused by this broadcast suggested that the ratings services were inaccurate. As for Welles, the publicity surrounding the "Worlds" broadcast had catapulted him and the "Mercury Theater" into the limelight. Suddenly, a sponsor, Campbell Soup Company, came forward. Still slotted in the same tough 8 P.M. time period opposite Edgar Bergen and Charlie McCarthy, the "Mercury Theater" now became the "Campbell Playhouse."

Welles appeared surprised that the broadcast had been taken so seriously. Far from expecting the radio audience to take the program as fact, he noted that "We feared that the classic H. G. Wells fantasy . . . might appear too old-fashioned for modern consumption." (8) How wrong he was. Yet Welles was still trying to get the audience to believe the broadcast. "Radio," he said cryptically, "was a voice from heaven and I wanted to destroy it. So it was a huge practical joke." (9) Never again would an Orson Welles manage to bamboozle so many people for so long over the airwaves. But a lesson indeed was to be learned, and it would be remembered for years to come. Radio, and later television, had a potential power that could drive people to the streets in panic.

While the Welles broadcast had been far more dramatic than imagined or intended, it was clear that serious drama did have a place on the new medium. Indeed, such programs gave CBS a new level of prestige in the latter part of the 1930s. The man who came to symbolize this development was Norman Corwin. While Archibald MacLeish and Orson Welles were only part-time radio artists, Corwin worked entirely within CBS. He helped to build a new self-confidence at the network, based on the notion that programming could be self-generated and still be of high quality. The Boston-born Corwin would become CBS's prime mover and shaker of the radio drama. He had started his career as a newspaperman, working for the *Springfield* (Mass.) *Daily Republican.* He became the *Republican's* radio editor while working as a newscaster for WBZ. Arriving in New York in 1936, he did a 15-minute program of poetry reading over WQXR. Corwin knew about CBS's "Columbia Workshop" and in 1938 became a director there. He had an idea for a series of broadcasts, adapting a number of nursery rhymes to radio, and to do the pilot, he needed the princely sum of $200. William B. Lewis liked the idea and decided to back Corwin. The show was called "Norman Corwin's Words Without Music," and it was aired on a Sunday afternoon following the New York Philharmonic concert. Then at Christmas 1938, Corwin produced his first program, "The Plot to Overthrow Christmas." The program became a classic, with its light verse not only parodying radio but mocking the powers of the rising fascism across the sea. Tongue-in-cheek but optimistic, lighthearted but a bit irreverent, the program gave Corwin a reputation as one of radio's bright new talents. There followed "They Fly Through the Air with the Greatest of Ease," another attack on fascism. The public loved it. Mail came streaming in. Corwin's picture appeared in *Time* magazine. On the strength of his past work, Corwin won the right to do his own series of programs under the aegis of "Columbia Workshop." The series was called "Twenty-six by Corwin." He did everything, coming up with the idea for the program, writing, it, directing it, producing it. As a result of that series and his other highly touted programs, Corwin was known as radio's poet laureate. CBS promoted its star. Paley loved him. "CBS told me," Corwin recalled later, "they never bothered to take ratings on my programs. 'We don't care,' they said, 'how many people are listening or not listening to your programs. We believe in it.'" (10)

In the late 1930s, CBS executives could make such statements; in later years they would hold totally contradictory views. Of course ratings didn't count for Norman Corwin. His programs were all sustaining. They had no sponsors. Hence, even if ratings had mattered a great deal—and in those days they did not—there was no one to bring pressure on CBS to cancel the program. Corwin's programs appeared popular, but few paid that much attention to exactly how many people were listening, because Corwin's programs gave CBS a programming identity. Whereas before the network represented little more than a series of studios for hire and a chain of affiliates stretching from the East to the West coasts, now CBS stood for the high-quality program, self-generated, self-produced. Just as it was beginning to establish an identity as a primary source in covering the news, so too was it acquiring a reputation as a source for programming.

five

"THIS . . . IS LONDON."

War was coming. Most of those who had been following events in Europe conceded that fact. H. V. Kaltenborn was an exception. He announced that he was so certain there would be no fighting that he was sending his son and new daughter-in-law to Europe on their honeymoon. But, if not all were as convinced as Bill Shirer that war was inevitable, many sensed that the Anschluss and Munich were preludes to more violent events. One man who remained uncertain during that summer of 1939 was Ed Murrow. Writing to Ed Klauber from London on July 26, he noted that "such plans as can be made have been made for covering the next crisis, which I remain convinced will not result in war." (1) Still, it behooved CBS to prepare its troops. Until 1938, its foreign staff had consisted of three correspondents, Murrow in London, Shirer in Berlin, and Thomas Grandin, hired that year and placed in Paris. It was time to find more American reporters who, as neutrals in the conflict, would be able to cover both sides of the coming war. The network by now had a group of stringers in various capitals. Paul White was sent to London that July to decide whether to hire more permanent staff. He approved only one additional foreign correspondent, and so Murrow hired a 26-year-old fellow who was doubling as city editor of the Paris edition of *The Herald*

Tribune and night editor of United Press. His name was Eric Sevareid. CBS was adding to its New York staff as well. Major George Fielding Eliot, an author and lecturer on military subjects, was hired to do news analysis. Elmer Davis, a freelance writer and Rhodes scholar, came aboard at first as a substitute for Kaltenborn who was vacationing in Europe! Davis's first assignment was to do a 5-minute evening news broadcast at 8:55 P.M. (Three years later, Davis was appointed director of the newly created Office of War Information of the U.S. government. He later appointed Ed Klauber as his deputy.). Eventually, CBS would have a full array of correspondents in place, including Cecil Brown in Rome and William L. White in Helsinki. Charles Collingwood and Howard K. Smith would be added to the London staff.

During the late summer of 1939 CBS executives in New York exhibited a sense of wishful thinking: no one wanted war, so war would not break out. Paul White had been urging Ed Murrow and Bill Shirer to organize a program that White wanted to call "European Dances." The two CBS European correspondents would go to night spots in Hamburg, Paris, and London and from each club broadcast an evening of dance music and entertainment. Shirer thought White's notion preposterous— it would illustrate a Europe dancing while slipping inevitably into war. Still, White insisted that Shirer go ahead with plans to broadcast a program from the St. Pauli nightclub district in Hamburg. It was scheduled for broadcast on the final Sunday of the summer—August 25. But, in the end, the show was never aired because Shirer and Murrow would not go along with the idea.

Bill Shirer had no doubts about the coming violence. He could peer across the street from his hotel room at the Adlon in Berlin as an antiaircraft gun was installed on the roof of I. G. Farben. He noticed more and more German bombers flying over the city. Even more significantly, he had an instinct that the developments could not go on much longer without exploding into war.

As the war drew near, Murrow, Shirer, and Grandin were doing four to five broadcasts each day. Whenever there was news from Europe, CBS would air a roundtable discussion from its overseas correspondents. In that last week of August, CBS would outdo NBC in shortwave pickups from Europe, eighty-one to seventy-nine. Some were willing to acknowledge that NBC often did as good a job as its rival, but, as Fred Bate noted candidly, "The difference was that CBS had something we didn't have— Ed Murrow." (2) There was another difference. NBC was still utilizing newspaper correspondents, Parliament members, and other public figures on its broadcasts while CBS relied upon its own correspondents who, in the words of *Variety,* were able to get "closer to the human element, and . . . get to essentials quickly, [and] interpret past and present as simply as possible for the ordinary listener." Often the two would converse, Murrow in London, Shirer in Berlin. At times they were able to circumvent the censors in both cities. Although they were supposed to obtain the censor's approval in advance for whatever they planned to broadcast, they discovered that by a change of voice tone here and there, they could communicate a great deal that the censor might not have otherwise permitted.

When war broke out, CBS found itself in the enviable position of having the story all to itself. Once Franklin Roosevelt had declared a national emergency to enforce neutrality, much of the broadcasting industry believed that it was time to cut back on broadcasting the news from Europe—to appear as neutral as possible. Although such thinking may now appear convoluted, both NBC and Mutual did in fact stop all broadcasting from Europe; for a time no war bulletins or unsponsored commentators were broadcast on NBC as well. That left CBS as the only network broadcasting from the scene in Europe. To some extent CBS followed the government's apparent wishes: it reduced the number of war bulletins and commentaries by H. V. Kaltenborn.

While enjoying the exclusivity, CBS correspondents were grinding their teeth over other frustrations. As Murrow and Shirer had long feared, the CBS policy of not permitting correspondents to use tape recorders was now coming back to haunt them. Bill Paley and Ed Klauber still believed that tape-recorded broadcasts could only bring harm to the network. The ban was, in Shirer's words, "an idiotic ruling that prevented American radio from doing the job it should have done covering World War II." (3) From the 1980s' perspective, when tape recorders have become accepted, and have allowed radio newspeople to function with great efficiency and imagination, such an attitude appears both strange and self-defeating. Yet that attitude was the prevalent one at the start of World War II.

From the earliest moments of the war, CBS issued warnings to its correspondents and analysts to broadcast fairly and objectively. Shortly after Britain declared war on Germany in early September, Bill Paley had Ed Klauber send out a memo to the CBS organization providing instructions on how to report the war. The chairman insisted that CBS be fair and factual, and its correspondents must maintain calm while at the microphone. Out of a sense of fairness, CBS would allow opposing viewpoints to be heard. For example, after President Roosevelt gave an address discussing his proposed revision of the Neutrality Act, CBS allowed thirty-four speakers with differing points of view to speak during the five-week period before Congress voted on the Act. (CBS's reluctance to take a partisan stance in favor of joining the war spilled over into programming; hence, it clung to the belief that there should be no dramatization,

---

no portrayal of emotion over the war. Grace Field was therefore kept from singing five Shakespearean sonnets over the air on the grounds that they contained "prophetic messages" about the war.) Throughtout the fighting, these warnings to broadcast objectively would be issued. Those warnings led Eric Sevareid to note, "We must not display a tenth of the emotion that a broadcaster does when describing a prize fight." For as long as the United States had been neutral, CBS did not want to appear guilty of pushing the country into war. "This was right," wrote Sevareid, "it was the only legitimate way to perform our function—but it was very hard." (4)

CBS News would flourish during World War II. Its correspondents were experienced; they knew the story, the newsmakers, and the turf. And they knew how to get the story to New York. Never was this more the case than the exclusive Bill Shirer managed to file in June 1940 when he "beat" Adolf Hitler on the announcement of the French-German armistice. Hitler had wanted to inform the world himself in Berlin of this major development. He had in fact ordered all the correspondents, foreign and German, flown back to Berlin from Compiègne. Hitler wanted the journalists present when he would announce the French surrender. The American press was perfectly willing to comply, aware of how difficult it would be to file from the spot of the signing. But Shirer decided to hang around, hoping to see the final scene in the armistice car. His were the instincts of a professional journalist. Perhaps, he thought, the French won't sign. He would not know if he were part of the pack of newsmen being routed back to Berlin. Whatever happened, it would be history, and the place for a radio newsman to give an eyewitness broadcast. He learned that all broadcasts from Compiègne would be recorded in Berlin and retransmitted to the United States only after Hitler had given his approval. By being at the scene, Shirer would beat the newspaper boys by many hours. At 6:42 P.M. the two delegations met in Marshal Foch's old railroad coach for the signing. Shirer, congratulating himself on his great fortune, watched every historic step. He saw the French representative, General Charles Huntziger, fighting back tears. And he could hear the pens as they scratched out the signatures. A minute of silence was observed for the fallen of both sides. The French then had to sign an armistice with Italy. Pipe in his mouth, Bill Shirer wrote his story on an old typewriter as German soldiers stood around indifferently. He set up his microphone near the army communications van some 30 yards from the armistice car. Rain was falling lightly. The German army and the Reichs Rundfunk had asked Shirer—and he had agreed—to make a joint broadcast to CBS and NBC. There was simply no time for CBS to make its own transmission as the precious phone line was desperately needed by the Germans. At 8:15 P.M. Shirer called both CBS and NBC but had no idea whether anyone at either network was even listening. "Hello CBS, New York. Hello NBC, New York. This is William L. Shirer in Compiègne, scene of the Franco-German armistice talks. In exactly 5 minutes from now we shall begin broadcasting from here on the results of the armistice talks. . . . Hello CBS, New York. . . ." When, after a few tries, CBS picked up Shirer just a minute before he was due to start, the Saturday skeleton crew had to scrounge around for someone to serve as an announcer. Elmer Davis was located at a restaurant on 52nd Street and urged to come offer commentary. Shirer spoke for the first 20 minutes and then the NBC stringer used the last 10 minutes. Shirer has noted that it may have been the first joint broadcast the two networks ever made. (5) (From the field, at any rate. Lowell Thomas, of course, had delivered the news for some time over both the CBS and NBC networks.)

At 12 noon the next day Shirer was awakened by banging on his door. It was Walter Kerr, the *New York Herald-Tribune* correspondent, who had been unable to get to Compiègne on Saturday. Having listened to shortwave rebroadcasts from New York that were largely CBS's, Kerr told Shirer that he had scooped the world. He offered Shirer his congratulations. For several hours Shirer's description of the armistice signing in Compiègne Forest was all that American listeners had on the story. Shirer was ahead of the newspaper correspondents in Berlin, and well ahead even of Adolf Hitler. The German Chancellor had only released the news at 11:30 P.M., more than three hours after the signing. The Berlin newsmen had to wait to get their stories out after Hitler's formal announcement. As Kerr related to Shirer, CBS in New York was at first troubled that no other news reports on the armistice were coming through. CBS commentator Elmer Davis pointed out that Shirer was still the only source for the story. But he noted, "Mr. Shirer is a very experienced correspondent and an extremely conscientious one. We expect confirmation from other sources shortly. In the meantime, stay tuned. . . ." Ed Murrow, upon hearing Shirer's broadcast, phoned Chequers to tell Winston Churchill the news. Churchill had not yet heard it. Although the source was Murrow, Churchill refused to believe it.

Ironically, what Shirer considered the greatest scoop of his career occurred in part as a result of a technical mishap that played beautifully into the newsman's hands. The German radio engineers in Berlin who were on the receiving end of Shirer's military phone line from Compiègne were supposed to direct his broadcast to a recording machine at the Reichs Rundfunk for recording. But they threw the wrong switch and instead channeled it into a shortwave transmitter at Zossen, a technical error that sent Shirer's words out automatically to—New York! Furious at being scooped by Shirer, Hitler ordered an investigation. Shirer was questioned by the army, Rundfunk officials, and the Propaganda Ministry. He insisted that he was not to blame. Was it only a technical error? Perhaps not. Some were convinced that the German army, angry at Hitler for taking all the credit for the German victory over France, were responsible for permitting Shirer's broadcast to get out.

Although Shirer escaped unharmed this time, the CBS correspondent found the atmosphere in Germany increasingly chilly. He had less and less desire to work in Germany, censorship being the principal reason. Shirer made clear to his superiors in New York that if censorship got too bad, he would feel compelled to leave the country. In April 1939 he had arranged with CBS to broadcast Hitler's speech at the launching of the battleship *Tirpitz* in Wilhelmshaven. Shirer had been in a German Broadcasting Company control room in Berlin where he had planned to introduce Hitler for the relay to New York. Soon after Hitler began speaking, someone—Shirer thought it sounded like Goebbels—had demanded that the CBS broadcast be cut off. The voice, trying to sound generous, said a recording of the speech could be made from the one the Germans were making. That was an extremely poor alternative to Shirer. He protested that listeners in the United States had probably become convinced that Hitler had been assassinated. At least, he said, let him announce that the speech had been interrupted due to technical difficulties and that Hitler was continuing his speech. But that attempt to scotch the rumors was vetoed. Fifteen minutes later, Paul White came on the line, just as Shirer had predicted, to pass on reports in the United States that Hitler indeed had been assassinated. Shirer tried to put White—and the American listening audience—at rest. But when White tried to hear Shirer on the circuit, German officials turned thumbs down. White wanted to know if Shirer was really free to speak, and the answer came back yes. Then why were you cut off, White asked? Shirer could only say in honesty that he did not know. He only knew that the order came from Adolf Hitler.

New York still thought it more desirable that he remain in Germany than leave. "Bill," cabled Paul White from New York, "We thoroughly understand, sympathize condition in Berlin, but feel we must carry on with broadcasts even if only reading official statements and newspaper texts." (6) Shirer thought this preposterous; he had not been hired to read official handouts or to regurgitate Nazi propaganda from the newspapers. Sarcastically, he told White to find himself a pro-Nazi American student and pay him $50 a week to read such items. CBS didn't need Shirer for that. During that spring, while the war was going well for Adolf Hitler, Shirer managed to tolerate the German censor. But by September, as the British bombing of Germany intensified and Hitler pondered whether to invade Great Britain, Bill Shirer was getting increasingly annoyed at the Nazis' interference with his reporting. They did everything they could to keep the ugly truth of the war from reaching Shirer's listeners. He was not even permitted to read the headlines from German newspapers over the air. Moreover, he had to use a lip microphone, so-called because it was held cclose to one's lips, thus eliminating all other sounds that might be picked up by the mike. The Germans had no desire for the outside world to hear the firing of antiaircraft guns ringing Broadcast House or, for that matter, the incoming bombs dropping nearby. That would have been an admission that the war was much closer to home than acknowledged. Sometimes the Germans insisted that Shirer enter an air raid shelter; he suspected that they did so to prevent him from broadcasting the British air raids. But that ban on Shirer hardly mattered; back in New York, Elmer Davis was telling CBS listeners—and the Germans heard him say this— that it was true that Shirer had made no mention of air attacks, but it was also true that the bombs around the CBS correspondent in Berlin were so loud that Shirer could hardly hear his own voice.

For Shirer, leaving Germany seemed inevitable. When he sent his wife and child out of the country, Shirer considered going with them, but Paul White again asked that he remain in Berlin. A German invasion of England seemed likely, and White wanted CBS to have a presence in Germany. For the next few months Shirer held on. But by December 5 he pulled out, by this time concerned that the Germans might turn on him.

Back in the United States, patriotism required that anyone who could, chief executive or bottle washer, should rush to put on a uniform. Bill Paley was no exception. In the early summer of 1940 an aide to President Roosevelt, James Forrestal, had offered him the government post of Coordinator of Inter-American Affairs. The CBS chief was grateful but insisted that he wasn't right for the job. From their work together at the Museum of Modern Art, Paley knew Nelson Rockefeller, and so the CBS chief suggested the future Vice President of the United States as his replacement. Forrestal accepted the recommendation, and thus began Rockefeller's career in politics. During that fall, Roosevelt still had Paley in mind for official work. And this time Paley couldn't refuse. The president asked him to use his background in radio to counteract Nazi propaganda and its influence over radio stations in Latin America. Thus on November 8, 1940, Paley left on a seven-week tour of South and Central America. The trip also benefited CBS, for Paley managed to sign up sixty-four stations to receive entertainment, cultural, and news programs from CBS in Spanish and Portuguese. In his official capacity, Paley investigated the influence of Nazi Germany wherever he visited and then reported back to President Roosevelt. It was always understood at CBS that if and when the United States entered World War II, the Paley-initiated network in Latin America would be turned over to the U.S. Government. That is just what happened. CBS began its broadcasts to Latin America in May 1942, but just six months later the U.S. Government took over the new facility. Ironically, the man then running this "CBS network" was Nelson Rockefeller, in his capacity as Coordinator of Inter-American Affairs!

As the war advanced, CBS intensified its coverage. In June 1941 the German army moved eastward to attack Russia. CBS sent Larry LeSueur via Archangel to the Soviet Union where he began shortwave transmissions from Moscow. During that same year Howard K. Smith joined CBS and went to Berlin. (Despite Shirer's difficulties, CBS still wanted a man on the spot.) Charles Collingwood also joined the network, working at first in England, and Cecil Brown went to the Far East for CBS. Meanwhile, CBS was getting ready for the inevitable American entry into the war. By the end of 1940, CBS would have thirty-nine correspondents around the world. By 1941, the number of correspondents and stringers had risen to sixty-five. They would work hard. From Pearl Harbor to VJ-Day, CBS Radio would present 37,500 broadcasts, or nine months of war-related programs in all.

CBS had kept war songs from the airwaves for some time. They were thought to strike too partisan a note. Now that the ban was lifted, it was possible to turn on a radio station and hear a medley of "Over There," "Tipperary," "Till We Meet Again," "K-k-k-katy," and "Pack up Your Troubles." The war songs, of course, were all from World War I. It hardly mattered. They reflected the new mood in the United States, a mood that suggested that soon American troops would be going "over there" once again.

The war would not impair CBS financially. In 1937, it had grossed $34.2 million with a net of $4.3 million. Even as the nation was switching over to a war economy, the network's gross was $62.2 million in 1942 with a $4.1 million net. Fully 724 CBS employees went into military service, including Bill Paley. By 1944, CBS had improved its financial situation so that it reported a gross of $84.9 million with a net of $4.7 million.

No man would arouse American sympathy for the plight of the British during those early days of war as much as Edward R. Murrow. His reports from Britain during those horrifying days of August and September 1940 would have a major effect on the American attitude toward the war. By bringing vivid descriptions of the Blitz of London into Americans' living rooms, Murrow managed to inject a sense of urgency and, most important, a feeling that Britain's war was fast becoming America's. Murrow had that most rare of commodities—credibility. He would advise his protégés to speak to their listening audience as if they were at a dinner table in the United States with a local editor, a banker, and a professor, talking over coffee. The idea, he would tell them, was to describe what the event was like, while the maid's boyfriend, who might be a truck driver, listened from the kitchen. "Talk to be understood by the truck driver," Murrow would say, "while not insulting the professor's intelligence." And that was precisely what he would do in his broadcasts; he would talk to everyone, the simple man, and the not so simple.

His broadcasts conveyed the fact that he was reporting the battle from up close. He avoided air raid shelters, telling friends that once he went near one, it would be a sign that he had lost his nerve. Murrow knew that the only real way to report on a story was to be there, to be up close, so that he could record the sights and sounds. Other newsmen, out of envy or perhaps guilt, would accuse Murrow of exhibitionism, of being "macho," of harboring a secret death wish. But the fact was that Murrow got to the story and others did not.

It began in 30 million American homes on Saturday, August 24, 1940 when Murrow described the first moments of the Battle of Britain. "This is Trafalgar Square," he opened. "The noise that you hear at this moment is the sound of the air-raid siren. A searchlight just burst into action, off in the distance, an immense single beam sweeping the sky above me now. People are walking along very quietly. We're just at the entrance of an air-raid shelter here, and I must move the cable over just a bit, so people can walk in." His voice was quiet, sober, no betrayal of excitement—or fear. Murrow had been in Europe since 1937, and now, in the words of his biographer Alexander Kendrick, had "definitely taken upon his shoulders the cares of the world." (7)

Murrow always wanted to get as close to the story as possible, whatever the dangers involved. As many as 1,000 German planes might be bombing London on any given day during the twelve-day September Blitz. Along with NBC's Fred Bate, Murrow wanted to do a live broadcast from a London rooftop during a German bombing run. The Air Ministry said no, on the grounds that Murrow's broadcast could not be censored properly. He tried to convince the ministry there would be no such problem. But they were not in a mood to listen. Nonetheless, Murrow put on a tin hat, took a sound man with him, and did a recorded broadcast of a raid from the rooftop of the BBC, a major military target. "I'm standing on a rooftop looking out over London," he began. "At the moment everything is quiet. For reasons of national as well as personal security, I'm unable to tell you the exact location from which I'm speaking. Off to my left, far away in the distance, I can see just that faint red angry snap of anti-aircraft bursts against the steel-blue sky, but the guns are so far away that it's impossible to hear them from this location." As he spoke, he could look across the street at the damaged building where the two floors directly above CBS's fourth-floor office had been wiped out by a recent air raid. The CBS correspondent was thrilled. Now he was getting the genuine sound of the Blitz. Other American newsmen got the sounds of the war from the safety of their basement. They would wait for the BBC to have someone thrust a microphone out over the roof, obtain the recording of the raid, and then use it as part of their broadcast. That was not Ed Murrow's style. Murrow finally appealed directly to Winston Churchill, who said yes. As luck would have it, when Murrow did his next live rooftop broadcast, his voice was drowned out by the sound of gunfire and the engines of the plane.

He would open his broadcasts by saying simply "This . . . is London." And he would close just as simply by saying, "So long, and good luck." Of all the broadcasts he did that month, perhaps the most moving came on September 22. "I'm standing again tonight on a rooftop looking out over London," he began, "feeling rather large and lonesome. In the course of the last fifteen or twenty minutes there's been considerable action up there, but at the moment there's an ominous silence hanging over London. But at the same time a silence that has a great deal of dignity. Just straightaway in front of me the searchlights are working. I can see one or two bursts of anti-aircraft fire far in the distance. . . . Out of one window there waves something that looks like a white bed sheet, a window curtain swinging free in this night breeze. It looks as though it were being shaken by a ghost. There are a great many ghosts around these buildings in London. The searchlights straightaway, miles in front of me, are still scratching that sky. There's a three-quarter moon riding high. There was one burst of shellfire almost straight in the Little Dipper.

"Down below in the streets I can see just that red and green wink of the traffic lights; one lone taxicab moving slowly down the street. Not a sound to be heard. As I look out across the miles and miles of rooftops and chimney pots, some of those dirty-gray fronts of the buildings look almost snow-white in this moonlight here tonight. And the rooftop spotter across the way swings around, looks over in the direction of the searchlights, drops his glasses and just stands there. There are hundreds and hundreds of men like that standing on rooftops in London tonight watching for fire bombs, waiting to see what comes out of this steel-blue sky. The searchlights now reach up very, very faintly on three sides of me. There is a flash of a gun in the distance but too far away to be heard."

It was pure Murrow, a calm, graphic voice, an eye for the colors as well as the madness of the moment. In the midst of war, he speaks so personally and hauntingly in such powerful images and sober tones that the listener in his living room felt as if he were alongside of Murrow. He was not only reporting back home to his "constituents," he was in effect creating a broadcasting style that would make CBS the supreme network in news coverage during World War II.

"The Murrow standard" was quietly being adopted at CBS. Murrow was so successful, why not imitate him? Everyone knew that Ed favored short, concise statements, and so short, concise statements became fashionable among CBS newsmen. Everyone knew that Ed spoke quietly, and that he uttered strong, direct phrases in that deliberate, measured delivery. That too became part of CBS's broadcasting value system. Of course, not everyone could be an Ed Murrow. A certain part of Murrow was unique, not open to cloning. Anyone listening to his broadcasts from the late 1930s and World War II will spot that uniqueness immediately, the undeniable sincerity, the sense of personal identification with the people whom he was describing (in this case, the British). But, most of all, it was his sense of humility. As he would often remark, because he spoke into the microphone this did not give him greater omniscience. That humility came through in his broadcasts, and his audience responded affirmatively to his self-effacement. He also had the wonderful quality of being able to kid himself, and thus, he could get away with kidding others. So when there was that famous slip of the tongue from Larry LeSueur in Moscow, calling a certain incident a "teapest tempot," Murrow in London cabled Paul White and asked if he would "Please purchase suitably-inscribed, old-fashioned enameled single-handled teapest tempot and present to LeSueur." (8)

In Ed Murrow, CBS had nurtured one of the most important men of the time. He was not simply a broadcaster. Perhaps only the President of the United States had more influence over the masses than he did. In early December of 1941, he wanted to use that influence in a way that he believed was in the interest of his country. And so he went home on December 2 and was feted by CBS at a gala dinner at New York's Waldorf-Astoria attended by 1,100. The dinner was Bill Paley's idea. He wanted to call attention to his star reporter, and of course to CBS. Murrow was not just an asset, he was the main reason why millions of people were turning to Paley's network. Thanks to CBS's European coverage, spearheaded by the Murrow team, the network was fast developing an identity as the place where one turned for excellence in broadcast journalism. And Paley was happy, eager to exploit Murrow. *Variety* called that dinner "the most celebrity-studded ever held for a radio employee." (9) Twice the audience rose in tribute to him. Murrow had a message to convey. America had to get involved in the war in Europe. Britain's future depended on it. Also on hand was Archibald MacLeish, who was considered the poet laureate of the Roosevelt administration, sitting to Murrow's right. (Bill Paley was to Murrow's left.) MacLeish introduced Murrow as someone who had "accomplished one of the great miracles of the world," destroying "the most obstinate of all the superstitions—the superstition against which poetry and all the arts have fought for centuries, the superstition of distance and time." Murrow, said MacLeish, had also gotten rid of the "ignorant superstition that violence and lies and murder on another continent are not violence and lies and murder here . . . ."

Four days later—on Saturday, December 6—Murrow planned a day of golf at Burning Tree with his wife Janet. Later there was to be a dinner at the White House and a private talk with Franklin Roosevelt. But an event was occurring thousands of miles away that would interfere with Murrow's plans. The news about the Japanese attack on Pearl Harbor arrived at the White House in midafternoon. Calling the White House, Janet Murrow was told that the dinner had not been scrubbed. It was hard to imagine. The United States had just suffered a major military attack and the president still planned to find time for Ed Murrow. He and Janet were told to come along anyway. Upon their arrival, they found harried men running to and fro. Meanwhile, Eleanor Roosevelt fed them scrambled eggs. It got late and so Janet returned to their hotel. Ed stayed behind, waiting outside the president's office on a bench in the hall, smoking cigarette after cigarette, as cabinet secretaries marched in and out along with members of Congress and the military. He saw their faces, their amazement, their fury. Finally, at 12:30 A.M., Roosevelt was free and wanted to see Murrow. Over beer and sandwiches in the Oval Office, Murrow and the president chatted about friends they shared in England, about morale there. The president made a big point of insisting to Murrow that Pearl Harbor had been a complete surprise. He then provided details on the losses at Pearl Harbor, the number of dead, the number of ships sunk, the planes. "On the ground, by God, on the ground!" (10) As the president spoke those words mournfully, he pounded his fist on the table with great force. Knowing these facts, Murrow now faced one of the great dilemmas of his career. He went over to the CBS office and told the people there that the situation looked grim. But, uncharacteristically, he did not file a story. He paced the hotel room for the duration of that night, sensing that he might have been handed the greatest journalistic exclusive of his life. But something inside him insisted that the president, while he had not said so directly, had meant the information to be off the record. Murrow still argued with himself whether duty required that he forget what he learned—or tell it. Ultimately, he decided to broadcast nothing, convincing himself that his middle-of-the-night conversation with the president had indeed been privileged. Later on, Murrow would have some regrets, wishing that he had gone with the story. Throughout his life, he would be asked about that evening and the remarkable conversation with the president. But he could not bring himself to divulge the details. He would say that he planned to include the details in the memoirs he would eventually write. Few believed that Murrow would ever stop long enough to write a book. (And indeed he never did.) It seemed more likely that Murrow simply could not bring himself to violate what he viewed as the president's trust.

The attack on Pearl Harbor would cause surprise to everyone, soldiers, politicians, and the American radio networks. WOR-Mutual was busy at the Polo Grounds, covering the professional football game between the Dodgers and the Giants. CBS was luckier as the news came off the wire just 5 minutes before its "World News Today" program, the regular Sunday roundup from foreign locations. Oddly enough, the public response to the tragedy was calm and quiet, a far cry from the panic that ensued on that October evening three years earlier when Orson Welles broadcast his famous fake reenactment of "War of the Worlds." It had been John Daly, then on the CBS staff and later the well-known moderator of the television program "What's My Line" who took the United Press copy off the wire and at 2:25 P.M. interrupted a network broadcast to say, "The Japanese have attacked Pearl Harbor, Hawaii, by air, President Roosevelt has just announced. The attack was also made on naval and military activities on the principal island of Oahu . . . ." Sixteen minutes later, Bob Trout in London reported that it was too early for British reaction. At 3:01 P.M., Elmer Davis went on the air with some direct news from Honolulu where witnesses reported fire and heavy smoke at the American facilities. Soon Bill Shirer was broadcasting from Berlin, where he pronounced, "We didn't want war with Japan, but now it's been forced on us and our people will learn one more lesson of these tragic times: that you cannot stay out of war merely because you wish to . . . ." CBS correspondents were stationed in Honolulu and Manila, Sydney, and Singapore, as well as Burma, Batavia, and Chungking. But W. R. Wills, the CBS Tokyo correspondent, became silent, as did the men in Singapore and Manila.

No longer could radio stay neutral. A performance of Victor Herbert's *Babes in Toyland* was canceled as being too frivolous; instead, Rise Stevens went on the air to sing the National Anthem. Kate Smith seemed to be singing the song continuously when she wasn't conducting War Bond drives. Like all other American institutions, CBS took on a war orientation. Characters on its dramatic programs confronted problems related to the fighting. "The American School of the Air" had war news, information, and instructions for the children; "Country Journal" provided farmers aid in solving wartime farming problems; "The Garden Gate" promoted Victory gardens, "Church of the Air" had chaplains do war-oriented broadcasts. Some company-owned stations went on a 24-hour-a-day schedule, serving as part of the air raid defense system; they also provided entertainment for defense workers on the overnight swing.

In 1943 alone, CBS provided some 17,000 hours of war-related programs, among them "They Live Forever," which were dramas about men who died in battle; "The Man Behind the Gun," dramas about the battles themselves; and "Womanpower," which described the role of women during the war. One popular show was "Our Secret Weapon," which trained its guns on the lies in Axis propaganda. Aired on Sundays at 7 P.M., it had a CBS announcer read a statement from a recent Axis broadcast, then Rex Stout would come on and expose the lie. One example:

Announcer (in a sharp German accent): "The best soldiers and officers in the United States Army are Germans. So are all the best baseball and football players."

Stout: "As you see, they've got the facts, no getting away from it. Take the six leading batters in the major leagues: Williams, Gordon, Wright, Reiser, Lombardi, Medwick. Some bunch of Germans. Also the great German prize fighter, Joe Louis."

Experiments in television advanced even though it was wartime. The great catalyst was CBS's engineer/inventor Peter Goldmark. Color television had been successfully developed as early as 1928, just three years after black-and-white television had been invented, but the color was primitive, and improvements were hard to come by. In 1939, the broadcasting industry was in a quandary: since the color systems were incompatible with black and white, the industry had to decide whether to develop color or black and white. Opting for color would have been facilitated by the paucity of black-and-white sets (3,000 in New York City and many fewer in the other large cities). But no one had the time or inclination to make such sweeping decisions.

In February 1940 RCA had come out with a prototype color system which it showed to the FCC. Soon thereafter CBS was working on its own because Peter Goldmark had gone to a movie one day. During a visit to Montreal in March Goldmark decided to take in a movie while waiting for the train back to New York. He saw *Gone with the Wind* and was so impressed with its technicolor that he immediately concluded that black-and-white television was inferior: "I could hardly think of going back to the phosphorus images of regular black-and-white television. All through the long, four-hour movie I was obsessed with the thought of applying color to television." (11) During the intermission he went to a corner of the lobby, took out his notebook, and began to calculate the requirements for color television. In the hotel and on the train he kept on filling his pages with equations. Getting Paul Kesten's approval to go ahead, Goldmark then developed what became known as "the field-sequential system of color TV." Some irreverently dubbed it, "Goldmark's whirling dervish." The system scanned the image, or field, that was transmitted through a sequence of colored filters—red, blue, and green. Those filters were built into a disc which rotated between the camera and the subject. Goldmark's color system scanned an image three times, once through each filter. While each image was photographed through a colored filter, it was transmitted as black and white. The color was added at the receiving end. There, another disc, spinning in synchronization with the camera, would add the red, blue, and green to those separate black-and-white images. Although separately colored, the resulting images passed so quickly across the screen that the viewer's eye mixed them together.

In August Goldmark demonstrated his new system to the FCC, which gave him a green light for more experimenting. The contest over color television had major implications for CBS and the rest of the broadcasting industry. But a final decision would have to await war's end. Due to the war, Peter Goldmark only returned to color television research in 1945. Had anyone taken the time to decide in favor of some color system in 1942, it might have been possible to discard black and white for color television. The CBS and RCA color systems were incompatible with black-and-white sets, so it made sense to make either black and white or color the industry standard.

CBS's first television news broadcast occurred in the spring of 1941. By the end of that year, the CBS New York station was airing two 15-minute television newscasts a day, Monday through Friday at 2:30 P.M. and 7:30 P.M. with Richard Hubbell narrating. Essentially, he provided "chalk talks." Standing with a pointer in front of a map, Hubbell talked about the main topic of the day, the war, describing what the latest information was from this front or that. He had little need for his maps to be precise: reception on the tiny, primitive sets was so poor that viewers could barely make him out much less the lines drawn on his map. On the day after Pearl Harbor, when the United States declared war on Japan, CBS's television station WCBW broadcast a nine-hour news special on the assault, with Hubbell anchoring. In those days it was not technically possible for the cameras to show President Roosevelt live: during his famous "Day of Infamy" speech to Congress, an American flag was placed in front of the camera and off camera a fan made the flag wave. Afterward, television was sharply limited as American industry was told to cut down on unnecessary production. Station building was stopped and only nine stations remained on the air. The three New York network stations cut down televising from four nights a week to just one. By the close of 1942, CBS and NBC had locked their studios, using only filmed shorts and a few live sports remote broadcasts as well as civil defense instruction films.

As the war progressed, London grew in importance to CBS. In 1942, it had developed into a hub for numerous foreign correspondents, the central point of transmission for all broadcasts from Europe, North Africa, and the Middle East. As the story grew in dimension, so too did the staff. Bill Downs of the United Press had gone to Moscow that winter for CBS;

Larry LeSueur had moved to Cairo; and a handsome, elegantly dressed Rhodes scholar named Charles Collingwood had taken up assignment in North Africa.

Charles Cummings Collingwood. He became one of the major figures of CBS News, and apart from Murrow, perhaps the next most exciting journalist within CBS. He had been at Oxford as a Rhodes scholar, studying Medieval law, but when war broke out in 1939 he had no desire to return home. Nor did he want to remain at Oxford when his own generation of Englishmen were all going to war. Collingwood came very close to joining the British Army. But instead took a job with United Press, remaining with the wire service for nearly two years in England and Holland. While working in London, he was assigned to cover the Blitz and would stand on top of the office roof, tin helmet on his head, a map of the city in his hand, trying to spot where the big fires were. He then sent someone to cover them, or went himself.

In early 1941 a "Mr. Morrell" from CBS called Collingwood. Or at least that was the name Collingwood understood from the note on his desk. In fact, he knew that Ed Murrow was a household name in the United States. But at first Collingwood couldn't conceive of Mr. Morrell being the same person as Mr. Murrow. Calling CBS, he asked for Mr. Morrell. "Oh," said Kay Campbell, secretary to Ed Murrow, "you must mean Mr. Murrow." Meekly, Collingwood conceded that he probably did mean just that. When the two men met, Murrow explained to Collingwood that he was looking for someone who could work in radio in the CBS London bureau. Murrow wanted someone with reporting experience who had not been "contaminated" by print. In other words, someone who could rid himself of print journalism's clichés. Murrow sensed that Collingwood was the right person. After hiring Collingwood, Murrow confessed to him that he had nearly not given him the job. It seemed that Collingwood, as always an impeccable dresser, had gone to the interview wearing a very loud pair of argyle socks. A great conservative when it came to clothes, Murrow could not figure out what this meant about Collingwood's character. He decided to take the risk anyway.

In 1942 Collingwood had become CBS's man in North Africa. This was a grand assignment; it was here that the Allies stepped foot for the first time on Hitler-held territory. Collingwood was known for his firm voice, his colorful reports, and, not surprisingly, his sartorial elegance. Actress Kay Francis, while on tour entertaining troops, said of Collingwood that he was the only man in North Africa who knew where to get a suit pressed. To Collingwood, Murrow was the embodiment of a professional journalist and, as with other CBS correspondents, imitation became the best form of flattery. If Murrow dictated his broadcasts to his secretary, Collingwood would do the same thing—and become a great correspondent like Murrow. But Collingwood found that dictating a broadcast took him more time than simply committing words to paper directly.

Like so many of the "Murrow boys," Collingwood would go anywhere and do almost anything for a story. Sometimes, such diligence worked. But at other times it led to embarrassing moments. One occurred when he was broadcasting live back to the United States from the Normandy beach on D-Day, June 5, 1944. Loaded down with an 80-pound battery pack on his back that enabled him to do the live broadcast, he would broadcast to a nearby ship, which relayed his voice to London, and from there it was relayed to New York. He had been describing where he was and what it was like. Men with uniforms were all around him. "There's a lot of firing going on in the distance. It's very difficult to tell what the situation is. It's quiet on this beach. There has been a first landing by troops who moved on and other ships are coming in. Let me walk up here. I think I see a navy officer down the other end who may have more information." Walking over to the man, Collingwood stopped and said, "Commander, excuse me, I'm Charles Collingwood of CBS. Can you give me any idea what's going on?" Suddenly, the next voice said, "It beats the shit out of me, Charley, I'm the NBC correspondent!"

They were called the "Murrow boys," a cachet that identified them as the prodigies of Ed Murrow. It identified them as a special breed of reporter, one with a solid educational background, with intense curiosity, and, above all, immense courage. Passing through this war would confer upon the "Murrow boys" a special identity card. Murrow would call them his "band of brothers." Those who were part of that band, part of that coterie of newsmen who had been part of the "big picture," had it made after the fighting. Walter Cronkite was not one of Murrow's boys, and those who were were quick to remind themselves that Cronkite was not one of them. Considering how much of an outsider he was at CBS, he would not do badly. Murrow had nearly lured Walter into CBS's net during the war, but lost him when United Press, upon hearing that Cronkite was being courted by the network, immediately gave him a $25-a-week raise.

One of the best known of the "Murrow boys" was Eric Sevareid. A young journalist from North Dakota, he had been working as the city editor of the Paris *Herald* by day and as night editor of United Press by night and was considered an outstanding newsman. Unsurprisingly, Ed Murrow learned about him.

The president of the United Press, Hugh Baillie, had just arrived from New York and offered Sevareid an excellent new post. The United Press man wavered. How, wondered Sevareid, could he continue to work for a place which was far more concerned with how much attention its story got among the world's newspapers than with writing quality. As he was brooding, Ed Murrow called, saying that he liked the way Sevareid wrote and he liked his ideas. Murrow noted that CBS's overseas staff comprised only Bill Shirer, Thomas Grandin, and himself, "but I think this thing may develop into something." Murrow seemed aware of Sevareid's anxiety about United Press. He promised Eric that CBS would apply no pressure to get scoops or anything sensational, just the genuine news.

There would have to be an audition of course. To say that Sevareid was nervous would be an understatement. The nervousness would in fact never go away even after years of radio and television work. The thought of auditioning before a microphone was shattering. The assignment was to read a speech on contemporary affairs he had just written in haste. His hands were shaking so violently, he recalled later, that he was sure listeners must have heard the rattling of the paper. However bewildered he may have been by Sevareid's performance, Murrow remained committed to high-quality newsmen. Their broadcasting voices were secondary considerations. Calming Sevareid, Murrow assured him that the job was his. Against the advice of friends, Murrow did indeed bring Sevareid on board.

Sevareid began his CBS reporting in France and stayed on until France fell in June 1940, moving afterward to England. His most harrowing experience occurred in the summer of 1942 while on on a C46 plane trying to clear the hump of the Himalayas en route to an assignment in China. The plane was known as a "flying coffin" and nearly lived up to its name when the left engine went dead. Passenger luggage was thrown from the plane and men clutched at parachutes. The pilot shouted at Sevareid but the CBS man couldn't understand what he was saying. Assuming that the pilot was urging him to parachute, Sevareid did just that, landing safely. He was not out of harm's way yet. Over the next few days he came upon some of the injured survivors. One of those survivors lightened Sevareid's day by telling him that he used to listen to his broadcasts. Soon things turned tense when the survivors were surrounded by twenty small, naked men with spears and knives who were chanting in unison. Sevareid fell back on something he recalled from childhood. Stepping forward, he raised a palm and said as earnestly as he could, "How!" It was meant as a gesture of friendship and he only hoped it would be so interpreted. Miraculously, the tiny spear carriers calmed down. Later, an American plane dropped leaflets warning the survivors that they were in an area of Naga headhunters and the group should beware. Eventually, a radio receiver was dropped from friendly planes. And later a rescue party arrived. Sevareid's ordeal was over. It would take several more weeks before CBS would find out that Sevareid and his fellow passengers were all right.

Perhaps the highest compliment that could be paid to CBS's European coverage came from Winston Churchill. In the middle of 1943 he offered Ed Murrow the post of editor-in-chief of the BBC with special responsibility for programming. Realizing that the offer had come directly from the prime minister, and that nominating an American was unusual, Murrow could not take the overture lightly. He flew home to consult with his colleagues. In the end, he turned it down. He could not leave CBS. Nor did he want to give up his war reporting for his American audience.

War reporting in general remained a sticky subject for the network. Around this time, one more controversy regarding the issue of fairness surfaced at CBS. The question was whether a correspondent had a right to editorialize. Network executives were never quite able to constrain on-the-air reporters from expunging their personal views from their reporting. Although Paley, Klauber, and White would insist on objectivity from their correspondents, they had at the same time given them the right to analyze and interpret events, and here and there, a correspondent would stretch his analysis to include personal points of view. Paley had learned a hard lesson from the experience he had had with Father Coughlin during the 1930s. He was also concerned about the effect of a CBS newsman's opinion making on a sponsor. As the number of advertisers on radio increased, the issue was focused even more sharply. CBS insisted that sponsors have no right to dictate to the network what was said or who would say it. But it would be nearly impossible to get a sponsor to renew its contract with the network if it were uncomfortable with someone's commentary. The network was beginning to show some concern during World War II, as illustrated by one incident revolving around CBS's Singapore correspondent Cecil Brown. In his news analysis one night in late August 1943, Brown offered an opinion in the wake of the Sicilian campaign and the Roosevelt-Churchill conference in Quebec. "Any reasonably accurate observer of the American scene at this moment," observed Brown, "knows that a good deal of enthusiasm for this war is evaporating into thin air." Paul White assailed him for not reporting factually and said his remarks were "dangerous to public morale." Brown was spreading "defeatist talk that would be of immense pleasure to Dr. Goebbels and his boys." White issued a memo to "CBS news analysts" that CBS published in New York newspapers as a full-page advertisement. It read: "Each of you has been chosen by us because of your background and knowledge, insight, clarity of thought, and special ability to make yourselves understood by vast audiences. We feel we have faced and met a considerable responsibility in your selection. We now feel that you must meet and face much the same responsibility in writing your analyses. For we have said to ourselves, 'We will not choose men who will tell the public what they themselves think and what the public should think.' And we ask that you say to yourselves, 'We are not privileged to crusade, to harangue the people or to attempt to sway public opinion."

". . . Actually, freedom of speech on the radio would be menaced if a small group of men, some thirty or forty news analysts who have nationwide audiences and regular broadcasting periods in which to build loyal listeners, take advantage of their 'preferred position' and become pulpiteers . . . ." Cecil Brown resigned over the issue. For his part, Paul White vowed that CBS would stop commentators from expressing any opinion. H. V. Kaltenborn tried to come to Brown's rescue, saying that his own spontaneous broadcasts at the time of Munich in 1938 hardly would have been allowed under the new harsh decree of 1943. The chairman of the FCC, James L. Fly, actually distanced himself from White's articulation of CBS policy by noting that the network could air opinion as long as it was so labeled. But Paul White stuck to his guns.

Bill Paley wanted a piece of the action against the Nazis. Ed Klauber had departed in August 1943. Paley chose to leave CBS in the hands of Paul Kesten, who had been number three after Paley and Klauber. Playwright Robert Sherwood, a friend of Paley's, had suggested his name to the Office of War Information, and within a few weeks, Paley was chosen to supervise the establishment of Allied radio broadcasting activities in North Africa and Italy. And so that fall, Paley, now 42 years old, joined a psychological warfare unit which went from New York to Miami, on to Brazil, Dakar on the west coast of Africa, later Marrakesh, and finally Algiers. He figured that he could give three to six months to the war effort and then return to CBS.

The following January 1944 Paley flew to London where he became chief of Radio Broadcasting within the Psychological Warfare Division of SHAEF—Supreme Headquarters, Allied Expeditionary Forces. SHAEF was preparing for the Allied invasion of France. One of Paley's assignments was to manage American English-based broadcasts in enemy territory. Paley ran both "black" and "white" broadcasts: "white" stuck to the truth, "black" did not. Once, conducting a "black" broadcast, Paley established a "German" radio station that presumably was located in Germany. In fact the entire operation was handled by Sefton Delmer, a bearded British news correspondent from a small village near London. Upon entering the gates of the "radio station," one spoke only German. Eventually the Germans began to trust the station so much that when other German stations were knocked out of action, they turned to this one, and only then did they receive all sorts of misinformation that led to chaos within German ranks.

Perhaps Paley's most complicated "white" broadcast had to do with the worldwide announcement he helped to prepare for the start of D-Day, the cross-Channel invasion into Europe. General Eisenhower had already prepared an official message for broadcast which included the following lines, "To patriots who are not members of organized resistance groups, I say, 'Continue your passive resistance, but do not needlessly endanger your lives before I give you the signal to rise and strike the enemy.'" A Paley colleague spotted the problem. The general can't say that, the colleague yelled out upon reading it. Those lines could mean that Eisenhower would give the men an order to endanger their lives needlessly. What to do? Ike would have to rebroadcast that part. But Paley learned that Eisenhower was too busy and had advised his communications aide to fix the problem up himself. But how? Perhaps, Paley thought, he could find someone who sounded like Eisenhower. But there was nobody around who qualified. There was only one thing to do. Risking Eisenhower's wrath, Paley beseeched him once more to agree to a rebroadcast. The general reluctantly said yes and, after Paley lugged all the equipment into a room, carried out the mission at 6 the next morning.

Recording Haakon VII, the king of Norway, proved just as difficult. The King insisted that only Paley be present for the recording of his D-Day message. So taken with emotion was the monarch that he couldn't get through an entire reading without breaking into tears. Paley kept telling him that it was all right, to take his time. After three or four unsuccessful tries, Paley finally told him just to go through the script from start to finish, weeping and all. Later, Paley and his editors managed to delete the weeping. General de Gaulle was no easier. He insisted on reading Eisenhower's D-Day message first. Discovering that Eisenhower had not mentioned him, de Gaulle said bitterly he had nothing to say to the people of France. It took the personal intervention of Winston Churchill to persuade the French leader to deliver the message.

Paley had planned to have the messages delivered once word arrived that the invasion was on its way to success. The plan was for someone to phone him and utter the code word "Topflight" as a signal that D-Day messages could be distributed. But, when the phone rang, an excited Paley, saying, "Yes?" merely heard a voice on the other end say, "Testing." Dejected, Paley put the phone down. Five minutes later the same thing happened, the phone rang and a voice said "testing." By this time Paley was angry. It happened a third time a few moments later. Paley exploded at the man, telling him that if he did it once more he would "knock your head off." (12) Paley ordered him not to call again until it was real. The man apologized. Some time later the authentic call came through, and seconds later, the world learned about D-Day.

CBS wanted comprehensive, factual coverage of the invasion. Paul White issued new instructions to his correspondents: "Give sources for all reports. Keep an informative, unexcited demeanor at the microphone.

Don't risk accuracy for the sake of a beat. Use care in your choice of words. Don't say 'German defenses were pulverized'; say 'German defenses were hard hit.' When you don't know, say so. . . . Exaggeration and immoderate language breed dangerous optimism." (13) He added that the only way to help the men at the front was to report factually, soberly, intelligently. He concluded that winning the war was a great deal more important than reporting it.

On D-Day, June 6, 1944, was radio's finest performance to date. In the 24 hours after the announcement of the Allied invasion, CBS devoted 16 hours to invasion news and commentary—3 hours from London alone. Paul White had difficulties, however, convincing the business people in the network to keep commercial programs off the air that day. The two NBC networks and Mutual canceled all programming, but CBS returned to soap operas at 10 A.M. and remained with them until 12 noon. In the early part of the war, even such monumental events as Pearl Harbor did not warrant a great deal of preempting. But CBS took seventeen commercially sponsored programs off the air to provide five full hours of D-Day coverage.

On May 5, 1944 CBS reopened its television studios with the debut of the CBS "Television News," hosted by Ned Calmer, giving a 15-minute wrap-up of the news, using newsreel film. Entertainment shows began at this time as well, with Worthington "Tony" Miner, a newly hired producer, trying to find which of CBS's radio shows, predominantly the quiz ones, would adapt to television quickly. CBS was in no rush to leap into television. It preferred to go directly to color without black-and-white television.

Believing that television was still experimental, it did not take part in the early bidding for new television station licenses in cities outside New York, limiting its television operations to its one outlet in New York City. The fall 1944 television schedule was largely empty: CBS broadcast the news at 8 P.M. on Thursdays and Fridays and a few other entertainment shows at week's end. If television were going to make it, clearly a great deal more enthusiasm would have to be devoted to this new medium.

six

"LET'S HEAR IT
FOR THE LORD'S PRAYER."

The war was over. The United States had triumphed and so had CBS. The *Motion Picture Daily* poll, canvassing 600 American and Canadian radio editors, had given some phase of CBS news coverage first place every year but one from 1938 to 1947. For the final three years of the war, *Motion Picture Daily* selected CBS as the network which performed the "Best news job in radio." The 1945 award mentioned CBS's coverage of VE-Day, VJ-Day (the Japanese surrender), and President Roosevelt's death. Also in 1945, CBS won the Peabody Award for its outstanding war coverage.

Aside from winning awards, CBS was busy helping the United States celebrate the glorious finale to the fighting. On May 8, Norman Corwin put together "On a Note of Triumph" to commemorate the end of hostilities. Listeners phoned in their congratulations to CBS—for both the program and for the end of war. A book edition of "Triumph," put out by Simon & Schuster, sold 50,000 copies within a few days. A Columbia Records album of the program sold out rapidly. That summer Norman Corwin once again supplied a script for a commemorative program of an American victory, this one over Japan. The program was called simply "August 14" and used Orson Welles as the narrator.

Ed Murrow's time in Europe was over too. Just prior to leaving England, he did a broadcast in which he praised England for fighting the war without giving up its principles of representative government and equality before the law. "Future generations who bother to read the official record of proceedings in the House of Commons will discover," Murrow said, "that British armies retreated from many places but that there was no retreat from the principles for which your ancestors fought." It was Murrow's way of saying thank you to the country he had come to love.

With the war's conclusion, Murrow had a dream which he shared with David Schoenbrun, just discharged from the American army and aspiring to become a CBS correspondent. Schoenbrun even had a place in mind from which to report: Paris. Murrow had in fact met Schoenbrun during the war and had expressed interest in the young man. With Eric Sevareid and Charles Collingwood going home, perhaps Murrow's interest might be turned into a firm job offer. With that hope, Schoenbrun flew from Paris to London to talk with Murrow. They met in the apartment house near the BBC studios on Hallam Street where Murrow had an office. Murrow asked Schoenbrun if he planned to return to teaching. No, came the reply, first he had a doctorate to do and there would be no time for teaching. "Well," said Ed, "one day I could give you the biggest classroom in the world." (1)

"Harvard?" asked David, apparently assuming Ed was joking with him.

"No," came the answer, "CBS News." And then Murrow spelled out his hopes. "We are going to make CBS the greatest news network in the world. We are going to inform and educate the people of America. They have lived almost all our history in isolation and know little or nothing of the world we live in. But now America is the world's greatest power, with enormous responsibilities and opportunities to advance the cause of democracy. It can no longer afford to be ignorant of the world. That's why I see CBS as a giant national classroom. I've been recruiting men with university backgrounds. Howard Smith was a Rhodes scholar at Oxford. So was Collingwood. That's the kind of man I want." There was a pause and laughter from Murrow. "You know, you can't teach a pear-shaped tone or a pretty face to think. But you can teach a brain to broadcast." Murrow's remarks were interesting, but Schoenbrun had a more immediate concern: his prospects of getting a job at CBS. His chances, Murrow insisted, were good. But he should not sit around waiting for the phone to ring. Nor, Murrow added, should he be surprised if he were called "out of the blue."

Murrow would dream of greatness for CBS News, and Schoenbrun would do his own personal dreaming of working for the network because radio had become, thanks to World War II, a national force. Ninety percent of all American families now owned a radio, more than owned

---

phones, bathtubs, or cars. A staggering 56 million radios were in use (but only 16,500 television sets). Someone figured out that the only activity Americans did more of than listen to radio was work and sleep!

As a result, CBS emerged from the war in reasonable financial shape. It was larger, wealthier, and far more ingrained in the public mind than in the past. Its revenues rose to $69 million and profits to $5 million. Before the hostilities, only one-third of its schedule had been commercially sponsored, but by 1945 that percentage had leaped to two-thirds. Armed with greater financial resources and better broadcasting facilities, NBC had continued to attract and employ entertainers far more easily than CBS. As a result, NBC still outshone it in audience ratings.

The top fifteen entertainment programs of the 1945–1946 radio season offered little joy for CBS. "Fibber McGee and Molly" was on top, followed by Bob Hope, "Lux Radio Theater," Edgar Bergen and Charlie McCarthy, Red Skelton, Jack Benny, "The Screen Guild Players," Fred Allen, "Mr. District Attorney," Walter Winchell, "The Great Gildersleeve," Eddie Cantor, Abbott and Costello, Jack Haley and Eve Arden, and Burns and Allen. Only two of these entries belonged to CBS: "Lux Radio Theater" and "Screen Guild Players." ABC had one and NBC had all the rest.

Precisely how to overcome NBC's ratings lead became the subject of a high-level debate at CBS, a debate that pitted the network's two top executives, Bill Paley and Paul Kesten, against one another. By all accounts, the debate never became bitter. In essence, the debate centered on what was the best direction for the network to take in selecting its entertainment schedule. With CBS in a lowly position vis-à-vis NBC, the debate had crucial significance. Paul Kesten wanted to turn CBS into an elite network, to avoid transforming the network into a truly mass medium. Kesten spelled all this out in a fifteen-page letter written to Paley in Europe after VE-Day. CBS, wrote Kesten, should be beamed, not to 30 million homes, but only to 10 or 15 million. The network should become "the one network that never offends with over-commercialism, in content, in quantity, or in tone . . . that presents superb and sparkling entertainment . . . (and) an important forum for great public figures and great public issues, for education, for thoughtful and challenging presentation of the news and the issues growing out of it. . . . To be the network that is never corny, blatant, common, coarse or careless, that is always bright, stimulating. . . ." (2) He proposed that affiliates make room for 10 hours of network broadcasting a day and then locate advertisers who would sponsor these nationwide shows. On the surface, it appeared that Kesten wanted to turn CBS into *The New York Times* of broadcasting, a high-quality enterprise which, by virtue of that high quality, would not reach the masses but was content in knowing that it was the best of its kind.

It was as if Paul Kesten sensed that the commercial impulses first on radio, but especially in television, would place a great burden on the network. And, in stating his doctrine, Kesten hoped that Paley would agree to avoid the handwriting on the wall. Kesten did not object to CBS's striving to become a mass entertainment network. He simply wanted to avoid the inevitable compromises and sacrifices along the way. Kesten wanted CBS to develop its high standards but feared the negative effects of overcommercialization. Kesten was indeed a prophet crying in the wilderness. He would have been pleased with much of what CBS did in later decades; he would have been saddened, however, that some of his warnings had been on the mark.

But Paley rejected Kesten's ideas. He saw them as tantamount to the abandonment of CBS's struggle to overcome NBC in the ratings war. Even in the immediate postwar world, ratings mattered enough for Paley to discard the Kesten doctrine. Radio, as far as the CBS chairman was concerned, was largely a mass medium—and that was that. "To survive," Paley wrote, "CBS had to give the majority of people the kind of programs it wanted to hear in popular entertainment." (3)

While Paley would triumph in the debate, this did not diminish the respect he had for Kesten. So much so that he was eager to give Kesten greater responsibility. He found Kesten warm and congenial, if a bit outspoken. Paley decided to promote him from executive vice president to president, putting him in charge of the network's daily operation. Paley, as chairman and chief executive officer, would deal specifically with radio and television development and new ideas on programming. The one glitch was that Kesten, bothered by his worsening arthritis, was in no mood to take over the presidency. Instead, he suggested that his protégé, Frank Stanton, be given the nod.

While Paley was away in the war, Stanton had helped Kesten run the company. Since joining CBS in the mid-1930s, Stanton had moved from research to general management, including the eight CBS-owned stations, becoming a vice president in 1942. Paley had found Stanton cool, shy, and reserved but knew him to be bright and effective. He accepted Kesten's proposal, and in September 1945 asked Stanton to become president. On January 9, 1946, Paley was elected chairman, and Stanton president.

This was an extremely important passage. Stanton would remain president of CBS for the next twenty-six years; he and Paley would provide a stability at CBS's helm lacking in rival NBC's camp where David Sarnoff would, on nine different occasions, shift around chairmen and presidents. Paley left the running of the network to Stanton, involving himself largely in the two areas where his instincts were sharply honed, programming and discovering talent, areas which he felt were the core of. broadcasting.

Paley soon got around to Ed Murrow, eager to capitalize on the magic of his name. Putting Murrow in charge of CBS News would give the news division just the luster that it needed in its postwar efforts. Murrow was reluctant. He had no real interest in becoming an administrator; the idea of being forced to fire someone was repugnant. Administrators were, in his view, glorified paper-pushers. After slogging around London and the Continent in a major war, the thought of being desk-bound seemed hideous. Yet Paley applied the pressure, and Murrow bent, agreeing to become vice president in charge of news and public affairs. The one discordant note concerned Murrow's relationship with Paul White. In his new capacity, Murrow would rank above White, in contrast with the previous years. White was given the title of director of News Broadcasts within the Public Affairs Department.

Murrow and Paley remained more than business acquaintances. They were close friends. Murrow's contract reflected their closeness: it permitted him to cancel the contract if Paley ceased being CBS's chief executive officer. Murrow's war feats had engendered in Paley a small case of hero worship toward Murrow. Accordingly, Murrow was the only employee exempted from Paley's practice of keeping his business and social lives separate. Indeed, in 1947 Ed and his wife Janet went to Bill's small wedding to Barbara Cushing. Thus, Murrow had an inside channel to Paley. In Paley, Murrow saw a cross between a father figure and an older brother: he would not make an important career decision without consulting Paley. (Once, he did brush aside Paley's advice—when the Democrats asked Murrow to run for the U.S. Senate seat from New York. Although Murrow felt, as a North Carolinian, he would expose himself to a carpetbagging charge, Paley told him to run. His heart in broadcasting, not politics, Murrow declined.)

The prestige CBS had achieved during the war made just joining the organization tantamount to success. Some, like David Schoenbrun, had long had a dream of becoming a CBS correspondent. It was time for David Schoenbrun's dream to be realized. In the fall of 1947 he was the Paris correspondent for a small news syndicate, the Overseas News Agency (ONA). He also engaged in freelance broadcasting for CBS News and the Mutual Broadcasting System. Schoenbrun had set off for Eastern Europe after his editors urged him to explore the situation behind the Iron Curtain. The morning after arriving in Prague, a telegram came for him. Schoenbrun thought its arrival less important than trying to protect himself against the Prague chill. He opened it diffidently and read it in growing amazement: "If you're interested in being CBS News Paris correspondent, please call me collect soonest. Edward R. Murrow, Vice-President, CBS News." The telegram made him forget the cold: "Suddenly, the room was warm. I jumped out of bed and began dancing around. I was wild with joy." (4) Later on the phone to Murrow, he crowed, "Ed, it's such a great post. I don't know why CBS is paying me. I ought to pay to be your Paris correspondent." Murrow laughed and said not to worry, Schoenbrun would pay a good deal, he would earn his keep.

CBS News had prestige, to be sure. Some of its staff were household names, better known than politicians. Those who joined the organization in the late 1940s, like Schoenbrun, were mesmerized by the CBS name. They were bigger than life, those CBS staffers. And Av Westin, a member of the founding generation of the television news staff but then in the summer of 1947 a junior copy boy, felt dwarfed by them: "I remember once breaking a really terrible rule. Murrow had the end office on the 17th floor at 485 Madison Avenue. When he was going to do his commentaries for his radio broadcasts, he would go into that office with [his secretary] Kay Campbell . . . I come bouncing along and I'm ready to make my 5 o'clock run down at Colby's. . . . So I committed the cardinal sin. Before the secretary could grab me and say, 'Don't go in there,' I was in there, asking can I get you anything. The glares and stares." (5)

What made young men like Av Westin dumbstruck then about CBS News and its correspondents in those days was an intangible quality that the "Murrow boys" had acquired as part of their war coverage. The "band of brothers" adopted the war's argot as their own: food became "rations," radio equipment became "gear." They even had their own "in" jokes. For instance, at the Philadelphia conventions in 1948 they put up little signs that said, "Don't be unbrotherly, brother." Above all, they had dual personalities: they could cover a war by day and show up at a formal banquet at night and not look the worse for wear. They liked a good story, and they liked good clothes. They would go anywhere for the story, but only to London for the clothes. As Av Westin said of one of the more senior "Murrow boys": "You felt that Charles Collingwood could step out of that bandbox suit, don fatigues or don a night jacket and he would put on a helmet and he'd be striding the lead tank." (6) Over at NBC, such compliments were rarely passed out.

After the war, relations between the United States and the Soviet Union deteriorated, and, falling in line with American policy, broadcasting executives wanted to make sure that commentary over the airwaves was devoid of left-wing propaganda, of a viewpoint that seemed sympathetic with the Communists. In this atmosphere of postwar patriotism, CBS was more inclined toward self-censorship. One of the first victims was William Shirer.

After his 1941 book *Berlin Diary,* based on his war diary, had become a best-seller, Shirer became a national celebrity. He undertook a weekly 15-minute program of news analysis, sponsored by J. B. Williams, the makers of shaving lotion. The program aired at 5:45 on Sunday afternoons and had attracted 5 million listeners. In early 1947, J. B. Williams passed word that it no longer wanted to sponsor Shirer's broadcast. It seems that he had been offering opinions that were clearly at odds with the conventional wisdom that acknowledged the existence of the Cold War. He was the only commentator to criticize the new Truman doctrine and American support for the Greek and Turkish government in their struggle against Communist guerrillas. In March, the sponsor dropped him. Murrow had to put Shirer in a different slot. Because Shirer had no sponsor, the pay would be much lower. Shirer was furious. He expected CBS to come to his aid. He was being censored—by a sponsor. Wasn't CBS opposed to such outside interference? Shirer turned the incident into a major controversy at CBS, charging that he had been gagged both by the sponsor and CBS. With eighteen months left to go in his contract, he resigned, resisting pleas from Murrow that he stay on. Supporters of Shirer's went to see Paley on Shirer's behalf; they also held a demonstration at New York's Town Hall. Shirer and Murrow tried to work things out over a lunch, but even after they agreed that Murrow would obtain from Paley a face-saving statement, Paley would not buy it. The chairman wanted Shirer out.

Some of the "Murrow boys" would meet grief after the war. One was George Polk. Considered one of Murrow's bright new recruits, Polk was in love with his work and not the byline. Polk, a Texan, had been wounded in the Solomons. He was thin, sandy-haired, and well liked among his colleagues for being unpretentious, kind, and honorable and a fine reporter. He sided with the underdog and disliked stuffiness of any type. Polk had approached Murrow in London in the fall of 1945 for work and a few months later was appointed CBS Mideast correspondent. A problem occurred at the outset when CBS's Doug Edwards, who had been requested by the bosses to make contact with Ted Berkman in Cairo, showed up in the CBS Cairo bureau. Though Edwards would also spend time with George Polk, confusion arose over just who was the new CBS correspondent in the region. With Edwards sent to talk with him, Berkman appeared the rightful CBS man. "But I'm the new CBS guy in the Middle East," said an astonished Polk. (7) When Berkman realized that Murrow himself had hired Polk, he gave way, eventually going to work for ABC.

Polk's job was to cover Cairo, Athens, and the rest of the eastern Mediterranean. During the winter of 1947–48 Polk was engaged in aggressive reporting, assailing both sides in divided Greece, eliciting protests from both the United States Aid Mission and the Athens government. He labeled the cabinet strongman, Populist Party leader Constantine Tsaldaris and his comrades "semi-Fascists" in a CBS broadcast. Writing in the December 1947 issue of *Harper's,* Polk described the Greek economic system as "rotten to the core." At CBS, Murrow gave Polk his full backing. In private notes to Murrow, Polk wrote darkly of being called a Communist, and of having his life threatened. Polk dismissed such threats, convinced that the worst that would happen to him would be expulsion from Greece. He went north to seek an interview with the guerrilla general Markos Vafiades. When Polk's young Greek wife, Rea, reached his room four days later, she found it in a mess, clearly empty for several days. She quickly passed word on May 8 that Polk was missing and that something may have happened to him.

Eight days later came word from northern Greece that a boatman in the harbor of Salonika, not far from the hotels and waterfront cafes, had come across a trussed figure in the shallows. The figure was wearing a camel hair jacket and U.S. Army trousers. It was the body of George Polk. His hands and feet had been bound. Behind one ear was a bullet hole. In Athens, the Communists were blamed. Furious at the murder, Ed Murrow said Polk's stories represented "clean, hard copy, well-documented. And his stories stood up—every last one of them. . . ." (8)

By September 1946 Ed Murrow had formed the CBS Documentary Unit, the framework for the documentaries that would in time become the most prestigious part of the CBS operation. With a mandate to tackle major national and international issues, the unit took as its first assignment a look at postwar Germany. Murrow also produced "As Others See Us," offering foreign comment on the United States, and "CBS Was There," the radio forerunner to television's popular "You Are There." On the latter show, CBS reporters played themselves, interviewing famous characters who stepped out of re-created historical events. They might interview Louis XVI at Versailles; other newsmen might interview members of the mob outside the Bastille.

"LET'S HEAR IT FOR THE LORD'S PRAYER."

Another Murrow-produced program, "CBS Views the Press," was a case of turnabout's fair play, with radio taking on the printed press. Narrator Don Hollenbeck might assail New York gossip columns (as total inventions); he might lash into New York newspapers for exaggerating a relief scandal. Suddenly on the defensive, some newspapers accused CBS of following the Communist Party line. After all, it was attempting to destroy one of America's great institutions—the press—so it must be acting under Communist orders.

Murrow, meanwhile, was growing restless for airtime. He had spent eighteen months playing the corporate official and had found it an uncomfortable experience. Both the unpleasantness surrounding the departure of Paul White and the controversy swirling about Bill Shirer had taken its toll. Besides, he was a newsman first and foremost and seemed delighted to return to being one. Paley, too, appeared quite pleased to have Murrow return to the broadcast studio.

Conveniently, Campbell's Soup, unhappy at the low ratings it was getting from Robert Trout's 7:45–8:00 P.M. newscast, offered CBS $1.5 million to have Murrow do the news at 7:45 P.M., representing the largest commercial contract drawn up for radio news. It was decided during the summer of 1947 that Murrow would resign as vice president and do network's main news program, the five-nights-a-week 7:45 P.M. broadcast. He returned to the microphone on September 29, providing just over 10 minutes of news, including pickups from outside the studio, using Charles Collingwood, Dorothy Thompson, and Winston Burdett. He also did just under 3 minutes of "think pieces" (Murrow's phrase). He received a ten-year contract for $130,000 a year—triple his previous income—plus $20,000 in expenses. His contract barred him from commercial television appearances. Murrow could easily live with that stricture: he thought radio more serious than television and doubted whether a commentator needed to be seen. During the following twelve years Murrow would make that program, in the view of his biographer Alexander Kendrick, "the most authoritative and effective news period on radio." (9) One person was disappointed: Bob Trout, replaced by Murrow, was upset and went over to NBC for some time.

Whereas David Sarnoff had returned from the war preoccupied with the idea of introducing television, Bill Paley was determined to replace rival NBC as the leader in radio entertainment. Paley believed firmly that the situation could not be changed until CBS gained control of the programs it put on the air. Most of its entertainment programs were produced and controlled by advertising agencies or outside producers. CBS could veto a show, but it could not keep a good one from going over to NBC. The solution, Paley thought, was for CBS to produce some of its own programs and then sell them to advertisers or sponsors directly. Thus, CBS would have more control over scheduling the programs as well. The new strategy would be revolutionary, risky, expensive. But Paley had a goal in mind. "I was determined that CBS would overtake NBC as the number-one radio network. I was not satisfied with second place. I would grant NBC its greater reputation, prestige, finances and facilities. But CBS had and would continue to have the edge in creative programming. That, I thought, would be the key to success in post-war broadcasting." (10) Taking a heavy risk, Paley announced in advance that the time slot for certain programs would be available only to those sponsors who purchased CBS programs in those time slots. Although the policy took two to three years to become reality, it began to prove itself: CBS put together thirty-six radio programs, twenty-nine of which were sponsored. Two of them, "My Friend Irma," with Marie Wilson playing the dizzy blonde lead role, and "Arthur Godfrey's Talent Scouts" hit the top ten. In time the other networks adopted CBS's strategy. Advertising agencies, which had been creating the programs, eventually gave way to the networks.

To deal a blow to NBC, CBS would have to find performers who could attract large audiences. Not coincidentally, the best place to find such talent was over at NBC. For years, Paley had been unable to create a formula that would attract the great performers. (Some argued that it was for that reason that he put such emphasis on the news division in the 1930s and 1940s). Paley was haunted by NBC's monopoly of the stars. He had always felt a special place in his heart for entertainment and programming. He had little knowledge of how the news department operated, but he did believe that he understood what made the entertainment world tick.

To succeed, however, to implement the strategy of turning CBS into a mass-appeal network, he would have to win over the talent that until now had been eluding him. For that purpose, Paley found some ingenious tax attorneys working for Music Corporation of America who informed him that it would be possible to change the way the big stars pay their taxes so they would earn even more money, and that would induce those stars to come over to CBS. Until then the stars were paying 77 percent of all their earnings above $70,000 in federal income taxes. The lawyers noted that the shows were owned by the entertainers themselves. By having the performers reorganize themselves into corporations, it would be possible to have their earnings taxed as capital gains at only a 25 percent rate.

That coincided with an offer in the summer of 1948 from the top executives of Music Corporation of America, the largest talent agency in the United States. Lew Wasserman, MCA president, and Taft Schreiber, MCA executive vice president, offered to have CBS purchase the "Amos 'n' Andy" program—then one of NBC's most successful and longest-running shows. "Amos" had been with NBC for nineteen years. Paley knew Freeman Gosden, who played Amos, and Charles Correll, who played Andy. Remember, he had tried to attract them to CBS in 1929 prior to their joining NBC. He would love to make up for that now. But the Wasserman-Schreiber asking price seemed too steep. MCA had proposed that CBS purchase the newly formed "Amos 'n' Andy" Corporation for $2.5 million. The talks were long and intense. The advantages to all sides were obvious: Gosden and Correll would get an immediate financial bundle for their families, MCA would have a fat agent's commission, and CBS would pull off a broadcasting coup. Paley believed that if he could win Gosden and Correll for CBS, he could lure such other entertainers as Jack Benny, Red Skelton, Edgar Bergen, and Burns and Allen.

By September the deal was finalized at $2.5 million. CBS acquired exclusive ownership to the show for twenty years. Gosden and Correll were to receive over $1 million each plus large annual salaries. They took over the Sunday 7:30 P.M. time slot. (Gosden and Correll would not play their roles on television. They had performed in an experimental broadcast at an RCA television exhibit at the New York World's Fair on February 26, 1939, playing their characters in blackface, but black actors would play their roles in the television version of "Amos 'n' Andy" in the early 1950s.)

In October, Wasserman offered Paley "The Jack Benny Show," using the same capital gains scheme. The Benny show had run on NBC for the previous sixteen years. Benny was America's outstanding comedian. Born Benjamin Kubelsky in Waukegan, Illinois, in 1895, Jack had always had a great ability to get people to laugh. A vaudeville performer for fourteen years prior to his radio days, he debuted over at NBC on October 1, 1934, using no props, no funny suits, just his own brand of self-deprecating humor.

In the late 1940s, Benny was earning $12,000 a week, quite a high salary, but less impressive considering the high tax bracket. CBS was to purchase the comedian's corporation, Amusement Enterprises, Inc., which included "The Jack Benny Show," plus some other productions. This resulted in a new CBS early evening lineup of "The Jack Benny Show" at 7 P.M. and "Amos 'n' Andy" at 7:30 P.M. on Sundays. Wasserman's deal with Paley for Jack Benny would cost CBS $2.6 million. At the last minute, Wasserman informed the CBS chairman that Benny had to back out of his deal. Upon hearing of the CBS negotiations, NBC had begun its own bargaining. Still determined to win Benny over, Paley found the comedian at a dinner party and the two agreed to talk the next morning. Unfortunately for Paley, he could not find Benny that next day.

Benny had decided to go off to rehearsal. Paley did locate Wasserman who informed him that NBC and Benny had come very close to signing only to have the negotiation explode over some minor legal point. What did this have to do with him, Paley must have asked himself? It became clear shortly. Wasserman explained that Benny had authorized him to let CBS know that if Paley were prepared to sign the same contract that Benny nearly signed with NBC, there could be a deal with CBS after all. Paley was thrilled. He conferred with his lawyer and eventually agreed. "Okay," said Wasserman with a sigh of relief, "All we have to do is change the name National Broadcasting Company to Columbia Broadcasting System." (11)

Meanwhile, Sarnoff was seething at Paley. Sarnoff might have been able to stave off Paley's tactics, but he refused to act aggressively. This, in effect, gave Paley a clear field. Sarnoff argued that he had made many of these stars and had taken risks with them when no one else was interested in their careers. To compete with Paley over these personalities would create a star system, Sarnoff felt, and that would ruin the broadcasting industry. He wanted no part of that. As furious as he was with Paley, Sarnoff was angrier at the stars for displaying such ingratitude by threatening to leave his network. Unwilling to run after comedy stars, as Paley was prepared to do, the NBC leader decided to stay put in New York. He also had qualms about the tax scheme Paley and his associates had cooked up, believing that it was legally and ethically improper. (Later, the Internal Revenue Service would declare that the CBS tack was indeed legal.)

But it was not over yet. Paley had waited until after the contract signing to hold a discussion with American Tobacco to whom Benny remained under contract for a few more years. The sponsor could have insisted that Benny remain with NBC. Paley saw Benny the morning after signing to offer congratulations, then flew on to New York where he ran into a wall of indifference from American Tobacco. He could not get a straight answer from them. There were more negotiations. So eager was Paley to close the deal that he agreed to a remarkable clause: if as a result of Benny's move to CBS the show suffered any loss in ratings, CBS would pay American Tobacco $3,000 a week per point lost in those ratings. With that cleared up, Jack Benny was on his way to CBS. Benny debuted on CBS on January 2, 1949, and his ratings were even higher there than on NBC.

The signing of Jack Benny was a major turning point for CBS. It sent a signal to both the entertainment and broadcasting industry that CBS was preparing to compete head to head with NBC, and, most important, in so doing, that it could entice stars from NBC. As a result, CBS would become the top network in entertainment. For the first time, it won the ratings battle that year, a prize it would keep in radio and then in television for the next quarter century. The Benny signing led to other Paley acquisitions, including Bing Crosby, Red Skelton, Edgar Bergen, and Burns and Allen.

Paley, meanwhile, was just getting started. After Jack Benny, he turned his attention to luring another big catch, Bing Crosby. Earlier, Crosby had left CBS and gone over to NBC. Then in 1946, he had switched to ABC. Warned by his own associates that Crosby had a reputation for being difficult, Paley now learned that indeed the singing star could be demanding. Crosby wanted to make sure that he would be giving the best possible rendition of a song. The only way to assure that was to prerecord his entire radio program. ABC was already pre-recording; CBS, however, along with NBC, remained adamant that the listener should hear only live entertainment. The two networks believed that if top-caliber programs could be recorded and sold directly to individual stations, it would spell the demise of networks. But Paley wanted to woo Crosby back, and so in 1948 he changed his view: realizing that the public didn't care about the issue all that much, he permitted prerecordings. Paley convinced Liggett & Myers, makers of Chesterfield cigarettes, to take Crosby on for a three-year, noncancelable contract at $20,000 a week. The top singer in movies and on radio at the time, Crosby could demand such a price. Liggett & Myers insisted, though, that Crosby cease his criticism of cigarettes. He agreed to that one easily. The sponsor also wanted him to carry around a pack of Chesterfields whenever he appeared in public. Complaining a bit, Crosby said to Paley, "But that'll make a bulge in my pocket, won't it?" "Yeah," Paley replied, "and so will the $20,000 a week." (12)

The Crosby deal was announced in mid-January 1949. The word was out, CBS was buying up the big stars—it wanted them, and it could get the sponsors for them. That very month Red Skelton came over and, in February, so did Edgar Bergen; then in March, Burns and Allen. These acquisitions were given a pejorative name. They were called the "Paley raids," but Bill Paley didn't mind being called a raider. He loved it in fact. Once at CBS, Jack Benny grew more and more popular. CBS quickly became the top network on Sunday evenings. The first Sunday night "The Jack Benny Show" was heard on CBS the network's total Hooper ratings jumped 53.3 percent over the Hoopers registered two weeks before, while NBC suffered a minus 34.8 percent setback for the night. Frank Stanton, the expert on audience research, had predicted that Benny would get 27.2. Benny racked up 27.8 percent. On Wednesday evenings the CBS lineup was weighty as well: Groucho Marx, Bing Crosby, and Burns and Allen. In 1949, CBS had twelve out of the top fifteen Hooper-rated programs and sixteen out of twenty in the Nielson ratings; its average-audience rating was 12 percent higher than that of any other network. As Paley noted with glee, "In short, that year, 1949, CBS became number one in radio." (13) CBS executives estimated that the reward for the star-stealing would be a $6.6 million increase over its $64 million of revenues in 1948. Lots of people wanted to believe that Bill Paley had somehow unfairly stolen David Sarnoff's talent. There was even a story put out that Sarnoff had phoned Paley after the raids to complain, how could he do this to him, hadn't they had an agreement that they wouldn't steal from each other? "Because I had to," came Paley's reply. The story is apocryphal. "It is a cute little story," Paley has written, "but it just never happened." (14)

The future of television remained unsettled. Experiments had been in progress since 1931. In one of those embarrassing bursts of enthusiasm, Bill Paley mistakenly predicted then that by the end of the next year (1932) television would be operating on a commercial basis. World War II had postponed all the main issues surrounding this exciting new medium: Should the standard be black and white or color? Should the RCA color standard be approved, or should CBS's? Peter Goldmark, the inventor/engineer of the CBS Laboratories, remained enthusiastic that his color standard would win FCC approval.

After the war, CBS operated two television stations, one in black-and-white that broadcast for 4 hours a week, the other an experimental color one. The two systems were incompatible. A decision would have to be made whether color or black and white would become the industry standard. At CBS, Frank Stanton and Paul Kesten had been pushing for the color standard; manufacturers of black-and-white televisions were, not surprisingly, urging black-and-white on Bill Paley. Loyal to the Stanton-Kesten team, Paley encouraged Peter Goldmark, now with a staff of one hundred people in the laboratory, to try to perfect his color system.

Matters came to a head in the summer of 1946 when RCA put its black-and-white televisions on the market. In September, CBS asked the FCC to authorize commercial color television, based, of course, on the CBS color system. CBS had commissioned surveys that showed that the public would be willing to put off buying black-and-white sets as long as it was confident that color was around the corner; it would also pay nearly 50 percent more for color. With only 6,000 black-and-white televisions around, the CBS gamble appeared reasonable. If the FCC gave CBS the OK, color would win the day. The issue of incompatibility would presumably fade as black-and-white sets eventually gave way to the new color ones. Complicating matters was the FCC's practice to continue accepting applications for new black-and-white television stations. Owning only one such station (WCBW in New York, which later became WCBS-TV), CBS was eligible to buy four more black-and-white stations in four other cities. Should CBS pick up the option? It was a tough decision. If the FCC turned down its bid to televise in color, the network would have lost a great opportunity to expand its black-and-white television operation. But, if it made applications for black-and-white stations now, that very act would appear to demonstrate a lack of confidence in Peter Goldmark's color system, something that would hardly help its case with the FCC. Stanton backed off from applying for the stations.

David Sarnoff went on the attack, hitting at CBS for its small screen size, the color degradation and fringing, and the lack of capacity for proper mobile coverage. He also noted that CBS's color would come up blank on current television sets. NBC's color system, when it was developed, would be able to work on black-and-white sets, albeit in black and white. Sarnoff was still in favor of electronic color unlike the CBS system, which involved a rotating wheel. Hence CBS's pictures could not be viewed on existing prewar black-and-white sets. But the NBC electronic system, Sarnoff acknowledged, was still five years off.

Again there was a CBS trial before the FCC, this time at the Tappan Zee Inn at Nyack, New York, overlooking the Hudson River, 40 miles from the color transmitter at the Chrysler Building in New York City. While the FCC chairman, Charles Denny, appeared to like what he saw, on January 30, 1947 the FCC still ruled, in a major setback for CBS, that more field tests were needed. Now the network had to look around for television stations, but they were in short supply, especially after the FCC's decision in 1948 to impose a freeze on building and licensing new television stations. In 1949, the FCC held hearings on color television, this time finding in CBS's favor, but the victory was pyrrhic; by now there were some 3 million black-and-white television sets, none of which were compatible with the CBS color system. It appeared that Peter Goldmark and CBS had, for the time being, lost the battle.

Apart from color television, Peter Goldmark had his mind turned to record playing. One evening in the fall of 1945, Goldmark and some friends in Westport, Connecticut, were listening to a record of Vladimir Horowitz playing Brahms's "Second Piano Concerto." Suddenly they heard a click recalled by Goldmark as "the most horrible sound man ever invented." Someone got up to change the record. The mood was broken. "I knew right there and then," remembered Goldmark, "that I had to stop that sort of thing." (15) Within three years he had invented the $33\frac{1}{3}$-rpm microgroove record, stamped from Vinylite to reduce surface noise. It immediately became known in the trade as the LP. Since 1948, the year the new record was introduced, the LP has grossed more than $1 billion for CBS. By 1973, more than one-third of CBS's yearly income from its record business came from long-playing records.

Goldmark's new record had major advantages over the 78-rpm disc: it revolved more slowly—at $33\frac{1}{3}$ rpm—permitting more than twice as much music to be stored in the same record space; the new CBS disc also had better sound quality. The first Columbia LP went over big, offering Bach to Harry James at prices from $2.85 for a 10-inch popular disc to $4.85 for a 12-inch Masterworks. CBS debuted the record at the Waldorf, but the reception was cool at first.

Trying to avoid competition, Bill Paley invited David Sarnoff to attend a trial of the LP. A joint venture might be in store. Some days earlier, Stanton had invited Sarnoff to a private luncheon to discuss this very venture. Now, accompanied by eight engineers, Sarnoff visited the CBS boardroom. Goldmark was nervous. He knew this was his day of judgment after years of hard work. Paley, dressed impeccably, smiling, explained that Goldmark would first play an ordinary 78 and then the CBS invention. Sarnoff grew more interested. Goldmark played the 78 for about 15 seconds before switching over to the new record. He put on the needle. As the first few bars were played, Sarnoff got out of his chair. After 10 seconds, Goldmark switched back to the 78 record. The eight engineers looked downcast. "I want to congratulate you and your people, Bill," Sarnoff said in a loud, emotional voice. "It is very good." (16) Paley proposed delaying the announcement of CBS's long-playing record so that RCA could join CBS in a joint venture. Sarnoff said he would think it over.

Soon thereafter, Sarnoff dropped a bombshell on Paley: NBC's own scientists had, after ten years of research, developed a new system that recorded at 45 rpm and featured an incredibly fast record changer. NBC's small 45-rpm disc had less playing time than did CBS's LP, but it would be easier to distribute and cheaper to produce. NBC put its 45 rpm on the market in January 1949.

With two new record formats joining the original 78 rpm on the market, the public became understandably confused. For its part, CBS had some major supporters for its new product: the influential National Association of Music Dealers as well as the three largest independents, Decca, Mercury, and London Records. Moreover, a number of RCA artists liked the LP's longer recording time and sound quality. Everywhere but in jukeboxes, the LP became the industry standard, dealing a staggering defeat to RCA. Over the years pop stars would take the place of symphonic and opera performers as the main source of record industry profits.

World War II had interrupted the development of television so that by 1946 only 6,000 television sets existed. With television sets costing as much as $3,000, only 225 sets were produced in the first eight months of that year. Yet television would finally come into its own in the late 1940s. A spurt of television manufacturing began that fall: 3,242 produced alone in September, 5,437 by January 1947, and 8,690 the following May. Major advertisers were still reluctant to go over to this new medium. As a result, television budgets remained tight. Puppets were used a great deal as were all sorts of animals, including snakes and ducks. The reason was economic. Puppets and animals came cheaply. They didn't need to be fed as did human actors. By 1946 some popular radio programs had moved over to television, among them "The Major Bowes Amateur Hour" and "Town Meeting of the Air." Still, television lacked a lot of programming. But the screens were getting sharper, less snowy, and larger—going from 7 to 12 inches, then to 14 inches. CBS Television still comprised just one station broadcasting six to ten hours a week, its experimental W2BXA (later WCBS-TV). Airtime was given away free, and people were charged only for the use of CBS's studios, sets, props, and costumes—with so few sets available, there seemed no point in charging. On June 19, television had covered the Joe Louis–Billy Conn fight. But December 31 of that year in a real sense was the night of television's formal birth. New Year's Eve parties were being televised for the first time as pictures were transmitted in eleven American metropolitan areas.

Americans now bought television sets in large quantities, 250,000 in 1947. Coaxial cable now linked New York, Washington, D.C., and Philadelphia. As a result, television advertisers leaped from 31 to 181. The opening of Congress was shown for the first time that January. During the summer the Zoomar lens was used for the first time in a CBS telecast of a baseball game between the Brooklyn Dodgers and the Cincinnati Reds. Thanks to the new lens, the camera could do more than simply show a close-up of the pitcher and catcher; now fans could take in a full-field long shot as well, creating new excitement for viewers. And later that year television covered the 1947 World Series.

By the end of 1947, CBS's programming had doubled that of the previous year and now stood at twenty hours a week. (By the end of 1948, it was up to thirty-eight hours a week.) Slowly, television began to cover certain events, notably sports, being easy, cheap, and entertaining. By 1948, a microwave link connected up Indiana, Kentucky, and Ohio. The start of television was truly the year 1948. CBS began producing its own programs and sending them out to the stations either via cable or on film through the mails. Now one could watch "Arthur Godfrey's Talent Scouts," the dramatic show "Studio One," and Ed Sullivan's "Toast of the Town."

One of CBS's most profitable assets, Arthur Godfrey, was something

---

of a phenomenon: he had two television programs, on Monday and Wednesday evenings, as well as morning radio and television programs. Not surprisingly, Godfrey earned $500,000 a year. He had been an obscure disc jockey in 1930 with a talent for engaging in easy patter. On April 14, 1945, he was given the assignment of narrating the network's radio coverage of President Roosevelt's funeral procession down Pennsylvania Avenue. Godfrey was taken with emotion. Rather than hold it back like other broadcasters would do that day, he evoked in his words just how troubled and frustrated the nation felt at losing its leader. When the new president passed in his car, a choking Godfrey called him the man who "just had such burdens fall upon him. God bless him, Harry Truman!" As Roosevelt's coffin came into sight, Godfrey simply broke down, sobbing into the microphone, and saying, "Oh God, give me strength!" His whole radio style had been based on sounding honest, natural, and never would he sound more so than on that sad day.

CBS had twenty-eight television affiliates in 1948, but on September 30 the FCC ordered a freeze on processing applications for new stations because of the problem of cross-station interference and the need for further study of the problem. At the time the freeze was announced, 37 television stations existed in 22 cities, with 86 others approved and thus permitted to go on the air. Another 303 station applications not yet approved were filed away until the FCC could work out the frequency problem. Once, the ban was lifted in the early 1950s, the number of CBS television affiliates would rise to 62.

The real thrust forward for television came in 1949. By midyear 1.6 million American homes possessed television sets and new televisions were purchased at an astonishing rate of 100,000 a month. (Only a decade later 50 million televisions had been bought.) By the end of the year CBS was showing all sorts of programs: variety shows, pop music, situation comedies, sports, mysteries, dramas, children's shows, quizzes, as well as news and public affairs programs.

Television news started on CBS in 1946 with one regular weekly Saturday night broadcast featuring Douglas Edwards. Edwards had started his career at the age of 15 in Troy, Alabama, and three years later moved to Atlanta radio station WSB as an announcer, later a newscaster. In 1938 Edwards moved to the Detroit radio station WXYZ. (CBS's Mike Wallace was a newscaster there at the same time.) At the very end of World War II, Edwards had been working for CBS in Europe. In May 1946 he returned to the United States and was asked to be a guest on a television program during his first week back. It was May 1946. Announcer Milo Boulton interviewed Edwards over the experimental CBS New York station's Thursday evening news program. "They apparently liked the way I acquitted myself in front of the camera," Edwards recalled. (17) As a result, he was chosen to narrate the Saturday evening television news. At that point, CBS television had news on Thursday, Friday, and Saturday evenings. Edwards's telecast could be picked up only in New York. In these pretelevision network days, CBS radio correspondents were the mainstays of television news. Edwards began work on Friday afternoons. A premium was placed on obtaining filmed reports of events occurring that week rather than relying upon stock footage. Recalled Edwards, "Perhaps a ship would be due. Somebody prominent was going to be aboard. We'd go and do interviews with them on the ship, depending on when the ship got in, because it took several hours to develop film in those days. We didn't try anything live. You wouldn't think of bringing your camera down. There was no minicam. Of course, no satellites. . . . But then we had material from the United Nations and guests from there. Mrs. Roosevelt, Abba Eban, the secretary of state, maybe, if he was in town. I would go over on a Friday afternoon or a Saturday morning and do an interview on film, bring it back and cut it, and put it on the air, as part of the 15-minute show. We used stock footage to illustrate topical points of the day's news. If it was an agricultural story, we would have flowing wheat fields on the air. . . ." (18) Soon Edwards took over the Thursday television news as well.

At one stage, CBS closed the experimental television station for six months. That did not deter Edwards and his small crew: "We continued doing the Saturday night news show rather ingeniously. Today it would be called cheating. What we did was take me up to Studio 9, which was the radio studio in those days, on the 17th floor at 485 Madison Avenue, and a cameraman put on 35 millimeter film various angles of me sitting before a microphone, obviously delivering a news script, everything except perfect head-on to avoid problems with lip-sync. We used that as a kind of insert technology. I would say, 'Well, I'm going to put two stories in this section,' where normally I would have been on camera live. 'I'm going to put three stories in here. I'll need 42 seconds of the film.' When that went on the air that Saturday night, we didn't prerecord it. I would come in and over the pictures of Edwards there would be stock footage made weeks before, I then would lay in a live narration of those three news stories." (19)

Once the television operation resumed, Edwards was back in the normal routine, doing the "World News Roundup" at 8 P.M. on radio while leading off with 2 minutes of news on the new 12 noon radio soap opera, "Wendy Warren and the News." After Edwards's 2 minutes, Wendy would read a minute of news, a commercial would follow, leading into the soap opera revolving around the life of Wendy Warren, girl reporter, wife of a big-city editor.

Edwards was the first of the radio newscasters who was genuinely not alarmed about switching to television. Many others were cautious. Apart from covering photogenic "special events" such as sports, political conventions, or congressional hearings, television was still not considered very practical for presenting news. It could offer the pictorial side but little more. Reflecting the views of other radio newsmen, Ed Murrow was skeptical of television as a news conveyor. "Most news," he once said, "is made up of what happens in men's minds, as reflected in what comes out of their mouths. And how do you put that in pictures?" (20)

The first real experience for television newscasting came at the 1948 political conventions in Philadelphia. Although only 400,000 sets existed by the summer of 1948, the number was sufficient to warrant interest on the part of the convention organizers. Television coverage of the quadrennial affairs began in 1940, but few were able to watch the telecast of the Republican convention in Philadelphia; war prevented television coverage of the 1944 convention. In 1948, coaxial cable reached only to the Atlantic seaboard so an Eastern city was the preferred choice for the conventions' locale. Philadelphia's Convention Hall was chosen, demonstrating at an early stage the power of television over the nation. Radio had until now dominated the conventions and still did in Philadelphia. But by the time the 1948 conventions were over, it was clear that television was on the map, so to speak, thus doing for television what the 1928 political conventions had done for radio.

An experienced newscaster was needed for the 1948 conventions and, though he was a junior member of the CBS News team (he was only 31 years old), Doug Edwards qualified. He had been anchoring television news twice a week in New York City for CBS so he was no stranger to the new medium. In contrast with later years, when television would have a standing equal to if not greater than the politicians themselves, in the year 1948, it was the new kid on the block and most looked disdainfully, if at all, at the people who were its pioneers. Edwards could expect little help at the conventions. Indeed, no one had even bothered to tell him about his assignment until he showed up in Philadelphia. In effect, functioning as an anchorman, Edwards was backed up by Ed Murrow and

---

historian-commentator Quincy Howe. Television, however, was not Murrow and Howe's first priority, and they conducted their interviews and offered analysis only after they freed themselves from their obligations to radio. Edwards's cramped enclosure was accessible, moreover, only by traveling the ignominious route through the radio studios.

Logistics for the television team were a nightmare: it was not yet possible for the anchorman to switch down to the floor and conduct interviews with politicians on the air. Correspondent and politician, sweating in the absence of air-conditioning, ran up to television's tiny quarters and held their interviews in those uncomfortable surroundings. Edwards was seated so far from the convention floor that he could not see the blackboard where the votes were being tallied. Improvising, he borrowed his daughter's Girl Scout binoculars.

Beyond the discomfort was the frustration Edwards and others felt at having to focus the camera on the podium for the most part. It was clearly a hardship to work for television. Ed Murrow and the other reporters arrived on the convention floor lugging around on their backs heavy voice transmitters with batteries, power, and sound. One or two cameras were set up around the hall to pick them up. The sound had to come through that backpack. Murrow would come off the floor soaking with sweat. One photo of Murrow shows him on the convention floor, looking like a man from Mars with antennas protruding every which way. In his right hand he is holding a huge microphone. Around his ears he is wearing a headset. He is clutching the battery pack, looking distinctly in need of a break. Even though the television reporters found the experience loathsome, *The New York Times* actually thought Edwards, Murrow, and Howe had accorded themselves well, commending them "for straight, adult reporting, seasoned with real humor . . . in a class by itself." The *Times* singled out Murrow for his ad-lib quips "that were far and away the most amusing words heard all week in Philadelphia, reflecting . . . a good-natured yet perceptive sense of detachment that was truly mature journalism." (21) By now the top commentator of the day, Murrow remained attached to radio. He was not about to abandon it for this new invention, if he could help it.

CBS decided to begin a nightly television news program that summer. In need of public service programming, the network wanted to make Douglas Edwards the regular newscaster. NBC would follow in February with its own nightly news show at 7:45 P.M. called the "Camel News Caravan." Edwards, however, was only lukewarm about taking on such a major television assignment.

Radio had been his meal ticket and he did not want to give it up. Edwards had been averaging $400 a week in the fees given newsmen routinely from sponsored broadcasts, representing most of his income.

Largely unsponsored, television, on the other hand, still could hardly pay its bills. Derisively scorning television as a medium devoted largely to roller derby and fake wrestling, Edwards was prepared to help it out once or twice a week. But even his work at the Philadelphia conventions had not convinced him to move over to television entirely. To drop radio would ruin his reputation, and why do that? Television was—what did the other radio journalists call it?—slumming. And so Edwards at first said no.

That did not stop CBS. Returning from a vacation, Edwards was called in for a chat with CBS president Frank Stanton. Edwards's fears were groundless. Stanton assured him; television would in time surpass radio in news coverage. "Doug, I guarantee you, if you do this television broadcast," Stanton said, "you'll soon be as well known as Lowell Thomas." (22) It is not clear whether Edwards wanted to be "as well known as Lowell Thomas," but Stanton's little speech was convincing. So was the fact that Stanton offered to double his salary. And to permit him to remain the news broadcaster for "Wendy Warren and the News."

Edwards found the offer acceptable, though he obviously felt little excitement. "I've been described as being pulled into television kicking and screaming," he has said. "It wasn't that at all. Just a little bit reluctant because I was worried about dry-running a lot of things, and then having somebody in the cool of the day come in and Edwards getting lost, really." (23) On August 15 CBS inaugurated the first nightly (five nights a week) television news program, from 7:30 to 7:45 P.M. Douglas Edwards was the anchorman, and he would remain in that slot until 1962, winning a Peabody Award in 1956 and several Emmy nominations.

But Edwards would have trouble at first. There were those at CBS who insisted that it was technically impossible to produce a nightly news program—it was simply too much work. Not helping matters, CBS was handicapped by its lack of resources. CBS was still dependent upon outside newsfilm suppliers for pictures. (CBS only began its own newsfilm operation in the mid-1950s.) It still divided its writers and other production personnel between its radio and television operations. NBC, for its part, had already invested in developing its own film crews and a full-blown staff for its television news and, accordingly, captured an early ratings lead.

At first called simply the "CBS TV News," the program became "Douglas Edwards with the News" two years later (in the fall of 1950), after CBS realized that Edwards had attracted his own viewing audience. Primitive by today's standards, the telecast employed no videotapes, no film reports on the same day's news from overseas or remote points within the country, no communications satellites, no field correspondents, and no camera crews. Recalled Edwards, "Some of the visuals were crude. We didn't go first class the way we do now. We didn't have tele-prompters. It was all done either from memory or from ad-libbing or from reading. Actually a combination of those three. One didn't get too far away from the planned script because if he did, he would throw the direc-tor a real curve when it came time to lead into a commercial or a piece of film." (24)

Although embryonic, CBS's television news took itself seriously. It was after all following in the tradition of Ed Klauber, Paul White, Ed Mur-row, and the "Murrow boys." Television news, like radio news in the past, would brook no interference from sponsors, from the government, or from anyone else for that matter. Meanwhile, the Edwards newscast, watched at first only along the East Coast from Boston to Washington, D.C., added station after station. Each time a new station hooked into the CBS television network, Edwards would open the show by welcoming them to the broadcast. By the end of 1951, when the West Coast was tied into the coaxial cable, he opened with these words, "Good evening, from coast to coast."

The guiding light behind the Douglas Edwards newscast was one of tele-vision's true pioneers, someone who remained in the shadows for years, inventing, improvising, always sensing television's potential, always un-derstanding that television was the one medium that was ideally suited to bring the news. Don Hewitt was the genius behind early television news, the man, in Av Westin's oft-repeated phrase, who invented the wheel.

Born and raised in New York, Hewitt loved the news business from childhood. His father had been an advertising salesman for the Hearst newspapers. No wonder that Hildy Johnson, the tough, wisecracking re-porter in *The Front Page* was an early idol. At age 19 in 1942, Don worked as a copy boy at *The New York Herald Tribune,* earning $15 a week. As it was wartime, he enrolled in the Merchant Marine Academy and spent World War II as a front-line correspondent in Europe for the War Shipping Administration.

Hoping to cash in on his wartime journalistic experience, Hewitt searched for a post as a foreign correspondent. Instead, all he could find was the job of head copy boy at *The Herald Tribune.* So, over he went to the Associated Press, where at least he was given work as a newsman: he was sent to the Memphis Bureau as night editor, remaining there for a year. During 1947 he edited the *Pelham Sun* in Pelham, New York, and then took work at Acme Newspictures, United Press's picture service.

Hewitt's big break came when Bob Rogow, an acquaintance of his from *The Herald Tribune* who worked at CBS Radio, contacted him to say that the network was looking for someone with picture experience. Strange, Hewitt thought, a radio network looking for somebody with picture experience. In fact, CBS Television was conducting the search. With only a mild understanding of television, Hewitt trooped off to the area over New York City's Grand Central Station where he found a staff of stage managers and artists. The sets and microphone booms enthralled him.

After News Director Bob Bendick hired Hewitt on the spot, Hewitt proudly informed Boyd Lewis, his boss at Acme Newspictures, the picture arm of the United Press, that he was moving to television. Television, asked Lewis? Why would he want to work there? It was only a passing fad. It had no chance of lasting. Hewitt later would say that Lewis had been half-right: it had been a fad, but it had also lasted.

When the Edwards news program debuted, Hewitt was one of several directors. On the fourth day, Edwards asked that Hewitt become sole director, and it was agreed. Hewitt experimented with using charts and maps behind the newscaster. One evening when he couldn't sleep, Hewitt took brown paper and cut out figures; he then taped them to his television screen and walked around the room, asking himself if someone were sitting 20 feet away, would those figures be big enough? Hewitt also was concerned with the way Edwards read the news. He tended to look down at his script. Hewitt preferred that he look up. He had someone copy the text from which Edwards would read in large black letters which were then held up in front of the newscaster. Eye level, however, was frequently off. Hewitt, at one moment of frustration, actually suggested that Edwards learn braille! Once he did that, he would be able to stare into the camera while reading the news with his finger. Edwards would have none of that.

Television entertainment was every bit as experimental in the late 1940s as was news. That led to a certain pragmatism. If something worked at NBC, it was worth a try at CBS. And vice versa. But CBS had a problem. It had been unable to find anyone like NBC's Milton Berle, television's most popular comedian. In time, it would find someone, someone who would seem as far removed from Milton as could be. Yet, for reasons that no one could fathom, this individual would prove to be one of television's greatest "entertainers." By the end of 1948, this unsmiling newspaper columnist named Ed Sullivan had television's most popular show, a variety program known as "Toast of the Town." (Ed was producer as well as master of ceremonies.) In 1955, the show was renamed "The Ed Sullivan Show."

He was born Edward Vincent Sullivan into an Irish family in Manhattan on September 28, 1902. He began his career as a journalist in high school covering sports part time for the *Port Chester Daily Item*. After graduation he took a full-time job with the newspaper at $10 a week. Much later in his career, when he was once asked to describe himself in a single word, Ed said, "reporter." His first column, "Ed Sullivan Sees Broadway," appeared on June 1, 1931, for the *Graphic*, a brassy scandal sheet. He delivered a bitter sermon to other Broadway columnists. "The Broadway columnists," he wrote, "have lifted themselves to distinction by borrowed gags, gossip that is not always kindly and keyholes that too often reveal what might better be hidden." He promised to give no space to phonies, to avoid mentioning divorces, and to praise a Broadway play if it so merited. "With the theater in the doldrums," he concluded, "it needs a decisive voice and I promise to supply it."

Sullivan began writing for the New York *Daily News* in 1932. That same year Sullivan did a program on CBS radio entitled "Broadway's Greatest Thrills," later renamed "Ed Sullivan Entertains," originating at New York City's "21" Club. Sullivan introduced a number of big stars to radio, including Jimmy Durante, Irving Berlin, Florenz Ziegfeld, Jack Pearl, Frances Langford, and Jack Benny. Sensing television's bright prospects, Sullivan was eager to have his own show and had in mind a sports interview program that would be called "Pros and Cons," with golf professionals advising viewers on how to improve their game. He mentioned the idea to Marlo Lewis of the Blaine Thompson advertising agency, who passed it on to CBS. The network replied that it was not interested in a golf show but it was considering a Sunday-night variety series. CBS producer Worthington Miner had "discovered" Sullivan after he had served, at Miner's initiative, as master of ceremonies for the 1947 Harvest Moon Ball, the Madison Square Garden ballroom dance event televised by CBS. Miner used Sullivan again in a 1948 Easter Sunday variety benefit. Recalling these events, CBS executives believed that Ed might be ideal as master of ceremonies.

He was hired as the temporary master of ceremonies, temporary inasmuch as he was a newspaper columnist with no performing ability. Sullivan, who certainly had wide personal contact with the entertainment world, insisted that he could produce a good show cheaply. By virtue of his *Daily News* column, he had the advantage of being able to plug performers—apparently fair recompense for appearing on his show. Still, the dour, humorless Sullivan was not exactly what the CBS brass had in mind when they sought a rival to Milton Berle—and as soon as a professional emcee could be found, Sullivan would be released. That was the original plan.

On May 21, 1948, CBS officially announced the new program, calling it "You're the Top." The title did not survive past the first press release. "Toast of the Town" premiered on Sunday, June 20, at 9 P.M. at New York City's Maxine Elliott Theater on 39th Street. A staff of thirty-five, including Ray Bloch's fourteen musicians, put the show on the air, working with a $1,350 budget. (By the late 1960s, the staff had grown to two hundred, the budget to $372,000 a week.) That opening night, despite an array of great talent, was something less than a smash. Sullivan introduced Broadway's Richard Rodgers and Oscar Hammerstein II (who refused payment), along with a pair of unknown comedians named Dean Martin and Jerry Lewis (who split the $200 fee) and a fight referee Ruby Goldstein who accepted $75. Apart from the cost of Ray Bloch's orchestra, the entire show cost $475.

His poker face and awkwardly dangling arms led themselves to kidding, but Ed Sullivan's "shew," as he called it, eventually was a great triumph. Not at first, though. Television reviewers were not kind. Emerson Radio, Sullivan's first sponsor, canceled after 13 weeks. Sullivan liked to say that it was no wonder he didn't smile much in those days. The most unpleasant moment came when he learned that CBS was trying to sell "The Toast of the Town" to prospective advertisers with or without him. Apparently, the Sales Department felt that sponsors were being frightened away by the press criticism of Sullivan. That was the low point of his life, Sullivan would say later. As it turned out, the optional offer had come from just one man, Jack Van Volkenburg, who had acted on his own initiative without the backing of either Bill Paley or Frank Stanton. Sullivan was quickly apprised of that. Matters improved quickly enough. By the end of the year, according to a Pulse survey, "Toast" was the top-rated show in New York City and Philadelphia. His first show was broadcast on only 6 stations. By the late 1960s it would be on 196. The competition couldn't keep up with him. NBC put up Perry Como during the 1949–50 season and later tried such stars as Bob Hope, Dean Martin and Jerry Lewis, Jimmy Durante, and Eddie Cantor. But Sullivan triumphed. "The Ed Sullivan Show" would run for twenty-three years, and many would call it the best variety program television has ever produced.

He introduced to television Louis Armstrong, Fred Astaire, Lionel Barrymore, Humphrey Bogart, James Cagney, Gary Cooper, Henry Fonda, Jackie Gleason, Bob Hope, Burt Lancaster, and Phil Silvers. Also, Julie Andrews, Maurice Chevalier, Noel Coward, and the Beatles. He had his largest audience watching the Beatles whom he introduced to American television on February 9, 1964, 73.7 million people, according to the Nielsen ratings.

The most controversial guest appearances were the three times

Elvis Presley came on "Toast," over a six-month period beginning in September 1956. Presley was paid the then-staggering sum of $50,000 for the three appearances, a record payment for Sullivan. At first, Sullivan was reluctant to book Elvis. He was known only in the Southwest; his hip-swiveling act did not seem proper for a family show. But then Presley appeared on Steve Allen, Sullivan's Sunday night rival, trouncing Ed in the ratings. Less than two weeks later Sullivan signed Elvis.

He had incredible influence with his audience. "All the Way Home" opened on Broadway on November 30, 1960 to fine notices but drew little box office attention. Enjoying the show, Sullivan urged everyone to go see it, paving the way for box-office success and a Pulitzer prize. Disturbed at Sullivan for violating its policy against providing unpaid commercials, CBS reprimanded Sullivan with a light slap on the wrist.

Once he became a major television star, Sullivan could not escape controversy. When he and Jack Paar engaged in their famous March 1961 feud, it was front-page news. The feud erupted over Paar's paying performers the $320 minimum union wage when the same performers were receiving up to $10,000 for a Sullivan appearance. Sullivan notified talent agents that anyone accepting the $320 figure for a Paar appearance would be paid the same on his show. For several weeks Sullivan and Paar traded insults, all of which became immediate news.

Sullivan got into a public tiff with Arthur Godfrey as well. In 1953 Godfrey fired singer Julius La Rosa from his program while on the air, another page-one story. Sullivan signed the singer, who had been getting $1,000 a week from Godfrey, for a "television comeback" at $30,000 for six appearances. The show, as Sullivan shrewdly realized, garnered a high rating. Sullivan did much the same thing when in 1955 Godfrey fired singer Marian Marlowe, signing her up for $3,000 an appearance. "It's nothing personal against Godfrey," Sullivan said. "If they'd fire him, I'd try to sign him up, too." To which Godfrey replied, "I'd certainly accept the offer." (25)

It was strange. Ed could not perform. He simply talked, and he didn't do much of that. But people loved the show. Ed Sullivan, this quiet man who could not sing, act, or dance, managed to entertain. He was, in fact, one of television's greatest acts. Indeed, when critics lambasted Ed, it was usually due to the fact that he was not a real performer in the classic sense, that he was on television under false pretenses, as it were. Alan King, the comedian, summed up Sullivan's talents tersely, "Ed does nothing, but he does it better than anyone else on television." (26). Still, some described him as television's most influential performer. He "performed" often with the little puppet personality the Italian Mouse Topo Gigio. "Hey, Eddie, keesa me good-night," the mouse's parting phrase, became part of the national lexicon. Burly truckdrivers, spotting Sullivan on the highway, would roll down their windows and say to him, "Hey, Eddie, keesa me good-night."

Sullivan had his faults. But they were overlooked as his television success crowded out any criticism. His awkward introductions of his guests and reactions to their performances became almost a trademark. He once said, "Let's hear it for the Lord's Prayer" after Sergio Franchi sang it on the 1965 Christmas show. He introduced Roberta Sherwood as Roberta Peters. New Zealand natives were, in Ed's words, "the fierce Maori tribe from New England." He made a pitch on behalf of the tuberculosis drive and concluded, "Good night and help stamp out TV." He called Benny Goodman a "trumpeter" and introduced Robert Goulet so frequently as a Canadian that few, perhaps even including Goulet himself, realized that the singer was born in Massachusetts. After presenting the Supremes with a long, flattering description of their talents, he brought them on camera, and promptly forgot the group's name. All he could do was say, "Here are the girls." But he was Ed Sullivan, and everyone promptly forgave him his gaffes.

Ed Murrow's relationship with Fred Friendly would alter the course of television. They got together, not because of radio or even television, but because of a record album. Fred was born in New York on 113th Street in 1915. His name was Ferdinand Friendly Wachenheimer, a mouthful which he would later shorten to just plain Fred Friendly. When, at age 22, fresh out of business school, he showed up for his first day at work at radio station WEAN in Providence, Rhode Island, Ferdinand Friendly Wachenheimer told the station manager his name. "He said we can't have a long name like that. What's your middle name? I told him my middle name, and I became Fred W. Friendly. That's all there is to that. And I've had that name 50 of my 70 years. I'm proud of both names." (27) At the Providence station he scripted a series of 5-minute programs—"mini-mini-documentaries," 5-minute portraits of great men and women, more than a thousand of them, called "Footprints in the Sands of Time" for which he was paid $8 per program.

It was only natural that his wartime experiences were mixed in with journalism. After being inducted in 1941, he was involved in the development of a panel competition, "Sergeant Quiz," which was used for testing American soldiers on knowledge gained in basic training. He traveled on behalf of the army's information and education section, setting up the quiz at various camps and lecturing to soldiers about the war's background. In 1943 Friendly became the overseas correspondent for the *CBI Roundup*, the Army daily for the China-Burma-India theater of operations (the Asian equivalent of *Stars and Stripes*). Friendly reported from all over the world on such events as the D-Day landings in France and the dropping of the atomic bomb on Hiroshima and Nagasaki.

Arriving in New York in 1946, he convinced NBC to do a television program in which a panel of well-known personalities would try to guess the authors of quotations taken from the week's news. A mere summer replacement, the program was well received and sparked the interest of rival CBS, which asked Friendly for a radio version. In 1947, Friendly and Jap Gude, who served as an agent for some of the major CBS personalities (including Ed Murrow, Walter Cronkite, Elmer Davis, and Raymond Graham Swing), had been reading Frederick Lewis Allen's popular social history of the 1920s, *Only Yesterday.* The book gave Friendly the idea of producing a history on records. Allen was approached to moderate the record, but he declined. Friendly thought of Ed Murrow. Over lunch with Friendly, Murrow loved the idea even though it was well known that talking records weren't supposed to sell: "That's a good idea, let's do it." (28)

So Gude, Murrow, and Friendly went to Goddard Lieberson, head of the classical part of Columbia Records. "In one of those accidents of history," says Friendly, "we went in there the day that James Petrillo pulled them out on strike. So the big recording facility had nothing to record. So Goddard said, 'pretty good idea. We need something to be recorded.' They gave us a $1,000 advance, which Ed said I should take because I was unemployed and he was gainfully employed." (29)

The album, called "I Can Hear It Now," was released in the winter of 1948. Friendly wrote the connecting narrative and chose the historic excerpts, culling 500 hours of recordings to produce a 45-minute album. It was an immediate, smash hit, selling 100,000 copies by Christmas. Friendly was amazed: "I who had never had more than $500 in the bank at one time, except for that stuff during the war—I went to the bank the day before Christmas with a check for $19,000—my share of the royalties." (30) Murrow, who was making $125,000 at the time in broadcasting, was probably not as excited about the new earnings. Undoubtedly, he was more thrilled to win a number of awards for the album, among which was the Newspaper Guild Page One Award. The album eventually sold nearly a half-million copies. This marked the first time that a nonmusical album had been a big moneymaker. (Later volumes were produced, and while they sold well, did not approach the original one in sales.)

Radio documentaries were spurred by the technical work that went into producing the album. Only when it became possible to edit audiotape were such documentaries feasible. Such internal editing was done for the first time with the album. It was a CBS Radio engineer named Joe Tall, working on the album with Friendly, who discovered a way to splice tape on a bias to make it all meet. Friendly had said to Tall one day, "Here's a Winston Churchill speech I want to use, but it's 8 minutes long and I want to get it down to 3 minutes." Friendly marked the script, showing Tall what he wanted to take out and what he wanted to leave in. And Tall managed it. (31) As Friendly explained, until then, records used to be uneditable: "If you had something, let's say, the Duke of Windsor's abdication or Churchill's speech, there was no way to edit it. You could take two records and make three records and then play them into a third record, but every time you made a stub, it would lose quality. But when tape came in, the precursor to that, big tape, or rich tape, it was possible to take the Duke of Windsor's speech, which ran 13 or 14 minutes, take the pauses out—he stuttered a lot—but also take out the redundancies, and with a razor blade, splice that." (32)

"I Can Hear It Now" was, as Murrow and Friendly liked to call it, a scrapbook for the ear, dealing with the years 1933 to 1945, describing many of the events which Murrow had personally covered. One heard the voice of Will Rogers, the cowboy comedian, making jokes about the Depression; Franklin Delano Roosevelt talking about fearing "fear itself"; Senator Huey Long expounding on "sharing the wealth"; New York Mayor Fiorella LaGuardia reading the Sunday comics during a newspaper strike; Edward VIII delivering his abdication message; and labor leader John L. Lewis talking about the Bible. Neville Chamberlain returned from Munich; Adolph Hitler shouted and ranted; and Charles Lindbergh gave his "America First" opinions. There were other remarks by Joseph Stalin, Dwight Eisenhower, and Winston Churchill as well as the sounds of D-Day, VE-Day, and VJ-Day, and of the burgeoning atomic era. And there was House Speaker Sam Rayburn, getting ready to introduce a fidgety Harry Truman as the new President of the United States. "Just a moment, lemme present you, willya—Harry?"

seven

"... An Old Team Trying to Learn a New Trade."

It was a time of fear and suspicion, of peeking into private lives, of insidious suggestions that people were what they were not. It emerged out of the smouldering embers of World War II when the United States believed that one enemy had been laid to rest but worried that another one would come to take its place. So pervasive was the fear that a new enemy was rising, even more monstrous than the first, that nothing was sacrosanct, nothing was taken for granted. Communism was the enemy, and, asserted its opponents, it lay within as well as without, inside American borders as well as far away in the Soviet Union, Eastern Europe, and mainland China. When the enemy was a foreigner, a Russian or a Chinese, he was easy to spot. But how could one spot the enemy within—when he was an American like all the rest of us? Why, came the answer, just look at the people who are different, who are unconventional. Look at the liberals. Look at the entertainers! Thus by its very nature, CBS became a special target of those on a Communist witch hunt. The spotlight shone brighter on CBS for another reason. Back in the late 1940s, Bill Paley had decided that CBS, and not the sponsors, theatrical producers, or ad agencies, should produce its own programs. There thus arose within the network a need for the very type of creative figure who would also be characterized as liberal and unconventional.

With the publication of a 215-page book called *Red Channels: The Report of Communist Influence in Radio and Television,* the broadcasting industry—and CBS—became a target of the Communist hunt of the early 1950s. On *Red Channels'* cover was a red hand clutching a microphone. Published by Counterattack, the newsletter of facts to combat Communism, and sold for $1, the book listed the names of 151 people who purportedly had infiltrated radio and television to "transmit pro-Sovietism to the American public." Days after *Red Channels* appeared, the war in Korea broke out. Broadcasting executives might have read the Counterattack book with mild bemusement had there been no Korea. But the international Communist conspiracy was on the move, forcing those executives on the defensive. The Korean hostilities seemed an all-too-real reminder that world Communism was a concrete, immediate danger.

Therefore, to be on the *Red Channels* list could prove devastating to one's career. Still, rather than a nest of infiltrators, the book provided an honors list of the most talented and respected people in the industry, among them writers, directors, and producers. Included were such well-known names as Leonard Bernstein, Oscar Brand, Abe Burrows, Lee J. Cobb, Aaron Copland, Norman Corwin, Howard Da Silva, Paul Draper, Howard Duff, José Ferrer, Martin Gabel, John Garfield, Ben Grauer, Dashiell Hammett, Lillian Hellman, Judy Holliday, Lena Horne, Langston Hughes, Burl Ives, Sam Jaffe, Garson Kanin, Alexander Kendrick, Gypsy Rose Lee, Joseph Losey, Burgess Meredith, Arthur Miller, Zero Mostel, Dorothy Parker, Edward G. Robinson, Robert St. John, Hazel Scott, Pete Seeger, Artie Shaw, Irwin Shaw, William L. Shirer, Howard K. Smith, Sam Wanamaker, and Orson Welles. As a result of their appearance in *Red Channels,* the careers of these men and women were often seriously harmed. The story is told that when Bill Paley met Zero Mostel years later, he complimented the actor on his talents, to which Mostel replied, "If I'm so talented why didn't you put me on your network." (1) But not every employer was intimidated. *Red Channels* contained the names of two overseas CBS correspondents. With his own news staff under attack, Ed Murrow stood by his men. "If you're in trouble, we're all in trouble," he told one of them. (2)

Not everyone at CBS mentioned in *Red Channels* was as lucky. Robert Lewis Shayon, who had been a producer for CBS, had been abruptly fired without an explanation. Betty Todd, a studio director, had been dismissed after being subpoenaed by the House Un-American Activities Committee and refusing to answer questions about her alleged membership in the Communist Party. The CBS television program, "The Goldbergs," became an object of controversy after one of its cast, Philip Loeb (who played Jake), was mentioned in the book. Its sponsor, Sanka, dropped the series "for economic reasons," and when the show was resurrected on NBC with a different sponsor, it was minus Philip Loeb. Gertrude Berg, star, author, and owner of the "Goldbergs" series, told *The New York Times* that Loeb had stated categorically that he was not and had never been a Communist. "I believe him. There is no dispute between Philip Loeb and myself." But her statement did not prevent Loeb's career from deteriorating. After his theater appearances were the subject of harassment, he took an overdose of sleeping pills. While the Loeb case received headlines, in other, less publicized instances, the professional careers of some radio and television artists also suffered setbacks.

Performers on Ed Sullivan's program were affected as well. In January 1950 Sullivan had booked a dancer named Paul Draper for a "Toast of the Town" appearance. Although Sullivan knew that Draper had been accused of being pro-Communist (a charge the dancer denied), he went ahead with the show. After Draper's performance, Sullivan's sponsor, the Ford Motor Company, and its advertising agency, Kenyon & Eckhardt, remained on edge. Their fears were realized when angry letters streamed in to Ford. As a result, it was decided that Sullivan would write a letter to the president of Kenyon & Eckhardt, William B. Lewis, which would then be distributed to the press. In that letter, dated January 25, Sullivan wrote in part, "I am deeply distressed to find out that some people were offended by the appearance, on Sunday's 'Toast of the Town' television show, of a performer whose political beliefs are a matter of controversy. That is most unfortunate. You know how bitterly opposed I am to Communism and all it stands for. You also know how strongly I would oppose having the program used as a political forum, directly or indirectly.

"After all, the whole point of the 'Toast of the Town' is to entertain people, not offend them. . . . If anybody has taken offense, it is the last thing I wanted or anticipated, and I am sorry."

The letter, so apologetic in tone, demonstrated the length that some of the biggest names in entertainment felt they had to go to escape from the devastating effects of the Communist witch hunt. As for Paul Draper, he discovered soon thereafter that he could not earn a living in the United States and so he moved to Europe. Ed Sullivan turned increasingly to Counterattack's staff for guidance about artists he planned to use on his show. If the entertainer had to explain anything, and Ed Sullivan still wanted to have him on the show, a Counterattack staff member and the artist would get together for a serious chat. Sometimes, sitting in Sullivan's living room, the staff member would give the artist the green light; at other times he would insist that the artist show greater proof of loyalty.

Having been attacked as an especially "Red" network, CBS sought to counter that impression. First, it hired former FBI agents to probe CBS employees. It then sought to assure its sponsors and others that it would not tolerate Communist members working for the network. Ironically, in contrast with Ed Murrow's daring attack on McCarthyism later, CBS at this time appeared the most aggressive of the networks in institutionalizing the practice of blacklisting. A policy guideline was issued, making clear that CBS would not knowingly employ anyone identified with "any philosophy not coincident with the best interests of the United States, its institutions and citizens." No one defined "best interests." In late December 1950 the network issued an in-house questionnaire that became known as a loyalty oath. Someone was asked, "Are you now or have you ever been a member of any organization listed as subversive by the Attorney General of the United States?" (The list of organizations, including the Communist Party, was printed on the reverse side of the questionnaire.) "If so, explain, and sign." CBS was the only network to use such an oath. The network said "wartime conditions" required the step. Still, CBS employees reported later that there was much dismay and a loss of morale. Bill Leonard, who at the time was a young television broadcaster and would become president of CBS News, recalled that "Like most of my colleagues, I was disgusted with the whole charade, ashamed of CBS for what we all considered to be abject knuckling under . . . but I had nothing to hide. The paper did not say one would be fired for not signing. But . . . I signed." (3)

Bill Paley came close to acknowledging that CBS adopted the practice of the loyalty oath; he called it in his memoirs an "in-house questionnaire." (4) According to Paley, the "questionnaire" was used to aid CBS in avoiding threatened blackmail, accusations, or pressures by outsiders. Only a handful of CBS employees refused to sign; one person resigned as a matter of principle. Between fifteen and twenty responded that indeed they had joined one of the listed organizations. Interviewed, they were permitted to remain at their jobs if their past associations were deemed harmless. But four or five were forced to leave either because of what they had done or because they had difficulty in explaining their past.

Years later, in discussing the "in-house questionnaire," as Paley called it, CBS officials at the time remained defensive on the issue. "Well," noted Frank Stanton, "It wasn't a happy period, certainly in Hollywood or in broadcasting. I don't believe that we, CBS, were any more concerned about the McCarthy influences than were our counterparts at ABC and NBC. I think perhaps our efforts to do internal housekeeping, if you will, received more attention in the press, but I doubt that what we did was a lot different than what others were doing at the same time. . . . Perhaps because we were a more liberal organization than NBC, and certainly more liberal than ABC, that we were singled out for more attention at that time by both the House Un-American Activities Committee and conservative groups such as AIM (Accuracy in Media) today." (5)

Through those dark days, the CBS news operation remained the crown jewel of the network. The correspondents from overseas who came trooping back home on January 1, 1950, were assembled for the annual year-end broadcast: Howard K. Smith from London, David Schoenbrun from Paris, Bill Downs from Berlin, Winston Burdett from Rome, and Bill Costello from Tokyo. They were joined by Larry LeSueur at the United Nations; Eric Sevareid, the chief Washington correspondent; and, of course, Ed Murrow, who was the anchorman. "It was," recalled Schoenbrun "a first-rate group of reporters. In those days, CBS News was not just number one, it was in a class by itself. Its competitors finally caught up with it and there is now a close race among the networks, but for a few brief years the Murrow team was nonpareil. There was CBS and then the others. It was a magic moment early in the history of television. . . ." (6) It was Ed Murrow, in Schoenbrun's view, his prestige and his integrity, that thrust the CBS correspondents into a league of their own. To his chagrin, Schoenbrun added that this too would pass. "Our day did not last more than a decade before the producers, managers, bookkeepers, and lawyers took over, but while it lasted it was dazzling."

Dazzling, because Murrow and his team would seemingly go anywhere, do anything—to get at the story. And Murrow always seemed to be out there, leading the pack. Thus, it was inevitable that the man who had carved out a reputation for himself in the London Blitz would a decade later be eager to cover the first American military encounter after World War II. So when Korea broke out in June 1950, it would have seemed unthinkable for Ed Murrow to remove himself from the fray. Drew Middleton, *The New York Times* military correspondent, had been visiting Murrow when the news came in that the North Korean Army had crossed the 38th parallel. Middleton asked Murrow if he wanted to go. No, he replied honestly, but he supposed he would have to. He took with him a progressive "single-system" camera that would capture sound as well as sight—until then the sound track had to be added later to film. Now, viewers would be able to hear the sounds of war as background to Ed Murrow's interviews.

In some respects, Korea was every bit as hazardous to a war correspondent as London had been. During his stay in Korea early in the summer of 1950, Murrow was "taken prisoner"—along with three other American correspondents—by American marines! The CBS man was traveling with *The New York Times'* Bill Lawrence, Mutual Broadcasting's Bill Dunn, and the *Afro-American's* James Hicks. On the way to meeting the 1st Division Marine Brigade, camped northwest of Pusan, their plane had skidded while landing at night and had almost gone off the runway at Chinhae. Murrow's companions wanted to sleep at the airfield. But he convinced them that they were better off trying to locate a Marine bivouac area to spend the night.

However, as the four-man journalist party made for the road, a voice shouted in the darkness, "Who's there?" Murrow identified himself and the others. The sentry asked for a password. None of them obviously knew it. "I have no orders to let correspondents through," said the marine. "Put your hands over your heads and don't move, or I'll blow you apart." He seemed to be quite serious. Although Murrow and his colleagues could not have known it, the marines in this unit were particularly trigger-happy, apprehensive that the enemy might be nearby. As part of their nervousness, they had already accidentally killed two of their own men and wounded several others that evening. Meanwhile, other sentries approached and eventually the reporters were taken off to a captain who recognized Murrow's name and voice from the radio. While spending the night at the bivouac, Murrow made sure to do a spot into his tape recorder. Later, he would concede that he had been more frightened that evening than at any time during World War II. "Maybe," he noted, "it was because I was older. In Europe I felt the same age and generation as those fighting, even if I wasn't. In Korea, I didn't feel that way." (7)

The sense of danger was not the only new troubling element for Murrow in Korea. There was his own agitated belief that the war, only seven weeks after the United States entered it, was not going well for the Americans. To be true to himself as a broadcaster, he felt he had to report his feelings to the American people. On August 14, 1950 he began his broadcast by saying, "This is a most difficult broadcast to do." He had never believed in offering criticism of the American military while it was engaged in battle. But this time he would do so. The views he would offer, the questions he would ask, sound strikingly similar to those of other American reporters covering another war in Asia nearly two decades later.

"The question now arises," he told his listeners, "whether serious mistakes have been made." While commanders were predicting six more months of difficult fighting, Washington was saying it could be wound up in the fall. Added Murrow: "To paraphrase the GIs in Korea—that ain't the way it looks from here. So far as this reporter is concerned," he said, "he doesn't see where or when this conflict will end. For this is not an isolated war, except in the purely geographic sense. It is isolated only for the men who are fighting it. When we start moving up through dead valleys, through villages to which we have put the torch by retreating, what then of the people who live there? They have lived on the knife-edge of despair and disaster for centuries. Their pitiful possessions have been consumed in the flames of war. Will our reoccupation of that flea-bitten land lessen, or increase, the attraction of Communism?" (8)

But before Murrow could put those questions to an American audience, he had to get past the editors at CBS. When those editors saw the transcript of Murrow's broadcast they went into a frenzy. In the newsroom at 485 Madison Avenue, news executive Wells Church took a look at the transcript which had just been printed on the teletype machine. He rushed a copy to the office of Ed Chester, director of news. Within minutes the transcript, like some hot potato that no one wanted to touch, was being whisked to the 20th floor and taken to Stanton. Some time later, Chester returned to the newsroom to say, "It's killed." Someone asked why, and Chester explained that the broadcast would give comfort to the enemy and could be used as propaganda by Radio Moscow. The executives had felt that Murrow had violated General Douglas MacArthur's order barring criticism of command decisions. Besides, said Chester, casting doubt where no doubt had ever been cast before, Murrow's sources might be unreliable. Ultimately, Paley took responsibility for the decision to rein in Murrow. He would call it later the most difficult experience he had ever had with his star broadcaster. Years later, Fred Friendly would note that the controversial Murrow nonbroadcast had a broader significance: ". . . It's not a terribly critical piece. . . . Certainly a man of Ed's credentials had every right to do that broadcast. But it was really—there's so much written about the bad blood between Murrow and the brass, usually overstated, but that was the first hint of any problem." (9)

And so no American radio audience ever heard Murrow's stinging words. They were supposed to be aired on the CBS "Evening News" program the night of August 14. The story got out. *Newsweek* broke it, saying, "Murrow's stormy objections brought the censorship problem to a head in the network's newsroom and for other Americans trying to report the war in Korea." Murrow considered resigning. He decided against it and would not go public with the incident. Privately, though, he vowed that he would never let such a thing recur. In later years, when he enjoyed the kind of independence and freedom to say and do on the air what was accorded to no other broadcaster, the quashing of Ed Murrow's views of the American role in Korea would be recalled with irony. It would have been uncharacteristic of Ed Murrow to fall totally silent no matter how eager his editors and bosses might have been to keep him in check. And so on his 7:45 P.M. news broadcast that fall of 1950, he would talk about his being in Korea, noting that he had been the only broadcaster who could talk from direct, personal experience—and he would warn his audience not to be unduly optimistic about Korea. He would try to impart the idea that Communism had a certain appeal to Asians. These remarks were not biting, but they suggested that it was impossible to keep a man like Murrow down for long.

Just as Ed Murrow was returning from Korea, Sig Mickelson, then the public affairs director at CBS, was giving consideration to luring Fred

Friendly away from NBC. Mickelson had been a former radio newsman and journalism teacher from Minnesota. He had run a very successful news operation at the CBS affiliate WCCO in Minneapolis. Paley and Stanton felt CBS's radio documentaries could be improved even more. Mickelson had suggested using "taped actualities," the format Murrow and Friendly had utilized so successfully in their "I Can Hear It Now" album. Fine, said the CBS executives, but then who would produce such programs? Jap Gude had been recently promoting Fred Friendly to Mickelson, and so Sig immediately mentioned Friendly as someone who had been doing fine work at NBC.

Ironically, Friendly's "The Quick and the Dead," a four-part series on nuclear weaponry, aired during the summer of 1950: it relied upon the style deemed by Paley and Stanton undesirable; the series was at least proof that Friendly had the talent for which they were searching. Over a Chinese meal in New York City Friendly and Mickelson chatted. Friendly said that what he really was hoping to do was a "Life Magazine of the Air." He understood that radio wasn't quite ready for that. In the meanwhile, he agreed to do a weekly radio documentary program to be called "Hear It Now." The idea of the program would be to recall the major events of each week, using recorded sound. Friendly would handle the editing; Ed Murrow would be reporter and narrator. Murrow and Friendly thought the program should last 30 minutes. Too short, said an enthusiastic Bill Paley. Take an hour. Do it right.

It was the first joint enterprise of Ed Murrow and Fred Friendly in broadcasting and premiered just as the Chinese Communists entered the war in Korea in late December 1950. The first program was a collection of news vignettes: a pair of marine privates in Korea talking about the retreat from the Chongjin Reservoir, a New York newsdealer explaining why he was unwilling to sell the Communist *Daily Worker,* the Duchess of Windsor talking about love. Aired at the prime 9 P.M. time, "Hear It Now" was heard on 173 stations. It won a Peabody Award almost at once and had unusually high ratings. Its format would become the standard for what would become "radio news specials." It would last only one season to be replaced by its television equivalent, "See It Now."

It was also in 1950 that a young man who later would have a major impact upon CBS News entered Sam Houston State Teachers College in Huntsville, Texas. Dan Rather was nearly 19 years old. During high school, the youngster had thought of working for a newspaper. Never during his college days did he imagine he would become a television personality, though he was intrigued by the new medium. During college he majored in journalism even though his father had warned him that there was little money to be made in such a profession. While at Sam Houston he found a mentor in Hugh Cunningham who taught journalism there. By the time he graduated Dan had been trained to be a newspaperman. His first job, however, was in broadcasting at the Huntsville radio station, KSAM. It is worth noting, given the fact that in 1980 Rather would sign a contract with CBS that was worth $2.2 million a year, that first job paid him the healthy sum of 40 cents an hour! At KSAM he broadcast sports, did the news, and combined it with covering executions at the state prison for the wire services. His mobile news unit was a 1937 Plymouth pickup truck.

By 1950 the United States was becoming televisionland. Three million people owned television sets. In the following twelve months another 7 million sets would be bought. But with 40 million radios in American homes, television still had a long way to overcome the older medium. During the spring of 1949 Hooper rating figures had indicated that 82 percent of the residents of Baltimore listened to radio while only 18 percent watched television. But the following May Baltimore became the first city in which television's evening audience (50.2 percent) was larger than radio's. (10) It was a sign of bigger things to come for television. By September 1951, viewers saw the first coast-to-coast television broadcast, President Harry Truman's address at the Japanese peace treaty conference in San Francisco. That broadcast went to 40 million viewers and was carried by ninety-four stations. Now that television had arrived, it seemed that nearly everyone wanted one. For the next five years television dealer sales averaged 5 million television sets a year. Correspondingly, Americans, particularly the youngsters, were spending an increasing amount of time watching the new medium. Not helping the situation was the invention of the television dinner in 1954. For a while in those days, people were puzzled why water consumption rose during the 3-minute commercial breaks. Then someone figured out that viewers were dashing into bathrooms all at once so as not to miss a minute of their favorite program. Viewers were spending an average of four to five hours a day taking in television. If the car had taken people from the home, television was bringing them back.

Television audiences remained small for a number of reasons. The most important one: during the late 1940s and early 1950s, the audiences were still small largely due to lack of abundant, high-quality programming and the poor quality of the reception. The picture was snowy, antennas were put up incorrectly, the early sets needed too many repairs, and there were too few repairpersons who really knew how to fix the sets.

Nonetheless, while television was going through its birth pangs, radio remained king. The major CBS radio stars (Ed Murrow, Arthur Godfrey, and Bing Crosby) had yet to move over to television. But, slowly, the entertainers would indeed make the shift, not with great enthusiasm, but with an awareness that the new medium would eventually become a major form of entertainment. Bing Crosby was disdainful of television, requiring as it did a performer to appear "live." In 1949, he wrote to Bill Paley: "Only one thing seems consistently apparent to me, and that is you just have to be twice as good on television as on any other medium. Anytime you let down (on television) for an instant you've lost your audience's interest, and it's a struggle to recapture it again." (11) In February 1951 Paley had persuaded him to make his debut on CBS Television but, to the chairman's chagrin, it was only a one-shot appearance. (It would take Crosby another thirteen years before he would agree to do a weekly television series, a domestic-situation comedy that ran on ABC for one season.)

Some wouldn't be able to make the transition from radio to television at all. No one ever imagined that white actors Freeman Gosden and Charles Correll would get away with playing "Amos 'n' Andy" on television—and they did not. "Here was a difference between radio and television we had not foreseen," wrote Bill Paley, "Gosden and Correll had created a warm and funny fantasy world in the listener's imagination on radio. When that world became visual, it also became concrete and literal. . . . We soon learned that creating television programs was a dynamic art with a life of its own. Producers had to find new forms or new variations on old forms. What worked on radio or on the stage or even in the movies did not necessarily work on the small screen." (12) Bowing to the inevitable, Gosden and Correll helped in the nationwide search for black actors to play Amos, Andy, the Kingfish, and others. Debuting on television in 1951, "Amos 'n' Andy" was an immediate smash hit. But, denounced as insulting to blacks by the NAACP, it lasted only two seasons. (The radio program lasted until 1960.)

Other stars, overly self-conscious, had trouble making the switch from radio to television. Edgar Bergen was one. He had grown careless during his radio days about not moving his mouth while throwing his voice to his wooden dummy pal, Charlie McCarthy. But that hardly mattered on radio. Television was a different matter. Bergen worried that he would be accused of moving his lips, of being a fraud. He didn't want that. He appeared on CBS Television only twice—during the 1950–1951 season. Ironically, his television audience didn't seem bothered about his lip moving. The comedian George Burns (of Burns and Allen) had other concerns about television. He was afraid there would not be enough for him to do if he and Gracie Allen simply redid their radio act on television. Bill Paley had an idea. Why didn't George alter the pace of the program by doing a monologue at the start, followed by a dialogue with Gracie? The idea appealed to both comedians, and the audience liked it as well. Burns and Allen appeared on CBS Television from 1950 until Gracie retired in 1958.

The same timidity about television affected Jack Benny. It would take him a full year and a half between his first talk with Bill Paley about moving over to television and his making a commitment to make the switch. Even when he finally agreed, it was only to appear on television once every eight weeks. In fact, Benny was a natural for television. He added new trademarks, the long stare, putting his hand to his cheek, and that famous fastidious walk. Still as stingy and vain as ever, on his first network television appearance on October 28, 1950, Benny brought the house down with his first set of remarks. Which was he more, stingy or vain? "I'd give a million dollars to know what I look like," he said with a straight face. Routinely the Jack Benny program ranked in the top ten for the next seven years. He switched to NBC in 1964 but lasted only one season.

By the fall of 1950, CBS was interested in developing an alternative to the variety show to compete more effectively against NBC. It thought of the sitcom. This way, it would not look as if the network were simply putting on 60 minutes of random activity. The only sitcom ready for that fall, however, was "The George Burns and Gracie Allen Show," and it only aired every other Thursday. CBS searched for more of the same. The search would be difficult, but would eventually pay off.

The network began to focus on a red-headed actress-comedienne named Lucille Ball.

"I Love Lucy" became the greatest comedy blockbuster television show of all time. Lucy played the housewife who would scheme with neighbor Ethel Mertz (Vivian Vance) to get good things from their husbands, Desi Arnaz and actor William Frawley. For four years it was the top-rated program; in two other years it was rated number two, and number three for two other years. (Lucy and Desi parlayed the television series into a show business empire. After the spring of 1957, the show was switched from a 30-minute weekly format to a 1-hour monthly one.) When during the 1952–1953 season, Lucy had a baby—in real life as well as on the show—the ratings soared to 68.8, triple what was generally considered a big success. "America's most famous baby," the baby was dubbed. Some would look at the program, at its huge success, and declare that television had finally been adopted as a significant part of American culture, that viewers had finally accepted the new medium. Some went so far as to date January 19, 1953—the airing of the "baby" show—as the moment when television became the most powerful medium in the country.

Lucille Ball had been born in Celoron, a town in upstate New York, on August 6, 1911. She dropped out of high school at the age of 15. Her future husband, Desiderio Alberto Arnaz y de Acha II, had been born in Santiago, Cuba, on March 2, 1917. During the 1930s she appeared in Hollywood films. In 1948 CBS Radio signed her to star in the radio pilot of "My Favorite Husband," a new situation comedy. A great success, the pilot turned into a series that ran for nearly four years. Lucy portrayed a scatterbrained wife always getting her husband involved in absurd situations. She appeared on television in 1949 with husband Desi, guest-starring on Ed Wynn's variety show. In one sketch they played a husband-and-wife team. The television programming executives at CBS liked what they saw. They wanted to transfer "My Favorite Husband" to television for the 1950 television season and were prepared to give Lucy the starring role. Lucy was willing but insisted that her Cuban bandleader husband Desi be on the show as well. Chairman Paley balked, asserting that Desi was not really an actor and, apart from that, had a thick Spanish accent, which would not go down well with American audiences. Lucy held her ground. She had traveled on too many one-night stands with her husband and yearned for a more normal married life. She hoped to have a child. Whatever their future, she declared, she and Desi would be together. Period.

Lucille and Desi tried unsuccessfully to convince producers and talent agencies to co-star them in a television series or film. She was told that the public wouldn't believe she was married to Desi. After all, what typical American girl was married to a Latin? In the spring of 1950 they took their husband-and-wife situation comedy act on the road to prove the naysayers wrong. They also formed Desilu Productions. Unable to get CBS backing for the pilot, Lucy and Desi produced the trial show themselves. She was five months pregnant. Lucy gave birth to her first child, Lucie Desiree Arnaz, a month before her fortieth birthday, on July 17, 1951. Finally, Bill Paley gave in and "I Love Lucy" premiered that October 15. It was not an overnight ratings success, though the critics seemed to like the show. Within a matter of weeks, its ratings soared.

Pregnancy was still a delicate issue for television in those days, and so Lucille Ball took a chance in dealing with this taboo topic, especially in a comedy format. But the "most famous baby in America" was born on that morning of January 19, 1953, Lucy's son, Desiderio Alberto Arnaz IV. That night on television, she gave birth (fictionally) to Little Ricky. An estimated 50 million people saw the show, which had actually been filmed in November. The show got a higher rating than the inauguration of President Eisenhower the next day. Two weeks later, Lucy was named Best Television Comedienne of 1952. "I Love Lucy" received an Emmy as well

---

for the Best Situation Comedy Show. A new contract was drawn up for $8 million, the largest ever signed in television until then.

In the fall of 1953, crisis struck Lucille Ball, and her rosy world appeared about to tumble. In September broadcaster Walter Winchell accused her in a broadcast of being a Communist. (13) Rather than cower, she dealt with the situation frontally, summoning the press and acknowledging that her grandfather, a furniture worker who had been active in labor and politics, had read the *Daily Worker*. He had indeed wanted her to join the Communist Party, and so she did, she asserted, not from any sense of political conviction, but merely to please one's grandfather. Confronted with her candor, the public accepted Lucy's version and forgot about the whole thing. Just prior to the next scheduled "I Love Lucy," before a standing-room-only audience of 300 there for the filming of the show, Desi addressed them: "I want to talk to you about something serious. Lucy has never been a Communist, not now and never will be." The audience broke into applause for a full minute. "I was kicked out of Cuba because of Communism. We despise everything about it. Lucy is as American as Bernie Baruch and Ike Eisenhower." Then he introduced his wife: "My favorite redhead, and that's the only thing red about Lucy and even that is not legitimate." (14) When the show ended, Lucy said, "God bless you for being so kind." Walter Winchell soon reported that Lucy had been cleared "one hundred percent."

Variety programs still loomed large in CBS's programming schedule in the early 1950s. And, even though the network had actually found someone to rival Milton Berle—the nonperforming, but highly successful Ed Sullivan—it still longed to showcase a talent equal to Berle's performing stature. CBS found him in Jackie Gleason. He had been born in Brooklyn, the son of an insurance auditor who disappeared when Gleason was 8 years old. Jackie dropped out of high school and began working as an emcee at carnivals and nightclubs. Signing Gleason up in 1952, CBS put him on Saturday nights. "The Jackie Gleason Show" had an extraordinarily high rating (42.5 in the Nielsen counting for the 1954–55 season). In 1952 he received a *TV Guide* citation as the best comedian of the year. "And a-way we go" became a kind of national chant after Gleason introduced it, his parting words following his opening monologue. He played a variety of characters and did them all astonishingly well: he was the poor soul, he was Joe the bartender, he was Reginald Van Gleason; but his greatest role was that of Ralph Cramden, the bus driver from Brooklyn who constantly searched for get-rich schemes. At first Cramden appeared in a Gleason segment called "The Honeymooners" and eventually the segment became an independent program. It was reported at the time

(1955) that the contract for the series, which was sponsored by the Buick Division of General Motors, called for him to be paid $11 million if the weekly half-hour shows ran for three years. It was said to be the biggest deal in television history until then. The first program was televised on October 1, 1955, with Gleason as Ralph, and Audrey Meadows playing his wife, Alice.

So successful was Gleason that he won a contract from CBS that called for a $7 million commitment for two years of shows plus a guarantee of $100,000 a year for fifteen years even if CBS never put him on the air. While demonstrating how badly the network wanted to keep Gleason under contract, the agreement nearly broke CBS. They called him "the Great One," a nickname that fit his girth (he once topped 280 pounds), his exuberance, his gregariousness (he called everyone "pal"), and above all, his self-confidence. "If I didn't have an enormous ego," he once said, "how in hell could I be a performer?"

The one performer who made the switch to television flawlessly was Arthur Godfrey. As early as 1949, he not only had his highly popular morning radio program but two evening television shows as well, "Arthur Godfrey and His Friends," an hour-long show on Wednesdays, and "Arthur Godfrey's Talent Scouts," which appeared for 30 minutes on Mondays. By the early 1950s, he was reaching over 80 million viewers and in 1954 accounted for 12 percent of the network's revenues. In a sense, Godfrey was a dream come true for CBS, a man who could go on radio and later television, prove so entertaining that he would attract a huge audience, and in doing so, guarantee high sales for whatever products advertised on his programs. And, indeed, Godfrey was known as an incredible salesman.

The story is told that when Ed Murrow and Fred Friendly were assembling material for their "I Can Hear It Now" album, they came across the famous Arthur Godfrey broadcast of President Roosevelt's funeral and included it in the album. When Godfrey plugged the Murrow-Friendly album on his program, the album became a huge seller. (Godfrey, of course, didn't get one penny for the promotion he did.)

In recognition of his talents, *Time* put Godfrey on the cover of its February 27, 1950 issue, declaring that "No one on the network air ever had the unbuttoned nerve to talk with his mouth full, use sloppy diction, give free plugs to non-sponsoring products or blithely ad-lib whatever popped into mind. Beyond such calculated flaunting of the rules of radio and TV, the thing that makes Arthur Godfrey remarkable as a hit entertainer is his relative lack of definable talent. He can neither sing, dance, act, nor perform with skill on a musical instrument. Yet today he is the top moneymaker and the outstanding personality on the air. From radio and TV, records, business investments, stocks and bonds, and other odds and ends, he gets close to $1 million a year. He earns $1,500 for every minute he broadcasts. He is seen and heard—and apparently loved—by 40 million people."

The Godfrey magic affected Bill Paley as well. One day in a conference Godfrey started selling the CBS chairman a product and Paley went right home and asked his wife if she had ever used it. A free plug by Godfrey was deemed so valuable that manufacturers, on the off-chance that he would mention their product, deluged him with all sorts of merchandise. Since the early 1930s the ukulele industry had been in the doldrums, but from the time Godfrey began to strum on his ukulele on the air, business picked up. Godfrey was, above all else, informal and because he was, others in radio would adopt the same carefree attitude. As *Time* noted in its cover story, "The listening audience can thank Godfrey for removing much of the starch and stuffiness from radio. He found the medium bustling with split-second efficiency, and slowed a portion of it to a comfortable walk. He helped clean up the high-pressure babble of machine-made commercials, and proved to a nervous, self-conscious industry that informality pays off." No better illustration of his informality can be cited than the line he became infamous for in kidding advertising men on the air: "Boy, the stuff they ask me to read!"

The entertainers were bringing in lots of money for CBS. The network's gross sales in 1952 totaled $251.5 million, and its profit before taxes was $15.9 million, an impressive gain from 1948, when gross revenues were $64 million, and 1949, when they were $91.9 million. There were other money-winners as well. Apart from sitcoms and variety shows, CBS was developing other forms of entertainment. It was during the early 1950s that the network offered a selection of drama programs, beginning with "Studio One," which won the 1951 Emmy for best dramatic show. Later in the 1950s, it produced "Suspense," "Omnibus," "The Lux Video Theater," "The Twentieth Century Fox Hour," "The U.S. Steel Hour," "The Best of Broadway," "Dupont Show of the Month," and "Playhouse 90."

In addition to the dramatic programs there were the episodic series, a form that had been used with great success on radio. By 1953 it had become the main staple in television programming. These series featured a number of continuing characters as well as a separate plot for each program; most used either mystery-crime or comedy formulas and almost all were live, or at least had begun as live series. One example was CBS's frequently top-rated "Man Against Crime," starring Ralph Bellamy, which ran from 1949 until 1954. Each episode, costing $10,000 to

$15,000 to produce, was written by one of a stable of fifty freelance writers. Sponsored by Camel cigarettes, "Man Against Crime" could not, according to the mimeographed instructions sent to writers "have the heavy or any disreputable person smoking a cigarette. Do not associate the smoking of cigarettes with undesirable scenes or situations plot-wise." (15) Cigarettes could never be puffed nervously, only smoked gracefully. And one could never give a cigarette to a character to calm his nerves—this could imply a narcotic effect to the product. Writers were given some rather incredible instructions on plot: "It has been found that we retain audience interest best when our story is concerned with murder. Therefore, although other crimes may be introduced, somebody must be murdered, preferably early, with the threat of more violence to come." Still, there was a practical problem. Given the flimsy sets, violence could only be staged briefly. Arson was forbidden—it being too much of a re-minder that cigarettes can cause fires. And no one could cough on the program, again because of a possible negative association with ciga-rettes. Doing the episodic series live stifled variety. The actors were lim-ited to five sets. Costume changes were unpleasant and unwelcome. Ralph Bellamy was constantly running from set to set between scenes. Eventually, "Man Against Crime" went over to film despite the higher costs.

The success of the CBS network stars—Jack Benny, Burns and Allen, Red Skelton, Jackie Gleason, Arthur Godfrey—attested to the sound judg-ment of the CBS brass, especially the keen insight of Bill Paley. Not that CBS as a network was particularly innovative in programming during the 1950s. Boldness and imagination were commodities found more in the NBC camp in those years. It was NBC under Pat Weaver who instituted the "Today" program in the early morning hours and the "Tonight" pro-gram late at night. Spectaculars and long variety programs such as "Show of Shows" were NBC products as well. Moreover, NBC pioneered the advertising concepts—particularly employing minute-long commer-cials rather than longer ones—that proved effective in amassing financial support for these innovative programs. Indeed, CBS lagged in the 1950s, giving the early morning and late evening hours to NBC by default, a situation that continues into the late 1980s. According to Mike Dann, who was chief of programming for CBS in the 1960s, "Paley's basic approach to broadcasting, being a smart professional in the conventional sense, was not to take gambles. Experimentation and development. He didn't understand that. . . . He would pay money for a sure thing. He would buy a 'Lucy' and pay the capital gains arrangements. He didn't care. [But] he wouldn't open up early morning programming. He wouldn't go for the 'minute' (advertising) plan. He wouldn't do anything innovative. . . . He was not a discoverer or creator of programs. Paley's genius, his ability, was that he gave programming a priority. He didn't care about sales . . . affiliate relations . . . administration, or Washington. He cared about programming. His great strength was to say that if it's not on the tube, it's no place. He loved programming. He loved programmers. . . . He himself wouldn't recognize a good script." (16)

With the kind of defects Dann mentioned, it would seem surprising that CBS amassed such strong ratings through the 1950s. Again Mike Dann: "Paley was very lucky in that he had no competition. Remember Paley grew up in an industry [in which] he had very little American competition. His biggest competition, NBC, was run by a man who thought that the advertisers and the agencies should really run the programming, should operate stations and he essentially liked the engineering aspects. . . . He [Paley] had a remarkable instinct for priorities. He ran the store. He had no stockholders to contend with. He made the broadcasting and later the record companies primary thrusts. He led the charmed life. Very few men in American industry ever enjoyed the luxury that Paley did as a broadcaster. . . . He was the General Motors of the broadcasting business. He had the money. He could do no wrong. Most of all you could pick up the phone and talk to Paley about programming at night, morning, afternoon. He'd discuss it anytime with you. And support you. The only thing in programming you couldn't tell him was how good things were. He liked to talk about what's wrong. That's what he said, 'I can only help you with what's wrong.' Not with what's right." (17)

In the early 1950s CBS continued its battle with RCA over color television. In October 1950 the FCC voted to approve CBS's mechanical non-compatible process as the nation's official color television system. Even though the Korean conflict had halted television's spread, 9 million sets had been sold by the time of the FCC decision, all of which would have to be discarded if the CBS system gained public acceptance. That led RCA to engage in a futile seven-month court battle to get the order rescinded. On May 28, 1951 the U.S. Supreme Court unanimously upheld the FCC ruling. CBS, assuming it had finally obtained victory, announced plans to broadcast 20 hours of color programs each week, starting October 15. On June 25, CBS broadcast the first commercial color network program in history, a one-hour show called "Premiere," with Arthur Godfrey, Ed Sullivan, Faye Emerson, and other stars. Bill Paley, Frank Stanton, and FCC Chairman Wayne Coy appeared briefly. But, without compatible sets, few watched the program, which aired in Boston, Philadelphia, Baltimore, and Washington.

Too caught up in the Korean conflict, the public could not contemplate getting rid of black-and-white sets in favor of color ones. Still, CBS went ahead with plans to market color television sets using the CBS system. Flush with the Supreme Court triumph, CBS wanted to move into the one field in which NBC had carved out a niche—the manufacture of electronic equipment. Certain that NBC would not manufacture color televisions that were compatible with the CBS color system, Paley sought a means for CBS to do the manufacturing itself. It was not a new impulse. He had returned from World War II determined upon building a diversified enterprise. For CBS to have been solely dependent on broadcasting, in his view, was problematic. Broadcasting, being government regulated, could become subject to new regulations that could adversely affect CBS. It was better, Paley believed, to get involved in businesses outside of the government's reach.

Thus, on June 15, 1951, CBS purchased Hytron Radio and Electronics Corporation of Salem, Massachusetts, one of the oldest manufacturers of radio and television tubes and the fourth largest in sales. The purchase came through an exchange of some $17.7 million of CBS stock. Considering that CBS had just $68 million in sales, the sale price was remarkably high. Hytron's two principal owners, Bruce A. Coffin and Lloyd H. Coffin, two brothers, became immediate millionaires as a result of the deal; both were elected to the CBS board of directors.

Almost from the beginning, the deal went sour. Paley had relied upon Peter Goldmark's positive reaction to Hytron. But within three months of the sale, Paley discovered that Hytron's inventory of vacuum tubes and television sets had been overvalued by millions of dollars. Then, at the insistence of the government, CBS suspended the building of color television sets in October 1951, ending the need for Hytron. The reason: the Korean conflict. (In 1961 CBS sold Hytron, losing an estimated $150 million.)

By the time the U.S. government had rescinded its order banning the manufacture of color television sets in March 1953, the number of black-and-white televisions had risen to 23 million, an insurmountable obstacle to CBS's incompatible color system. With great enterprise, Peter Goldmark invented a converter device that could be attached to existing black-and-white sets, but by this time RCA had its own color system that could transmit to existing black-and-white sets without a converter. The final blow to CBS came in December when 200 engineers from 91 manufacturing firms produced a refined color system based on the RCA system. That same month the FCC adopted the new system.

Although Ed Murrow had appeared on television as early as the 1948

political conventions, only in 1951 did his first serious introduction to the new medium occur. So influential was he that, in coming over to television, Murrow would legitimize it for others. Not that Murrow had been pleased to go on television, essentially an inferior means of breaking news, in his opinion, to radio—nothing more than the reciting of captions for photographs and film. For those reasons, he would stay away from narrating television news even after his television days began.

Television was of course less sophisticated than radio in the early 1950s. It could not get to fast-breaking stories quickly; live coverage required large mobile vans and miles of cable, not to mention days of advance planning. In this presatellite era, getting film of news events overseas could take a week. Even within the United States, where plane connections were still limited, it could take 24 hours to get film on the air. As a result, much of early television news focused on staged, predictable events, particularly events that occurred in New York or Washington.

When Ed Murrow went on television, he in effect put television news on the map. (Although Murrow constantly told friends that he had no desire to go into television, that the way he wrote and projected himself was designed for radio, some of those friends sensed that he was dead wrong. "Television," observed Fred Friendly, "was invented for him." (18)

It was only natural that Murrow and Friendly would want to adapt their "Hear It Now" radio program to television. When Murrow met representatives of Alcoa, the Aluminum Corporation of America, sponsor of the program, he was asked what were his politics, and he answered that was none of their business. The Alcoa officials were sensible enough to understand that Murrow meant what he said. They promised they would give Murrow and Friendly a free hand. Murrow's independent spirit may have put Alcoa off, but it needed him badly, coming off a losing antitrust suit. Some public relations people advised the firm that it would do a good deal for its image if it involved itself in television and if it could get Ed Murrow to star in an Alcoa-sponsored program. So Alcoa approached Murrow and Friendly and said that it would sponsor "See It Now," which was to be a half-hour documentary. Alcoa and CBS sealed the deal in time for the third program. The first two were sustaining.

On November 18, 1951 Murrow televised the first "See It Now" program. He sat on a swivel chair before two monitors that could be viewed by his live audience, Murrow called on one camera to bring in the Atlantic Ocean, on another to bring in the Pacific Ocean. Suddenly there were pictures of the Golden Gate Bridge and the San Francisco skyline followed by the Brooklyn Bridge as part of New York's profile. He was making use of the recently developed coast-to-coast broadcasting facilities that were a combination of coaxial cable and microwave relay. Some thought it smacked of gimmickry, but there was a fascination with the new toy that led to such playfulness. If all Murrow was doing was letting someone sitting in his living room gaze at two oceans at once, that seemed enough wizardry to justify the excitement over television. "Good evening," said Murrow, stern, cigarette in his fingers, "this is an old team trying to learn a new trade." The old team had been in the foxholes of World War II, had created and then mastered radio journalism. Now they were involved in something new, the new trade of television news. The team consisted of Murrow and Friendly, one the reporter and analyst, the other the technician, producer, and organizer. Friendly would describe his relationship to Murrow in military terms. "He's the company commander. Everything I edit, I edit with Ed's eyes. I write with his fingers." (19) The new coast-to-coast link made Los Angeles suddenly available as a city from which television programs could originate. As a result, performers who had moved East to host the top variety shows on CBS (and NBC) now went back to the West Coast.

Also on that first program, Murrow, in New York, and Eric Sevareid, in Washington, talked about the war in Korea; Howard K. Smith did the same via a prefilmed phone conversation with Murrow. That half-hour would enter broadcasting history, suggesting the true potential of television. "Both in itself and in its effect on the medium," wrote Murrow's biographer Alexander Kendrick, "it was perhaps the most significant television half-hour presented on the home screen until then." (20)

Daniel Schorr, then a young correspondent for CBS, recalled coming upon Fred Friendly early in the "See It Now" days. "I was taken to his 'See It Now' shop at the back of 485 Madison Avenue. Since I had been living in Europe for the previous four years and didn't really understand television at all, I had no idea what was happening in television. . . . So I asked Friendly, what do you do back here? He said, 'We don't know. We're trying to invent something.' And while he tends to exaggerate, as Fred does, to dramatize his lack of knowledge, whatever, but I remember him saying, 'We are fooling around with an hour on television.'" (21)

"See It Now" was supposed to last only thirteen weeks, but thanks to the honors paid to it, the Murrow-Friendly documentary program lasted seven years. The main reason for the program's success, even in the view of rivals, was Edward R. Murrow. Those who watched would sense that here for the first time was an attempt at confronting the power and potential of television. The man who worked most closely with him, Fred Friendly, noted: "I don't think that broadcast journalism would have been what it is except for Murrow. I'm talking about television journalism. Because he had a chance, with whatever I did to help him, to set a course. People looked at that as a benchmark . . . I guess there was a compulsion about Murrow when he was on the air that this is the most important subject in the world I'm telling you about, an involvement, I guess is the best word." (22)

"See It Now" had the feel of a news magazine. Each week three or four subjects were tackled during its 30 minutes; occasionally a program would focus on one subject only, whether it was Trieste, Lt. Radulovich, a Big Four foreign ministers' conference, or the recognition of Communist China. During the first season of 1951–52 the show was aired from 3:30 to 4:00 on Sunday afternoons, what Murrow called "that intellectual ghetto" of programming time. (23) The following two seasons, 1953–54 and 1954–55, it shifted to the 10:30–11:00 slot on Tuesday evenings; thereafter, until July 1958 when it ended its run, "See It Now" was on irregularly—eight times a season with the programs 60 or 90 minutes long.

Murrow could never quite get used to the distinct physical discomfort of performing on television. He found television's hot lights uncomfortable. They made him sweat. He didn't like the makeup. Murrow and his crowd had disdained early television news as containing too many frills. With its directors, technicians, bulky cameras, blinding lights, the emphasis appeared to be on show business and glitz—not news. Worst of all, the requirement to use makeup suggested there was something unmanly about appearing on television—and Murrow and his bunch, imbued as they were with all that World War II machismo, had great difficulty getting used to this new world. A journalist worth his salt donned a trench coat and went off to risk his life covering war. But makeup? That and all the other rough edges made television unpleasant to contemplate. Oh, Murrow yearned for radio, with its directness, its facelessness, the control over his material that it gave him. As for television, the cameras, lights, setting, producers, directors, coordinators, and stagehands—all seemed to be disturbing him, getting in his way of reaching the audience with the story. It was all that paraphernalia that seemed to be in charge, not him. For that reason, among others, he would never give up his nightly radio news broadcast. How ironic all this was.

For all his complaints about television, the man seemed to have been born to the medium, with a personality and looks that gave him superstar quality. Murrow may not have liked television, but he had the personality and appearance of someone perfectly suited to television. "His eyes," wrote Murrow biographer Kendrick, "were deep-set and grave, his mouth and chin purposeful—a baritone timbre of voice, straightforward address, and serious interest, with an occasional Mephistophelian smile." (24)

Because of Murrow (and Fred Friendly as well), "See It Now" broke new ground. Its reporting was the most realistic yet devised for documentary film. It was also the first program to shoot its own film rather than use archive film material or film already shot for the newsreels and for daily news programs. Differing from other documentary programs, "See It Now" sent its cameras out without a prepared script, striving to be spontaneous—and authentic. Dubbing was forbidden. So was the use of actors. Interviews were not rehearsed. Murrow and Friendly would shoot as much as twenty times as much film as would be used. The classic illustration of this was a four-week journey on the famed Orient Express—from Paris to Istanbul, with stops in Milan, Trieste, Belgrade, and Salonika—which was pared to a 9-minute, 34-second segment. Cost appeared to be of little consequence: programs could cost $100,000. At times CBS had to pay a portion of the bill as the sponsor would pay only $23,000 a week plus $34,000 for the purchase of airtime. Although "See It Now" was frequently in the red, it did not seem to matter, so great was its prestige. Everyone realized that, compared with the high-cost entertainment shows and "spectaculars," with their big-name stars and lavish productions, the ratings for these serious documentaries would be small. (That first Sunday afternoon the program had 3 million viewers; it would never reach more than 7 million.) But in the early 1950s, no one expected a documentary program to attract a huge audience.

The program went from strength to strength. Occasionally, "See It Now" would do longer presentations as was the case with its Christmas show in 1952, marking the first full-hour program as well as television's first full-length combat report. For two and a half years, the day-to-day coverage of the Korean war had been based largely on Washington-issued battle reports with some government-supplied combat footage. None of this conveyed the war in human terms. And none of it could have communicated the central fact of the fighting: the existence of a stalemate. "See It Now" was about to convey all this in the most ambitious enterprise yet undertaken by television. Involving nearly everyone connected with the "See It Now" pool of camera and sound personnel, the show sent to Korea a fifteen-member camera crew, Murrow, and four other CBS correspondents: Bill Downs, Larry LeSueur, Robert Pierpoint, and Lou Cioffi. Five camera crews filmed on the front line in the midst of the Siberian winter, working in near-zero temperatures, snow, rain, and sleet.

Ed Murrow was reporter and executive field producer. One marvelous photo of Murrow from that journey shows him decked out in army fatigues, replete with black army boots and a tin helmet; beside him is a black soldier; Murrow is holding a mike, talking into it while the soldier smiles, holding a gun. They are surrounded by other American troops. It was a new experience for American television audiences, the reporter at the front, sending back his report soon after it happened.

The most famous shot came as a result of an attempt to get lots of film of a foxhole being dug. That old front-line landmark had come to symbolize World War II, and Friendly and Murrow wanted to present it as a symbol of the Korean fighting as well. Murrow found a sergeant from Nebraska hacking away on his twenty-fourth birthday with a shovel upon a ridge. Cameraman Charlie Mack filmed the soldier's boots, the young man's hands holding the shovel, and the shovel digging into the frozen earth. Friendly made it the show's opening and it became a classic of wartime television coverage. He recalled that "nobody knew anything about doing sound in cold weather. . . . Nobody'd ever done sound. We went up to the top of old Baldy and Pork Chop Hill with two and three hundred pound recorders. . . . Now, I can remember Ed and I saying to Johnny Mack and Leo Rossi and Palmer Williams, 'We want to get the sound of a guy digging a foxhole in Korea.' You remember that scene, when we ran a guy digging a foxhole for four and a half minutes? I can remember people saying, 'Well, you don't want to bring that sound equipment up to the top of Old Baldy. What you do is, you do a silent picture of that, like it was done in World War II, and when you come back to New York you put in the sound effects.' We said, 'No, we want to do that live.' Not live but recorded with real sound. Now, today, everybody does it that way. Nobody would put in any fake sound. I would like to think that the fact that Murrow and I were so stubborn in those days and said, 'If we have a guy digging a foxhole, we want to make it happen that. . . . What we didn't understand was that nobody'd ever run equipment like that in that kind of weather, and the oil would coagulate and dials would freeze and everything else. But we had a hardy bunch of guys who were a band of brothers under Ed." (25)

But that wasn't the end of the story. The odds that the film would prove usable in those days was only fifty-fifty. "How are you doing?" Friendly in New York asked Murrow in Korea, after the famous foxhole filming.

"Well," said Murrow, "if there's anything on the film we'll be all right." (26) There was, as it turned out, something on the film. The Christmas in Korea program was shown on December 28, and Jack Gould of *The New York Times* the next day called it "one of the finest programs ever seen on TV . . . a unified mosaic that gave the persons sitting thousands of miles away at home a sensation of participating in the ordeal. . . ." *Variety*'s headline read: "Murrow's Korea: The New Journalism. Even a battlefront brought into the parlor."

In a certain sense, the program supported the American war effort, but in showing the sacrifices and frustrations of the American boys, it had another effect as well. There was footage of soldiers saying that they thought the war a lot of nonsense, something that would have been unthinkable in wartime radio broadcasting. Murrow ended the show: "There is no conclusion to this report from Korea because there is no end to the war."

There would be other significant "See It Now" programs, Murrow interviewing Harry Truman about Douglas MacArthur; MacArthur talking about Truman. Murrow interviewing Nikita Khrushchev in the Kremlin. "See It Now" was also the first television program to discuss the danger-

---

ous relationship between lung cancer and cigarettes, an irony, given Ed Murrow's own heavy cigarette habit.

The balance between radio and television was shifting in the early 1950s as television became increasingly more important. Toward the end of 1951, a directive was issued by CBS President Frank Stanton to CBS Television News to look for ways to get more serious. In 1951, television and radio at CBS were split into separate entities, each with its own president. That put pressure on radio to show a profit on its own, creating what some thought was an unhealthy competition between these two media, a competition that would have some bizarre dimensions. (Until late 1965, for example, CBS Television could not be used to inform its audience that a certain special event was to be broadcast over radio, and vice versa.) Sig Mickelson became head of a newly-formed News and Public Affairs Department within the CBS Television Network Division. In effect, Mickelson had been given a mandate to inaugurate a fully blown television news operation for CBS. Mickelson asked for $2 million to build up the television operation, and Jack Van Volkenburg, then president of the network's new television division, gave it to him.

From the start, Mickelson was under a handicap—with only thirteen people working for television news—four producers, two graphic artists, four technicians, two producer-directors, and newscaster Douglas Edwards. They worked out of a corner of a floor at 485 Madison Avenue and had to run to the studios at Liederkranz Hall, eight blocks away. When Mickelson was given a budget to hire reporters exclusively for television, he hired Harry Reasoner and then Charles Kuralt, two men who would become giants of CBS Television News. He also hired Ernest Leiser and Les Midgley as producers.

Television was beginning to cover politics more aggressively by the early 1950s. No better illustration of that exists than the effort CBS made to cover Dwight Eisenhower's kick-off of his campaign for the presidency in June 1952. Bill Paley, who counted himself as a friend of Eisenhower, wanted CBS to cover the announcement live. Sig Mickelson did some checking and found that unfortunately it would have cost thousands of dollars, requiring the laying of a cable from New York to Abilene, Kansas, site of the Eisenhower announcement. The event was planned for June 4. It proved a disaster. A torrential rainstorm soaked Eisenhower and his manuscript. Efforts to get him to speak in a nearby barn failed. But the next day he planned to hold a news conference at the Abilene movie house. At first, it appeared that CBS's television cameras would not be permitted inside. The print journalists didn't want to allow television coverage, arguing that the presence of the cameras and the crews would be disruptive. There was much discussion, but in the end David Schoenbrun, brought in especially from Paris because of his close friendship with Eisenhower, was permitted inside.

The presence of television at that Abilene press conference proved highly significant. For as Sig Mickelson has written, "It created the first crack in the then existing impenetrable barrier between the printed press and representatives of television. . . . The conference also pointed the way toward later live television coverage of presidential conferences" (which would get under way in 1961 under President Kennedy). (27)

Television news was fast making inroads. Covering major news conferences was but one example. Covering political conventions was another. But the presence of television at a convention inevitably worried politicians. While an increasing number of them understood the importance of television, no one had quite figured out how to conduct a convention with the whole world watching. At the 1952 Democratic convention, held in Philadelphia, all delegates and alternates were provided with instructions noting that, "You will be on television. Television will be watching you. There are to be no empty seats, no sleeping, and good behavior is urged." Newspapermen had been covering political conventions for years, but now the politicians had to adjust to the presence of television. At the Republican convention that year, reporters hovered around the senator from California, Richard M. Nixon, after he was nominated for the vice presidency. Suddenly, Don Hewitt instructed his floor man to hand over his headset to Nixon so that Ed Murrow and Walter Cronkite could interview him directly from their booth. At that time, it was a revolutionary notion for a politician to talk live on television. Print reporters had to wait. Richard Nixon, it so happened, was just as eager to talk to the new television boys as they were to interview him, sensing that through television he had a quick pipeline to the entire nation. Thanks to Hewitt's initiative, CBS had an exclusive—and television had injected itself in a new way into the goings-on of the politicians. (CBS Radio and Television still behaved like competitors toward one another. At the Democratic convention, CBS Radio News managed to bug an important caucus and obtain a recording that turned out to be a good story; however, it refused to share the recording with CBS Television News.)

As television news took on a new acceptability, its pioneers came under pressure to improve the technology. Accordingly, Don Hewitt kept inventing. Once during the 1952 conventions he had stopped for breakfast at a diner. In the back of his mind was the continuing problem of how best to identify the hundreds of delegates on the convention floor without having to interrupt Walter Cronkite's commentary. Sitting down to eat, he spotted a sign with movable letters, advertising the day's specials—hamburger 35 cents, soup 20 cents. The waitress asked him what he wanted to order. Without blinking an eye, he replied that he would like the entire board—and he paid $20 for it. Thus was born the "super," the letters that were superimposed on the television screen.

One novelty at the 1952 convention was the anchorman. Television would have, for the first time, a major presence at the two conventions, and so, it was felt, the camera should focus on one key personality—to give the coverage of the four-day-long conventions some sense of orderliness. Besides, someone would be needed to keep talking throughout the entire proceedings. Someone would be needed to serve as anchor for the reporters on the floor. One prospect was Robert Trout, who had been handling conventions for CBS since 1936. Sig Mickelson had another choice. His name was Walter Cronkite.

Walter Cronkite was the only rising star at CBS News who had not been part of the Murrow crowd. He had found reporting more exciting than his studies so he dropped out of the University of Texas in his junior year. For a short time he was a radio sportscaster and would replay football games with wire service copy and a sound effects man. Employing a rich imagination, he would improvise complicated descriptions of players and cheerleaders. Sometimes he pretended to recognize friends in the stands. On one occasion, the wire machine broke down and he had to keep the game going on for another 20 minutes, using his imagination completely! "I marched them up and down the field—with frequent and protracted time outs," he recalled. "When the wire finally came back, I discovered that Notre Dame had scored. I had them on their own 20-yard line. I had to get them all the way back downfield to score in a hurry." (28)

He had almost been one of Ed's "boys" back in the fall of 1942. As a London-based reporter for United Press, Walter caught Murrow's eye; after a friendly lunch, he was offered a job with CBS. Murrow and Cronkite shook hands on the starting salary of $125 a week plus fees. But the United Press immediately offered him a $25 a week raise. Walter was so impressed by the gesture and so smitten with the fast-paced wire service life, that he decided not to quit. To Ed Murrow, Cronkite's decision smacked of lunacy, but he could do nothing about it.

Remaining with the wire service throughout World War II, Cronkite covered the North African landings and then, from London, the air war. After the Allied invasion, he was put in charge of United Press's coverage of the Low Countries: frequently, he reached towns ahead of liberating Canadian troops. "I got a lot of garlands and heard a lot of welcoming speeches," remembered Cronkite. "The Canadians were not amused." (29) For the next two years, largely unpleasant, he was United Press's Moscow bureau chief. He returned to the United States with a promise that soon he would be named United Press chief in Europe. But, failing to get a raise in 1948, he headed to Kansas City where he had spent part of his childhood; while there, he was hired at $250 a week to work in Washington as the radio correspondent for a string of Midwestern radio stations. He was dubious about the whole thing, telling his friends at the time that newspapers, not radio, should be covering the news. But the pay was good. His aim was to return to Kansas City as the general manager of KMBC, the Kansas City CBS radio affiliate.

A year and a half later, Cronkite got a call out of the blue from Ed Murrow. Would he be willing to cover the Korean war for CBS? Yes, said a happy Walter Cronkite. He never got there. The television news director of Washington, D.C.'s WTOP, a new CBS affiliate, suddenly confronted by a manpower shortage, asked Walter to report on the Korean story each night—from Washington! Briefed daily by the Pentagon, Cronkite used chalk and a blackboard to explain the military situation. He was a superb explainer. He had information, presence, a sense of authority; in short, he possessed an unbeatable professionalism.

Sig Mickelson had been offered a list of one hundred reporters, among whom was Walter Cronkite. He had assigned Walter as anchor for the network pool coverage of the Japanese Peace Conference in San Francisco in September 1951 and had been impressed with him, enough so that now he wanted him for the convention job. Walter supplied an audition film and on that basis won the job.

Now he would be tested at the conventions. He was discernibly different from the Murrow group, not sophisticated or intellectual, not genteel. He eschewed deep analysis, loved hard news, and actually said "Gee Whiz" when an exciting event occurred. He had done his homework and learned who the important delegations were. He had a degree of professionalism that others lacked. He had one other quality that few possessed, endurance. He rarely became fatigued, and considering that others would wither a short time after working under the hot television lights, Cronkite was indeed an unusual find. He had the gift of gab as well, always something to say, always there when confronted with a few minutes of empty air. What he had to say was generally clear, thoughtful, and colorful. And it sounded authoritative. It sounded as if you could trust him. Which, as it turned out, most Americans did. CBS did well in the ratings contest for the conventions that year. And Walter Cronkite was given the credit. There was a wonderful moment when some of the Murrow radio crowd inched over to Walter to let him know that they would be happy to take on assignments for television. It was their way of saying that Cronkite was acceptable—and that television was acceptable. That meant a lot. One thing it meant: Walter Cronkite had become a full-fledged star.

Television was not content merely to bring the personalities into one's living room instantaneously. It wanted to do more—to report on the outcome of a presidential election instantly and not have to wait hours or even days for all the votes to be tallied. In 1952 CBS planned to do this through the use of computers. One giant public relations exercise for the network, the computer gambit would boost CBS's prestige enormously—if it worked! If it failed, the network would have egg on its face.

The exercise was the result of a barter accord between CBS and Remington-Rand. (30) CBS had asked Remington for several hundred typewriters and adding machines to use on election night; in return, the network gave its promise that it would focus its cameras on the Remington-Rand logo. A Remington-Rand public relations man proposed to CBS that one way of retaining the audience's attention throughout the tiresome vote count would be to attempt to predict the winner using a computer. At the outset, network officials believed that the machine would be little more than a show business gimmick. "We're not depending too much on this machine," anchorman Walter Cronkite told his reporters. "It may be just a side show." He thought for a moment and added, "Then again it may turn out to be of great value to some people."

With that uncertainty, CBS prepared for election night. Meanwhile in Philadelphia, engineers programmed UNIVAC I, building algorithms to help the computer analyze election returns and voting patterns in the previous two presidential elections as well as voting trends dating back to 1928. The task was so monumental that engineers employed three computers—one to process the data on the air, a second to check the first, and a third to serve as a backup in the event that one of the other two "crashed." Using a teletype line, the data went back and forth to New York. The engineers labored right up to airtime.

Then at 6 P.M. Eastern time CBS went on the air. The data were entered on three magnetic tapes. One tape was placed on the second computer to check for accuracy with the other two. A program was also used to assure that no precinct reported more votes than voters and that each new total was higher than the last one. Then it happened. Three hours later UNIVAC I made the Republicans exceedingly happy by predicting a landslide win for Dwight D. Eisenhower, running counter to what a lot of political pundits were saying at the time. Charles Collingwood, the CBS man assigned to report on what the computer was spewing out, told anchorman Walter Cronkite that when he asked UNIVAC for a prediction, "he [UNIVAC] sent me back a very caustic answer. He said that if we continue to be so late in sending him results, it's going to take him a few minutes to find out just what the prediction is going to be. So he's not ready yet with the [new] predictions, but we're going to go to him in just a little while."

Obviously, computers don't talk like that. They don't even talk. Collingwood was stalling for more time. It was not clear whether he was deliberately not telling the truth or was being misled. But it seemed likely that the computer was about to have the last laugh. The UNIVAC engineers were in a panic, refusing to believe what the computer was telling them with just 7 percent of the vote in the machine. UNIVAC insisted that Eisenhower would triumph overwhelmingly, winning the Southern states, almost an unthinkable feat for Republicans.

CBS begged for something to put on the air, but the engineers refused until they could check the program more thoroughly. They did so. And then incredibly, Arthur Draper, Remington-Rand's director of Advanced Research, ordered the engineers to alter the program so that it would conform with what the pundits were saying! Now, UNIVAC was reporting that the Republican nominee would capture 28 states and 317 electoral votes, a more modest victory; again the engineers played with the program so that Eisenhower led by just 9 electoral votes. Finally at 10 P.M., they went on the air with a prediction.

One hour later, the computer decided that Eisenhower was running way ahead of the Democratic nominee, Adlai Stevenson, no matter what the programmers had tried to do to its brain; it reported a landslide. Collingwood told the audience, "An hour or so ago, UNIVAC suffered a momentary aberration. He [the computer] gave us the odds on Eisenhower as only eight to seven . . . but came up later with the prediction that the odds were beyond counting, above 100 to 1, in favor of Eisenhower's election." Collingwood then turned to Arthur Draper in Philadelphia and asked him to explain "what happened there when we came out with that funny prediction?"

Draper meekly said, "We had a lot of troubles tonight. Strangely enough, they were all human and not the machine. When UNIVAC made its first prediction, we just didn't believe it. So we asked UNIVAC to forget a lot of the trend information, assuming it was wrong. . . . [But] as more votes came in, the odds came back, and it is now evident that we should have had nerve enough to believe the machine in the first place." With 7 percent of the vote in, UNIVAC gave Eisenhower 438 electoral votes; in the end he actually got 442, only a 1 percent margin of error. Undoubtedly, the UNIVAC experience would encourage CBS—and others—to rely upon computers as the competition for coming up with final results at election time intensified.

The CBS evening news remained under the steady anchor of Douglas Edwards, although the conditions under which he and his team worked were far from ideal. They occupied a crowded place on 42nd Street over Grand Central Station. The broadcast studio, thirteen blocks from Grand Central, was a converted German singing club named Liederkranz Hall. This required the staff to hustle into a cab every night at 7:20, trying to rush the broadcast material to Edwards in time for the start of the nightly news. This did not always work out. Once, when film of Queen Elizabeth's visit to Bermuda was arriving at Idlewild airport, the film director sensed that, owing to heavy traffic, time would not allow getting the film from the lab to the studio by 7:30 P.M. So the director improvised, setting up a portable processing machine at Liederkranz. Unfortunately, the machine failed and the film rolled out, dripping wet. The film editors stretched the film of the Queen's arrival all over the men's room floor until it had dried.

Edwards's newscast was the poor relation at CBS News, due largely to the awesome prestige of "See It Now." Murrow's documentary program was able to command the best equipment and triple the number of staff. Moreover, Murrow staff members received higher pay than their colleagues at CBS Television News. No one believed that it was important to pump money into Doug Edwards's nightly newscast. To work for Edwards was in effect a demotion.

Television news programs in the early 1950s had a good deal of chatter to them—due in part to television being a child of radio, due in part to its inability to communicate pictures easily. As yet there were no television correspondents; it was left to the radio correspondents to file stories for television. Most of the film in the early 1950s came from Telenews, the inexpensive syndication service. Don Hewitt found, however, that only 20 percent of it was usable; the rest of the news show was devoted to Edwards reading the news, aided by photographs, maps, and drawings, or conducting an interview.

Hewitt's greatest innovation was the double projector system. A true revolution, it gave producers and correspondents greater flexibility in covering news for television. Until the innovation, almost all television news stories were shot on silent film. Once the film reached the shop, the correspondent recorded the "voice-over" narration on an audiotape, and the two elements were combined to form the finished piece. Then the sound camera became popular, enabling the correspondent to record his sound track on the film as it was being shot on the scene of the news story. Sound and picture could then be recorded at the same time, offering immediacy: the reporter could now be shown at the scene, doing his spot.

Clear-cut progress over silent film, the new "voice-over" method was still limiting. Because sound and picture were recorded on the same film, the camera was required to focus on the reporter and his exact location.

Then along came Don Hewitt's double projector system. One day in the early 1950s, Hewitt and his film editors were looking at some footage of a speech given by Senator Robert Taft on the swollen federal budget. Although a significant piece of oratory, the speech seemed dull. Hewitt wondered out loud if it might be possible to retain Taft's sound track and illustrate it by cutting away to still photos or charts. "Talking heads" could, in this way, be used less, a welcome step forward. He was told, technically, yes it was possible. Later that day, while working on another project, Hewitt concluded that it would also be possible to cut away to film. All that was needed, his film editors advised Hewitt, was to use a second projector! Adopting that technique, it became possible to take a reel of picture on one projector and combine it with a reel of narration from the sound camera, on a second projector, and by mixing the two, produce a better story in terms of words and pictures. One great advantage: film could be shot on location and the reporter could do his narration at a later stage.

Hewitt was a genius at graphics. When the Soviets launched *Sputnik* in 1957, he built a makeshift rig, taking an ordinary globe and attaching a motor to it. Stretching a wire clothes hanger out in a straight line, he then fastened one end of the hanger to the bottom of the globe and on the other end attached a ping pong ball which had small spikes glued on to it. Once the motor was turned on, the globe would turn slowly, giving the impression that *Sputnik* itself was rotating in the heavens. The exhibit proved somewhat clumsy for Doug Edwards when he used it on his evening newscast. Still, to viewers, the Hewitt-created *Sputnik* served to make space technology slightly more comprehensible.

So inventive was Hewitt that he was forgiven for bending the rules every once in a while. One morning during the early 1960s he rushed off with a film crew to cover a New Jersey prison riot. Arriving after the event, Hewitt saw before him the choice of returning to New York empty-handed or taking the initiative. Could he simply take some background shots, he asked prison officials? No, came the terse reply. Then, relenting a bit, they allowed Hewitt and his crew into an area from which they could view part of the prison interior where inmates had congregated. Hewitt had to promise that he would not talk to the prisoners. He did so. Eyeing a dozen inmates, Hewitt decided to spring into action. "Are you rolling?" he asked a cameraman out of the side of his mouth. Hewitt gazed at the prisoners, and, placing his left hand in the crook of his right arm, thrust his right fist upward, action finger extended, the classic "Up yours" gesture. In response came catcalls, obscenities, along with tin cups and plates banging against the prison bars—in short, lots of usable footage of a "riot." When angry prison officials raced up to Don, he insisted that he had kept his word—he had not said a word to the inmates! (31)

It was not just Don Hewitt's lively imagination that gave CBS News its special character in those days. It was the conviction that there was something special about the network, something that carried over from the founding days of broadcast news in the late 1930s and World War II. When Dan Schorr joined CBS in 1953, he sensed this: "You felt you were joining a very elite group of newspeople, Murrow's people. . . . CBS acted and felt unique. I recall somewhere in the '50s, watching NBC, and seeing a story on NBC that we hadn't had. And I wished we had had, and when I said something to someone on the desk, 'Have you been watching NBC?' his reply was, 'No, NBC watches us.'" (32)

eight

"THE FAULT, DEAR BRUTUS, . . ."

Few chapters in CBS's history are as controversial as the one involving Edward R. Murrow and the series of programs he would do in the early 1950s on McCarthyism. By this time, Murrow was such a luminary, his views on almost anything held in such widespread respect, that he appeared to have carte blanche in what he could put on television. No other figure on television enjoyed so much independence; after him, CBS would impose the kind of controls that would make it all but impossible for another Murrow to surface. In Fred Friendly's apt phrase, there could not be an Ed Murrow today. (1)

As co-producer of "See It Now," Murrow was technically responsible to Sig Mickelson. In fact, Murrow had near total autonomy. Ed had watched the witch-hunt against Communism with growing pain. He had seen a few close friends lose their jobs over the McCarthy scare. Yet, by the time Murrow got around to examining McCarthyism on television, Ed would acknowledge that he was somewhat late. Few would blame him. The rest of the nation was reeling from the senator and no one until then had had the temerity to act. Still, Murrow wanted to be 100 percent certain that he was doing the right thing. He sensed the raw power of television and he asked himself repeatedly whether it was right to turn that power on a single issue or a single man and go on the attack.

Eventually, he decided to go on the attack—believing McCarthyism a cancer that was spreading.

He began in October 1953 by producing a program on "See It Now" about a 26-year-old University of Michigan student who was a meteorologist in the Air Force reserves, Lt. Milo J. Radulovich. He had been classified a security risk after his father and sister had been accused by unidentified sources of radical leanings, especially of reading "subversive" newspapers. The Radulovich program was television's first attempt to focus on McCarthyism. It was also the first time a nationally televised news broadcast had engaged itself in controversy. When the shadow of scandal hovered over Radulovich, he had been asked to resign his commission; when he refused, an Air Force board at Selfridge Field ordered his separation on security grounds. One October day at lunchtime, Murrow handed Fred Friendly a wrinkled clipping and asked him to read it. The two men agreed to send reporter-producer Joe Wershba to Detroit to gather more information about the case. Wershba read the transcript of the Air Force hearing and talked to Radulovich, his family, and their neighbors. Persuading the Radulovich family and friends to talk on camera was no problem. But the Air Force refused to let a spokesman defend its actions in public. This presented a dilemma to Murrow and his team. How could they do the program if they could only film one side? Would that not be essentially unfair?

Murrow wondered whether he ought to drop the program rather than offer only one version of what happened. Others might have dropped the program. Not Ed Murrow. By scuttling the project, he thought, he would be permitting one side, by its silence, to hold a veto power over broadcast discussion. But even as he was determined to go ahead, there were new pressures awaiting him. An Air Force general visited Murrow and Friendly, and reminded Murrow that he was considered a friend of the Air Force; the general was cordial and restrained, but his message was hardly subtle: Murrow should drop the Radulovich program.

If anything, the pressure spurred Murrow and Friendly to do the program. Their enthusiasm for the show led them to ask CBS to take out an advertisement in *The New York Times*. But CBS was skittish and said no. So the two men paid $1,500 out of their own pockets and placed the advertisement in their own names. The Radulovich program would test Murrow's vaunted position of power and independence at CBS. He was very much aware that he was placing himself in a ticklish situation. He knew that what he would say at the end of the program—the "tailpiece" in the lexicon of television documentaries—would have a crucial bearing on the public's response. "Leave me enough time because we are going to live or die by our ending," he said. "Management is going to howl, and we may blow ourselves right out of the water, but we simply can't do an 'on the other hand' ending for this." (2) Murrow and Friendly knew only too well how Paul White, the wartime head of the CBS News Department, would have felt about the Radulovich program. He would not have felt good. In controversial issues, White believed, the audience should never learn where the analyst stood. This case was different. Neutrality, Murrow decided, was simply out of place: "We can't make the air force's case if they won't help us. Besides, some issues aren't equally balanced. We can't sit there every Tuesday night and give the impression that for every argument on one side there is an equal one on the other side." (3)

When it came time for the program, Murrow demonstrated that the newspaper Radulovich's father had read was harmless. A Serbian-language newspaper read in Yugoslavia, it expressed support for Marshal Tito, the Yugoslavian leader, hardly demonstrable proof of being a Communist as Tito himself had little affection for the Soviets. Murrow concluded the program with an offer to the Air Force to reply, adding: "Whatever happens in this whole area of the relationship between the individual and the state, we will do ourselves; it cannot be blamed upon Malenkov, Mao Tse-tung, or even our allies. It seems to us—that is, to Fred Friendly and myself—that this is a subject that should be argued about endlessly . . . ." When the program ended, "See It Now" staff members and engineers, tears in their eyes, crowded around Murrow to shake his hand. Phones rang; congratulatory telegrams and letters arrived; some newspaper columnists assailed the program but more praised it. CBS management was deafeningly silent.

Most significantly, Lt. Radulovich was cleared of being a security risk. The announcement came in a statement filmed for the "See It Now" program on November 24. Murrow introduced Secretary of the Air Force Harold E. Talbott who said that he had reviewed the Radulovich case and had decided he was not a security risk. "I have, therefore, directed that Radulovich be retained in his present status in the United States Air Force." It was a great victory for "See It Now," for Murrow, Friendly, and the others.

All this while, Ed Murrow had been a recognizable star within the news broadcasting field; he had never become a national sensation. That only occurred once he began to moderate a program far afield from the news, one that seemed totally out of character for him. After Murrow paid two "television visits" to a celebrity's home as part of "See It Now," the idea arose that he adopt that format to a fully fledged program. It was called "Person to Person." When movie star John Cassavetes, who was a guest on the new show, asked Murrow why he was doing it, Ed replied honestly, "To do the show I want to do, I have to do the show that I don't want to do." It aired for the first time on October 2, 1953. If "See It Now" was a gourmet dish, "Person to Person" was pablum: it avoided contention as if it were indecent to intrude upon the celebrities' time with such unpleasantness. The formula clicked. "Person"'s ratings were higher than those of "See It Now," and it became a top-ten show. The reason? In the words of broadcasting historian Eric Barnouw, the show had "a *Vogue* and *House Beautiful* appeal, along with a voyeuristic element." (4)

Each Friday evening Ed Murrow sat in an easy chair in the studio, famous cigarette in hand, talking breezily with guests from all walks of life. Seated in their living rooms, the guests had to endure the disagreeable reality of television producers and cameramen arriving on the scene and dumping their paraphernalia all about. No one objected. The exposure was well worth the bother. For Murrow, "Person to Person's" popularity served as a shield of immunity against the slings and arrows that were tossed at him over "See It Now."

On the opening "Person to Person," Murrow visited baseball player Roy Campanella, and then conductor Leopold Stokowski and his wife, the former Gloria Vanderbilt. Three cameras and ten miles of wire connected each home with the studio, and wireless microphones enabled the hosts to move around their homes, followed by cameras, as they showed paintings, played piano, or pointed out trophies. Awkward and unexpected moments were inevitable. When Krishna Menon, the Indian delegate to the United Nations, was asked a question by Murrow that appeared to imply criticism of Indian policy, the ambassador said, "That is an improper question for you to ask me." Undaunted, Murrow corrected the politician: "Perhaps it is an improper question for you to answer." When John F. Kennedy, then a U.S. senator, appeared with bride Jackie, Murrow asked him about his wartime ordeal as the commander of PT-109. "An interesting experience," the future president said. "Interesting?" replied Murrow. "I should think that would be one of the great understatements."

Murrow managed to entice the Duke and Duchess of Windsor into making their first television appearance on "Person to Person," but the conversation was dull and superficial. More colorfully, after waiting two years, he finally landed Marilyn Monroe for the show (she took five hours to put on her makeup). Murrow had actually wanted that program to feature Marilyn Monroe and Dr. Albert Schweitzer, or if he couldn't get Schweitzer, financier Bernard Baruch. But he had to settle for conductor Sir Thomas Beecham. The show still garnered high ratings. Not every program went so smoothly. When A. C. Neilson, the father of the ratings system named after him, gave a demonstration of the recording device which enabled him to estimate television audience sizes, it didn't work.

At one stage, it appeared that there were too many celebrities crowding the show, and so Murrow brought on a mailman and a farmer. But the audience complained, arguing with some justification that if they wanted to meet simple folks, they could visit their own relatives. Murrow brought back the celebs, visiting Anita Ekberg, Admiral Richard Byrd, Lawrence Welk, Liberace, Pat Weaver, Billy Graham, Jane Russell, Eddie Fisher and Debbie Reynolds, Dr. George Gallup, and Hal March. During 1956 he had 93 guests. By the time the show ran its course on June 26, 1959, he had gone through 500.

Ever since the spring of 1953 Murrow and his colleagues at "See It Now" had been contemplating doing a program on Senator Joseph McCarthy and his investigations. "See It Now" had instructed its camera crews to begin compiling filmed records of all the senator's speeches and hearings. No firm date existed for the airing of the material. Murrow was hesitating. Senator McCarthy had given his first speech in March 1950, and here it was three years later and Murrow had still not engaged the senator. Although he had done the Radulovich program in the fall of 1953, he could not bring himself to go forward against McCarthy. It was clear to Murrow that, were he to go after McCarthy, he would have a nearly impossible time demonstrating fairness. He also worried that a CBS show on the senator might only serve McCarthy's purposes rather than cut him down to size.

Television in the early 1950s was still experimental in many ways, still nervous about whether it was right to take on governmental and public figures. This was long before Vietnam, long before Watergate, long before it would become acceptable for someone to appear on television and denounce the people in Washington.

It was remarkable. "See It Now" was about to launch a full-scale attack against one of the most powerful institutions in the country—the U.S. senator from Wisconsin—and the power to undertake such an act rested purely with one man, Edward R. Murrow. That could have never happened in later years. Fred Friendly, looking back to that early period, would say that Murrow, were he around today, would not be doing television documentaries; he would most likely be working for a place like National Public Radio. (5)

By February 1954 Murrow was moving toward a decision to do the show. Some believed that he may have been spurred by word that the army was planning to go after McCarthy. Whatever the reason, the program was scheduled for airing on March 9, 1954. Feelers were put out whether CBS would place an advertisement in advance of the program and again, as with Radulovich, the answer was no. Up to the last moment, Murrow had his doubts. He had informed Paley he was doing the broadcast and asked him if he wanted to see it.

"Are you sure of your facts?" Paley asked Murrow. "Are you on safe ground?"

"Yes, I am," replied Murrow. "No question about it."

"In that case," Paley said, "I'll wait until everybody sees it." (6)

Paley did suggest to Murrow that he grant McCarthy equal time, and Murrow, believing this was only fair, agreed. Paley expressed concern that McCarthy might try to counter Murrow by digging into his past. Accordingly, Paley won Murrow's approval to hire an attorney who did his own investigating. He found nothing. Just before the program was aired, the CBS chairman phoned Murrow to say, "Ed, I'm with you today and I'll be with you tomorrow." (7) Sig Mickelson was asked if he wanted to see the show. He had not screened anything done by Murrow and Friendly before. He said no, too. Mickelson and Paley reflected the general CBS view: stay clear of the Murrow program, don't identify with it, avoid giving the impression that Ed had the company's blessing. As the show was about to be aired, Murrow and Friendly could not find anyone at the middle-management level to take an interest in what they were doing.

Ed was worried. Paley had asked him if he was sure of his facts; he did not ask whether Murrow was sure he was going to be fair to all sides. CBS had a long-standing policy against newscasters indulging in personal opinion. It had not always been easy to keep everyone in line. No one, not H. V. Kaltenborn, not Cecil Brown, not William Shirer had gone as far as Murrow planned to go in expressing a point-of-view.

Realizing the program's significance, Friendly and Murrow were tempted to tell their sponsor, Alcoa, that they wanted to run the commercials at the start and finish and eliminate the middle break. But rather than alert Alcoa to what was in the works, the two broadcasters went ahead and changed the timing of the commercials themselves. Just as the program was to start, Friendly leaned over to Murrow and whispered, "This is going to be a tough one." Yes, Murrow replied, "and after this one they're all going to be tough." (8) Friendly was so nervous that when he went to start his stopwatch in the control room at the beginning of the program, he missed the button.

The program was a mixture of McCarthy appearing on film and Ed Murrow refuting his charges. There was nothing new in seeing the Wisconsin senator on television, spewing forth his venom. What was new was the Murrow attack on him, marking the first time that the mass media had examined what the senator was saying, and assailed him for it. There on the screen was McCarthy warning that if this fight against Communism "becomes a fight between America's two parties, one party would be destroyed—and the Republic cannot endure very long under a one-party system." There he was now questioning a witness: "You know the Civil Liberties Union has been listed as a front for . . . the Communist Party?"—and there was Murrow chiming in: "The Attorney General's List does not and never has listed the A.C.L.U. as subversive. Nor does the F.B.I. or any other federal government agency."

Murrow had worked out the concluding part endlessly. He knew that what he had to say then would make or break the broadcast. Six times he rewrote the "tailpiece" until he was finally satisfied. "Earlier, the Senator asked, 'Upon what meat does this our Caesar feed?' Had he looked three lines earlier in Shakespeare's *Caesar* he would have found this line, which is not altogether inappropriate: 'The fault, dear Brutus, is not in our stars but in ourselves.'

"No one familiar with the history of this country can deny that Congressional committees are useful. It is necessary to investigate before legislating, but the line between investigation and persecuting is a very fine one, and the junior senator from Wisconsin has stepped over it repeatedly. His primary achievement has been in confusing the public mind as between the internal and . . . external threat of Communism. We must not confuse dissent with disloyalty. We must remember always that accusation is not proof and that conviction depends upon evidence and due process of law. We will not walk in fear, one of another. We will not be driven by fear into an age of unreason, if we dig deep in our history and our doctrine, and remember that we are not descended from fearful men, not from men who feared to write, to speak, to associate with, and to defend causes which were for the moment unpopular.

"This is no time for men who oppose Senator McCarthy's methods to keep silent, or for those who approve. We can deny our heritage and our history, but we cannot escape responsibility for the result. There is no way for a citizen of a republic to abdicate his responsibilities. As a nation we have come into our full inheritance at a tender age. We proclaim ourselves—as indeed we are—the defenders of freedom, what's left of it, but we cannot defend freedom abroad by deserting it at home. The actions of the junior senator from Wisconsin have caused alarm and dismay amongst our allies abroad and given considerable comfort to our enemies, and whose fault is that? Not really his. He didn't create this situation of fear; he merely exploited it, and rather successfully. Cassius was right: 'The fault, dear Brutus, is not in our stars but in ourselves.' . . . Good night, and good luck."

Few other television programs would have such an impact. Don Hollenbeck, delivering the news that night at 11, concluded by saying, "I want to associate myself with every word just spoken by Ed Murrow." Once the program was over, viewers expressed their enthusiasm for Murrow. By 1:30 A.M. the network had received over 1,000 telegrams, all in favor of the show. More than 2,000 phone calls came in as well. This was the greatest mass response to a network television show, outdoing even the famous "Checkers" television speech given by Vice President Richard Nixon. Nineteen hours after the McCarthy program was aired, the phones at CBS were still ringing. A few days later, riding in a car with Eric Sevareid, Murrow was stopped by taxicab drivers who wanted to congratulate him. He walked into places as well where people rose and saluted him.

Ironically, Murrow's network seemed far less pleased. "Good show, sorry you did it," was the way Murrow described his CBS colleagues' reaction to the show. Inflamed, some CBS board members demanded that Paley rein Murrow in. But the CBS chairman quietly came to Murrow's support, meeting with him every day to figure out how to respond to personal attacks. It was Paley who had suggested that Murrow respond by saying that history would one day decide whether he or McCarthy had served their country better. And Ed did just that. In his memoirs, Paley deftly skirted the issue of whether he actually liked the McCarthy broadcast. He gave Murrow and Friendly credit for exposing the senator's more diabolical methods, but he fell short of any direct praise of the program. Revealingly, Paley suggested that McCarthy damaged himself more in his reply to Murrow than in the original Murrow broadcast.

The response to the program was at times exuberantly pro-Murrow. "In a sense, you are his Zola," wrote columnist Harriet Van Horne in a private note to Murrow, "and thus we are all in your debt. Your 'j'accuse' was quiet and cool, and therefore the more effective. Considering the climate of opinion we live in these days, you are an extraordinarily brave man." (9) Author Laura Z. Hobson blurted out at the television screen when the program was being shown, "Bless you, damn it, bless you." *The New York Times'* Jack Gould called it the next day "a superb and fighting documentary . . . a long step forward in television journalism." Phone calls came in from such people as former President Harry Truman, U.S. Senator Mike Monroney, comedian Groucho Marx, and Bishop Bernard Sheil of Chicago. Scientist Albert Einstein even wrote a letter asking to see Murrow. Artist Ben Shahn sent Murrow and Friendly two original drawings he had done just after the program with an inscription to the two men. The only call Murrow felt obliged to make was to Archbishop Cushing of Boston. The archbishop was to be a guest on Murrow's "Person to Person" show the following week, and Murrow asked him if he might now be embarrassed and would like to postpone the interview for a few months or indefinitely. "Mr. Murrow," said the archbishop, "you and I have a long-standing engagement. I expect to keep it."

Not all comment was positive. Gilbert Seldes, the critic for the *Saturday Review,* assailed Murrow and Friendly for calling the show a report when it was an attack: "In the long run," wrote Seldes, "it is more important to use our communications systems properly than to destroy McCarthy . . . ."

At first, McCarthy turned down CBS's offer to reply. Vice President Nixon was given the time: somewhat ambiguously, he urged McCarthy to be true to the Republican Party's philosophy. Murrow and Friendly could not tell from that what the official view of the Eisenhower administration was toward the program; if they feared that the president might signal his associates to blast away at CBS for taking on one of his party members, they were quickly assuaged when that same week Treasury Secretary George Humphrey appeared as a guest on "Person to Person." (After writing his 1967 book "*Due to Circumstances Beyond Our Control . . .*," Fred Friendly sent a copy to Eisenhower. The former president replied that he had been glad to read about the Murrow-McCarthy broadcasts because he had never known about them at the time. He had also never known that he had had such allies as these two broadcasters. (10)

Two days after the program, McCarthy appeared on the radio to unearth a blast at the "See It Now" host. Appearing on the Fulton Lewis, Jr., radio broadcast, the senator said: "I may say, Fulton, that I have a little difficulty answering the specific attack he [Murrow] made, because I never listen to the extreme left-wing, bleeding-heart element of radio and television." On his next radio broadcast, Murrow replied: "The Senator may have me there. I may be a bleeding heart, not being quite sure what it means. As for being extreme left-wing, that is political shorthand, but if the Senator means that I am somewhat to the left of his position and that of Louis XIV, then he is correct."

Ed Murrow seemed to take the reaction, pro and con, to the program in stride. He tried to suggest, though few would believe him, that he hadn't said anything new about McCarthy, he has said nothing that hadn't been said on radio before. But that was the very point. While those things may have been said on radio, no one had taken note of them. But, when said on television, everyone stood up and paid attention. That was the power of television. Just how powerful? A new Gallup poll noted that McCarthy's popularity had dropped suddenly from its all-time high in January—undoubtedly the result of the "See It Now" program. McCarthy's downfall would accelerate. On April 22, the Army-McCarthy hearings opened and were shown live on television for the next two months. Later, the U.S. Senate voted to censure McCarthy by a vote of 67–22 for conduct that was described as "contemptuous, contumacious, denunciatory, unworthy, inexcusable and reprehensible."

After it was all over, Murrow would acknowledge that what had helped him face the opposition to the McCarthy program was the new popularity and respectability he had gained from doing the "Person to Person" program. What had helped him also was the sympathy and encouragement from his sponsor. Not that Alcoa was thrilled at what Murrow was doing, but officials there seemed to understand that sometimes it was necessary. After the first of the McCarthy programs, Irvin W. Wilson, president of Alcoa, told Murrow that he wouldn't ask him not to do such programs. He would simply ask that he not do them every week. Murrow's reply was honest enough: he and Friendly wouldn't do such programs every week either. Public opinion was polarized, and accordingly Alcoa received lots of angry mail. Its dealers were pressured. Newspaper columnists denounced the company. In time, even Murrow's mail was 5 to 4 against him, but Alcoa stuck with him.

McCarthy finally did reply on April 6, 1954. It cost CBS $6,336.99 but the network had no choice—it had to be fair. "Now, ordinarily," McCarthy said, "I would not take time out from the important work at hand to answer Murrow. However, in this case I feel justified in doing so because Murrow is a symbol, the leader and the cleverest of the jackal pack which is always found at the throat of anyone who dares to expose individual Communists and traitors." Some thought his reply ineffectual, some the opposite. Frank Stanton called Friendly into his office and showed him the results of a CBS-commissioned poll. It showed that 59 percent of those questioned had seen the McCarthy rebuttal program or heard about it, and of those, 33 percent believed that McCarthy had in fact raised doubts about Murrow or proved him pro-Communist. Friendly responded that, had the poll been 5 to 1 in McCarthy's favor and 10 to 1 against Murrow, there would have been greater justification for having done the March 9 telecast. Stanton appeared disturbed that CBS's business relationships might be affected by all this strife, as evidenced by the poll; Friendly, for his part, was angry that someone had thought it important to commission the poll in the first place.

Murrow was still obviously worried about how history would record what he had done. Remembering Paley's advice on what to say, he talked to newsmen on April 6 after the McCarthy reply: "When the record is finally written, as it will be one day, it will answer the question, Who has helped the Communist cause and who has served his country better. Senator McCarthy or I? I would like to be remembered by the answer to that question."

There would be one more in the sequence of broadcasts related to McCarthyism, but this one would only come on January 5, 1955—just after the Senate censure of the senator had finally condemned him to moral defeat. The broadcast, a 30-minute interview with J. Robert Oppenheimer, a creator of the atomic bomb and critic of the hydrogen one, provided a forum for one of the senator's victims. It seemd to be Murrow and Friendly's way of letting the supporters of McCarthyism know that there could be, indeed should be recompense paid to those who suffered under the senator from Wisconsin.

Oppenheimer had been a true victim of the senator. In his April 6 reply, McCarthy charged that the hydrogen bomb had been delayed eighteen months by traitors in the U.S. government, a reference that was taken to include Oppenheimer. Soon after that he was stripped of his security clearance as a consultant to the Atomic Energy Commission's general advisory committee. Murrow and Friendly originally had a different focus in mind in conceiving "A Conversation with Dr. J. Robert Oppenheimer." The program was supposed to be about the Institute for Advanced Study at Princeton, New Jersey, of which Oppenheimer was director. But, after examining the series of filmed interviews with Institute personalities, Murrow and Friendly agreed that only the two-and-half-hour interview with Oppenheimer was worth airing.

To get it on television would not be easy. For one thing, Oppenheimer objected, saying that his colleagues at the Institute would be miffed at his getting so much attention. Murrow had to phone him and announce that the interview was running, whether Oppenheimer liked it or not. Afterward, Murrow said, he was sure Oppenheimer would agree that the interview had been good for him and for the Institute. Murrow and Friendly showed the interview to Bill Paley just before airtime, simply because they were so proud of it. Meekly, they admitted that it ran 2 minutes over the limit. Brimming with enthusiasm for the show, Paley said it would be all right to run it over. Of course, technically that was impossible. The phone company pulled the network's lines 30 seconds before the show concluded.

During the interview, the scientist did not refer to the security ruling but instead talked about the implications of increasing government control over research and its relationship to the freedom of the human mind and man's future on earth. At one stage, Murrow asked Oppenheimer whether it was true that humans had already discovered a method of destroying humanity. "Well," he replied, " I suppose that really has always been true. You could always beat everybody to death. You mean to do it by inadvertence?" Yes, Murrow replied. "Not quite," said Oppenheimer. "Not quite. You can certainly destroy enough of humanity so that only the greatest act of faith can persuade you that what's left will be human." He spoke about the danger of nuclear fallout as well: "I'm not worried about it. I tend still to worry about war rather than peace. I think . . . the scale of things in these experimental undertakings is . . . so vastly smaller and their location so much more secure than . . . what you'd expect if . . . the battle were joined, that we do well to worry about the latter before the former."

The show was highly praised. Lots of messages flowed in. The one Murrow and Friendly liked the best came from Princeton. "You were right as often, Robert." CBS took some heat—for putting that "traitor" on the air. Some now called it the "Red Network." The Oppenheimer broadcast became a classic. Murrow and Friendly produced a 48-minute version of the interview for universities and colleges. There were sad consequences for Oppenheimer—he was hailed by the scientific community for his display of humanity; but right-wing groups were so noisy in protest against him that it was only in the early 1960s that CBS felt it could safely put him back on the air again.

The handwriting was on the wall for documentary programs. Audiences watching entertainment programs were increasing, drawing sponsors in their wake. Those sponsors had little interest in a "See It Now," not unless it could attract money the way a highly rated quiz show did. The year 1954 was the year of the Quiz Show: "I've Got a Secret," "Stop the Music," "Place the Face," "Name That Tune," "What's My Line?," "Twenty-one," and "The $64,000 Question." CBS had introduced "Question" in 1955, and within a few weeks it had become television's most popular show, outdoing even " I Love Lucy." As soon as Ed Murrow saw "Question," he realized that his labors were about to be pushed aside. When, on June 7, he sat in the control room and for 5 minutes watched the debut of "Question," which had preceded "See It Now," he turned to Fred Friendly and asked, "How long do you think we're going to hang on to this time period now?" (11) It was no secret that CBS could earn three to four times as much by putting a highly rated quiz show in the "See It Now" time slot. What was more, at $100,000 a shot, "See It Now" was expensive. Soon thereafter, sure enough, the decision was taken to scrub "See It Now." Meeting with Murrow, Bill Paley told him, "I've got great news for you, Ed. We want your program to be an hour." Before Murrow could decide whether the news was really "great," the chairman delivered the knockout punch: "But it won't be on at 10:30 Tuesday night. It'll be on eight to ten times a year." Wags began calling it "See It Now and Then."

It was all the result of "The $64,000 Question," a program produced by a independent production firm owned largely by Louis G. Cowan. "Question" would boost Cowan to a position of supremacy at CBS. A few weeks after it was aired, Cowan went to work for CBS as a senior adviser in programming. He was a creative troubleshooter, and he did so well at it that three years later he became president of the CBS Television Network. As the president of CBS Television, he gave warm support to both Murrow and Friendly, making sure that time was found for news specials, resisting the growing commercial pressures. Once, he clashed with Paley, agreeing with the news division that a United Nations debate should be shown live. The occasion was the 1958 Lebanon crisis. Eisenhower had sent in the marines, and war seemed possible. Paley laced into his network president, contending that Cowan was wasting money; Cowan retorted, melodramatically perhaps, that he had joined CBS purely because

Bing Crosby

Frank Stanton (left) and Bill Paley

Black Rock, CBS headquarters in New York City

rson Welles and cast
rform "The War of the Worlds"

Paul White (standing) is huddled with (seated from left to right): Ed Murrow,
Maurice Hindus (an authority on the Soviet Union), Robert Trout, and
Hans V. Kaltenborn

Ed Murrow (left) and Bill Shirer

Bill Paley (left) and Arthur Godfrey

Ed Sullivan is flanked by the four Beatles

Portrait of Walter Cronkite

Douglas Edwards

"I Love Lucy"

The "60 Minutes" cast (left to right): Ed Bradley, Mike Wallace, Morley Safer, Don Hewitt, Harry Reasoner, and Diane Sawyer

Dan Rather reports on the TWA hijacking of June 1985

Portrait of Larry Tisch

Peter Goldmark with color television receiver, January 1, 1946

Jackie Gleason

Portrait of Jim Aubrey

M*A*S*H cast—the 4077th—including (front row, far left): Hawkeye (Alan Alda), prepares a hearty reception when they hear a rumor that Marilyn Monroe is coming to visit the unit, April 18, 1963

"All in the Family": Carroll O'Conner and Jean Stapleton

Jack Benny

Fred Friendly (left) and Ed Murrow during the "See It Now" days

"Beverly Hillbillies" cast

of the network's strong tradition of service, nurtured by people like Ed Klauber and Ed Murrow. Where was that sense of service if the network ignored such major issues?

Billed as the largest jackpot program on radio or television, "Question" made its sponsor Revlon ecstatic. "The $64,000 Question" reached the number one spot in the ratings within six weeks. No program had risen so speedily in years. By September, the commercial for Revlon's Living Lipstick was scratched from the show after it had been sold out and stores had begun phoning the factory with desperate pleas for more shipments. Hal March, the program's master of ceremonies, asked the public to be patient. Las Vegas casinos emptied during the program. In White Sulphur Springs, West Virginia, a convention of wholesale druggists took a break to keep track of contestants' progress. Once, an announcement was made at the convention: "The Marine (Captain Richard S. McCutchen) has answered the question!" The druggists cheered wildly. Riding on the success of "Question," the next season "The $64,000 Challenge" was introduced by the same production firm. Winners in "Question" would go on to compete in "Challenge." Thus it was that 11-year-old Robert Strom, with a speciality in electronics, won $224,000. The greatest money-winner, however, was Teddy Nadler, a 49-year-old former civil servant from St. Louis, who had never earned over $70 a week but won $252,000 on "Challenge."

By 1955, the money was rolling in to television in large quantities. And CBS, thanks to a highly successful programming schedule, was grabbing a large part. The audiences were getting larger, accounting for higher revenues for CBS. Since 1951, the number of televisions in homes had tripled, and the number of affiliates had doubled. CBS Television had become the largest single advertising medium in the world. Its ratings were incredible: in 1955 CBS had seven of the top ten shows: "The $64,000 Question," "I Love Lucy," "Toast of the Town," (renamed "The Ed Sullivan Show" that same year), "The Jack Benny Show," "December Bride," "I've Got a Secret," and "The General Electric Theater." The top network in popularity that year, CBS would remain number one in audience ratings for the next twenty-one years. Helping the network was a new adult Western, "Gunsmoke," a favorite of Bill Paley's. The show, which debuted in 1955, appeared in the top ten for thirteen years and had many imitators. But at first the show's producers had trouble finding someone to play the starring role of Marshall Dillon. Heavyweight William Conrad, the original Marshall Dillon who tamed Dodge City on the radio program, was not a candidate for the television role. Few auditioned, believing there was little to be gained by playing a television marshall. They were of course dead wrong. John Wayne was thought to be a natural for the television marshall, but, in demurring, he suggested an unknown actor named James Arness, then under contract to Wayne's production company. Until then Arness had done little—his largest role had been playing the title role in "The Thing." He had played a 250-pound vegetable from outer space.

Those CBS correspondents who had the chance to work overseas in the 1950s knew that they were following in Ed Murrow's golden footsteps. There was a great tradition to uphold. In upholding it, they had a lot of fun—and frustration. "It was absolutely marvelous," remembered Ernie Leiser, who had been stationed in West Germany for CBS from 1956 to 1960. "In the first place there was a great premium then on being a specialist in a country and I was pretty much a specialist on Central Europe, especially Germany. You could really get into a subject. The other delightful part was that there was not the trans-Atlantic phone communication on a daily or hourly basis that there is now. There were no satellites, no videotapes. So what you would do is—mostly you were on your own. You would dream up stories, film them with your camera crew, and in effect put together a piece for the 'Evening News.'" (12)

Daniel Schorr was overseas for CBS in those days too. He had began his journalism career at the age of 12 when he organized a four-page mimeographed monthly in the Bronx Jewish Center where he had been studying Hebrew. A year later Dan interviewed the police after observing a suicide leap outside his family's apartment-house window. He phoned the *Bronx Home News* and collected his first five dollars as a reporter. There followed work on his college newspaper and stringing for the big-city newspapers. His mother wanted him to be an attorney; she was suspect of journalism as a respectable profession. But it was too late. In 1953, while doing radio reports from Holland, Schorr reported on a major flood and soon came to Ed Murrow's attention. Invited to join CBS News in Washington as a staffer, Schorr hesitated, believing broadcasting to be less serious than print journalism. Realizing that his long-standing ambition to write for the *The New York Times* was not achievable, he accepted the CBS job. Upon arriving in Washington, Schorr spent the next eighteen months covering the State Department and Senator Joseph McCarthy.

Soon thereafter he went abroad, this time for CBS Radio, experiencing a number of difficulties common to foreign correspondents at the time. Recalled Schorr: "You were never quite sure whether you were going to broadcast that day. Anything like sunspots, magnetic interference or whatever would simply blot out the show." (13) But there was a good part: radio correspondents had more time on the air than today, the average spot lasted 2 minutes rather than today's 15 or 30 seconds.

In the summer of 1955, Schorr arrived in Moscow soon after NBC had placed its own correspondent, Irving R. Levine, there. Sending letter

---

after letter to Soviet leader Nikita Khrushchev, asking him to allow CBS to be represented in the Soviet Union, CBS only managed to put its own correspondent in Moscow once the Soviets granted visas to all newsmen who wished to cover West German Chancellor Konrad Adenauer's visit to the Soviet Union. The good news was that Schorr finally had his visa. The bad: it was good for only one week—for the duration of the Adenauer visit. Schorr managed to stay on in Moscow, but he was never able to open a full-scale bureau there. The obstacle was CBS, not the Soviets. Although it was several years since the McCarthy period and network blacklisting, the network was still jittery.

After a short delay, Schorr was permitted to broadcast from a studio in the Central Post Office, but that turned out to be little more than a glass telephone booth that did not keep out the nearby noise. When a New York technician asked Schorr if he had anything to deaden the sound, Dan took a fur coat, put it on, buried the microphone inside it, and suddenly the sound was acceptable. Unfortunately, because he had the fur coat over his head, Schorr couldn't read the script. It was too dark. Ad-libbing was unthinkable: the script had already been approved by the censor. New York said to go ahead anyway. But before he did, Schorr shouted out, "I'm going ahead. I'm going to do what is substantially in the script. But if I change a word here or there, it is only because I am ad-libbing. But I don't intend to give any other information." That little speech was meant for the listening censor. To his gleeful surprise, he was not cut off.

He tried to negotiate staying longer. Even after the Soviets let him remain, he realized he was at a disadvantage: NBC's Irving Levine was allowed to broadcast from Radio Moscow; Schorr was not. At first Schorr had no idea why. Then, someone in the Soviet Foreign Office explained that no one knew what the Columbia Broadcasting System meant. Where was Dan Schorr from? Was he from the country Colombia? From America? Levine gained an advantage as well because NBC was regarded in Moscow as the "national" broadcasting arm of the United States of America.

Another complication for Schorr had to do with shipping CBS film out of the Soviet Union. Because the U.S. government would not permit Soviet film crews working in the United States to ship their film to Moscow, the Soviets reciprocated by not permitting Dan Schorr to ship CBS film out of the Soviet Union. To get around this seemingly unsurmountable obstacle, Schorr hit upon a scheme that he employed once or twice a week until he left Russia at the end of 1957. Locating American tourists returning to the United States, he asked them to take the film with them—surreptitiously. So severe was the restriction that he and Irving Levine collaborated in the ploy. Once a tourist was found, a cable was sent to the CBS office in Paris or Brussels advising time of arrival and asking the office to grant the "usual courtesy." When asked why a tourist would engage in such a seemingly dangerous act, Schorr replied with a twinkle in his eye: "Irving Levine and I were very important people. They [the American tourists] had seen us on television back in America. We were very romantic. . . . We would tell them, this is film; it depends on you whether Walter Cronkite will have the story or not. It was a big adventure. We were also able to tell them that nobody has been stopped. They rarely refused." (14)

In June 1957 Schorr conducted a free-wheeling interview with Khrushchev, arranged by Frank Stanton, inside the Kremlin over "Face the Nation." Predicting that "your grandchildren in America will live under Socialism," the Soviet leader proposed a "small step" toward disarmament and offered the first public hint of the Sino-Soviet feud. With Stalinist excesses still in Americans' minds, President Eisenhower reflected a certain irritation at CBS when he assailed the network for giving the Russian leader access to an American audience. At a news conference, Eisenhower suggested that CBS was nothing more than "a commercial firm trying to improve its commercial standing."

Paley, in an internal memo, retorted that the Khrushchev interview was "one of the most outstanding broadcasts ever carried on radio and television." (15) Frank Stanton was also firmly in Schorr's corner. "I come from a commercial organization," he told the National Press Club. "A major duty of that organization is to report the news." CBS picked up some major awards for the Khrushchev interview. Supporting the network, *Variety* hailed CBS as "the undisputed strongman of television journalism . . . within the past year the web has had a lineup . . . comprising Khrushchev, Nehru, Tito, China's Chou-Enlai, Egypt's Nasser, Israel's Ben-Gurion, and Burma's U Nu, all in interviews with CBS correspondents or with Ed Murrow on "See It Now."

Eventually Schorr lost the right to report from the Soviet Union, apparently for defying censorship too often. He was back in the United States in 1958, hoping for a visa to return to Moscow. Schorr went on a lecture tour, and owners of CBS stations, who tended to be right-wing, treated him warmly as the person who had stood up to the Communists. He went on to cover the United Nations, Warsaw, Geneva, Paris, Havana, Germany, and Eastern Europe.

In the mid-1950s a future CBS personality was building a reputation through a bold, new interview program on television. Interview shows had tended to be dull, with host and guest engaging in banal, insignificant chatter. Mike Wallace was determined to change all that. Becoming part detective, part tough guy, part journalist, Wallace believed that a "third-degree" approach with a guest could elicit intriguing information and make for a lively interview. Using the aggressive tack, he became known as "Mike Malice" and, just as sweetly, "The Grand Inquisitor." It all started in the fall of 1956 with Wallace's "Night Beat" program, a small show seen only in New York City and its surroundings, on which he did face-to-face interviews. Wallace was 38 years old but had been in broadcasting for 17 years.

He had been born in the Boston suburb of Brookline (his real name: Myron Leon Wallace), the son of Russian-Jewish immigrants. He had gone to the University of Michigan where he intended to study English as a prelude to a career in teaching or law. But in his sophomore year he dropped in on Morris Hall, the University's broadcast center, and soon thereafter dropped English for Speech and Broadcasting. He came upon a mentor, Professor Waldo Abbot, who explained to him the fundamentals of broadcasting. Abbot also arranged an announcer's job for Wallace at a small station, WOOD, in Grand Rapids, following the young man's graduation in 1939. Wallace did more than announce; he took part in the news, quiz shows, and commercials. After nine months he moved on to Detroit and WXYZ, a major broadcasting outlet. Again, he was a man for all seasons, dabbling in announcing, narrating, even doing a little acting. Wallace also read news items from the wire services.

In 1941 Wallace was in Chicago, his home for the next decade except for two wartime years when he served as a naval officer in the Pacific. Discharged in 1946, he did news, soap operas, and panel shows and was then hired to do the interviewing on the Chicago station WGN's "Famous Names" broadcast five afternoons a week from the Blackstone Hotel. For the most part Wallace interviewed show business personalities about their latest play, movie, or nightclub act. In the late 1950s he teamed with his wife Buff Cobb on a Chicago radio talk-show called "The Chez Show." By the spring of 1951 CBS had brought the program to New York and called it simply "Mike and Buff." It lasted three years. In 1954 he appeared in 100 performances of a broadway comedy called "Reclining Figure." Although acting had seemed attractive at first, he would tire of the stage. Later, when he had become a highly successful CBS news correspondent, Wallace appeared uncomfortable when his past was brought up, the "Mike and Buff" show, the commercials, the acting. That image wasn't in keeping with his wish to be considered a serious news correspondent, and only that. Just as "Mike and Buff" were going off the air in 1954, his marriage to Buff Cobb ended as well. Audiences watched them quarrel on the air, and thought it was all in fun. Apparently it was not. In 1955, Wallace began anchoring the Channel 5 evening news programs at 7 and 11. Scrapping that format during the summer of 1956, the local New York City station replaced it with "Night Beat." It lasted two years, and in that time it became one of the most talked-about programs on the air. Wallace managed to put his guests on the spot. A New York milliner named Mr. John was asked why there were so many homosexuals in the fashion industry. His embarrassed reply: "That's not worth talking about." When Mike asked Elsa Maxwell why she had never married, the high-society partygiver, admitted, "I was never interested in sex, quite frankly. It never interested me. I was never interested for one minute, ever." When underworld figure Mickey Cohen appeared on "The Mike Wallace Interview," the ABC program which was a network-wide successor to Channel 5's "Night Beat" in 1957, Wallace noted that he engaged in killing to which Cohen replied: "I have killed no man that in the first place didn't deserve killing." "By whose standard?" Mike asked. "By the standards," Cohen responded, "of our way of life. And I actually, in all of these killings—in all of these what you would call killings—I had no alternatives. It was either my life or their life." Cohen also made comments about the Los Angeles police chief and members of the police department that led ABC to issue a public apology over the air.

Another rising CBS News star was Harry Reasoner. He was 31 years old in the summer of 1956 when he joined CBS Television News. Reasoner was the first television reporter to be named a CBS correspondent. He had been a public relations man, had written news for a radio station, and had served for three years in the Far East as an officer of the U.S. Information Agency. Then in late 1954 he began working in television news. CBS's Sig Mickelson, a teacher of his at the University of Minnesota, had advised him to get some experience and so Harry became news director of KEYD-TV in Minneapolis. Reasoner said it was a good place to learn about television "because when I did something badly, there weren't many people out there to notice." (16)

Informing Mickelson that he was felt he was ready, Reasoner was offered a job in 1956 as a summer replacement on the CBS television news assignment desk for nineteen weeks at $157.50, half what he was making at the television station. He said no. Then a week later, urged on by his wife, he took the job. In those days the assignment desk was more important than it would be later, for deskmen not only kept track of the news and made assignments, but also reported the news. At that time almost all film stories were silent and were routinely shot by freelancers. The film would be flown to Washington or New York, processed, and then used. It soon became clear that if television news was going to compete favorably with newsreels, the reporter—and not the cameraman—would have to be responsible for editorial content and the direction of the story. Hence, the assignment desk began sending reporters out to do stories. The trouble was that few were eager to work in television news: the audiences were too small, the equipment was too unreliable, it took too long to edit the film. All this created an opportunity for Harry Reasoner. He got his break in the winter of 1957.

It was then that he was called from the "ratty and depressing" (his words) quarters of television news in the old Grand Central Building to 485 Madison Avenue, where radio news operated, where Murrow had an office, and where the executives were. John Day, Mickelson's director of news, offered him a job on the Sunday afternoon television program that resembled *The New York Times'* "News of the Week in Review" Sunday section. Reasoner was named a CBS news correspondent—the first to be named from television news. He had the same title as Murrow and Howard K. Smith. "I walked out onto Madison Avenue in as impervious a state of euphoria as I have ever known," Reasoner noted. (17) The job paid $175 a week, plus a $75 advance and guarantee against fees. The fee system, since done away with, gave extra money to anyone who did a network news broadcast ($50), a radio news report ($25), or a radio news broadcast ($75). Walter Cronkite, the anchorman on the Sunday night 15-minute television news broadcast got quite a large fee ($600), but the largest at CBS News went to radio news broadcaster Lowell Thomas ($800 a night, five nights a week). At this juncture, television news still rated lower than radio news.

In December 1957 Reasoner was sent down to Cape Canaveral in Florida to cover the launch of the Vanguard rocket. The launch was considered a military operation, and so the time of the blast-off was classified. Newsmen were not allowed closer than ten miles of the site, forcing them to hang around a motel hoping to pick up gossip. CBS cameraman Paul Rubenstein learned that the Vanguard would be launched on December 6 between 8 A.M. and 12 noon. "We worked out an elaborate plan," Reasoner recalled, "to ensure that, while Russia might have beaten the United States, no one was going to beat CBS News." (18)

The regular CBS News correspondent, Charles von Fremd, and cameraman Rubenstein, went to a beach with an unobstructed view ten miles away from the launch. Von Fremd's job was to get film and describe events for the evening television news. Locating himself in von Fremd's beachfront cottage in front of the motel, Reasoner was to get word to New York of the launch via an open line for a morning bulletin. Reasoner could barely see Vanguard from outside the cottage. His eyes hurt, it was hot, and he was afraid he would not even recognize a launch, never having seen one. Then at 10 A.M. he saw a flash of flame and watched as the slender, white rocket started to move. "There she goes," he shouted to von Fremd's wife Virginia, who was holding the open line to New York. "There she goes," Virginia shouted into the phone. "There she goes," the executive in New York repeated. Immediately putting down the phone, the executive dashed away to get the bulletin on the air. CBS had beaten the other two networks. But Reasoner realized that something was wrong with the launch. Soon after he had shouted, Harry watched as the rocket leaned and then with lots more flash and smoke than before, exploded on ignition. He raced for the phone and yelled, "Hold it." But there was no one listening. "It was the first really elaborate attempt by CBS News to cover a Canaveral launching," Reasoner recalled. "We got better later." (19)

By 1957 television's quiz show phenomenon was flourishing. The American Research Bureau ratings for July reflected their omnipresence. Five of the top ten shows were quizzes. "$64,000 Question" was number one, "Gunsmoke" number two, then "I've Got a Secret" (CBS), "Twenty-one" (NBC), "The Ed Sullivan Show" (CBS), "What's My Line?" (CBS), "Lawrence Welk" (ABC), "$64,000 Challenge" (CBS), "Alfred Hitchcock" (CBS), and "Studio One" (CBS). A year later all this would change as quiz programs would become the focus of the greatest scandal in the history of television.

It began with a man named Ed Hilgemeier. He was a part-time butler and bit actor, aged 24, who had been a standby contestant on the daytime version of CBS Television's quiz show "Dotto." Standing in the wings awaiting his turn on camera on May 20, 1958, Hilgemeier had noticed a notebook dropped by the woman contestant preceding him. In the notebook were the same questions she then answered on stage, collecting $4,000. He notified the woman's opponent and filed a protest with the show's producers. When he was given $1,500 to assure his silence, he appeared prepared to forget the whole thing, but then he learned that the losing contestant had been given a higher payoff—$4,000. Consequently, on August 7 he filed a complaint with Colgate, the show's sponsor. No one knew of any of this; so Colgate's August 16 announcement canceling the weekday morning "Dotto" on CBS as well as the Tuesday evening version on NBC surprised most people, especially because no reason was supplied. Ironically, District Attorney Frank Hogan announced on August 25 that his office planned to probe into possible illegal actions on the part of the "Dotto" producers. That same day Teddy Nadler set the record for quiz show prize money by winning $252,000 on "The $64,000 Challenge."

Soon after "Dotto" was terminated, Charles Van Doren, a contestant on NBC's "Twenty-one" quiz show, had racked up $129,000. He had been put on the spot, however, by Herbert Stempel, who claimed that he had been asked to lose to Van Doren. Van Doren denied that he had been given any answers in advance. (Late in 1959 Van Doren finally acknowledged that what Stempel had charged was true.) Allegations of rigging increased, and by September 1959 a number of quiz shows were dropped, including "The $64,000 Challenge." Two months later, "The $64,000 Question" was off the air. CBS and NBC contended that bad ratings, not the rigging charges, had been the cause for dropping their quiz shows. The two networks insisted that most of the quiz shows had been produced by outsiders, that they had no control over how the shows were produced. There were many admissions of rigging on the part of contestants, producers, and others. All those indicted pleaded guilty and sought the mercy of the court. They were given suspended sentences, and while President Eisenhower called the quiz show rigging "a terrible thing to do to the American public," the average viewer apparently didn't seem to object that much, according to public opinion polls.

The rigging introduced a new low in morale at CBS. Someone would have to be blamed, and Lou Cowan appeared the best bet. It was he who had invented "The $64,000 Question," and even though he claimed that he knew nothing about the rigging, he became a convenient scapegoat: he was forced to resign as television network president in December 1959. Publicly, Frank Stanton had observed that he believed Cowan when he declared himself ignorant of what was going on. But behind the scenes, Stanton was working to get Cowan to resign. Advised to cite reasons of health, a believable excuse as he was indeed not well, Cowan would not go quietly. He went public, insisting that he was in fine health and the only reason he was leaving CBS was that the company had edged him out.

Worried that Washington might exploit the quiz show scandals to tighten control over broadcasting, CBS launched a campaign to assure the viewing public that it was not being duped while watching network programs. Frank Stanton, speaking on behalf of his network, said on October 16 to the Radio-Television News Directors Association in New Orleans, that CBS would institute new practices to get rid of what he called the "hanky-panky" of the quiz shows: "We accept the responsibility for content and quality and for assurance to the American people that what they see and hear on CBS programs is exactly what it purports to be." This was meant to apply to all programs, not just quizzes. New rules were introduced at CBS, requiring such now-familiar announcements as "This program was prerecorded" and "Participants in this program were selected and interviewed in advance." When Stanton said that everything had to be "what it purports to be," he meant it. So much so that he ordered canned laughter and applause to be identified as such. The quiz scandal led to rapid changes in television scheduling. In August 1959 the Nielsen ratings reflected those shifts. CBS's "Gunsmoke" was first followed by "Have Gun—Will Travel" (CBS), "Rifleman" (ABC), "I've Got a Secret' (CBS), "Peter Gunn" (NBC), "Best of Groucho" (NBC), "Alfred Hitchcock" (CBS), "Joseph Cotton" (CBS), "Wyatt Earp" (ABC), and

"Frontier Justice" (CBS). Westerns had surged into the forefront, but CBS continued to dominate the ratings with six shows on the list. Significantly, the game shows were gone.

All this coincided with the gradual demise of a great cultural hero, Edward R. Murrow. By 1957 he had reached the height of his public career. *Time* magazine, putting him on the cover on September 30, called him television's outstanding journalist. He had received all the awards offered. His income was well over $300,000 a year. When a stockholder asked why Murrow was paid more than Bill Paley or Frank Stanton, the CBS chairman replied candidly: "His value seems to be higher." (20) *Time's* lead in its cover story was itself one of the great tributes to this man: "Amid the trite and untrue that shed a honky-tonk glare from the nation's T. V. sets come moments that pierce reality and live up to television's magic gift for thrusting millions of spectators into the lap of history in the making. As television moved into its second decade, chances were that some of the best of such moments would come from a dark, high-domed man with a hangdog look, an apocalyptic voice and a cachet as plain as his inevitable cigarettes."

Unfortunately for Murrow, by the spring of 1958 "See It Now"'s days had become numbered. With all its awards, prestige, and headline grabbing, it remained a hard sell. CBS officials doubted they could keep it on the air any longer. The occasion for dropping the show was a program Murrow and Friendly did on the question of statehood for Alaska and Hawaii. Hardly one of the great blockbusters of television history, the statehood program created sufficient controversy to provide the network with an excuse to drop the series.

Harry Bridges, the Hawaiian labor leader, held Marxist beliefs and that was enough to convince some Congressmen that legislators from the State of Hawaii would fall under Communist control. Bridges appeared on "See It Now" and called one of the Congressmen "crazy" for holding such thoughts; when the Congressman demanded the right to reply, CBS granted it without consulting Murrow or Friendly. The two men felt that CBS had in effect repudiated them; Murrow made it clear that he could not do any more "See It Now" programs under these circumstances. That was meant merely as a threat: he simply wanted to convince the network not to fire him, but to consult with him on such matters. Approaching Paley, Murrow found that his long-time friend had become distinctly uncomfortable with all the fuss surrounding "See It Now."

"I don't want this constant stomach-ache," Paley said.

"It goes with the job," replied Murrow.

But Paley would have his way. There would be no more "See It Now" programs. Come the fall, Murrow would continue with "Person to Person," and he and Friendly would inaugurate their "Small World" show. The final "See It Now" show appeared on July 9, 1958, and dealt with the reemergence of Germany as a world power. It had been television's most honored series, winning three Peabodys, four Emmys, and a host of other awards. The official reason for scrapping it: the show simply cost too much money. Some were angry, notably John Crosby, television critic for *The New York Herald Tribune*, who wrote: "'See It Now' . . . is by every criterion television's most brilliant, most decorated, most imaginative, most courageous and most important program. The fact that CBS cannot afford it but can afford "Beat the Clock" is shocking."

By the fall, "See It Now" was no longer around, and the quiz show scandal was unfolding. With Murrow narrating, "Small World" debuted in October with an international conversation between Pandit Nehru in New Delhi, Aldous Huxley in Turin, Italy, and Thomas E. Dewey in Portland, Maine. The quiz show scandal remained in the headlines that fall as Murrow prepared to get something off his chest. He had become somehow larger than the network in many eyes, and that gave him the right, as he interpreted it, to speak out about what was troubling him, and what was troubling him more than anything else was the broadcasting industry itself. He was appalled at what it had become, with its $1 billion in revenues a year, with the country flooded with televisions and radios. It was such a huge and powerful force. He wanted the industry to use that power for good, but, in his view, it was wasting its opportunity.

And so the speech he was about to deliver would be one of the industry's most famous public tongue lashings. Murrow had sent advance copies of his remarks, delivered in Chicago that October, to radio and television news directors, to news agencies and television editors, as well as to *Variety*. But not to Bill Paley, Frank Stanton, or any of the other CBS brass. In that speech, Murrow said that both radio and television had both "grown up as an incompatible combination of show business, advertising and news. . . . The top management of the networks, with a few notable exceptions, had been trained in advertising, research, sales, or show business. But by the nature of the corporate structure, they also make the final and crucial decisions having to do with news and public affairs. Frequently they have neither the time nor the competence to do this. . . . And if there are any historians about fifty or a hundred years from now and there should be preserved the kinescopes for one week of all three networks, they will there find recorded, in black and white or color, evidence of decadence, escapism and insulation from the realities of the world in which we live. . . . During the daily peak viewing periods, television in the main insulates us from the realities of the world in which we live." He suggested that each of the twenty or thirty large corporations which dominate radio and television give one or two of their regularly scheduled programs each year over to the networks and say in effect: "This is a tiny tithe, just a little bit of our profits. On this particular night we aren't going to try to sell cigarettes or automobiles; this is merely a gesture to indicate our belief in the importance of ideas." In conclusion he said that "Unless we get up off our fat surpluses and recognize that television in the main is being used to distract, delude, amuse and insulate us, then television and those who finance it, those who look at it and those who work at it, may see a totally different picture too late. . . . If we go on as we are, then history will take its revenge and retribution will not limp in catching up with us. . . . This instrument can teach, it can illuminate; yes, and it can even inspire. But it can do so only to the extent that humans are determined to use it to those ends. Otherwise it is merely wires and lights in a box. There is a great and perhaps decisive battle to be fought against ignorance, intolerance, and indifference. This weapon of television could be useful."

Paley's relationship toward Murrow, once so warm and reverent, had soured in the past year; the relationship would suffer even more as a result of the speech. Paley felt he deserved better from Murrow. After all, he had made him rich and famous. The Murrow speech did have one positive effect: at the end of 1958 CBS presented five full-length news programs: one reviewing the year's events, another United States–Soviet relations, another on Communist China, and two on trends in the arts and sciences.

In the wake of the Chicago speech, Murrow was further castigated for narrating a CBS radio documentary on January 19, 1959—"The Business of Sex"—on the cozy relationship between prostitutes and big business. Reacting to the program angrily and self-righteously, American business defended itself and focused its wrath on Ed Murrow. Because the producers had promised the call girls anonymity in return for spilling details of their behavior, Murrow could not defend himself and the program properly. Later, he promised himself that he would never narrate a program over which he did not have complete editorial control.

The fuss surrounding "The Business of Sex" had the result of speeding up his plans to take some time off from CBS. On February 16 he announced that he would take a one-year sabbatical, beginning in July, "to spend a year traveling, listening, reading and trying to learn" without the need to gaze at the clock.

Just as Murrow was learning to get along without CBS, the network was plotting to move forward without him. In early 1959, stung by criticism that the company was interested only in profits, CBS had come to realize that it had a mounting public relations problem on its hands arising from the quiz show scandals. It sought to convince the public that it was interested in more than just making money. (21) A special five-man committee met secretly to draw up a new major public relations campaign that was meant to restore CBS's image. Recommended were internal seminars, a weekly half-hour program on television itself, and a fresh effort to explain CBS to the outside world. The committee proposed a news special presented at midweek in prime time once a month. No one apparently said so—it did not need to be verbalized—but the intention was clearly to get along without Murrow, indeed to demonstrate that CBS could in fact function nicely without him. A way would have to be found to groom others to replace Murrow on the air.

A way would also have to be found to replace him as unofficial spokesman for the broadcasting industry. It was hoped that Frank Stanton would somehow take over that job. He was already a highly public figure. Stanton seemed more reliable. There was no longer room at CBS for a maverick like Murrow, especially one who turned on his own industry, on his own network. The time had come for CBS to exhibit firmness, not to let its broadcasters go unrestrained. The advantage of promoting Stanton as CBS and industry spokesman was obvious: he would not carp about the industry; he would do what he could to build it up. He was a corporation man, and that was what the network needed right now.

Looming on the horizon was CBS's fresh attempt, planned in the spring of 1959, to schedule a series of documentary programs that would maintain the network's prestige without indulging in wild controversies. It was to be Murrowism without the fire and brimstone. In May 1959, Stanton had vowed publicly that CBS would offer a program that would "report in depth on significant issues, events, and personalities . . . ." The program would be aired six times during the next year, beginning in the fall, and every other week the year after; within three years it would run weekly. Sig Mikelson, head of the news department, called Friendly at his home in the Berkshires in June and asked to see him the next day. Expecting some dreadful news, Friendly arrived in New York, figuring that the network was going to terminate his contract, or some such thing. But Mickelson simply handed him a press release about Stanton's speech and said, "We want you to produce this." He assumed that what Mickelson had meant was that CBS wanted Friendly and Murrow to produce the new documentary series. No, said Sig, it was not to be that way. Appealing to Paley, Friendly asked why cut Ed out? The chairman replied that there was nothing wrong with letting Howard K. Smith or Eric Sevareid handle the narration of the program. In the end, Friendly gave up the fight: Murrow's planned sabbatical made him almost entirely unavailable for the show. And so "CBS Reports" was his, and his alone.

As for Murrow, on June 26 he hosted his last "Person to Person" program, the 250th he had done. His 499th and 500th guests had been Hugh Baillie, the former head of the United Press, and Lee Remick, the actress. Lost in the shuffle of his tiffs with the network was the fact that "Person to Person" was an unquestionable success: of all the programs shown on the air in the past six years, it was still the only one around in its original format. Murrow had brought in $20 million for the network. He was imitated and caricatured and had become, by virtue of "Person to Person," one of the most well-known people in the United States. At around this time Murrow ceased doing his nightly radio broadcasts as well, ending a 12-year run. He began his leave of absence on July 1.

But, even out of the country, Murrow's problems with CBS remained. When Stanton asserted on October 16 in New Orleans that CBS assured viewers that what they saw and heard on CBS was "exactly what it purports to be . . . ," Jack Gould of *The New York Times* asked Stanton to provide some details of what he had in mind. Stanton replied that he had meant dubbed applause and laughter as tricks—and these would henceforth be eliminated. Stanton then turned on the "Person to Person" program, asserting that while the program's producers tried to give the impression that it was being done spontaneously, it was in fact rehearsed; that is, an element of phoniness prevailed there too. Stanton argued that either the guests should not be given advance questions or the audience ought to be informed that the show was indeed rehearsed. The following Friday evening, Murrow's replacement on the show, Charles Collingwood, had been told to provide a disclaimer, namely, that "advanced planning with our guests" is required to determine "what we will show, what we will discuss and in what order" as well as to arrange for the personnel and equipment needed for the program. In London, Murrow was apprised of what Stanton had said. He issued a statement, saying, "Dr. Stanton has finally revealed his ignorance both of news and of requirements of television production. . . . He suggests that "Person to Person," a program with which I was associated for six years, was not what it purported to be. Surely Stanton must know that cameras, lights and microphones do not just wander around a home. Producers must know who is going where and when and for how long. . . . The alternative . . . would be chaos. . . . I am sorry Dr. Stanton feels that I have participated in perpetrating a fraud upon the public. My conscience is clear. His seems to be bothering him." All that Stanton (with Paley's backing) could do was to have Ralph Colin, the CBS general counsel and a member of the CBS board, fly to London to demand that Murrow either apologize or resign. Colin returned to New York empty-handed. Murrow would neither say he was sorry nor leave CBS voluntarily.

Toward the end of July CBS News announced that Friendly would become executive producer of "CBS Reports." Sig Mickelson, then CBS vice president and general manager, said it would be the most important programming project ever undertaken by CBS News. The new documentary, destined for the usual low ratings, was aimed at getting good grades from

Congress and television critics. The first program aired on October 26, 1959 and was called "Biography of a Missile," the life story of a 76-foot Juno 11 missile. Ed Murrow served as narrator and Fred Friendly was executive producer. (Murrow had completed the work on it before beginning his sabbatical.) "Fascinating and instructive," said *Variety.* "CBS Reports" appeared only twelve times. (But as Stanton had proposed, it went biweekly the second year, and weekly the third.)

nine

"No One Will Be Killed. No One Will Have a Brain Tumor."

The early 1960s were known for the predominance of television comedies, and in that field CBS clearly held sway. Just as the Westerns were fading in popularity, along came rural comedies. Some thought them an embarrassment to the network. Back in the late 1940s Bill Paley had been asked by Paul Kesten to adopt an elitist approach to broadcasting, to avoid the temptation of seeking the lowest common denominator in order to appeal to the most people. Paley had scotched that idea then; and fifteen years later he was laboring to implement his own brand of mass entertainment. What kind of entertainment was not particularly important. What mattered was what worked. And what worked was roughly the equivalent of what the public wanted. When it came to figuring out what the public was after, Bill Paley felt he had a special sense. "That's been his gift," said George Schweitzer, who until the summer of 1987 was CBS vice president for communications. "As stately and as cultured as he is, with all of his worldly experience and his love of art, and his participation in many of the finer cultural aspects, he understands, and has always understood, this is a mass-audience business, that it goes beyond New York. That you have to appeal to a broad spectrum of tastes of a population of over 200 million people. That has been his success, his ability to look beyond the cultural world." (1)

Paley was the classic pragmatist. "He liked success and hated failure," said Michael Dann, who as CBS programming chief in the 1960s worked closely with Paley. (2) But there would be a price to pay. Certainly not in dollars. In other ways, primarily prestige. But that didn't seem to matter, not when weighed against the amount of money that could be earned from attracting larger and larger audiences. The network had always wanted to make money; but, now, thanks to the potential of reaching millions of new viewers, there was more to be made. Ratings took on mythical importance: the higher they were, the larger the share of audience; and more audience meant greater network profits. The quality of the program was secondary. If people watched it, that was all that really mattered. Whoever figured out what programs would appeal to a mass audience would become a demigod around the network.

James Aubrey would become that demigod. He had taken over as CBS president in December 1959. Only 41 years old, he was soon so highly regarded that people spoke of him as a likely successor to Frank Stanton. For a time Stanton himself held that view. What is more, there was even talk that Aubrey might replace the chairman when he finally stepped down. Paley himself acknowledged that point.

The son of an advertising executive, Aubrey had grown up in the Chicago suburb of Lake Forest, was educated at Exeter and Princeton, and in 1944, at age 26, married an MGM starlet, Phyllis Thaxter. A space salesman for magazines for a while, he moved to broadcasting in 1948, acquiring a job as a time salesman for the CBS Radio and Television stations in Los Angeles. By 1956, Aubrey had become the manager of CBS's Hollywood programming. Stymied at CBS, he became vice president for programs and talent at ABC, earning $35,000 a year. During his nearly two years there, he acquired a reputation as a specialist in the filmed series, making "Maverick," the rural comedy "The Real McCoys," and an urban adventure series, "77 Sunset Strip." Few broadcasting historians have been kind to Aubrey. One caustic portrayal came from David Halberstam who wrote that Aubrey was "a man so nakedly open about what he was and what he wanted—that is, the greediest side of the network so openly revealed and displayed—that even the other hucksters were embarrassed. What differentiated him from the others was not so much that he was worse than they were as that he did it with such abandon and with so little apology." (3) Aubrey's boss, Bill Paley, had a very rosy view of him—at the start, at any rate. Aubrey was, in his view, "bright, aggressive, good-looking and he had a sophisticated charm when he chose to use it. Above all, he showed us that he had a sure, self-confident instinct for the kind of television programs that would appeal to a mass audience. He had also a good sense of business and administration. He was a hard-driving man, tenacious and goal-oriented . . . ." (4) (Once, Paley was asked by a British interviewer how a man of such good taste, a man who appreciated art, and who was friendly with such great intellects could defend programs like Aubrey's "Beverly Hillbillies." He grew furious and looked as if he were going to stalk out of the studio. Instead, he sat there, insisting that he put nothing on the air of which he wasn't proud. But he was clearly shaken, and his annoyance appeared to suggest that he might have felt there was a trifle something to the interviewer's question.)

What was Aubrey's secret? CBS was moving away from live programming (emanating in New York) and falling in love with the filmed series (located in Hollywood). Aubrey fell right in line with that shift, exploiting the fact that the filmed series, which often attracted mass audiences, were less risky than was live programming. He was young, aggressive, some said arrogant. Arrogance in his case was his early boast that he would double CBS's $25 million yearly profits. To go along with his boasting, Aubrey had an entertainment philosophy. In a famous memorandum, he is said to have noted that the ideal elements for a prime-time television program were "broads, bosoms, and fun." (5) But Aubrey denied authorship of what some came to call the Aubrey dictum.

Between 1960 and 1965 Aubrey could rightfully take credit for every entertainment program that appeared on CBS. He brought to television such shows as "The Beverly Hillbillies," "Gomer Pyle," "Petticoat Junction," "The Munsters," and "Mr. Ed." "The Andy Griffith Show," an example of this new comedy form, premiering in 1960, soared nearly at once to the top ten and remained there throughout the decade, even after 1968 when Griffith left the show.

The most famous of the rural comedies was the "Beverly Hillbillies," which debuted in September 1962 and within one month became the most popular program of the season. The number one program for 1963 as well, it remained in the top ten for a long time, considered the most popular program of the mid-1960s. The focus of the show was a mountain clan named the Clampetts who had come to sophisticated southern California from the Ozarks. Having struck oil, they arrived in Beverly Hills on an old flatbed truck loaded with jugs of corn liquor. Their prime purpose in life was outmaneuvering the Hollywood hotshots. When Granny Clampett decided to fish in the swimming pool of her fancy estate, she caught a toy plastic fish. "There's Beverly Hills fer you!" she proclaimed, "All flashy an' show on the outside, but nothin' inside where it counts." Despite their new environment, the Clampetts remained unchanged and that proved the basis of the show's humor. There were word plays and devilish sexual innuendo. "Do you like Kipling?" someone asked. "I don't know—I ain't never kippled," came the reply. When the son of the Beverly Hills banker called on Elly May and asked, "Is Elly May ready?" Granny replied that "She shore is! She's been ready since she was fourteen!"

If some critics disliked the exploitation of hillbilly types, they seemed to miss the point. The message seemed to be that the Clampett clan had kept its ways and seemed uncorrupted; it was in fact Beverly Hills and its money-oriented society that was being lampooned. Beyond that, the program's admirers were grateful that here was a show that was different from the others: it lacked violence, it lacked ugliness. As "Hillbillies" director Richard Whorf proudly asserted, "You know that no one will be killed. No one will have a brain tumor." (6)

Just why one formula worked in programming—and another one did not—few could explain. Few tried. For Paley, what mattered was whether a lot of people were out there watching. Mike Dann was vacationing one summer at Martha's Vineyard when a phone call came in from the chairman. "You know," said Paley, "'The Munsters' is just not our kind of show. It's not a CBS show." Dann thought to himself. Exactly what is a CBS show? This was a network that had spawned Westerns, then quiz shows, then "Beverly Hillbillies"–type entertainment. Where was the common denominator? "Gee, Mr. Paley," Dann replied, "I can't get another show ready. It's late August." Then, as if he had not heard a word, Paley admonished him tersely, "Well, do something about it."

"The Munsters" went on in the fall of 1964 and was a big hit. About a week after the pilot ran—the same one Paley had seen and hated—the chairman saw Mike Dann in a CBS corridor. This time his mood was all bright and cheery. In an obvious reference to "The Munsters," Paley said, "It's a good thing you fixed it, because that other one was awful." Dann could not bring himself to admit that "The Munsters" pilot was identical to what Paley had seen. Nor did he need to admit it. Paley didn't care. Paley didn't even remember. He only had in mind that the public liked what CBS was offering.

The Aubrey dictum worked miracles. In the 1962–63 season, CBS had eight of the top ten programs; seven were comedies. In 1962, the television network was providing 60 percent of the company's total sales of $500 million. By 1963, CBS had a perfect 100 percent score in the daytime field—twelve out of the top twelve daytime shows belonged to the network. The 1963 Nielsen ratings for February 1963 showed the following: "Beverly Hillbillies" (CBS), "Andy Griffith Show" (CBS), "Red Skelton Hour" (CBS), "Candid Camera" (CBS), "Ben Casey" (ABC), "Bonanza" (NBC), "Lucy Show" (CBS), "Dick Van Dyke Show" (CBS), "Danny Thomas Show" (CBS), and "Gunsmoke" (CBS). That same year Paley was said to be worth $48 million. (It seemed that CBS just couldn't stop making money: its investment in the Broadway musical "My Fair Lady" brought in $33 million as of 1964). Whereas NBC and ABC could only charge $41,000 and $45,000, respectively, for a minute of prime-time advertising, CBS by 1964 was charging $50,000—that meant $1 million in revenue each night. It was not hard to tell why Jim Aubrey had such a reputation. In 1964, CBS profits had indeed doubled—the stock sky-rocketed as well, soaring from $17 a share when Aubrey assumed the network presidency to $42 at the time of his dismissal in February 1965.

Inevitably, CBS News would suffer from Aubrey's success. In his view a financial drain, he took concrete steps to dilute the importance of CBS News. In 1962 he circulated a decree that the news division would have to cut back on its habit of preempting prime-time shows for special news-oriented occasions. Aubrey made no secret of his disdain for the news side. To Fred Friendly, who became president of CBS News in 1964, Aubrey groused, "They say to me, 'Take your soiled little hands, get the ratings, and make as much money as you can.' They say to you, 'Take your lily-white hands, do your best, go the high road and bring us pre-stige.'" (7) Always trying to cut the news division down to size, Aubrey was adept as self-promotion. At annual budget meetings he would use color slides to describe CBS Television's financial achievements. Significantly, the cost of the news division was put in bright red. "You can see, Mr. Chairman," Aubrey would say, "how much higher our profits could have been this year if it had not been for the drain of news." (8)

None of that talk was smart, not smart at all. It was as if Aubrey had walked into a church and started to denigrate religion to the clergy. No one could deny the logic of Aubrey's thinking, but he did himself little good by coating the news division in mud, the same news division which Bill Paley had built up, which had brought CBS so much glory when glory was in great need. With a soft spot in his heart for the news side, Bill Paley didn't want to hear anyone put it down. Jim Aubrey had made a mistake. He had misunderstood what Paley was all about, what mattered to the chairman. It was not only money. Indeed, Paley may have felt a bit embarrassed by the profits that flowed in from the entertainment side. Some in the news division felt he did. How else to explain the large sums spent on the news in those days. As Daniel Schorr has noted, "Paley had a very good sense—and in some ways I don't consider what he did in news as being at all consistent with what he was doing in television. Sometimes it seemed as if it was a compensation for it. He would put on high-rated shows which were not necessarily very serious and intellectual shows and then to make up for that he would give the news department its head." (9)

It was hard for CBS to admit that Aubrey, the man who could whistle and dollar bills would pour forth from the skies, was anything but perfect. Long after he had gone, Frank Stanton would continue to dismiss critics who suggested that the excellence of CBS had somehow been under-mined by the Aubrey days: "It was Aubrey, for example, who covered the opening of the Lincoln Center thing . . . I think that 'Playhouse 90' was probably one of the best things that we had on our schedule, that was on during that period. I'm not saying that I like all the situation comedies that we put on, but 'Lucy' was certainly, you know, it's one of the things people look back and say, 'Why don't we have more like it now?' Jackie Gleason was on at that period. Red Skelton was on at that period. These are the big (shows), in the top ten shows of the period. I don't find anything that I would be embarrassed about as far as our image was concerned. We were strong on entertainment, and we were strong in news." But hadn't rural comedies like "Beverly Hillbillies" brought the network a good deal of criticism? Snapped Stanton: "Nobody loved it except the people." (10)

The popularity of the first set of rural comedies spawned others such as "Green Acres," "Hee Haw," and in the same vein, a rural-type variety program known as "The Glen Campbell Goodtime Hour." The network also had its share of doctor, spy, and police dramas, but comedy and especially rural comedy monopolized the schedule. CBS presented so many variations on these down-home themes during the 1960s that it became known as the "Hillbilly network."

Aubrey's downfall came as a shock to him but to few others. Some of his actions had proven unpopular, particularly dismissing veteran CBS celebrities such as Arthur Godfrey and Jack Benny. To his critics, he became the "Smiling Cobra." He appeared to divert from the successful formula he had devised in planning the 1964–65 entertainment schedule. No one could account for his behavior. Aubrey scheduled four totally new shows without waiting for pilots to be made, and scripts or stars to be selected. The four were "The Baileys of Balboa," "The Reporter," "The Cara Williams Show," and "Living Doll." Three of the four shows happened to be produced by Keefe Brasselle, a long-time Aubrey acquaintance. When none of the programs lasted the season, Aubrey's record was suddenly, sweepingly marred. Additional rumors surrounding his personal life made it inevitable that he would not be around much longer.

The decision to let him go was taken in February 1965. The exact reasons were mysterious then and remain so today as the principals refuse to talk about the causes for his dismissal. All that Frank Stanton ever said publicly was that he had decided on firing Aubrey after concluding that he no longer felt him qualified to take over the network. The task of dismissing Aubrey was carried out by Frank Stanton one Saturday morning. Caught by surprise, Aubrey demanded to appeal the decision to Paley. Informed by Stanton that the chairman was ill, confined to bed with a bad back, the exasperated Aubrey insisted and Stanton placed a phone call. Aubrey left, presumably for Paley's hotel suite, but 40 minutes later Paley called Stanton asking what had happened to the newly fired Aubrey. The walk should not have taken more than 5 minutes. Growing concerned, Stanton looked in Aubrey's (former) office in vain; he asked the security guards downstairs if they had seen Aubrey leave, but they had not. Stanton checked the men's room. According to one report, he then walked around the full perimeter of the building. (Years later, recalling the incident, Stanton acknowledged that he had been worried about Aubrey, but he did not recall walking around the exterior of the building.) But Aubrey was nowhere to be found. Returning to his desk, Stanton waited another half-hour before receiving a welcome phone call from Paley to say that Aubrey had finally arrived. Aubrey had simply taken a long walk in Central Park to gather his thoughts.

With the entertainment side managing so well, CBS was intent as well on building a new, serious image in its public affairs programming. The early 1960s brought "CBS Reports" to the fore as the more company-oriented replacement of "See It Now." There was little difference between "Reports" and its predecessor, except that "See It Now," of course, was strictly an Ed Murrow package. "Reports" had the same aggressive attitude toward the news as Murrow's "See It Now." Among the personality interviews on "CBS Reports" were talks with Walter Lippmann, in which he pronounced on national and international affairs; Carl Sandburg, reviewing Lincoln's prairie life and telling the story of Gettysburg as the cameras toured the battlefields; Dwight D. Eisenhower, reflecting upon the presidency and returning to the Normandy beaches with Walter Cronkite to make a special program in 1964.

Getting Walter Lippmann to do the "CBS Reports" interviews was quite a challenge. (11) Late in March 1960, Fred Friendly, who was the executive producer of "Reports," had asked the great pundit if he would like to appear on television. "I wouldn't," was Lippmann's terse reply. He felt a mixture of contempt and suspicion toward the media. Rarely did he turn on his own set except for the occasional political event such as the conventions. Television, in his unflattering words, was the creature, the servant, and indeed the prostitute of merchandising. Well, countered Friendly with great shrewdness, the only way to improve television was to get people like Lippmann to help develop its potential. That induced Lippmann to agree to a lunch with Friendly and CBS newscaster Howard K. Smith. Meanwhile, Lippmann said he would ponder Friendly's proposal. Ultimately, Lippmann taped a one-hour interview on the condition that should he decide after watching it that he was not satisfied, it would not be broadcast. Reluctantly, Friendly went along. Furthermore, Lippmann insisted at first there be no commercials. Later, he relented but stipulated that no dog food, deodorants, or soap commercials break into the show. (In the end the show went unsponsored.) CBS sent Lippmann a check for $2,000, taped the show on July 7, 1960 (when Lippmann was nearing 71 years old), and televised it August 11, not long after Eisenhower's inept handling of the U-2 spy plane incident and the aborted summit meeting in Paris with Khrushchev. Lippmann was asked what qualities he thought a leader ought to have. He should have, he felt, the "ability to see what matters in the excitement of daily events . . . to be able to see through the latest headline to what is permanent and enduring." Churchill had this "second sight," as Lippmann termed it, and so too did de Gaulle and Teddy Roosevelt. "The ability to see which way the thing is going is the basis of great leadership. The President cannot, himself, act on everything. He had to decide. So his mind must be judicial." Stirring words, but how would the audience react?

Here was the network trying to elevate the level of television. But was that enough to elicit favorable comment? Indeed it was.

That first Lippmann interview became front-page news. "To have the sage of Washington up close and ad-libbing," said the *Saturday Review,* "revealed not only his urbanity, which was to be expected, but yielded a bonus in the impression of kindliness and personal warmth never apparent in the intense concentration of his logical, impersonal prose." Congratulatory letters streamed in. Once again, television—and CBS—had offered a public figure whose words carried weight. When J. Robert Oppenheimer appeared, however, the atmosphere and the ugly charges hurled at that eminent scientist clouded the network's presentation. This time, there was none of that. Walter Lippmann was the dean of the intellectual world, and when CBS brought the nation an entire hour of his thoughts and analysis, it was providing the kind of program that Ed Murrow had preached about in Chicago a few years earlier. It was still in the days before rural comedies reached their heights, before anyone had dubbed CBS the "Hillbilly network." But the Lippmann interview and the entire "CBS Reports" series would serve as something of an antidote to what would come from the entertainment side.

(CBS sent Lippmann another check, this time for $3,000 and offered him a five-year contract. Clearly pleased by all the new attention, Lippmann agreed. He even used his Washington attorney, Oscar Cox, to get better terms: $15,000 a year for one program each year, and $10,000 for each additional one. All in all, CBS ran six more interviews, on the average of one a year, showing the final one on February 22, 1965. The Lippmann interview won a special citation from the Peabody Awards committee in 1962. The set of interviews was later published in book form. "My God, what syntax!" exclaimed an amazed Lippmann upon reading them.)

Occasionally, a "CBS Reports" program drew the fire of critics. That happened with "Harvest of Shame," which was aired on the Friday after Thanksgiving Day of 1960. "Harvest" explored the problem of America's migrant workers, lashing out at the indifference that permitted people to live so terribly. To make the point ever sharper, the program had been deliberately scheduled for Thanksgiving week—a time when most Americans were sitting down to a large meal, a meal which had come to them thanks in part to the harvest gathered by the migrants. Murrow, who by this time had returned from his sabbatical, was the narrator and David Lowe, the producer. The focus of the program was the plight of the migratory farm workers, black and white, forced to labor under inhumane conditions in order to feed people who were much better off. CBS's cameras followed the path of migrants as they traveled the harvesting route in rundown caravans. These were people mired in squalid conditions, with no hope of awakening to brighter circumstances. Mothers had to leave their children alone in rat-infested hovels, unable to afford to send them to a day-care center. Parents explained that they could give their infants milk no more than once a week.

The public reacted with surprise and shock at what CBS had uncovered. After the program was aired, "CBS Reports" was accused of having slanted and distorted the story, magnifying the problems, ignoring the other side of the question as if there could be some legitimate explanation for the migrant workers' travail. Farm organizations were predictably annoyed, charging the network with "highly colored propaganda" and "deceit." Spokespersons for the farmers even insisted upon equal time, while shopkeepers at the Florida winter camp of the migratory workers threatened to boycott the sponsor's cigarette brand. In response to the criticism, Richard Salant, who became president of CBS News in early 1961, noted that "The price of avoiding angry letters is blandness; the price of blandness, in this field at least, is public indifference; and we cannot afford those prices either."

"Harvest" would be Ed Murrow's last major documentary at CBS. A few months later the new president, John F. Kennedy, appointed him director of the United States Information Agency. (The nameplate on Murrow's CBS office remained for three years after his departure, so much of a fixture was he.) He took a pay cut from $200,000 to $20,000 a year. Oddly enough, in his first few days in the new job, Murrow asked BBC Director-General Hugh Carlton Greene, as a personal favor, not to broadcast "Harvest of Shame," even though it had already purchased the program. Now that he was in charge of America's image abroad, Murrow apparently felt that the nation would be better served by not exposing such problems to foreigners. Pressure came too from President Kennedy who was concerned that, given Murrow's new role in the U.S. government, the BBC's televising of "Harvest" could give the erroneous impression that the new administration in Washington was scornful of farm interests. Whatever the case, the BBC chief ignored all requests that the program not be shown. Later, Murrow would admit that he had regrets about his own request of the BBC.

As the new director of the USIA, Murrow found the job less than thrilling. The president had enticed him with the promise that he would be part of his inner circle, a promise that went unfulfilled. On his visits to Washington, Bill Paley would get a mouthful of complaints about the president from the disgruntled Murrow. Resignation, however, was out of the question until Murrow was forced to do so in January 1964, suffering by then from the lung cancer which would claim his life fifteen months later.

Television news got a big push in the early 1960s. The networks hoped to placate the FCC following the quiz show scandals of the late 1950s by developing the "serious" side of television—and that meant not only documentary programs but news as well. Then too Newton Minow, the new FCC chairman, favored public television and believed that the networks should engage in public service programming. In his famous address before the National Association of Broadcasters in 1961, Minow called television "a vast wasteland" and warned that license renewals would not be automatic in the future. In that same year the networks doubled the number of hours of news, documentaries, and other informational programs on television. The next year, CBS and NBC began planning to expand the early-evening newscasts from 15 to 30 minutes.

Helping CBS and the other networks in their effort to give emphasis to news coverage was the new technology of the early 1960s. By accelerating the speed with which news could be transmitted, that technology brought a veritable revolution in the way television news worked. Now, news from all parts of the globe could be covered with a degree of seriousness that was not possible before. In the past, it could easily take days for television footage of important news events to reach New York for broadcasting. In some cases, transportation and communication were so poor that some events were not aired at all—despite huge investments of time and effort by television personnel. Until satellites, film had to be flown in from overseas, limiting television news to the speed of jet planes—and their schedules. As late as August of 1961 when the East Germans put up the Berlin Wall, it would take two full days for the first film to be seen by television viewers.

Satellites were about to change all that, beginning with *Telstar*, the first communications satellite, which went into orbit on July 10, 1962. With *Telstar* it became possible to make same-day transmission from overseas. *Telstar* was a nonsynchronous "bird," which meant that it spun around the earth every hour, changing its position in the sky. Space technology was not yet sophisticated enough to place a synchronous satellite in orbit, which would have the advantage of being much more available. Visible from a transmitter at Goonhilly Downs in England and from a receiver at Andover, Maine, *Telstar* had a "window" of 11 to 14 minutes each hour. To celebrate the arrival of the new technology, the three American television networks pooled resources to produce a 14-minute program and beam it to Europe. Chosen as executive producer of the show was Fred Friendly.

Soon there would be that first synchronous satellite. It was called *Earlybird*, and it was launched in April 1965. *Early*, unlike the more limited *Telstar*, was visible 24 hours a day from transmitters and receivers on both sides of the Atlantic. (Once Hong Kong and Bangkok established satellite links with the United States, the Vietnam fighting turned into the nation's first television war. Thanks to the satellite, viewers saw President Nixon appear live at China's Great Wall. They also watched events develop after masked terrorists held the Olympic Village in Munich hostage. Fifteen minutes after correspondents in Jerusalem learned that Israeli soldiers had crossed into Lebanon to halt Palestinian Arab incursions into Israel, they were on the air live to describe the early moments of the "Litani Operation.") But the cost of using the "birds" was so high that only in the 1970s did they become routine. At first satellites were used only once or twice a week: the first 10 minutes, costing $3,500, was simply too high for networks to use them more at that time. Along with videotape, the satellites now enabled the television networks to compete with newspapers in covering that day's major events.

Once the news could be brought in more quickly and thoroughly, there was reason for the networks to boost their news departments. CBS fell in line. Until the early 1960s, CBS News had domestic bureaus in only three cities: New York, Washington, and Chicago. For film reports from elsewhere in the United States, the network had to rely upon freelance cameramen as well as employees of its affiliates. But then in 1962, CBS News opened bureaus in Los Angeles, Atlanta, and Dallas, putting in its own correspondents and camera crews in those cities.

By the early 1960s, CBS News was clearly in trouble. Throughout the 1950s, thanks to Ed Murrow and Fred Friendly, it had been the leading network for news. But pressures were being brought to bear on CBS News from all directions. One was Jim Aubrey and the disdain he felt toward the news division. Another had come with the rise of two fresh personalities working for NBC, Chet Huntley and David Brinkley. Introduced as a co-anchor news team in 1956, Chet and Dave had turned the "NBC Evening News" into a serious rival for the CBS news program with Douglas Edwards. Finally, the old CBS veteran correspondents were slowly leaving the scene. By the late 1950s, Murrow was flickering on and off the television screen. Changes were being made among the news executives to try to counter CBS News's difficulties. First, Sig Mickelson's deputies left; then Mickelson himself departed (in February 1961). Taking his place was Richard Salant, whose ascendancy was a major break with the past. CBS News had always been run by men steeped in journalism. But here was Salant, Stanton's executive assistant, taking over the reins.

By the time of the 1960 political conventions, Huntley and Brinkley's superiority was in great evidence. Bill Paley was furious that the NBC anchor duo had knocked CBS off the pedestal at Los Angeles, where John F. Kennedy was nominated for president, CBS attempted at the Republic convention in Chicago to bolster Walter Cronkite by teaming him with Ed Murrow. It didn't work. Ed, for his part, found ad-libbing a strain. He appeared indifferent and fatigued. Walter wasn't overly pleased to have to share the spotlight with someone else. The executives over at NBC were jubilant at the pairing of Murrow and Cronkite, seeing in it CBS's acknowledgment that Walter needed boosting. During the conventions, the NBC news team had garnered a 51 percent audience share, almost unheard of, while CBS got 36 percent and ABC, 13 percent.

There were new faces as well at CBS around this time. One belonged to a man who had enjoyed a mildly successful career in radio and television in the past but who in the early 1960s was turning his thoughts more and more to television news. At the time Mike Wallace had been doing commercials for Parliament cigarettes. He was determined to break into big-time television news—and that meant a network. Approaching Joseph Cullman, the head of Philip Morris, he explained that he would no longer do the cigarette commercials. Concerned that Wallace was committing a foolish act, one that could lead straight to unemployment, Cullman suggested that he not let go of the commercials until at least he had latched on to something in television news. "Didn't that make sense," Cullman asked? "No," said Mike politely, "because they won't believe, they won't even listen to me unless I can give them proof that I'm serious about this." And so Mike quit the cigarette commercials. After listening to Mark Goodson, Wallace also turned down a chance to be a host on a new Goodson-produced show to be called "Match Game." Altogether, Wallace had refused $150,000 in income for the 1962–63 season in his talks with Cullman and Goodson. He wanted to have a clean slate when he approached the television networks. By having one, he just might be able to convince them to take him on as a television news correspondent.

In the fall of 1962 Wallace wrote letters to Dick Salant of CBS, Jim Hagerty of ABC, and Bill McAndrew of NBC, acknowledging that his career had been checkered but saying he had firmly decided that he wanted to work exclusively in news; as a necessary first step, he wrote, he had cut himself off from all other sources of income. At first Wallace's "come-clean" strategy appeared to lead nowhere. In February 1963 he was about to accept an offer to become the television anchor for the evening and late-night newscasts at KTLA in Los Angeles. Before he could reach Los Angeles, however, Salant called Wallace and asked to see him before he left for the West Coast. Salant picked up the phone, impressed at a remark he thought Wallace had made. In fact, Wallace never said it. But Salant had heard that Wallace had informed Philip Morris that he had wanted to purchase his Parliament commercials to keep them off the air. No matter. Salant went ahead and offered Mike the job, working for the local television station, WCBS, and doing an interview series on the radio network. He would be paid $40,000 a year. Wallace was thrilled. He was about to embark upon one of the most illustrious careers in television journalism.

By the early 1960s fierce competition erupted over Douglas Edwards's news anchor job. Even after Huntley and Brinkley had taken over in the mid-1950s, Edwards had held his own in the ratings; but by 1962, the momentum had switched to NBC. Edwards had been at the job for fourteen years, and there was general acknowledgment that it was time for a change.

Eric Sevareid was a candidate. So was Howard K. Smith. As commentators, rather than straight reporters, they certainly had a chance. But both in their own way had irritated CBS executives by taking views which the network's management found distasteful. Smith had been long admired by Bill Paley. He had been proud of Smith's weekly radio news analysis from London on European affairs, broadcasts which had brought awards and prestige to CBS. He had taken outspoken stances from his perch in London and had escaped major criticism, but then when he replaced Eric Sevareid as the chief Washington correspondent for CBS in 1957, he became the object of scorn from everyone, it seemed, including Congress, the White House, and Wall Street.

Paley waited impatiently for the right opportunity to come down on Smith hard. It came in May 1961 when a documentary was made on Birmingham, Alabama. Smith was on the scene when a mob of bullies, wielding ax handles and whips, had stopped a bus and brutally beaten up civil rights workers who were riding to a rally. Smith had been born and grown up in New Orleans and he hated Southern racism. Watching unarmed men and women being clubbed horrified him. What particularly incensed Smith was the indifference shown by the Birmingham police force. It conjured up old memories of the rise of the Nazis. Smith had watched such scenes when he was the CBS correspondent in Berlin during World War II. In his closing commentary on Birmingham, Smith quoted Edmund Burke, saying "the only thing necessary for the triumph of evil is for good men to do nothing." Convinced that Southern stations would not carry the program, Fred Friendly and other CBS executives asked Smith to kill his tailpiece. Angrily, Howard said no. But the pictures spoke volumes, insisted Friendly, making the tailpiece unnecessary. Smith bristled at the thought that his words were superfluous. He insisted on meeting Paley to complain. That was precisely what the CBS chairman had been waiting for. He listened patiently to Smith as he conducted a brief lecture on what CBS's policy should be in the realm of news analysis. Paley then spoke. He chided Smith for not understanding that networks were not free to say or do whatever they wanted, as were privately owned newspapers and magazines. CBS was licensed by the government, Paley reminded him, and therefore had some obligation to rein itself in. The chairman had one more thing to say to Howard Smith: he was through at CBS. In October 1961 the network announced that he had been dismissed.

That cleared the path for Walter Cronkite. Considering how popular he would become, it is ironic to recall that when Cronkite replaced Doug Edwards in April 1962, thousands wrote in to the network, protesting the change. Ironic, too, because, unbenownst to the television audience, Edwards was coming in for some criticism from his colleagues at CBS. They were distributing memos urging that he be replaced. They felt that somehow he no longer seemed right for the job. Yet the audience had been used to Edwards, used to getting their news from him, and they resented someone else stepping in. Edwards had become almost a part of many American families. It would take some time, but Cronkite would grow on the viewing public. He had been given the job precisely in order to improve CBS's ratings, and he would do that. It would take until late 1965 before Walter Cronkite would take over the ratings lead from Chet and Dave, but once he did so, he held onto it until he stepped down in 1981. In time, Walter Cronkite, the friendly native of St. Joseph, Missouri, famous for his avuncular manner, his trustworthiness, and of course his stamina, would become CBS News's leading personality during the 1960s.

He became known for his devotion to the hard news story, and not for his intellectual range (as were Charles Collingwood and Eric Sevareid). No blasé observer of events, Cronkite was just your average person who might be sitting with you in the living room watching television. He seemed comfortable, and no matter how bad things were, if Cronkite could hand-deliver the news to you, it would somehow be OK.

"No One Will Be Killed. No One Will Have a Brain Tumor."

Above all, he prided himself on being able to report the news quickly. Doug Edwards had been a reader of the news, and quite a good one. But he had not taken control of the news operation as such—he had not taken the title of managing editor, as Cronkite would. Walter Cronkite was a wire service man, he had it in his blood, and because of that, he would turn the "CBS Evening News" into a replica of the wire services: just as the daily news "budget" of the Associated Press or United Press International gave the top stories of the day, so the "CBS Evening News" would do the same. And, just as *The New York Times* tried to be a newspaper of record, Cronkite wanted the "CBS Evening News" to be the broadcast of record. Ernest Leiser, who would become executive producer of the Cronkite show in December 1964, noted that had Walter been given his way the entire news show "would have been a series of very short hard-news reports. And he would have been on camera for half the show which, as good a broadcaster as he is, wouldn't have worked." (12) With that wire service blood flowing, Walter liked breaking stories. "He used to be very impatient," recalled Burt Benjamin, who was Cronkite's executive producer, "if you would come in and say, 'Jesus, that's a great piece on the front page of *The New York Times*. He'd say, 'We should have had that yesterday, not today.'" (13) So much so that he hated to step outside for a bite to eat. In the true wire service tradition of preferring to hang around the office just in case some big story might break, he would feel guilty being away from the office too long. News broadcasters, in his view, had to be reporters first. "Everything else," he once said, "in electronic journalism should be built on this base: a solid belief in—and ambition to be—a newsman, not a disc jockey, not a soap salesman . . ." (14)

He was a tough editor as well, deciding which CBS news personnel he liked, which he disliked, grilling reporters whether they were truly sure of their facts. He wanted to know everything. Once he turned to Bill Overend, a writer on the "Evening News" who had been working on a minor environmental story, and said, "Bill, would you find out when life began?" (15) Overend called a researcher, and they came up with a figure. CBS's reputation grew because of Cronkite's no-nonsense approach to the news. Another Cronkite talent was his sense of balance. He appeared to give all news items the same weight, avoiding intonations that might imply degrees of significance. Viewers reacted positively to this unwavering delivery. In short, Walter Cronkite radiated a kind of steadiness as well as a sincerity and that counted with his audience. He would become a true American institution. So much so that the Swedish even called their anchormen Cronkiters.

In the late 1960s Cronkite remained his usual indefatigable self. Huntley and Brinkley had never gotten interested in the space race, and so when it came time to televise the dramatic live space shots, one of the major stories of the 1960s, others would fill in for them. Not so with

Walter Cronkite. He loved the story, loved space, studied the job, and mastered its terminology and folklore. And, once he got on the story, it was impossible to get him off. With Chet and Dave yielding precious airtime to others, Walter had the field to himself. And he took advantage of it. During the Apollo XI lunar walk, CBS stayed on the air for 30 consecutive hours, and Walter was on air all but 3 of them. He concluded the live coverage at 6 P.M. and then anchored the "Evening News" at the regular 6:30 P.M. time. Later that night at 11:30 P.M. he returned to do a special when the astronauts were leaving lunar orbit.

What lay at the basis of Cronkite's success? *Chicago Sun-Time* television columnist Ron Power believed that "somewhere in the collective consciousness of people in this country is the ideal composite face and voice of the American Man—and Cronkite has it." Paul Klein, a former audience researcher at NBC, thought that viewers had stuck with Cronkite because his rational rhetoric provided a buffer of sanity between the often-frightening news images on their screen. (16)

By the fall of 1963, the feeling was growing among CBS news executives that there was too little time in the 15-minute evening slot to report the news fully. As Ernest Leiser, assistant general manager of CBS News, wrote in a memo to CBS News President Richard Salant and CBS News General Manager Blair Clark, "The next great advance in television news will be the half-hour network news broadcast each weekday night in prime time. CBS News proposes to be the first to take this major step in the coming of age of television journalism. Our aim is as simple as it is exciting. We propose to leave off the compressed tabloid treatment of hard news on TV and to give our viewers instead the television equivalent of an authoritative and complete daily newspaper. We will deal with more news, of more kinds, and give that news more meaning.

"A whole, vast array of stories now goes totally uncovered, or brutally synopsized, on the nightly news broadcasts of all the networks. Big developments in business or science, or in the basic patterns of American living now go unnoticed, just because there is not time to deal with them in 12 minutes (15 minutes less commercial announcements) of regular programming. We skim off the top of page one, and we must do so at a pell-mell pace that leaves the viewer dizzy and only fleetingly aware of what he has seen and heard. For pace, we sacrifice change of pace. There is no time for the stories of human interest, of whimsy and nostalgia, of 'civilization reporting,' which are often more genuinely important than the headlines of politics and disaster, and which are longer remembered. And we now cannot cover even the big headline stories in the depth and dimension the American people deserve." (17)

Leiser's plea was noted, and a decision was taken to extend Cronkite's "Evening News" from 15 to 30 minutes. Designed to boost CBS's presitge in the news field, the news expansion was for Bill Paley an opportunity to reclaim the lost glory that had been taken away by Huntley and Brinkley. Around CBS, the belief was that the NBC co-anchors were a passing phenomenon; there was confidence that the network, thanks to its group of high-quality correspondents, could retrieve a part of that glory and reemerge as supreme in the news field. The expanded news would give television news a new power, a new potential. But there were problems to overcome. Going to 30 minutes would not be greeted warmly by the CBS affiliates: yielding those 15 minutes to the networks meant that the affiliates couldn't sell commercials. Thus, by way of compensation, CBS promised to give the stations more money from the commercials sold during the network news show. Apart from the problem with the affiliates, there was genuine doubt in some quarters that viewers would want that much news. How would CBS fill so much airtime? Would it require more stories or would the stories it did have to be expanded? With expanded evening news, new field staffs were required, more bureaus, more stories. The 30-minute slot had arisen in response to the view that there was more important news than a 15-minute nightly show could accommodate. But, ironically, once the 30-minute news programs arose, new demands were made for more news and that, along with the development of the new satellite technology, would mean a fresh boost to television news. Chosen to anchor the expanded coverage was Walter Cronkite. He had some competition from Charles Collingwood, but it was apparently not a serious challenge.

On Labor Day of 1963, Walter Cronkite and his CBS News team, which included Eric Sevareid in Washington, D.C., began the first 30-minute network news show. Highlighting that first night was a Cronkite interview with President John F. Kennedy, conducted that morning at the president's summer retreat at Hyannisport, Massachusetts. Cronkite asked Kennedy about the growing war in Vietnam where forty-seven Americans had been killed. Also on that history-making program was a young field reporter named Dan Rather who described a confrontation between police and blacks in the South. The 30-minute format would endure, but CBS won no great applause at the outset for introducing it; indeed, when Cronkite's ratings did not soar as a result of the new format, Paley turned on Salant as the man who had promoted the idea, kicking him upstairs. Once CBS expanded the "Evening News" to 30 minutes, more reporters would have to be hired and more domestic bureaus opened. As late as 1961, CBS News still emphasized foreign reporting. In 1962, domestic bureaus were opened to supplement the existing ones in Chicago and Washington. And so, though he may have looked as if he was handling the program on his own, Cronkite eventually had over fifty CBS correspondents and staffers contributing to the "Evening News" program.

Cronkite had become the master anchor. He was, in his own view as well as others', unique, and he had no interest in diluting whatever it was that he offered viewers. By illustration of that, he refused to watch the Huntley-Brinkley nightly news for fear of having some of their style rub off on him.

It was standard for CBS correspondents to become eyewitnesses to history. That was their job. Occasionally, some of them became part of the history. In this case, it happened to David Schoenbrun, who, toward the end of 1961 had been offered the job of CBS bureau chief in Washington. Once in the post, he found life in Washington far different from working as a CBS correspondent in Paris. Schoenbrun used to send cables offering news stories to Don Hewitt for the Cronkite evening news, or Hewitt would cable, requesting news reports. It was simple enough, and there was no real conflict. It was up to him, as the CBS man in Paris, to explain Charles de Gaulle to viewers, and that was that. No one at CBS would have had the temerity to question anything David Schoenbrun would say over the air. But in Washington things were different. He would phone Don Hewitt before 12 noon to discuss an analysis piece for the "Evening News," and then after he wrote it, David would send a telex copy of it to New York. At that point, Cronkite, as the managing editor of the "Evening News," would read Schoenbrun's piece and then discuss it with Hewitt. Only then—about two hours before airtime—would Cronkite and Hewitt set up an afternoon conference call with Schoenbrun, perhaps disagreeing with something he had written, and proposing changes in the script.

By September 1962 he had begun his own news show on Sundays called "Washington Report with David Schoenbrun." Soon thereafter would come his biggest moment in television. On October 22 President Kennedy had announced at 7 P.M. on television that the Russians had put missiles into Cuba, 90 miles off American shores, with the purpose of "none other than to provide a nuclear strike capability against the Western Hemisphere." Kennedy pledged to remove the missiles. In the coming days the Soviet leader, Nikita Khrushchev, sent a letter to the president, offering to remove the missiles if Kennedy would in turn pledge not to invade Cuba. A second, harsher letter had come unexpectedly from the Soviet leader. After some deliberations among American officials, a response was drafted to the first letter as if the second had somehow not existed. The Soviets were told that they had to reply by the next day, Sunday, October 28.

Early that Sunday morning, David Schoenbrun began writing the opening material on the missile crisis for his "Washington Report" when the news came off the wire that Moscow had announced a decision to dismantle the missiles, crate them, and return them to the USSR. This certainly appeared to indicate that President Kennedy had won his confrontation with Khrushchev. With the Soviets having caved in and the missile crisis apparently over, Schoenbrun let out a whoop of joy. Racing back from the wire machines to his office, David called Pierre Salinger, Kennedy's press secretary, at home at 9:15 A.M. Salinger's wife said Pierre was asleep, the first time in two weeks, and she was not about to wake him.

"Wake him," screamed David. "Don't argue, it's great news, we've won."

"We did?" She screamed. "I'll get Pierre."

A few moments later, Pierre Salinger came to the phone, still half-asleep, and said, "David this better be good or I'll beat the hell out of you."

Laughing, David declared, "Pierre, K has backed down. He's pulling out the missiles. Your boss has won." Salinger quickly got off the phone to inform the president who was at church, promising to give David something for his 12 noon show in return for the favor of waking him up with the great news. Schoenbrun could not have been more excited. No one had wanted his ghetto time (the phrase, as noted earlier, that television officials used for the time on Sundays when potential viewers were otherwise busy with church and a large midday meal), so there he was with the only news report on any network on this momentous morning. He had phoned Marvin Kalb, the CBS man in Moscow, to arrange for him to give a situationer to lead off the show and then he would ask Kalb a series of questions.

At 12 noon Schoenbrun was on the air, announcing that the missile crisis had just ended. He then switched to Marvin Kalb in Moscow. This was still the 1960s and so there were no direct satellite pictures. A still portrait of Kalb was shown as he started to broadcast on a radio circuit. As he was describing the scene, Soviets congregating around the Kremlin, talking in low tones, digesting the Soviet defeat, a little bulb next to Schoenbrun's phone lit red. It was a signal from the control room that something was wrong and that he should go right to a commercial break to get an urgent message. Interrupting Kalb, Schoenbrun said that he had to take a short break and he would get right back to him. On the screen came a standard noncommercial appeal for funds for some disease. Picking up the phone in anger, Schoenbrun heard Pierre Salinger's voice.

"David, I'm speaking from the Oval Office. . . . The meeting [of the Kennedy crisis team] adjourned to watch your show. The President is right next to me. Please do not let Kalb run on about a Soviet defeat. Do not play this up as a victory for us. There is a danger that Khrushchev will be so humiliated and angered that he will change his mind. Watch what you are saying. Do not mess this up for us."

Rather than react contemptuously to this indisputable attempt by the government to influence his broadcast, Schoenbrun expressed delight. "It never occurred to me for even a microsecond," he wrote later, "that a President ought not to be cutting into a live news program to tell a broadcaster what to say." (18) Instead, he thought the president's judgment was right on the mark, that it was certainly proper for the president to warn him, and he was eager to comply. The conversation with Pierre Salinger had taken no more than 15 seconds. Hanging up, Schoenbrun yelled to the floor man to put Kalb back on the line when the commercial ended. The anchorman was certainly in a quandary. He could not let on that the White House had broken into the broadcast to demand a change of reporting from one of CBS's men in the field. But, agreeing with Salinger and the president, Schoenbrun understood that the missile crisis, seemingly over, could just as quickly be renewed. He sought to walk a delicate tightrope.

"Marvin," Schoenbrun began, "I wonder if people in Moscow are getting some of the thoughts I'm hearing here in Washington today? That this is not a defeat or victory for any power, it is a victory for all mankind, a victory for peace?"

Kalb was sensitivie enough to catch on right away. "Well," he replied, "not generally, David, not yet, but there are a few people at the top who understand what a great moment this is for everyone. It will get through to the masses of the people quickly. The Russian people value peace as much as any people. They will rejoice when the realization sinks in that this is a great day for everyone."

Few decisions would give CBS News President Richard Salant more satisfaction than the one to bring Mike Wallace to work for CBS Television News in March 1963. At first, resentment flared against Wallace. He had been an entertainer, a maker of commercials, and those roles appeared to have little to do with broadcast journalism. So he would have to prove himself. Wallace adopted a low profile, putting most of his energies into his radio interview series, "Personal Closeup"; among his guests during the early weeks were Noel Coward, Jimmy Hoffa, Jack Benny, Moshe Dayan, and a young writer named Gloria Steinem. The series was well received, and consequently, the program's name was changed to "Mike Wallace At Large." For the next twenty years the radio show would remain a staple of the CBS radio network. In the summer of 1963, CBS decided to begin a news program during the midmorning slot on weekdays. It sought an anchor man. Harry Reasoner believed he was eminently qualified. He had been backing up Cronkite on the weekday evening news program and hosting a midmorning news and feature program called "Calendar," which seemed similar to the new morning program. So when the

"No One Will Be Killed. No One Will Have a Brain Tumor."

job went to Wallace, Reasoner was miffed. The show, called "CBS Morning News," was aired at 10 A.M.

To attract a large audience, producer Av Westin told Wallace that the broadcast would have to grab people by the ears and not the eyes as midmorning viewers were likely to have sets on while doing household chores. As a result, Westin flooded the morning news with consumer-oriented stories and features for women. The show dealt candidly with sexual subjects: birth control, infidelity, veneral disease, menopause, and pap smears. Engaging in such subjects was a daring departure for television in the early 1960s. For two years the program stayed in its midmorning time slot; then in August 1965 it was suddenly moved to 7 A.M. CBS executives realized they could make $1 million more by putting on "I Love Lucy" reruns in the Wallace time slot. Another reason for the switch was NBC's highly popular "Today" program. CBS had always had difficulty in attracting a large audience for the early morning hours. NBC's "Today" show grabbed the ratings early and stayed out in front down through the years. In various ways and at various times, CBS had made special efforts to seize the audience from "Today" but with little luck. Although both Wallace and Westin angrily protested, it was to no avail. Wallace was going to be used to go up against "Today."

But it didn't work. The morning news program didn't fare well in its new time spot, having lost its special identity and a good deal of its audience. Wallace did the 7 A.M. show for nearly a year and then decided to move on. The hours were most unpleasant. He had not liked getting up at 5 A.M. for the 10 A.M. show but getting out of bed at 3 A.M. for the 7 A.M. show proved downright painful. During the summer of 1966, Wallace abandoned the morning anchor and joined the ranks of general-assignment correspondents.

Dan Rather began talking with CBS about work in early 1962. His agent told him that CBS was offering $17,500, but he was sure in a day or two he could get them up to $22,000. Rather said that he would prefer to start at the lower figure simply because he felt better about starting at that salary than a higher one. The next morning Rather started a career that would take him to the height of the profession of television news.

It was March 1962. He had been told to report at 10 A.M. He was to hang around the news desk and handle the loose ends. At the very moment he was walking through the door, a jetliner went down in Jamaica Bay a few seconds after taking off from Idlewild (later renamed Kennedy) Airport. The plane had ninety-five passengers plus a crew and no one survived. Dan yelled out to the man in charge of the desk that he had covered plane crashes and perhaps he could help. But the correspondent,

Dave Duggan, and cameraman, Herbie Schwartz, had already started racing for the door. Rather received approval to try to catch up with Duggan and Schwartz. When he did, Duggan told the new CBS man that the best thing he could do was to stay out of the way. By the time they reached the airport, Duggan had asked Rather if he thought he could handle the radio portion of the assignment. Thrilled, Rather said he could. With no phone in sight, Dan went out to the highway, flagged a man in a phone company van, and explained his problem. Climbing a pole, the man hooked up a phone and soon had it working. From then on Rather did hourly reports over radio on his first CBS assignment.

Although told he would be kept in New York six months, within six weeks Rather was off to Dallas to head up the CBS Bureau. Soon after beginning television assignments, Rather uncovered a new, unexpected problem. Makeup. Sometimes a television correspondent like Rather had to apply his own makeup without the luxury of relying on a makeup person in the studio. That meant the correspondent would have to carry his own compact. Once in 1962, Rather boarded a flight from Memphis to Birmingham and placing his coat on the overhead rack found himself in great embarrassment when the compact fell out and landed on the floor in the aisle. A stewardess quickly retrieved it and asked to whom did the compact belong? Rather gave her a stare as if to say what would he be doing with a thing like that? She looked around at the other (female) passengers but no one spoke up. Rather was panicky for the rest of the flight. He realized that he had to do a piece almost as soon as he landed and he needed the makeup. But there was no way he was going to ask the stewardess for his compact back. So he walked off the plane, and did the piece without his makeup. (19)

Rather's greatest moment in the early part of his career would come in Dallas on a November afternoon in 1963. Until almost the last moment he had not planned to be there that day. As the chief of the new CBS Bureau in New Orleans, Rather had been asked to organize CBS's coverage of President Kennedy's precampaign swing through Texas. But, as it turned out, Friday, November 22, 1963, happened to be the ninety-eighth birthday of John Nance Garner, the Texan who, having served as vice president of the United States from 1933 to 1941, compared the vice presidency to "a pitcher of warm spit." CBS had decided that Rather should fly to Dallas that morning and send a story on Garner from there.

At the last moment, Rather learned that one of CBS's film drops along the parade route of the presidential motorcade in Dallas was still uncovered. It was the last such drop on the route. The motorcade was due to end at a railroad overpass just beyond an old brick building with a name no one had heard of—the Texas School Book Depository. The caravan would then move onto the Stemmons Freeway, pick up speed, and head for the Trade Mart where the president would deliver a luncheon speech.

Close to 12:30 P.M. Dallas time Rather picked out his spot on the other side of the railroad tracks, beyond the triple underpass, 30 yards from the later-controversial grassy knoll. He held a yellow grapefruit bag for the CBS film that would be tossed to him by a cameraman in a truck rolling along with the motorcade. This was not exactly a dream assignment for a television correspondent but because it was the president he was willing to do it. The motorcade was running late. The president should have been there by now.

Suddenly, Rather saw a police car dash off, taking the wrong turnoff, in a blaze of speed. Then he thought he saw the presidential limousine go by him. He did not see the president. But he thought he had seen the first lady and Texas Governor John Connally who were riding in the same limousine. He could not be sure. Later he would remember that at no time did he hear any shots. Behind him there was confusion and noise. All Rather could think of doing was to head back to KRLD, the CBS radio affiliate. Standing where he was, he could do nothing, find out nothing. As he passed the railroad tracks, he saw people lying on the grass. Some were screaming, some running, others were pointing. The police were all around. "Don't anybody panic," a voice yelled out, but it appeared that was all everyone was doing. (20)

Back at the radio station, Rather got on the open line to the Trade Mart. Rather yelled to everyone to turn up their police radios full blast. Once they did, one of the police radios made a reference to the Parkland Hospital. Rather phoned there quickly, and, astonishly, learned from a hospital operator that the president had been shot. This was a key moment for the CBS man. Until now, he had had his suspicions, but nothing solid to go on. Now, at least, he knew that something devastating had indeed occurred. But before he would allow himself to report the shooting as fact to CBS he had to nail the story down. Seconds later Rather was somehow able to get a doctor at Parkland on the line; he verified that Kennedy had been brought in. Then incredibly, the doctor volunteered that he understood the president was dead. Rather let people in the Dallas radio station know that he had been told that Kennedy had been shot. Shot. That was all. Cautiously, he held back the other, more significant part of what the doctor had said.

To pass that along, Rather would need something official. Calling Parkland again, this time he got a Catholic priest on the line. Yes, the priest said, the president had been shot and was dead. Was he certain of that, Rather asked the priest? "Yes, unfortunately, I am," came the reply. Seconds later, Rather was on the phone to Eddie Barker, who was the news director at KRLD, at the Trade Mart. Barker said he was with the chief of staff of Parkland and he had told Barker that Kennedy had been shot and was dead. Unbenownst to Rather, on the phone line were three CBS people listening in from New York, one of whom asked him what precisely had happened. Barker came on and said to Rather that he had been told the president was dead to which Dan replied, "Yes, yes. That's what I hear, too. That he's dead."

Suddenly a voice came on the line asking "What was that?" At this point, Rather thought the voice belonged to Eddie Barker, but it did not. It was in fact a radio editor in New York. Rather said, "That's my information, too. That he's dead."

"Did you say 'dead'?" asked the radio editor. "Are you sure, Dan?"

"Right, dead. The president definitely has been shot and I think he is dead." Still assuming he was talking to Eddie Barker, Rather added, "That's the word I get from two people at the hospital." At that instant, the CBS man in Dallas heard someone in New York announce around the radio desk that Dan Rather says the president is dead. There then came the voice of Alan Jackson over CBS Radio saying the president of the United States is dead. The "Star Spangled Banner" was played, an automatic step in such situations. CBS Radio had a beat of 17 minutes over the other networks. But, as far as Dan Rather down in Dallas was concerned, the radio should never have rushed out with the news. Nor should it have created the solemn mood by playing the national anthem. Shouting into the phone, Rather said he had not authorized a bulletin saying Kennedy was dead; indeed, he had authorized nothing. But, said the editors in New York, you had said, hadn't you, Dan, that the president was dead—and twice at that? Horrified at what had happened, Rather quickly reviewed his sources and decided that what those sources had told him would stand up if he had to announce the death of anyone—save for the president of the United States! The president was different. Announcement of his death would automatically plunge the entire nation into mourning, indeed into national crisis.

Now on the phone to Rather came two senior CBS News executives, Ernie Leiser and Don Hewitt, asking if the president's death had been officially announced. The two men wanted to clear the way for television to pass on the tragic news, but they were not prepared to authorize a television announcement unless the White House had confirmed Kennedy's death. Rather said no, as yet there had been no official announcement. Leiser and Hewitt then asked if Kennedy was in fact dead. Again, Rather said yes, he believed that to be the case. How did he know, they asked? Rather passed on to them the details, with whom he had talked, what they had said. Eddie Barker jumped on the phone line and urged New York to announce the president's death over television, but New York would not budge.

Meanwhile, at CBS Television headquarters nearly everyone other than Walter Cronkite was literally out to lunch. As he so often did, Cronkite was sitting at his desk, finishing a light lunch of cottage cheese and canned pineapple when Ed Bliss, who was the editor of the Cronkite news program, burst in, waving a piece of United Press wire copy and shouting that the president had been shot. It was 1:40 P.M. in New York, an hour later than Dallas. Cronkite jumped up from his chair, grabbed the UPI copy, shouting, "The hell with writing it. Just give me air." Heading for a small announcer's booth a few feet down the hall, he gave himself instructions: don't break up, control yourself. Cronkite interrupted the soap opera "As the World Turns" with the first, fragmentary news that the president had been shot and that his wounds were serious and "perhaps could be fatal." Cronkite's was the first announcement over television, beating ABC by 2 minutes and NBC by 5. On the screen was a bulletin slide while he spoke. It was still not possible to put a newsman on the air immediately.

Finally, at 2:30 P.M. New York time, came the official announcement, more than 30 minutes after CBS Radio had reported the death of the president. It was Walter Cronkite who announced President Kennedy's death over television. His voice this time broke and he was forced to wipe a tear from his eye. Don Hewitt, who was directing the continuous coverage, asked Charles Collingwood to take over. In later years, no one would have probably dared to suggest that Cronkite be replaced at such a moment. Indeed, some admirers of Cronkite have suggested that it was he himself who asked to be relieved. But that would have been most unlike Cronkite. That night Harry Reasoner handled CBS's prime-time coverage.

Thus began perhaps the single most dramatic event shown on American television, four days of intensive coverage of the events surrounding the assassination of the president of the United States. Prior to that dramatic weekend, television news had covered some live events, such as the conventions, but never before had television covered an event of such significance as the aftermath of the Kennedy assassination as it was happening. During the four days of the funeral, the television networks lost $40 million. Credit for taking the nation through one of its worst crises went to television as a whole, and television news in particular. As Fred Friendly put it, "Television was the glue that held the country together. I think we might have viewed the assassination as a conspiracy. We might have thought that some black did it . . . that some enemy did it . . . that Castro did it. Some people still believe that. But I think television on the air for four days straight, no commercials, held this country together, and there was a big enough staff to do that right." (21)

Just as so many millions of American would be shocked and transformed by the Kennedy assassination, so too was television, and with it CBS. Because of that weekend, television news would rise to become the major element in American journalism. Thanks in part to those four days, Americans would turn increasingly to television for their news.

Frank Stanton was in the dining room. Upon hearing the news from Dallas, he quickly alerted everyone that CBS was canceling all programs except those related to the news and the tragedy. It was the first network to decide to do so. It was, in retrospect, a bold decision. "I was criticized by a lot of people who were hurt economically," noted Stanton. "Some of our affiliates thought we were being stupid. I don't think anybody went public with that kind of criticism, because as it turned out, they would have looked pretty foolish." (22)

Once he made the decision to stay on the air continuously, Stanton realized that he had given himself a new problem. "What the hell do you do for programming when you've got 18 hours a day of open airtime?" he asked himself at the time. (23) He had gone through Franklin Roosevelt's death, and he recalled the calls he had from Jimmy Durante and Red Skelton and others who told him, "You know, we can't go on." In those days, programs were live and there wasn't anything ready to substitute for the live shows. And so CBS had to improvise. But at least Stanton had gone through that experience, probably alone, he believes, of all the broadcast executives in 1963.

And it helped him when it came to making decisions at this time. "I realized that one of the things I needed for that weekend, at least I thought what I needed, was some good music from distinguished orchestras that could fill the time, because I didn't think we could go on talking." (24) So that Friday afternoon one of the first things he did was to call the head of television programming to ask if he could get some of the great orchestra conductors, Eugene Ormandy, Leonard Bernstein, and others, to agree to take on this sad, but vital task. Recalled Stanton, "I wanted to stockpile about 8 or 12 hours of distinguished music and get it recorded and ready to go so we could use it at various times in the schedule, realizing full well that some of it we would repeat, because we couldn't come up with music for the whole time." (25) Goddard Lieberson, who ran the record division, approached Bernstein. CBS brought the musicians into studios, and asked them to play a repertoire of classical music that would be suitable for that horrific weekend. But, in the end, CBS used only 4 hours of the music on the air. It eventually became clear to Frank Stanton that the viewing audience wasn't interested in listening to music. He noticed that when news of the tragedy was on, even repeats of previously shown material, the audience shot up.

The search for usable film of the assassination soon began in earnest. No one had such film or so it appeared. Finally, the local Dallas CBS affiliate produced a name, Abraham Zapruder. Zapruder was, in Dan Rather's colorful phrase, one of history's great accidents. Having shot film of Kennedy's motorcade, Zapruder had no idea what he had or what the value of it was. CBS arranged for Eastman Kodak to process the film. By Saturday morning, November 23, with a lawyer advising him, Zapruder had suddenly become acutely aware of just what he possessed. To Rather, CBS had a moral claim to the film, having helped Zapruder to process it. But would Zapruder agree? Or would he make a deal with someone else first? When Rather walked into the lawyer's office he was shocked to find Dick Stolley of *Life* magazine. The rules of the game were explained by Zapruder's lawyer: the two men could look at the film without taking notes and then give a bid. Rather thought quickly. The bidding was secondary. Once he had seen the film, the important thing to do was to get to the station and describe what he had seen over national television. The Zapruder film, the only actual footage of the Kennedy assassination, automatically ranked as historic—and Rather knew that if he could be the first to describe it on television, he would have a major exclusive. After gazing at the remarkable film, Rather prepared to make a mad dash for the radio station but not before telling the lawyer that he had no authority to make a bid. That was the job of CBS in New York. He sought a promise, however, that Zapruder would not make a final decision until CBS had a chance to make an offer on the film.

Seconds after arriving at the studio, Rather was put on the air. He did make one error, leaving out the part about the movement of the president's head. In the film the president's head lurched slightly forward, then exploded backward. The CBS man described the forward motion of Kennedy's head but overlooked mentioning the violent, backward reaction. Later Rather went back to the lawyer's office, planning to offer $10,000 to show the film once on CBS. But upon arriving he was told that the film had been sold to *Life*. Rather was furious. CBS offered to rent the film from its new owners for $100,000 for one showing that weekend but was refused.

Dan Rather's presence in Dallas, his quick-witted coverage of the complicated, mind-boggling events, his diligence and energy under pressure, brought him into the national spotlight and thrust his career at CBS forward. He had become one of the network's stars.

ten

"RIDING OFF INTO THE TWILIGHT LOOKING FOR THE BLACK HATS"

CBS had been occupying the building at 485 Madison Avenue since 1929. But now, a little over three decades later, it had outgrown the place. The decision was made not simply to move into a new building, but to build the place from scratch. The new building was a very definite symbol of the growth CBS was undergoing. But it was more than that. The building at 485, with its lack of air conditioning, its antiquated style, its dankness, had given CBS employees a distinctly second-class feeling compared to NBC, housed in its majestic building at Rockefeller Center. Moving, then, would be a step up.

The building, to be located in New York City, would be designed with aesthetics in mind. When nothing was available on Madison Avenue, Paley and Stanton concentrated on Sixth Avenue and found a site there on the east side of the avenue going from 52nd to 53rd Streets. It was in fact only two blocks from the previous location and had the virtue of being situated in a major business center. Sandwiched between ABC's New York headquarters at 1300 Sixth Avenue and NBC's at Rockefeller Center, the new CBS building along with the other two naturally became known as broadcast row.

The new building became the obsession of one man. Frank Stanton

---

put his heart and soul into the planning. Armed with all those profits from the Jim Aubrey era, CBS would put $40 million into the new edifice. Eero Saarinen, a creative force who was one of the country's finest architects, was commissioned to design the building. He was chosen in part because of his design of the TWA building at John F. Kennedy International Airport in New York. The CBS building was the first skyscraper Saarinen would design. He told Paley in a letter that the building would be "the simplest skyscraper statement in New York." (1) It would soar out of the ground and appear to reach for the sky. Upon seeing a mock-up of the building in Detroit, Paley at first was thrown off by the building's austerity. But it grew on him, and in July 1961 he gave the architect the go-ahead on the final design.

Soon after that, however, Saarinen, at age 51, died. Paley chose to stay with the Saarinen firm. Stanton took Paley to New Rochelle to see the mock-up before the Saarinen firm was given the final green light. Granite was chosen over other materials even though it was more expensive. This was a building that was meant to last a hundred years so what did it matter? The granite would retain its harsh beauty without deteriorating. The granite Paley and Stanton wanted was to be dark, but not look polished or marblelike. People were sent to Africa, Japan, Norway, and Sweden, to check out different types of black granite. Paley checked out different types on his trips to Europe. Eventually they settled on a Canadian black granite from a quarry in Alma, Quebec. Thanks to the dark black color, the granite-faced building became known, understandably, as "Black Rock." Everyone from Paley on down referred to the building by that nickname. By the end of 1964, CBS employees began moving into the forty-story building.

The interior struck everyone as anonymous and uninteresting except for the 35th floor where Bill Paley had his offices and executive conference rooms. There, he placed dark green carpet and softened the atmosphere by placing examples of modern art on the walls. Along the lengthy corridors he put more paintings as well as sculpture. The suite had something of the atmosphere of a museum. Meanwhile, Stanton was attempting to create a uniformity within the building that presumably would encourage efficiency and discipline. He had a hand in choosing every desk (except Paley's) and every office television set. His instructions reflected the desire for a sameness: there could be no paintings, photographs, or posters on the walls except those that came from the art department's special collection. Stanton chose a special typeface to indicate floors in the elevators. It was said that he walked around the building on Saturday mornings with a screwdriver in his hand to assure that the grooves in the screw were parallel to the ground. It was also said that he put sensors in the chairs of his secretaries so he would know whether they were at their place of work. Stanton, for the record, denied doing these things.

The top people at CBS felt a building of grandeur was needed. The network, in the 1960s, was moving in all sorts of directions, and it would need a magnificent building not just as a symbol of its diversity and size but as a central headquarters worthy of its name. Flush with the profits that had been coming in because of the Aubrey triumphs of the early 1960s, CBS was in a new mood to expand.

Diversifying was hardly new at CBS. Between its founding and the late 1970s, the company would acquire over forty firms, always trying to remain within the field of communications. Dating all the way back to the late 1920s, the establishment of the radio network was followed by the purchase of a talent agency, the manufacturing of records and then television sets and musical instruments; eventually, CBS became involved in books and magazines, and as unlikely as it seemed, a major league baseball team. Beginning in 1956 when CBS put money into the Broadway musical *My Fair Lady*, CBS invested in more than forty theatrical productions, most of them Broadway shows.

By 1962, Paley and Stanton and the board of directors were interested in branching out some more. With cash in hand, it made sense to diversify. But, as Paley noted, it made sense to broaden CBS beyond broadcasting, subject as the network was to possible governmental regulation. A company acquisitions specialist was hired as were a number of business consulting firms.

One of CBS's strangest acts of diversification came in 1964 when CBS bought the New York Yankees baseball franchise for $11.2 million (acquiring 80 percent of the team). Over the next two years, CBS bought the other 20 percent for another $2 million. The Yankees had had the best record in baseball and were on their way to winning their fifth straight pennant and ninth in the previous ten seasons. In their forty-two-year history they had won twenty-eight American League pennants and twenty World Series. "We figured," said Paley in retrospect, "that by owning a professional baseball team we would gain a deeper insight into the world of professional sports, upon which we were spending millions in television rights each year." (2)

Owning a baseball team was not like owning a radio or television network. Bill Paley and the executives he chose understood the need for good programming and did something about it. But, no matter how much they understood the need to win baseball games, they were in no position to improve the Yankees' hitting or fielding. They were far too removed from the playing field for that to happen. To make matters worse, the Yankees' future looked less and less impressive. They had fewer super-stars, their player development was slipping, and by 1964, the Yankees were losing their attraction. The lowly New York Mets were outdrawing them.

If CBS thought the Yankees would revive, there was little hope of that. In the eight seasons after CBS purchased them, the Yanks finished second once and fourth or worse the remainder of the time. During six of those eight years, the Yankees lost money. (In 1973, Paley eagerly dumped the team for $10 million.) Paley noted with little enthusiasm later that because CBS had amortized its investment over the years of the own-ership, the sale had created a small profit of $5.4 million after taxes. It was little consolation for what appeared to be one of CBS's less successful attempts at diversifying.

In the summer of 1967, CBS bought the book publisher, Holt, Rine-hart and Winston for $221.8 million. With that purchase, CBS became a major publisher of elementary, high school, and college textbooks and trade books. The magazine *Field & Stream* was also purchased then. And in 1968, CBS bought W. B. Saunders Company, the largest publisher of medical textbooks in the world. After that came the purchase of a Mexi-can firm, Editorial Interamericana S.A., the number one publisher in the world of scientific and medical books in Spanish and Portuguese. Other special-interest magazines were purchased, including *Road & Truck, Cycle World, Sea, Pickup Van & 4WD,* and *World Tennis.*

In 1971 CBS bought Popular Library, Inc., making it a publisher of paperbacks, including novels and reference works. Then in January 1977 it bought Fawcett Publications, a major publisher of mass-market paper-backs; with that purchase it obtained *Rudder* magazine, *Mechanix Illus-trated,* and *Woman's Day* magazine, with a circulation of over 8 million. The next purchase came in December of that year when CBS bought 80 percent of Doin Editeurs, a French medical and science textbook pub-lisher.

In addition to publishing, CBS in 1966 bought Creative Playthings, which made high-quality educational toys. It also bought a decade later Wonder Products, which made the Wonder Horse riding toys. In the sum-mer of 1978 CBS acquired Gabriel Industries, a large toy company. By that time CBS had cornered an important part of the toy market. It moved into other areas as well, making full-length feature films and becoming the second largest maker of musical instruments in the United States.

Diversification worked well. It had taken CBS forty-two years to achieve the level of $1 billion in annual sales. And in 1969 it had reached that level. (Between 1971 and 1979, more than half of all CBS sales had come from nonbroadcasting activities.)

As the 1960s wore on, spinoffs became the catchword of television entertainment. Paul Henning, producer of "Beverly Hillbillies," started the process rolling with "Petticoat Junction" debuting in the 1963–64 season. In the fall of 1964, CBS spun off "The Andy Griffith Show," and "Gomer Pyle, U.S.M.C.," starring Jim Nabors, was born. ABC was getting stronger in the mid-1960s: only "Gomer Pyle" and "Gilligan's Island" counted as CBS triumphs in the 1964–65 season. Jim Aubrey took the unprecedented step in midseason of revamping the schedule, making eleven programming changes for the winter of 1965. He did not introduce new shows; he merely altered time slots in a bid to improve ratings. It worked: CBS's ratings improved marginally, enough to give it a ratings victory for the 1964–65 season. As the 1965–66 season began, CBS and NBC tried to appeal to the large number of viewers who by now had purchased color television sets. In the fall of 1964, NBC had begun the first major color season; then, in the summer of 1965, the networks started to cover live news events in color. That fall NBC was televising almost all its programs in color; CBS had reached the halfway mark. During the fall of 1967, the top ten list was still crowded with perennial favorites such as Ed Sullivan, Red Skelton, Jackie Gleason, Lucille Ball, Andy Griffith, "Gunsmoke," and the "Beverly Hillbillies." In its fall 1967–68 season, CBS sought to modernize its schedule. The results were disastrous. The main entry was "He and She," starring the real-life husband and wife team of Richard Benjamin and Paula Prentiss. A ratings failure and clearly ahead of its time, the show was canceled after one season. In four years similar efforts would hit paydirt. It was around this time that CBS stopped plans to do an American version of the bold British sitcom, "Till Death Do Us Part," which had been on in England for the previous two years. While CBS managed to win the 1968–69 season, it appeared to be having difficulty coming up with new hits.

"You know, Fred," said Harry Reasoner, "you are an executive in the sense that Willie Sutton is a banker." (3) Nonetheless, in March 1964 CBS News had a new president—Fred Friendly. He had been the beneficiary of Bill Paley's dismay at the continuing bad ratings experienced by the "CBS Evening News." At the wrap-up of the Huntley-Brinkley news, NBC had been touting the program as having the largest daily news circulation in the world. Paley was hurt by that. Often he asked Friendly when Cronkite was going to be first. All that Friendly could answer was: when we switch Walter over to a better time spot than 6:30 P.M. (Indeed, when in late 1965, that happened, Cronkite shot up to number one in the ratings.)

But, meanwhile, Paley had watched in recent years as the news division slipped, and he wanted it back on top. Because of the bad ratings, Richard Salant was out as the president of news (he was asked to become a special assistant to Frank Stanton) and Friendly was in. There was some question why Friendly would take such a job. He would be paid less than when he was executive producer of "CBS Reports." His predecessors had all left the job in disappointment and frustration. Friendly turned to Murrow for advice and was told to take the job but make sure that he wouldn't have to report to a ten-man committee. Friendly thought that good advice. He was now in charge of a $30 million news organization. It was said by some, who were aware of his connections to Ed Murrow, that Friendly had been appointed to repair CBS's prestige in the news field. When Bill Leonard asked Paley years later why he had made the switch, the chairman replied, "I thought the place needed shaking up, and maybe Friendly could do it." (4) Admittedly, it was an odd choice. Friendly had the reputation of being a maverick, of being more closely tied to Ed Murrow and his legend than to anyone else at CBS, and of being a difficult person for whom to work. As *Time* magazine noted, he was a "homely, rangy fellow who tosses around in his chair as if it were stuffed with thumbtacks, Friendly stews, fusses and frets over everything he does. . . . His friend Carl Sandburg once remarked: 'Fred always looks as if he had just got off a foam-flecked horse.'" (5)

Just what kind of news chief would Friendly be? No one could be sure. But three weeks into the job Friendly faced his first severe test when an earthquake struck in Alaska. It was the first major news story under his presidency. And the results were, from CBS's viewpoint, a disaster. NBC reporters and camera crews moved to the scene quickly, providing Chet Huntley and David Brinkley with detailed film reports. As Friendly learned to his distress, the "CBS Evening News" has used stories rewritten from wire service accounts. He insisted that such a thing never happen again: furious at the Los Angeles Bureau for not getting a correspondent to the scene quickly, Friendly was prepared to fire someone simply to make a point, but backed off at the last moment.

Friendly made his presence felt quickly on the issue of putting bulletins on the air. For years it had been the policy of CBS and the other networks that the news department had the automatic right to interrupt the entertainment schedule if the news warranted. To avoid complaints from irate viewers, advertisers, or affiliates, the networks made sure not to overdo the bulletin privilege. But Fred Friendly had an itchy trigger finger when it came to bulletins. In his view, the news came first, and no one was going to tell him differently. On one occasion CBS News broke into a soap opera with a bulletin reporting a train derailment in West Virginia: it turned out to be a freight train and only four persons had been slightly injured. Another time NBC broke several minutes ahead of CBS with a bulletin that President Johnson had been rushed to the hospital. Livid with the CBS assignment desk editor, Friendly told the man he was fired even before he could go on the air with the delayed bulletin. So, in full view of the American people, the young man read the bulletin, tears streaming down his face. Viewers were startled not so much by the news that Johnson was ill—it later turned out to be nothing serious—as by the fact that the voice giving out the news was a man obviously crying!

Walter Cronkite had been anchoring political conventions since 1952 and had been the mainstay of the CBS news team. But the Huntley-Brinkley team had raced off with the ratings during the Republican convention in San Francisco in July 1964. To the CBS brass, a change of players appeared necessary for the upcoming Democratic National Convention to be held in Atlantic City in August. A decision was made to replace Walter Cronkite and to put in his place the 55-year-old Robert Trout and the 36-year-old Roger Mudd. It was hoped that Trout, with his experience, and Mudd, with his youthful looks, would manage to compete with Huntley and Brinkley. Fred Friendly argued that removing Cronkite would damage morale, but he was newly installed as CBS News president, only a few months in the job, and as such lacked the clout to take on the higher-ups, including Bill Paley.

Suffering an obvious career setback, Walter was magnanimous about the change, saying he wasn't insulted. The country, however, reacted more emotionally. "We Want Cronkite" buttons appeared in Atlantic City. Viewers let CBS know of their anger at the removal of Walter. CBS officials would later acknowledge that they had overreacted by blaming Cronkite personally for the bad ratings. The real reason appeared simply to be the charismatic quality of Chet and Dave.

By 1968, Cronkite was back as CBS's convention anchor. Cronkite's temporary decline was soon forgotten as he went on to anchor the network's coverage of every political convention from 1968 until 1980. After that, Dan Rather, succeeding Cronkite on the evening news, also inherited the convention anchor assignment. Aiding Cronkite on the floor during that period were Rather, Mike Wallace, and Roger Mudd. It was during those years that CBS overtook NBC, returning as the leader in broadcast journalism.

Apart from the Cronkite controversy, one incident involving CBS correspondent Daniel Schorr caused the network great discomfort during that

---

summer of 1964. Early during the Republican convention, Schorr, who was then CBS's man in West Germany, sent in a filmed report that was aired the weekend before the convention. The report noted that Barry Goldwater had planned a vacation trip to West Germany immediately after his expected presidential nomination. Goldwater was to be the guest of his friend, Lt. Gen. William Quinn, commander of the United States Seventh Army. The senator would stay in Berchtesgaden, Hitler's former retreat and now an American army recreation center. Schorr also reported that the likely Republican nominee planned to link up with the German right wing.

To Goldwater's associates, here was direct evidence that CBS was trying to undo the Arizona senator's presidential run. Goldwater's anger toward CBS did not start in San Francisco. At the time of the Kennedy assassination, Goldwater had learned that in those first traumatic hours of broadcasting, Walter Cronkite had read a piece of wire service copy that indicated that Goldwater, unmoved by the president's death, was going about his normal business. In fact, the senator was in Chicago in the process of taking the body of his mother-in-law to Muncie, Indiana, for burial when he heard the shocking news.

The Schorr report, denied by Goldwater, had an explosive impact in San Francisco. Supporters of Goldwater's chief rival for the nomination, William Scranton, eagerly reproduced the text of Schorr's broadcast and quickly circulated it to delegates. Calling in three network news officials, Fred Friendly told them that "Dan Schorr has given me a clubfoot at this convention." Should Schorr be recalled, Friendly asked? Discharged? Reprimanded? Recalling Schorr was ruled out; that would have appeared as if CBS were giving in to pressure from Goldwater. Phoning Schorr, Friendly told him that Goldwater had denied the story. The story, insisted Schorr, was true.

Friendly demanded that Schorr issue a retraction. Again, Schorr refused. Unfortunately for Schorr, he was forced to admit that one error had crept into his broadcast: it was untrue that Goldwater had tried to link up with the West German right-wing. Rather, it had been a West German initiative to seek out the senator. Schorr offered to clarify that point in a subsequent broadcast, in effect to apologize for that portion of his report. But even that would not satisfy the CBS brass. Paley repeatedly asked Friendly if he had fired Schorr yet. But Friendly could not bring himself to do so, worried that it would lower morale among the other CBS correspondents. Goldwater, for his part, was incensed, vowing never to speak into a CBS microphone again and barring the network from his convention hotel suite. Returning to New York that fall, Schorr sought Walter Cronkite's advice on whether to resign. "I thought of resigning last summer," Cronkite told him, referring to his temporary suspension in Atlantic City. "But then I decided that it doesn't make sense to quit because of the action of some executive who may be gone in the next shakeup a week from now." (6) Cronkite's argument was persuasive: Schorr remained with CBS.

There were some interesting historical footnotes. The following April 1965, Goldwater did show up in West Germany, commenting on his arrival in Stuttgart that this was "the same trip that I canceled last year after a reporter loused it up." Schorr was on hand at the airport with a camera crew, but Goldwater refused to be interviewed. Sally Quinn, in her book, *We're Going to Make You a Star,* complained that President Lyndon Johnson had vetoed her father's promotion and kept him from becoming army chief of staff because of the Goldwater-Schorr incident. And, when Goldwater appeared on the Dinah Shore television program in 1977, he said, "Schorr has never apologized to me and I won't talk to him." Goldwater asserted that Schorr should be tried for espionage for having made public the so-called Pike report, the suppressed report of the House Intelligence Committee. Goldwater also called Schorr a son of a bitch. That phrase was cut from the tape. Schorr himself appeared on a subsequent Dinah Shore show in keeping with the FCC fairness rule to say that he had apologized for the one erroneous sentence but still felt it odd that Goldwater would have wanted to "start his career as a presidential nominee by going to Germany." (7)

By 1965, as American troops were pouring into Vietnam, the television networks were building up their resources there. It is often forgotten, but during the early phase of the American fighting in Vietnam, the television networks treated that American effort with kid gloves. The correspondents essentially backed what the American soldiers were doing, and their stories reflected that attitude. Sympathy for the American combat effort in Southeast Asia extended to the corridors of power within CBS. Frank Stanton was often in touch with President Johnson and appeared to identify with his Vietnam policies. When in January 1966 CBS correspondent Murray Fromson mentioned American air bases in Thailand on the air, bases which had acted as a springboard for American bombing of North Vietnam, Stanton protested to CBS News President Fred Friendly, asserting that all correspondents had agreed to embargo that information. (The CBS bureau chief in Saigon, Sam Zelman, denied this was the case.) Friendly then suggested to Stanton that the North Vietnamese knew they were being bombed, so what purpose was served by keeping the Thai involvement off television? When Stanton argued that the U.S. Government would be embarrassed, Friendly replied that was undoubtedly correct.

There would be other embarrassments that would lead to a deterioration of American support for the war. The most significant one in the early days, occurring in August 1965, was CBS correspondent Morley Safer's disturbing report about a village that was said to have helped the Vietcong and had to be punished.

The son of Austrian Jews, the Toronto-born Safer joined the news staff of the Canadian Broadcasting Corporation in 1955. By the early 1960s he was working for CBS's London Bureau, where for three years he covered nearly every major story in Europe, the Mideast, and Africa. CBS then asked him to go to South Vietnam. As a bachelor, he seemed a logical choice.

Safer's report showed a marine flicking his cigarette lighter to set its huts afire. Cronkite and Ernie Leiser, his executive producer, hesitated and worried for hours over whether to run the now-famous sequence. Were the pictures fair to the United States? To the Marines? Or was their message somewhat out of balance? In the end, it was decided that the pictures were simply too good to pass up. As *Time* noted over a year later: "The very sight of Safer, gaunt and haggard, out there in the midst of battle, brought the war to the screen with undeniable immediacy." (8) When Safer said, "This is what the war in Vietnam is all about," *Time* noted that it seemed a reminder of Ed Murrow's radio reporting from London during World War II. So powerful was this scene that some viewers would later recall that they turned against the war after watching it. Others, most especially the American government, were annoyed at CBS for showing such an event. The Defense Department made Safer *persona non grata*. CBS backed up its correspondent even though some at the network felt uncomfortable by his report.

Fred Friendly came under fire from another quarter in the American government—from Arthur Sylvester, a senior public relations figure in the Defense Department, berating the CBS News president for allowing Safer to hire South Vietnamese television cameramen. Presumably, these cameramen were to blame for Safer's anti-American television footage. (9) At the same time, Friendly met someone else in the American government, a far more senior official, who pointed an angry finger his way and asked, "Don't you ever make a decision on what's good for the United States of America?" To which Friendly replied: "I'm never so smart that I can tell, in that split second decision-making, what's going to be good for the United States of America." After he resigned from CBS in February 1966, Friendly was invited to a Gridiron Club dinner in Washington. As he left, people gathered around him to offer their congratulations on the tough stand he had taken in resigning. One person appeared and broke the mood. It was Arthur Sylvester.

"Well," he said, "we got rid of you. Now we've got to get rid of Morley Safer." (10)

Soon thereafter, the consensus on Vietnam began to come apart. In January 1966 the Senate Foreign Relations Committee planned to hold hearings into American policy in Vietnam. Fred Friendly urged live CBS coverage. In an intranetwork memo he wrote that "Broadcast journalism has, once or twice every decade, an opportunity to prove itself. Such an opportunity were the events leading up to World War II; such was the McCarthy period. The Vietnam war—its coverage in Asia and in Congress—is another such challenge." The man Friendly would have to convince was John A. Schneider, who had only recently been appointed group vice president, Broadcasting. Friendly's proposal to cover the hearings would be Schneider's first major challenge in his new post.

During the first week of the hearings with Secretary of State Dean Rusk testifying, none of the networks chose to broadcast live. Fulbright had permitted a pool camera to represent all three networks at the hearings. The networks could show the proceedings live or use edited portions for their news programs. However, on February 2, Friendly learned from CBS Washington Bureau Chief Bill Small that beginning the next day at 8:30 A.M., NBC planned to preempt regular programming to televise the testimony of David Bell, head of the Agency for International Development. For NBC, the decision to preempt was far easier than for CBS which possessed most of the morning audience; its advertising rates were double those of NBC. So CBS stood to lose much more money. John Reynolds, the CBS Television Network President approved Friendly's proposal to put Bell on live, but advised him to keep the coverage to no more than a half hour. Friendly went way beyond that, leaving the AID man on the air live into the afternoon hours, costing CBS $175,000 in lost revenue. Meanwhile, NBC had decided to provide live coverage of George Kennan, a major critic of American policy in Vietnam. But Schneider would not commit himself. And so at 10 A.M., on February 10, NBC began showing the Kennan testimony live while CBS screened a rerun of "I Love Lucy" followed by a rerun of "The Real McCoys." Schneider explained later that he had decided against showing Kennan because very few "decision makers" (his own phrase) were at home in the daytime and the hearing would confuse the issue for many people. Stanton noted in newspaper interviews at the time that Kennan was not an important enough figure to be given live coverage. Friendly was horrified.

According to Friendly, Stanton tried to calm him down saying: "You and the news division have accomplished so much in these twenty-four months; why not compromise on this one issue?"

"Because, Frank," Friendly says he replied, "this one issue is Vietnam. We are going to be judged by the way we cover Vietnam." (11) Stanton, however, denies that such an exchange occurred.

In the back of Friendly's mind was the decision in the summer of 1964 to remove Walter Cronkite as convention anchor. Friendly had learned a large lesson. Then it had been virtually unthinkable for him to disobey the wishes of Bill Paley. "But," said Friendly in the summer of 1987, "I should have. And obviously, self-serving as this may sound, that had a lot to do with my decision in 1966. Because all I could see was the Cronkite thing all over again. And I knew this time if I refused that order, a year later they'd get me on something else."

Everyone in the news division supported him, Bill Leonard, Gordon Manning, Walter Cronkite, Eric Sevareid, Bill Small, all of them. Some said they would resign with Friendly, if he wished. But Friendly held them back. He would go. This time he knew it was the right thing. "I was convinced that whatever integrity I had would go out the window if I did that. They would have known that they could do anything they wanted with me after that. . . . It was an easy choice . . . because staying would have been impossible. . . . It was a simple decision because it was black and white." (12)

Although some of his friends implored him not to leave, Friendly resigned on February 15. It was front-page news. Coming as it did just ten months after Ed Murrow's death, the Friendly resignation appeared to signal an end to a major era of television. "Cataclysmic" was the word *Variety* used to describe Friendly's departure. In his "Dear Bill and Frank" letter of resignation to Paley and Stanton, Friendly said that he had resigned because CBS News did not carry the Kennan hearings. "I am convinced," he wrote, "that the decision not to carry them was a business, not a news, judgment." He added that "I am resigning because the decision not to carry the hearings makes a mockery of the Paley-Stanton Columbia news division crusade of many years that demands broadcast access to Congressional debate. . . . We cannot, in our public utterances, demand such access and then, in one of the crucial debates of our time, abdicate that responsibility. . . . I now leave CBS News after sixteen years, believing that the finest broadcast journalists anywhere will yet have the kind of leadership they deserve. . . ." (Replacing Friendly was Richard Salant, returning to his old job.)

Friendly's colleagues two decades later saw things slightly differently. They did not believe that he resigned only because of the Kennan–"I Love Lucy" flap. They suggested that his departure was long in the making. He was disturbed at losing too many battles to the business people, and he could see the handwriting on the wall. Then, too, his colleagues were convinced that the CBS brass, from Paley and Stanton on down, were gunning for him, were eager to see him stub his foot. Said one: "He was charging like a raging bull headlong for the cliff, and they stepped back and said, keep running, Fred." (Friendly's confrontation was not greeted at the time with sympathy from some CBS correspondents. Harry Reasoner, for example, believed that John Schneider's practice of alloting 30 minutes of prime time each night for a digest of that day's Vietnam testimony was perfectly acceptable. And, what was more, more than three times as many people watched it as would have during the daytime.)

Discussing the Kennan–"I Love Lucy" dispute during the summer of 1987, when the Congressional hearings on Irangate focused for so long on the intriguing personality of Lt. Col. Oliver North, Frank Stanton had this to say: "We didn't have anything like that [the North hearings] when Friendly left. We had nothing of the Constitutional nature that was represented by the [North hearings]. . . . That particular day nothing happened in the [Vietnam] hearing. . . . Friendly argued that he wanted them on. But he didn't know, and neither did I know what was going to happen. But our advanced intelligence was that the heat was out of the hearing. . . . The sad part of Fred's position at that time was that we were taking prime time out of circulation and taping the highlights of what happened in the day, and putting it into prime time, when the audience is measurably two to three times larger than the audience in the morning, at the time of the daytime serials. So that if it had had the kind of dramatic thrust that the North hearing had, or that others have had subsequent to the Vietnam hearing, no question that the judgment would have been to put it on, but it didn't have that. It had petered out. . . . The public wasn't being denied anything because I believe one of the other networks was carrying it, in addition to public broadcasting." (13)

To the average viewer, the debates at CBS over how to handle news stories in the 1960s were distant and of little seeming relevance. What did matter was the heightened amount of violence on the screen as foreign war and urban riot, political assassination, and street crime became the most obvious metaphors for the troubled decade. Television, predictably, was blamed for showing it all, for focusing on the bad and forgetting the good. The answer of television officials was unwelcome, however reasonable: the bad is what makes news. The good, however worthwhile showing, had no business being portrayed as news. One man at CBS differed with all that. He believed that there was room for televising, if not good news, then at least a more tranquil, untroubled part of America that was out there, waiting for a journalist with a little imagination to find. The man's name was Charles Kuralt.

Kuralt's association with CBS started early—at the age of 14. He had triumphed in an American Legion contest in 1948 for his essay entitled "Voice of Democracy." He went to Washington, met President Harry Truman, and that evening listened as Ed Murrow, a judge in the contest, read his essay over the CBS radio network. At age 22, the North Carolina–bred Kuralt, having graduated from the University of North Carolina, took a job as a reporter for the *Charlotte News*. Again, he won a writing prize—the Ernie Pyle Memorial Award. This time Sig Mickelson, running the CBS network news at the time, wrote him a congratulatory letter and invited Kuralt to come to New York to apply for a job. He showed up two days later and began working as a radio writer for CBS in the fall of 1956. After a writing stint on the Doug Edwards television show, he became a reporter on the assignment desk and the next year, a correspondent. Kuralt's chief backer, Sig Mickelson, who promoted him as the next Ed Murrow, made him the star of the weekly prime-time television program, "Eyewitness," in 1960, much to Walter Cronkite's displeasure. Cronkite wanted the job for himself. Jim Aubrey, by now ensconced as CBS Television Network president, was dismayed at the choice of Kuralt for a prime-time television series; he wanted someone with more star quality, perhaps even a big-name actor. In a compromise, Kuralt was replaced in January 1961 with Cronkite. Kuralt might have been chosen to replace Doug Edwards in 1962 had it not been for the fact that Aubrey remained unenthusiastic about him. For the next few years, Kuralt worked as Latin America correspondent. He returned to New York in 1964 in search of a good job with the network.

The idea for that new job had come to Charles Kuralt one night in 1965 while he was flying across the United States on assignment. A few days later, he was in New York where he raised the idea with the CBS management. He proposed that he and a camera crew go around the country in leisurely fashion. Whenever they come across something interesting, in a feature rather than news sense, they would do a story. At first, the idea fell on deaf ears. Fred Friendly, who listened to Kuralt's idea, had little love for news coverage of the casual and the seemingly frivolous side of life. "That's the worst idea I ever heard of," he told Kuralt, mincing no words. Kuralt got the subtle hint, dropped the idea—for the time being—and returned to covering the hard news.

But, once Friendly resigned as CBS president in February 1966, Kuralt decided to give the idea another shot. This time, Richard Salant and Gordon Manning, two senior CBS executives, and Ernie Leiser, the executive producer of the Walter Cronkite evening news show, gave the suggestion a sympathetic ear. Kuralt was told that he could spend three months on the project. Some skeptics thought he would be back long before that with little to show. He was given a camera crew and in October 1967 Kuralt and his team set out in a newly equipped camper for Vermont and New Hampshire. When Cronkite introduced Kuralt's "autumn leaves" piece, a look at the display of fall colors in the New England states, on the evening news, the anchorman noted that this was the first of a series special reports that would be called "On the Road with Charles Kuralt." Other features followed, and soon no one could remember that Kuralt had been given three months on a trial basis. The "On the Road" series went on until 1980 when Kuralt became the anchorman of CBS's morning news show. "On the Road" gave birth to several prime-time specials and won every major award available to television journalism. The shows were well received largely because of Kuralt's great skills as a reporter and writer. Gary Gates, in his study of CBS News, wrote that "with his plump, slouchy build, his cherubic face, and his deep voice that seemed always to be on the verge of a hearty chortle, Kuralt came across as a big, friendly bear of a man. Which he was. Although he had spent almost all his adult life in New York and other large cities, he still had the down-home, 'just-folks' personality of a good ol' boy from rural North Carolina." (14)

The good 'ol boy was, therefore, the good news person at a time when the airwaves were otherwise filled with ugly shots of war in Vietnam and messy violence on the streets of America and elsewhere. As Richard Nixon and Spiro Agnew bore down on the press for being arrogant, powerful, and unelected and, of course, for being purveyors of only the bad news, Charles Kuralt proved of inestimable value at CBS.

For all the sunshine Charles Kuralt would deliver to the viewing audience, it was still a grim world out there. War was raging. American soldiers were fighting and dying. The nation appeared to have lost its direction. The times were remarkable and led some to take extraordinary steps in response. Walter Cronkite was one. Under normal circumstances, he would have never dreamed of doing anything but deliver the news as objectively and fairly as he could. In earlier days, CBS correspondents, from Hans Von Kaltenborn to Edward Murrow, from Cecil Brown to Bill Shirer, felt it possible, felt compelled, to inject their personal opinions into broadcasts. But that era was over. Or so one thought.

Now, in early 1968 Walter Cronkite would step out of his role as unbiased anchorman and in doing so would have a profound effect on swaying public opinion against the American role in the Vietnam war. Not that Cronkite was totally confident that what he planned to do was proper. He mulled the decision over with CBS officials and heard from them only expressions of support for leaving his traditional role in this instance. You have to be true to your profession, they would tell him. There was a major story out there, and you should tell it like it is.

And so he went to Vietnam and while there met his old friend, Creighton Abrams, then the deputy commander of American forces, eventually to take over from General William Westmoreland. Abrams's candor shocked Cronkite. The military man spoke honestly about the dimensions of the catastrophe, leaving Cronkite with the impression that if someone as high up as Abrams had such doubts about what America was doing in this Southeast Asian conflict, then perhaps it was indeed time to reexamine the situation. On his final night in Vietnam Cronkite dined with correspondents on the roof of the Caravelle Hotel in Saigon. He kept asking them how it all could have occurred. Peter Kalischer said simply that the lies had been going on from the start, that the United States was nothing more than an intruder in the lives of the Vietnamese.

When Cronkite returned to the States, he broadcast a half-hour news special which he wrote himself. In late February and early March, during four consecutive nights, Cronkite offered reports on his Vietnam journey. He said in one report that the American effort wasn't working and that putting in a few thousand more troops would not change things. It was time, in his view, to start thinking of getting out. He ended the broadcast by noting: "We have been too often disappointed by the optimism of the American leaders, both in Vietnam and Washington, to have faith any longer in the silver linings they find in the darkest clouds. . . . For it seems now more certain than ever that the bloody experience of Vietnam is to end in a stalemate. . . . To say that we are closer to victory today is to believe, in the face of the evidence, the optimists who have been wrong in the past. . . . It is increasingly clear to this reporter that the only rational way out then will be to negotiate, not as victors, but as an honorable people who lived up to their pledge to defend democracy, and did the best they could."

The Cronkite telecast was undeniably a turning point, and in later years CBS's coverage would contain more criticism of American tactics. An anchorman with a long record of trust was declaring that the war was over. In Washington President Johnson, after the Cronkite broadcast, told George Christian, his press secretary, that Cronkite's program had affected him deeply. If he had lost Walter, and apparently he had, then almost certainly he had lost Mr. Average Citizen. And then, there was little more he could do in Vietnam. The president was in fact losing others in the television media as well. Two weeks after Cronkite's Vietnam program, on March 10, NBC's Frank McGee moderated a special one-hour broadcast, noting that the war in Vietnam was being lost, if judged against the Johnson administration's reasons for pursuing the conflict. He added that the war's initiative had passed from the United States to the Vietcong and the time had arrived to decide whether it was a futile policy to destroy Vietnam in an effort to save it. There is good reason to believe that Johnson's decision not to run for reelection, announced at the end of March 1968, was prompted in part at least by the Cronkite broadcast. As Sam Roberts, who had been a producer on the Cronkite evening news program for fourteen years and was a former foreign editor for CBS, noted, "It was totally out of character for Cronkite to do that. Totally out of character. Cronkite was a right-down-the-middle newsman. Almost to the point of finding somebody who says the world is flat. You know, we really had to be very careful that we were representing all points of view carefully in a story properly and fairly. For him to come back from Vietnam, step out of the reporter's role into a commentary role was totally unprecedented. . . . Everyone was very proud of him. Very much, very much. . . . It was very much the right thing for him to do, for him to say what was on his mind." (15)

A few weeks after his television broadcast, Cronkite received a visa to travel to North Vietnam. He had waited a year for the visa to come through, and he was quite pleased. Now he would be able to file a report from the other side. But something was not just right. Cronkite sensed that his going now would give the wrong impression—as if he had received the visa as a reward for his broadcast. Cronkite gave the task of going to North Vietnam to Charles Collingwood.

Vietnam would spur controversy elsewhere at CBS. This time the incident would occur, not on a news program, but on one of the network's most popular entertainment programs, "The Smothers Brothers Show."

The Smothers brothers had begun performing folk songs in San Francisco in 1958. Unlike other folk singers of that time, they studiously avoided political involvement. Ironically, they had little interest or sympathy for the radicalism of folksingers Pete Seeger and Woody Guthrie. Folk singing became highly popular in the 1950s and 1960s, and Tom and Dick's career blossomed. They appeared in clubs around the United States, debuting on television on the Jack Paar "Tonight" show, Tommy on guitar, Dick on bass fiddle. Trying out comedy, Tommy played the dumb one: he would flub lines, lose his temper, shout at his younger brother, who acted rational and well adjusted. Some of Tommy's lines became their trademarks: "Mom always liked you best," was one.

The Smothers brothers' television program had been around for a few years. Back in the winter of 1966, Sunday night prime time was dominated by one show, NBC's family Western, "Bonanza." CBS wanted to unseat the Cartrights and had tried such stars as Judy Garland and Gary

Moore but no one had succeeded. Then along came Tommy and Dickie: their prime time one-hour variety program became highly rated. At first the program contained some explicit material, explicit at least for the time. But material was still carefully edited. For example, the first line of a song they had wanted to sing went: "The first time ever I lay with you." But the CBS censor vetoed the line. When actress Nanette Fabray asked Tom, playing Romeo, "Did you get that girl in trouble?" in a line from a "Romeo and Juliet" satire, that line was also excised. Yet a few years later, once "Laugh-In" and Johnny Carson's "Tonight" show loosened things up, being slightly blue was OK. In a mock poll conducted on the February 25, 1968 show Dick Smothers asked Pat Paulsen, who played an advertising executive, about the quality of television programs:

Dick: "What do you think is the most important concern for an advertising agency?"
Pat: "The most important thing is to find the right program for the right advertiser. For instance, one of our clients was the Dearform Brassiere company, and we linked them up with the perfect show."
Dick: "And what was that show?"
Pat: "The Big Valley."

Jokes on the race issue were aired as well. On that same show, Dick Smothers and black actor Scooey Mitchell engaged in this dialogue in which Scooey is a black television viewer improbably named George Wallace:

Dick: "Tell me, Mr. Wallace, are you still having trouble with that name of yours?"
George: "Yeah, it's a drag. People keep calling me and asking if I'm running for president."
Dick: "Well, are you running?"
George: ". . . No, I'm not running anywhere. Not unless he wins. Then I'll run."

Given the Smothers brothers' liberal attitude toward what should be aired on television, it was no coincidence that they would throw their support behind Pete Seeger's attempt to sing a highly controversial anti-Vietnam song as a way of protesting the American effort in Vietnam. Seeger had a long, unpleasant battle in getting on television. After his name had appeared in the *Red Channels* list, he had rarely appeared on television. In 1966, Seeger had appeared on the CBS television Sunday morning program, "Camera Three." His personal goal was to break through the television blacklist that kept him from making prime-time appearances. Finally, in 1967 he received an invitation to appear on the Smothers brothers' variety show.

Naturally he planned to sing on the program. The question was whether CBS would give him carte blanche to sing what he liked. The nation had become openly divided over Vietnam, and Seeger wanted to use this prime-time program to convey his opposition to the fighting. When Tom Smothers asked him what he wanted to sing, Seeger listed several songs. "I'd also like to sing 'Waist Deep in the Big Muddy,'" he said. (16) "Waist Deep" was a new composition which he had written as an attack upon President Johnson and the Vietnam war. The attack was indirect; he used parable to make the point. The song told of a World War II incident in which a commanding officer ordered his platoon to forge the Big Muddy river while on a routine training march. Not aware that the river was both deep and dangerous, the commander nearly drowns the entire platoon before being swept away himself. In the key sixth stanza, Seeger related the incident to current events: "All you have to do is read the newspapers to realize that we are once again waist deep in the Big Muddy, while the Big Fool says to push on."

Although Columbia Records had recently released a Seeger album with "Waist Deep" as the title song, CBS was not eager to have it sung on the television network. Some listeners, CBS's chief programmer Michael Dann explained to Tom Smothers, might interpret the sixth stanza as an attack on Johnson and his handling of the war. Replied Tom: "Oh, don't be ridiculous." At that stage, some CBS executives suggested a compromise whereby Seeger could sing "Waist Deep" but leave out the sixth stanza. No deal, said Seeger. Defending his guest, Tom Smothers explained, "That stanza is the whole point of the song. He's got to sing the whole song." At the taping session for the September program, Seeger sang "Waist Deep" in its entirety. But Mike Dann ordered that the song be deleted from the final tape. A furious Pete Seeger went public, phoning a *New York Times* reporter to provide details of what had occurred. "It's important for people to realize that what they see on television is screened," he said, "not just for good taste, but for ideas."

Tom Smothers then invited Seeger to return for the February 25, 1968, show. Did he want to try "Waist Deep" again, Tom asked? "Yup, I sure do," came the answer.

"Let's go for it," replied Tom.

What could have happened between September and February to change the minds of CBS executives? For one thing, as stars of a highly popular program, the Smothers brothers had a good deal of clout. For another, everyone agreed that it was better to avoid any further bad publicity. So this time, Mike Dann and the rest of the CBS brass gave in. Seeger was allowed to sing the song on television. It was one more indication that the American public had grown weary of the war. Only one minor incident occurred in Detroit where the local CBS affiliate director had previewed the tape and erased the "Waist Deep" section.

The Smothers brothers' program was canceled in April 1969. The reason given was technical: it was claimed that Tom Smothers had reneged on his agreement to make program tapes available for prescreening. When the tape of the April 14 show, featuring an appearance by Dr. Benjamin Spock, the antiwar activist, arrived allegedly several days late, CBS leaped at the chance to end the program. The timing—three months after Richard Nixon was inaugurated as president—gave rise to speculation, on Tom Smothers' part, that Bill Paley was not eager to subject the new president to the inevitable jokes that would crop up on the Smothers brothers' show. Tom Smothers, however, had a theory that Paley was interested in being named American ambassador to London and was merely trying to smooth the path. Whatever the truth, Paley was not appointed. There was still a court case over the cancellation of the show. The brothers alleged that CBS had violated their contractual agreement. The U.S. District Court in California agreed and awarded them $776,300.

The year 1968 was traumatic for many Americans. It was traumatic as well for CBS. One example was the assassination of civil rights leader Martin Luther King, Jr., in April. In neither of the two Kennedy assassinations (in November 1963 and June 1968) had there been any fear or danger of a nationwide panic. Such was not the case in the King assassination. And so CBS knew it had to handle the story gingerly. Robert Wussler, in charge of special events for CBS News, was in his office that day. He had been at a meeting arranging coverage of the 1968 conventions when word came that Martin Luther King had been shot. Frank Stanton called and said that whatever Wussler did, he must make sure that coverage of the assassination aftermath went uninterrupted. Stanton clearly sensed what might happen if television appeared to be downplaying the story. CBS stayed on the air from 11 P.M. to 1 A.M. and then throughout that morning gave 5-minute updates every 20 minutes and arranged a roundtable discussion with black leaders moderated by Dan Rather.

No event symbolized the turmoil of the times more than the Democratic convention in Chicago that stormy summer. The anti-Vietnam protest movement had been growing. The American establishment was coming under increasing attack as the major villain of the Vietnam folly. One obvious symbol of that establishment was the police. While young protesters were engaged in violent confrontation with the police outside the convention hall, reporters were having their own problems on the inside. On the second night, one of Chicago Mayor Richard Daley's security men punched CBS correspondent Dan Rather in the stomach and knocked him down. In a rare moment of emotion, Walter Cronkite, anchoring the convention, lost his temper, and in a voice filled with rage, observed: "It looks like we've got a bunch of thugs in here. . . . If this sort of thing continues, it makes us, in our anger, want to just turn off our cameras and pack up our microphones and our typewriters and get the devil out of this town and leave the Democrats to their agony."

CBS News did not pack up and leave. But things did not improve all that much. The very next night Mike Wallace, another CBS floor correspondent, experienced his own difficulties with Daley's guards. It began when Alex Rosenberg, a delegate supporting Minnesota Senator Eugene McCarthy, was dragged off the floor for speaking rudely to a security agent. Wallace tried to follow them to get the story. As they moved off the floor and out of camera range, a police officer shouted at Wallace to stay away, saying this was none of his business.

"Certainly, it's my business," said the CBS man. "This is a public place." That argument had little appeal to the policeman who grew angrier by the second. Wallace flashed a big smile to try to calm the man. "Officer, what are you getting so upset about?" Wallace then lightly tapped the officer under the chin, hoping to soften him up further. The gesture may have been well intentioned but it was misinterpreted. The policeman responded by slugging Wallace on the jaw. The correspondent's knees buckled. He was clearly stunned. But he remained on his feet. At that stage another policeman told Wallace that he was under arrest. Why, he asked, by now astonished at the scene. For assaulting an officer, came the reply. "Assaulting an officer? For crissakes, I chucked him under the chin. What the hell. . .?"

The officer who had struck Wallace told another officer that the CBS man was under arrest for slapping him. By this time two other policemen had grabbed Wallace under each arm and led him away past a group of still photographers who snapped away at this latest incident of the Chicago mayhem. The next day the picture of Wallace's "arrest" made newspapers around the country. In fact, he was in custody briefly. Richard Salant hastily arranged to see Mayor Daley who offered neither an apology nor an acknowledgment that the officer had been wrong in slugging the correspondent. Daley did agree, however, that under the circumstances, the decision to haul Wallace into custody was a bit much. He could re-sume his duties on the convention floor and after washing his face and combing his hair, he did just that. (17)

ᴓᴓᴓᴓ

Over the years, television's conventional wisdom increasingly held that documentary programs, while boosting a network's prestige, could not make money and were therefore not really worthwhile. The idea that one of these documentaries would become popular and turn a profit was so far-fetched in the 1950s and 1960s that no one even raised such a prospect. Both the news and entertainment side understood that documentar-ies were "loss leaders"; they put CBS into the daily newspapers with their controversial headlines, they made people sit up and admire what Ed Murrow and Fred Friendly and others were doing. But they were costly. Too costly. If anyone had ever suggested that it would be possible to pro-duce a television documentary program that could actually bring money into the network, he would have been laughed out the door—until Don Hewitt turned his attention to a new concept in news documentaries.

The story really began just after the 1964 conventions when Fred Friendly, president of CBS News, decided to change executive producers in the Cronkite evening news program. He wanted someone who would pay more attention to the news. With his flair for graphics and far-sighted inventiveness, Don Hewitt had been fine in his day; but in Ernie Leiser, the new executive producer, Friendly was confident that news would come first. (Friendly would say twenty years later that the Hewitt-Leiser switch was the best decision he had ever made.) Sometime in 1965 Friendly called Don Hewitt into his office and, in his best diplomatic lan-guage, said, "Don, the Cronkite news is not big enough for you. You prac-tically invented this business, and I'm going to set up a special unit just for you."

Hewitt reacted well, though Friendly's plans for him sounded a bit too vague. He informed his wife to tell her the good news. "Don, dear," she said, "you just got fired." (18)

He thought about quitting, but his loyalty to CBS was too strong. So he remained a producer, involved with such programs as "Omnibus" and "Town Meeting of the World." While doing that, sometime in 1967 Hewitt began thinking about the idea that would eventually become "60 Min-utes," the most successful news documentary program in the history of television. The idea emerged from Hewitt's conviction that the equivalent of a magazine was needed on television. What was also needed was to personalize the story by having the reporter essentially take the viewer along with him in his probing. Hewitt had noticed while a director of several "See It Now" episodes that the audiences were more interested in Ed Murrow and what he found out than in the subject matter itself.

The evening news programs were already the television equivalent of a daily newspaper, an electronic front page so to speak. Hour-long documentaries, the more boring of which Hewitt liked to call "snoozers," were closer to nonfiction books, and like a book, they examined a subject in depth. But no one had tried the equivalent of a magazine which would examine several stories on a wide range of topics, weekly or biweekly. The magazine approach would take into account the short attention span of the viewer.

Hewitt proposed the idea to Richard Salant, president of CBS News after Friendly's resignation in early 1966. "Why don't we try to package 60 minutes of reality as attractively as Hollywood packages 60 minutes of make-believe?" Hewitt asked him. (The name "60 Minutes," casually used then by Hewitt, would stick.) At first, Salant was concerned that Hewitt's new program might be viewed as competition for CBS's news and documentary people. Why add strain? Why add more worry about who would do which news story? Others disliked focusing "60 Minutes" on a single individual, as Hewitt was proposing to do. They questioned whether the viewing public would be willing to latch on to more news stars. Bill Leonard, the vice president in charge of documentaries, liked Hewitt's idea, however, and was able to convince Salant to come aboard.

In February 1968 Salant gave Hewitt the go-ahead to produce a pilot. Perhaps, Salant thought, the program might be put on every other Tuesday at 10 P.M., alternating with documentaries opposite the highly rated "Marcus Welby, M.D." Contemplating how much it would cost to produce the new Hewitt program, CBS executives wondered whether it was worth getting involved in another "loss leader" situation. In the back of their minds was the fact that during the 1967–68 season the three networks were spending $250 million for the production of their nighttime entertainment. That was $20 million higher than the previous season. This was considered a legitimate expense: sponsors, after all, were lining up to buy time on "The Smothers Brothers Show" and other entertainment programs. But sponsors stayed away from documentaries. Then too there was the sad memory of what had happened to a recent prime-time public affairs program called "Who, What, When, Where, Why," with Harry Reasoner. Low ratings killed it off in 1967.

Who should be the program's moderator? Hewitt thought immediately of Harry Reasoner. He had the right personal touch. Bob Chandler, a vice president of CBS News, thought of Mike Wallace as a partner for Reasoner. Hewitt told Wallace that the format of the show would give him a chance to do the kind of interviews he used to do on "Night Beat" and that of course appealed to Mike. But during the early part of 1968 Wallace had not been giving much serious thought to taking part in the "60 Minutes" project. Wallace thought Richard Nixon had a strong chance of winning the presidency the following November, and should that happen, he was confident that he would become the CBS White House correspondent.

Things took a strange turn when, a week after the New Hampshire primary, Len Garment and Frank Shakespeare, two Nixon aides, delivered a message to Mike Wallace from Nixon.

"The boss would like you to join up, to come aboard and work with us," said Garment. Skeptical, but intrigued, Wallace asked, "To do what exactly?" (19) Garment said he was not certain but he imagined that it would be either press secretary or communications director. Wallace turned to Frank Stanton for advice. Stanton, however, had little to say of comfort, warning him that if he took the offer he would be compromising his standing as a newsman. Wallace would have difficulty returning to journalism after being the spokesman for the president. Listening to Stanton's advice, Wallace gave up the idea and did the "60 Minutes" pilot that spring. Even after he began working on the show in earnest over the summer, he remained ambivalent, thinking all the time about what might happen to his own career should Richard Nixon win the presidency in November. Wallace was bothered that he had missed out on a chance to become the CBS White House correspondent. He doubted that "60 Minutes" would last more than a season or two, certainly less time than a Nixon presidency.

When Richard Nixon won the presidency that November, he offered Wallace the post of White House press secretary. Flattered and intrigued, Wallace this time sought Don Hewitt's advice. As with Stanton, Hewitt had little positive to say. "That doesn't make any sense," Hewitt told him. "You don't want to go from being Mike Wallace to being a press secretary, even a White House press secretary. It's the kind of a job a nobody takes so he can become a somebody." (20) That was enough for Wallace. He told Nixon that he was sorry, but he could not accept the press secretary offer.

On September 24, 1968, "60 Minutes" debuted, alternating with "CBS Reports." Hewitt at first had little hope. The time, which had not been of great help to "CBS Reports," scared him. Why should he be able to do anything better with it? He was unfortunately right. Ironically, few viewers saw the show. That was a shame as Hewitt managed to lead off with an exclusive: CBS cameramen had been permitted to remain in the hotel rooms of Richard Nixon and Hubert Humphrey on the nights that they had won their parties' presidential nominations the previous summer. Viewers saw Nixon conduct a political seminar for his family as the balloting occurred; Hubert, more emotional, rushed to kiss the screen when he received the nomination. There followed on that initial "60 Minutes" a Mike Wallace interview with the nation's number one cop, Attorney General Ramsey Clark. Then appeared an offbeat film called *Why Man Creates,* the work of an inventive filmmaker named Saul Bass. At first, the ratings were low, and the critics were not entirely in love with it. There were some warm reviews, however. The next day *The New York Times* said it was "something television has long needed. Not all the segments were of equal interest, but one doesn't expect that in a magazine." *Time* magazine in its October 4 issue called it "a good cub reporter's try." But other critics thought the stories dated and the magazine format pretentious. They were not overly enthusiastic about the multitude of producers either.

For a while thereafter "60 Minutes" moved in the lower level of the Nielsen ratings; CBS displayed such little confidence in it that the show was frequently preempted. As a result, it was never seen two fortnights in a row until December 1969. But then in 1972 the show was moved to the Sunday 6 P.M. slot. That meant that it would never be shown during the football season. It also appeared to mean disaster to Don Hewitt. As Bud Benjamin, who had been a producer of documentary programs at CBS, recalled, "I'll never forget it. Hewitt came into my office disconsolate. He said, 'This is the end. They are trying to give me a message.' But I told him, 'Don, you're wrong. I lived in that time. We used to have very big audiences on 'Twentieth Century.' Sometimes we got a 30 share, a 32 share. There's an audience out there.'" (21)

As late as 1975, the program was still suffering from low ratings. It was only in that year that Oscar Katz, a vice president in the entertainment division, suggested moving "60 Minutes" to the 7 P.M. Sunday slot. That was a time that had been specifically set aside by the FCC as part of the prime-time access rule for either public affairs or children's programming. As a result, ABC and NBC would routinely show something for the children. This meant that "60 MInutes" had little opposition in that slot on the largest viewing night of the week.

The decision to shift "60 Minutes" to Sunday 7 P.M., in the eyes of many, was one of the most important in the history of television. The program finished the 1975–76 season in fifty-second place, but by the following fall it had enjoyed such a steep rise that it was allowed to "bump the network": it would be shown in its entirety in the Eastern time zone whenever football finished and the rest of the Sunday night schedule was simply bumped back. In the first year in its new time, the program won its time period, by the second year it was in the top ten, by 1980 it was the most watched program in the United States!

When that happened, those who remembered how much of a pioneer Don Hewitt had been in the early days of television suggested that there was an inevitability about Hewitt's success with "60 Minutes." As Robert "Shad" Northshield noted, "Don Hewitt is the most successful producer in the history of television news, but only for the last twenty years.

. . . There was never any question, by the way, that someday he was going to be the first great one, and he certainly is. He's not only the first great one, but he is still the greatest one." (22)

The program's success was due as well to the decision, taken perhaps unconsciously early on, that there would be no hosts or moderators, just reporters—and those reporters would go anywhere and everywhere. Sometimes one reporter would take one side of a story, and another would take the other side. This allowed each reporter to adopt a more subjective viewpoint than he might have done had he been the only reporter on the story. Working with another reporter, he could be confident that the other side of a story (or other sides) would be covered. For instance, Harry Reasoner covered the Catholic side and Mike Wallace the Protestant in Ireland; Wallace took the Israelis, and Reasoner handled the Arabs. A few months later they reversed roles. In the Biafran civil war, Wallace visited Lagos and Reasoner traveled to the Biafran side of the war zone. Unfortunately, Wallace came down with a bout of dysentery. Reasoner fared worse: he got shot at. "60 Minutes" focused on corruption as well, and 20 percent of the stories dealt with one swindle or another. That led Morley Safer, who would join the program as a reporter later, to joke that no con man thought he had made it until he had been on "60 Minutes."

In 1970 Harry Reasoner left the show. Morley Safer was asked to replace Reasoner and agreed on the condition that he could return as CBS London bureau chief, his current job, if "60 Minutes" was canceled. Such was the lack of confidence about the show's future in those days. But, as the ratings improved, confidence increased. And soon everyone, inside and outside the program, began analyzing why the show had done well, why it had captured the public's attention—when so many other news documentaries had not. Everyone had an opinion. But, as Don Hewitt said in a *Playboy* magazine interview, "There's no recipe. . . . The reason nobody else can fake this cake is that there's no recipe for it. And that's why the network leaves us alone. . . . You know, it could fall apart. If a big gust of wind came along, it might blow the whole thing over, and they don't want to mess with it. The corporate brass get to testify before the Senate on how much of a national institution we've become—but they have no idea how the hell it works!" (23) In that same *Playboy* issue, Diane Sawyer, who joined the program in 1984, noted that in her first week she kept looking for hints about how things worked: "And then it occurred to me, it's like . . . it's like going to a mixer; there's no form. There are just simple communications, and you find a producer in the hall and you say, 'What do you think about. . .?' And maybe he'll say, 'I don't like it,' and then you'll walk on to the next producer and say, 'What do you think about. . .?' and he'll say, 'I love it!' and you've got yourself a story." (24)

To Bud Benjamin, who in 1975 became executive producer of the Cronkite news program, "60 Minutes" hit the mark because it has been "extremely well-produced, and particularly during its early days, it was extraordinarily provocative . . . it's a western. Those four people, now five, are the white hats, and every week they ride off into the twilight looking for the black hats, doctors who rip people off, phony cancer institutes, car dealers who are cheating. It's a western." (25)

eleven

"Damn Truman, Damn Stalin, Damn Everybody."

The early 1970s would be good years for the network. After reaching $1 billion in sales in 1969, it would take CBS only another seven years to reach the $2 billion mark—in 1976. And, by 1978, sales at CBS passed the $3 billion mark for the first time. The company had grown to 27,842 employees in 1972 and had a net income that year of nearly $93 million. But the past was fast catching up with CBS. It would now have to fight harder than ever to remain at the top of the broadcasting industry.

For thirteen straight years—1955 to 1968—CBS had routinely captured the ratings race in the television entertainment field. It was a remarkable achievement. It was profitable. But, as the executives at CBS realized all too well, there was no telling how much longer the streak would last. And for that reason, as the new decade was approaching, there were worried faces around the network. The worry began as a result of the 1968–69 season when NBC had edged CBS out in the ratings by a mere .3 of a point. The following fall of 1969 remained problematic for CBS as all its new sitcoms failed. In January 1970, buoyed by the situation, NBC announced that it would make no changes in its prime-time schedule. Concern arose by February that CBS might not come out on top in its prime-time schedule, something that had not happened since the mid-1950s.

Mike Dann, the feisty programming chief at CBS, decided it was time to take action. He brought sixty of his programmmers together and challenged them to put CBS ahead of its rival by April 19 when the official 1970 television season ended and the networks began reruns. The next "100 days," as the period became known, would prove whether CBS could put its act together. "I knew Paley wouldn't stand for that," said Mike Dann. "I never said I was going to do the hundred days. I never said anything to Paley about it. I knew what he wanted. And I took over promotion, advertising, scheduling, and with the help of a brilliant program department, laid down the hundred days, and we won easily. And that kind of sophistication was typical of CBS. You couldn't do it today, because everybody's just as smart." (1)

During the "100 days," series that were doing poorly (such as "Get Smart") were preempted as frequently as possible. Dann used imagination, taking movies such as *Peyton Place* and *The African Queen*, which had already run on television, and promoting them as specials. He did the same with National Geographic documentary films. Trying to beat NBC at its own game (of showing specials), Dann put the movie *Born Free* on and the results were astounding: it garnered a 34.2 rating, meaning that roughly 40 million people were watching or 53 percent of the viewing public. Dann was getting away from the traditional strength of CBS—the regular series—but something extraordinary was required, and he delivered. When it was over, Dann announced that CBS had won by .2 percent. NBC claimed that it had won, arguing that it had been ahead on March 22, the date when NBC began 40 percent of its rerun schedule. A consensus has developed, however, that in fact CBS was the winner. Soon thereafter, Dann left CBS to go to work for public television's Children's Television Workshop.

Replacing Mike Dann was another phenomenon, a 32-year-old named Fred Silverman who since 1963 had been head of the network's daytime programming. Silverman became vice-president in charge of program planning and development. Born in September 1937, Silverman was the son of a television repairman, raised in the New York City borough of Queens. In 1958 he received a bachelor's degree from the Syracuse University School of Speech and Dramatic Arts. And then he took his master's degree in communications at Ohio State University in the speech department. In 1959, he did his master's thesis on the ABC television network. It ran over 400 pages. He had pinpointed the steps ABC had taken between 1953 and 1959 to improve its ratings, noting that ABC had done well with programming aimed at young audiences.

As opposed to Jim Aubrey's programming strategy, which had been to attract the most viewers possible, Silverman suggested that programmers try to reach a certain slice of the population, a slice who advertisers felt would be best suited to purchasing their products. He advocated concentrating on teenagers and the younger generation ages 18 to 34. If ABC were to follow his guidelines, he could assure a rosy future for the network even though it had constantly been losing money. Ironically, when at last ABC took over the ratings lead in 1975, it was none other than Fred Silverman who was director of programming as president of its entertainment division.

Although he sent his master's thesis to all three networks, Silverman got no response. So he began working at WGN, the major independent Chicago television station, boosting its ratings by recycling old movies in new formats. Soon thereafter, he signed on as a staff producer at WGN-TV, an independent outlet in Chicago. After devising a number of alternative programming schemes, he became director of program development, helping the station to capture first place in its local Friday evening ratings. Completing three years with WGN, he moved on to New York City's WPIX-TV early in 1963.

It took only six weeks before Mike Dann, who had seen Silverman's master's thesis and was impressed, hired him to run the network's moneymaking daytime schedule. Silverman was then only 26 years old. He had near autonomy, and so he replaced weary situation comedy reruns with first-run animated cartoon series. He also changed the concept of Saturday morning children's programming. His "Children's Film Festival" won a Peabody Award. In July 1966, Silverman was named vice-president in charge of daytime programs. Then in 1970 he became CBS's chief programmer.

By the early 1970s, it was not easy for CBS to stay on top. Even though the network had dominated the entertainment schedule since the mid-1950s, remaining the major programming force was no easy trick. Each season one had to start all over, each season the programming executives had to read the tea leaves correctly. The situation was made all the more difficult because of an economic downturn from which all the networks were suffering at this time. Pretax profits for all three networks for 1970 totaled $50.1 million, $43 million less than in 1969. In the first three months of 1970, advertising sales at the networks had dropped by almost 4 percent. Network minutes were being sold to advertisers at half price.

The year 1971 brought an even greater hardship when Congress passed a law banning all cigarette advertising from television. Network revenues plunged by 15 percent in January 1971 and 9 percent in February. But for 1971, the first full year of the ban, pretax profits were at $53.7 million. Some predicted that over $150 million in annual network revenues would be lost. But by 1972 profits again rose to $110.9 million and were more than double that figure only two years later as the demand for broadcast2703$$1103g advertising time available kept increasing. To attract new clients, particularly advertisers with small budgets, CBS reduced the minimum amount of time they could buy from 60 to 30 seconds. The other networks soon followed suit.

Apart from the economic pressures, CBS programmers confronted other burdens. One had to do with the shifting nature of the American population: demography was making CBS a network for the aging. Bill Paley contended that as early as 1965 he had sensed that CBS was on a perilous path, its entertainment successes blinding it to the new reality of the era, that the audiences of its top-rated programs comprised an increasingly older set of people at a time when the country was in turmoil and the young appeared on the verge of making their voices heard. Beginning in the late 1960s, the country had been experiencing a youth revolt spearheaded by the antiwar movement, and somehow television would have to take that into account.

AS CBS entered the 1970s, it was brimming over with rural comedies and Westerns. Five of its shows were among the top twenty: "Gunsmoke," "Mayberry R.F.D.," "The Red Skelton Hour," the "Beverly Hillbillies," and "The Glen Campbell Hour." A sixth, "Hee Haw," was ranked 21. Where others might have been calm and content, pointing to the programs' continued success, CBS executives were justifiably nervous. The high ratings were illusory: they would not last. The older generation was faithful—but many of them wouldn't be around much longer. So a grand strategy was mapped out, one that would modify the CBS programming strategy, aiming not at the old folks, or the people who lived in the rural hinterlands, but a brand-new viewing audience, the young, urban generation.

The two leading proponents of this strategy were Robert Wood, the CBS network president, and Fred Silverman. Wood knew that he would have to convince Paley of the merits of making sweeping changes in programming, and the task would not be easy. After all, CBS was still the number one network in the entertainment field. Wood told Paley, "A parade will be coming down the street and you may watch it from your rocking chair, collecting your dividends, and it will go by you. Or you might get up from that chair and get into the parade, so that when it goes by your house you won't just be watching it, you'll be leading it." (2) Paley agreed, and so Wood went to work, deruralizing the schedule and jetti-

---

soning some familiar and popular talent. A new action-packed schedule was created to attract those young viewers. The programs that were being discarded appealed to low-income viewers. Replacements for these programs tended toward the dramatic series based on socially significant adventures and variety shows with youthful irreverence. In a word, these programs were "relevant." They were designed for the "Now Generation."

CBS was not alone in this rethinking. During the fall of 1970, all three networks produced programs that focused on young interns, young storefront lawyers, young criminologists, young psychiatrists, involved teachers, and involved ministers. CBS's efforts in revamping its schedule in the early 1970s would eventually lead to success. Robert Wood and Fred Silverman would make some mistakes, but that was inevitable as they believed in not putting all of the programming eggs in one basket. They missed the boat on the so-called "realism" programs. "Beacon Hill" was a failure. But Wood and Silverman managed to change the nature of television programming. The grand change came with the 1970–71 entertainment schedule when Wood canceled thirteen series. He dropped such long-standing favorites as Ed Sullivan, which had been around for twenty-three years, "Lassie," seventeen years, "Mayberry R.F.D.," eleven years, the "Beverly Hillbillies," nine years, Jim Nabors, five years as "Gomer Pyle" and another two years in the role of a variety host, "Hogan's Heroes" and "Green Acres," both six years, and "Hee Haw," two years. Paradoxically, a number of these shows remained highly popular, but the decision had been reached to clear the way for a new kind of programming. Wood selected eight new series.

The most important replacement arrived in midseason. Its debut on January 12, 1971, has become one of the more important benchmarks of broadcasting history. The name of the program was "All in the Family." No program would symbolize the change at CBS more than "Family." Along with a number of like-minded programs, "Family" touched on a whole set of subjects that had never been mentioned on television entertainment fare before. Until this show, television had been the last bastion of morality and prudishness. It had been taboo to talk about alcoholism or abortion, breast cancer or premarital sex, impotence or menopause. That would change. It would change because of "All in the Family" and other similar shows that it spawned: "Maude," "The Jeffersons," and "Good Times" were but three. Because of these programs, the nature of television entertainment was altered radically.

It began in 1968 when Marc Golden, a CBS programmer and a former CIA agent, visited England. He worked for Mike Dann and was responsible for reading scripts and giving a first reaction on all program ideas received by the network. (The number of programming ideas reaching the networks would soar from 800 a year in the late 1960s to 2,000 a year by 1979.) Golden took in an episode of the BBC's huge comedy hit "Till Death Us Do Part" and roared with laughter. Already two years old, the program was deliberately outrageous. The star was Alf Gannett, who played a foul-tongued, prejudiced dockwocker, who particularly enjoyed taunting his liberal son-in-law. When Golden showed an episode to colleagues back at CBS, the response was positive. One CBS executive thought Jackie Gleason would be perfect for the lead in an American version. Mike Dann authorized CBS to purchase the rights to "Till Death," but Norman Lear, a balding, slightly built comedy writer, had beaten him to it.

Lear, who was 46 years old and was just completing his latest film, "The Night They Raided Minsky's," had read about the British series in *TV Guide* magazine and was quickly reminded of his own stormy relationship with his father. In an unusual step, without having seen an episode or even having read a script, Lear grabbed the rights and concluded a deal for an American version. He persuaded ABC's programming executives to finance the production of a pilot which would be called "Those Were the Days." Chosen by Lear for the lead role was Carroll O'Connor. He would play Archie Bunker, a character who would be as likable as Alf Gannett and equally outrageous. ABC was not prepared, however, to go so far out on a limb. A previous unsuccessful attempt at off-beat humor—a program called "Turn-On"—had left the network gunshy. A test audience thought Archie Bunker quite abrasive. Airing the new Norman Lear program looked to ABC like an act of suicide, especially after "Turn-On."

Early in 1970, Sam Cohen, who was Norman Lear's agent, took the pilot to Mike Dann and Irwin Segelstein. They were even more enthralled with the American version than they had been with the original British show. What they saw in that pilot was a cantankerous 50-year-old foreman from a working-class section of Queens for whom Jews were "Yids," Puerto Ricans were "spics," blacks were "spades," and Chinese were "Chinks." Archie Bunker's prejudices were international—he had no trouble putting down everyone! He described his son-in-law Mike Stivic as a "Polack pinko meathead"; his daughter Gloria was a "weapin' Nelli pinko and an atheist." Wife Edith got off easy—she was simply a "dingbat." That same pilot showed a scene of son-in-law Mike zipping up his fly as he and Gloria walked downstairs after making love at 11 o'clock one Sunday morning. Archie then said to Mike, "when your Mother-in-law and me was going together, it was two years. We never. I never. I mean there was nothing. I mean absolutely nothing. Not till the wedding night." A pause. The camera turned to Edith. "Yeah," she said with a straight face, "and not even then."

The man whose approval was ultimately needed didn't like the show at first. Bill Paley called it vulgar. He was troubled and offended by the insults and the foul language. Some CBS executives, perhaps sensing how Paley thought, believed that the program would benefit from changing Archie into a mild-mannered man supportive of his family. That would appeal to audiences more. But, of course, that had not been Norman Lear's premises. It would certainly take some courage on CBS's part to air the show as Lear conceived it. Bob Wood, the network president, argued to Paley that CBS could afford to take a risk. It still was on top of network programming. What was more, it was clear, said Wood, that a new wave of comedy was taking over the airwaves in the 1970s.

Paley eventually gave in but ordered that "All in the Family" be put on at 9:30 on Tuesday evenings—directly following "Hee Haw" and just before "60 Minutes." In this way, if "Family" floundered, it would not pull down other shows and ruin an entire evening for CBS. There then began disputes over what could be left in the show. The CBS censor was acting like a prude: he didn't want Mike and Gloria's postcoital Sunday morning scene to be shown nor did he wish any reference to the Bunkers' wedding night. The censor would not allow the phrase, "Goddamn it" in the script either. Lear stood his ground for the most part but made clear that he intended to put "Goddamn it" into the show in a later episode.

When the program finally debuted, CBS prepared for the worst. Bob Wood issued a news release saying that "It's time to poke fun at ourselves." CBS executives passed word that something new was going to happen, real people would be seen in a comedy situation. CBS hired extra phone operators to field the complaints expected to stream in once the program ended. Senior CBS executives remained at their desks all evening, waiting for phones to ring, readying their responses for the press and offended opinion leaders. At 9:30 on that January evening in 1971 an announcer said, "The program you are about to see is 'All in the Family.' It seeks to throw a humorous spotlight on our frailties, prejudices, and concerns. By making them a source of laughter we hope to show—in a mature fashion—just how absurd they are."

On that debut Archie said, "If your spics and your spades want their rightful share of the American dream, let them get out there and hustle for it, just like I done. . . . I didn't have no million people marchin' and protestin' to get me my job."

Edith shook her head in agreement. "No, his uncle got it for him."

Later Archie said, "I wouldn't call your black beauties lazy. It just happens their system is geared slower than ours, that's all." When son-in-law Mike objected to the phrase "black beauties," Archie countered: "It so happens, Mr. Big Liberal, a black guy who works with me has a sticker on his car that says, 'black is beautiful.' So what's the matter with black beauties?" Edith added, "It's nicer than when he called them coons."

To everyone's surprise, only 1,000 phone calls reached CBS opera-

---

tors in five cities, and, even more surprisingly, more than 60 percent said they had liked the show. Only in New York was there much displeasure where 287 of the 511 callers denounced the show's vulgarity and prejudice. The ratings were only a 28 that first time and "Family" received only mixed reviews. But by the seventh episode the show had doubled its ratings. At the insistence of Paley, who by now had an obvious change of mind, "Family" was renewed for the fall and was given the 10:30 P.M. Monday slot. In May, Lear and his "Family" staff collected three Emmy awards. The same month, when the entire cycle of shows went into repeat telecasts, "Family" became the number one rated show. In time, the critics enthused about the show. According to Cleveland Amory, writing in *TV Guide,* "Family" was "not just the best-written, best-directed and best-acted show on television, it's the best show on television."

In the spring of 1987, sixteen years after "Family" debuted, Norman Lear was eager to explain just what had caused the huge success of the program: "There were these myths. One was that the working man comes home and doesn't want to be reminded of his problems. So you don't deal with them (on television). Another is that the average intelligence of the audience is 13 years old. So don't give them anything to think about. The third was that anything deemed by the New York–Los Angeles establishment to be controversial will cause a knee-deep reaction in the middle of the country and an overreaction in the Bible Belt. So you had to fight each week with something that flew in the face of it. They saw that states didn't secede from the union because Archie Bunker diapered his grandson and that his wife made love and spoke of it." (3)

"Family" remained the number one show for five straight years. In time the program would change. Mike and Gloria would leave in 1978. Edith, in 1979. With feminism asserting itself increasingly, Edith took on a more assertive and aware character. She even went to work in a home for the elderly. Archie remained his old self, but at times appeared to mellow. He had less to say about hippies and pinkos; more down-to-earth themes, such as the eroding of his earning power by inflation, concerned him. But he was always the ever-irascible Archie.

❧❧❧❧

Ratings surged for CBS in the fall of 1971. Although it had some disappointments, the network led the ratings by nearly a point. Saturday night was the big hit with "All in the Family" leading the way. Other programs that evening—the new "Dick Van Dyke Show," "Funny Face," and the "Mary Tyler Moore Show"—also scored well.

CBS was shifting from cornball comedy to programs that were geared for a better educated, more affluent group, youthful and sophisticated. This was an audience that still was anchored in the antiauthoritarian mood of the 1960s. It still was embarked on a search for the authentic. What CBS wanted to show were people, who, while clinging to those values, were not really caught up in politics, but rather in their own lives. And often their own lives would put them in confrontation with an invisible or arbitrary authority. It was that confrontation that was the underlying thrust of "All in the Family," "M*A*S*H," and "The Mary Tyler Moore Show," the three comedies that reflected the new CBS direction.

On that same Saturday night list during the fall of 1971 was "The Mary Tyler Moore Show," setting a new standard for the kind of breezy, articulate comedy that got away from rural people and geography. In fact "Mary" had debuted the previous fall. Coming as it did before "All in the Family," it proved to be the first CBS hit of the early 1970s to combine modern attitudes with the fundamental comedy elements that were so familiar from "I Love Lucy" and the "Honeymooners." "Mary" was a symbol of the new, independent career-minded woman, a role not yet seen on sitcoms. Some worried that the audience would not accept a character over 30 who was not married. She was described as having come off a broken love affair. That was more acceptable than saying she had just divorced. That might have implied that she had divorced Dick Van Dyke to whom she had been married on the "Dick Van Dyke Show."

"Mary" paved the way for yet another wonderfully witty comedy called "M*A*S*H," which debuted in the 1972–73 season. Based on a film of the same name, it dealt with the 4077th Mobile Army Surgical Hospital. The unit contained a set of zany, irreverent army doctors stuck in the quagmire of the Korean conflict. Although the parallel with Vietnam was hardly lost on anyone, the show became a hit as much for its bright comedy as for its antiwar theme. Larry Gelbert, the writer of the show, explained that the show had several messages. One of them was simply that war is futile. Another was that things had reached a terrible state when people had to kill each other to make a point. "We wanted to say," observed Gelbert, "that when you take people from home they do things they would never do. They drink. They whore. They steal. They become venal. They become asinine, in terms of power. They get the clap. They become alcoholics. They become rude. They become sweet, tender, loving. We tended to make the war the enemy without really saying who was fighting." (4) This was epitomized in a line that came from Klinger while he was under fire: "Damn Truman, damn Stalin, damn everybody." (5) During its first season, 1972–73, "M*A*S*H" hovered around a discouraging 26 in the ratings, but word was passed that Bill Paley liked the show. Sandwiched between "All in the Family" and "The Mary Tyler Moore Show" on Saturday nights, "M*A*S*H" became the fourth most popular prime-time program for 1973–74. The producers of "M*A*S*H" tried at one stage to persuade CBS to drop the show's laugh track, which they felt was distracting. Viewers were expected to laugh more easily if there was a laugh track. When testing showed that such was the case, the "M*A*S*H" laugh track stayed. The program lasted eleven years, ranking in the top ten for all but two of those years, and became one of the most widely syndicated shows in television history.

Another new kind of program came to CBS in the early 1970s. This one was called "soft," lacking as it was in sex and violence: the relationship of the characters was what counted, characters who for the most part were decent individuals. "The Waltons," depicting the life of a large family in rural Virginia during the depression, reflected this trend. It began as a two-hour Christmas special in 1971 called "The Homecoming." The special had the blessing of the CBS chairman: Paley called it the best film he had ever seen. By the fall of 1972, "The Homecoming" had turned into a series but was placed in a bad time slot (Thursday 8:30 P.M., opposite ABC's "The Mod Squad" and NBC's "Flip Wilson Show"); its ratings hovered in the mid-20s. But then CBS began promoting it, and suddenly "The Waltons," drawing more than 30 percent of the viewers, shot up to number two.

The 1972–73 season featured seventeen new action adventures as a whole generation of police shows arrived. In the fall of 1973 Fred Silverman came up with a big winner about a cop with a shaved head and a flattened nose who sucked on a lollipop and seemed gentle as a lamb—but wasn't. His name was Theo Kojak played by actor Telly Savalas. In its first year "Kojak" reached number seven in the ratings. Apart from police shows, Silverman took on variety shows as a new challenge. They had been in eclipse after shining in the 1950s and 1960s: in the 1969–70 season there had been sixteen variety programs on the air, but two years later only two remained, "The Ed Sullivan Show" and "The Red Skelton Hour." Watching the "Merv Griffin Show," a late-night talk show on CBS, one evening in the spring of 1971, Silverman cast his eye on two of Merv's guests, a husband and wife singing team named Sonny and Cher. The "Sonny and Cher Comedy Hour" debuted on August 1, 1971 at CBS and attracted a 42 rating. By 1973, it had reached the top ten.

Much of the success of CBS during the early 1970s was attributable to this fellow whom people called "The Man with the Golden Gut." Fred Silverman was indeed astonishing. In 1970, the year he had inherited Mike Dann's job at CBS, the network had logged only four shows in the top ten. That total rose slowly in the beginning, from five to six in the subsequent two years. But then in the 1973–74 season CBS had nine shows in the top ten! That marked the first time that CBS had achieved such a record in a decade. In the 1974–75 season CBS would nearly repeat that achievement, garnering eight top-ten shows. Altogether, starting with the fall of 1970, CBS had placed thirteen new weekly series in the top ten as well as three others within the top twenty.

To appreciate the significance of those figures, one should recall that the Silveman era had gotten off the ground as CBS was canceling a host of highly rated shows. The risk had been formidable, and Silverman and CBS had come through with flying colors. (Silverman had been earning $250,000 in 1974 but after twelve years with CBS was still only a midlevel executive. ABC offered him $300,000 a year salary, a $1 million life insurance policy plus lots of other perks, and Silverman went over to ABC in May 1975 to become head of programming there.)

But, by the mid-1970s, CBS's entertainment schedule was weakening. The 1976–77 season did not go well for CBS: ABC led with a 20.9 rating followed by NBC with 19.6; CBS came in third with 18.7. By the spring of 1977, ABC had seven of the top ten shows. CBS had only two, NBC, one. In the fall, CBS did even worse, dropping to third place.

While the entertainment side of CBS grappled with the changing 1970s, the news division confronted a major test of its right to the same legal protection traditionally given to print journalism. That test would come as a result of the CBS documentary, "The Selling of the Pentagon," aired on February 23, 1971. Ever since the early days of broadcast journalism, radio and later television correspondents fought for the right to be protected in their work by the First Amendment, which guarantees freedom of the press. The First Amendment has been considered a vital shield for newsmen from forced disclosure of their sources. Now, in "Pentagon," CBS was about to throw down the gauntlet, arguing that broadcasters were no different from print journalists, deserving of the same rights, the same protection. For years, the print newsmen had argued (always behind the backs of television correspondents) that somehow the men with the cameras and the soundmen were professionally inferior to them.

"Pentagon" had been written and directed by Peter Davis, and focused on the huge expenditure of public funds—partly illegal—to promote militarism. The documentary presented evidence that the Defense Department was spending tens of millions of dollars in public relations allocations each year solely to "sell" the Vietnam war to the American public. It alleged that the military could hide its mistakes easily because news emerging from the Pentagon was under such tight control.

Major issues were at stake as a result of the broadcast. First, there was the image of the military-industrial establishment. But, more important, the way Congress handled the subsequent probe into the program raised the intriguing question of whether television news programming deserved protection under the First Amendment to the Constitution.

The hour-long documentary began when Bud Benjamin, who at the time was a CBS producer of documentaries, came upon a film made by the Atomic Energy Commission on the peaceful uses of nuclear energy.

Wondering why CBS couldn't get extraordinary film like that, he showed the film to Richard Salant. Then, talking to Bill Leonard, Salant and Leonard realized there was a story worth doing on the government's efforts to sell itself to its own taxpayers. Writer-producer Peter Davis was asked to probe the matter. Davis returned with this conclusion: all other government agencies' selling efforts were of little note compared to the Pentagon's own public relations activities. Davis had come across a book on the subject of the Pentagon's public relations techniques written by J. William Fulbright, the former head of the Senate Foreign Relations Committee. That book, written in November 1970, became the basis for "The Selling of the Pentagon."

The documentary started with a dramatic explosion caused by a rocket being fired by a jet plane streaking across the sky; other explosions followed, and then there were shots of infantrymen running and firing rifles. Roger Mudd, the narrator, noted that this was not Vietnam. Instead it was North Carolina and what was going on was "an exercise in salesmanship—the selling of the Pentagon." The action shots wound up with a look at civilians sitting in a reviewing stand being addressed by an officer who explained what they had just witnessed. Such military displays were what the program was all about—and what the program was assailing. Mudd stated that the free flow of information was essential to democracy, and "misinformation, distortion, propaganda all interrupt that flow. They make it impossible for people to know what their government is doing, which, in a democracy, is crucial." The Pentagon estimated its public affairs budget at $30 million in 1971. But CBS quoted a Twentieth Century Fund estimate that put the figure closer to $190 million, exceeding by more than $40 million the combined total cost of all three networks' news coverage.

Reaction was swift—even before the program was over. Fourteen minutes into the documentary, one caller accused Mudd of being an "agent of a foreign power." Thirty-seven minutes into it, an Air Force colonel called to proclaim that "The next time I see Mudd I'm going to take the nose off his face." (6) The defense establishment was predictably irate; so were politicians. Vice President Spiro Agnew charged CBS with "propagandist manipulation." One Congressman added that the show was "the most un-American thing I've ever seen on the tube." There was criticism of CBS's editing methods, but significantly none related to the program's main revelations. Television critics praised the show; Pentagon reporters thought it didn't go far enough. They would have preferred that CBS deal not with just the selling of the Pentagon, but also with how difficult it was to obtain accurate information from that institution. CBS repeated the telecast, displaying its confidence in its findings, gave air time to the critics, replied to them—and won a Peabody and some other awards. The Pentagon, acknowledging the truth of what CBS was addressing in the program, withdrew some of the more jingoistic—and unprofessional—propaganda films it had been circulating.

A House subcommittee was convened to look into the documentary. In the course of that probe, the "Pentagon" case turned into a major confrontation between the subpoena powers of the federal government and the freedom of the press. The subcommittee, headed by Rep. Harley O. Staggers, subpoenaed CBS's notes and outtakes (film and tape gathered for the program but not actually used over the air) involved in the production of "Pentagon." Frank Stanton declined to make the notes and outtakes from "Pentagon" available to the subcommittee, claiming Congressional harassment and incompatibility with the First Amendment. The case no longer dealt with what CBS had alleged in the program; it now centered on the news judgments and editing which were alleged to have resulted in distortion. Stanton observed acidly that inasmuch as the federal government licensed broadcasters, such subpoena actions, if allowed to stand, would have a particularly "chilling effect" upon broadcast journalism. The issue, Stanton had said, "boils down to one central and vital question. Is this country going to continue to have a free press or is indirect censorship cynically masquerading as a 'federal standard' to be imposed upon it? The issue is as simple as that—and as crucial."

Why had Stanton taken such a courageous stand? According to Ernie Leiser, "He (Stanton) was just a man of principle. He didn't have any background in news either. But he was a man of very considerable morality, and he realized the importance of CBS News. He hated the other programming, the other crap that CBS Television was putting on the air, and he liked, he was interested in news, and he was determined to protect its independence. He risked going to jail to protect the integrity of, the independence of CBS News." (7)

The "Pentagon" case was all the more troublesome, coming at a time when the Nixon administration was already hinting that the press might have to be regulated if it did not shape up. This was the same administration that had sought to exercise prior restraint in the "Pentagon Papers" case, when *The New York Times* obtained and printed Pentagon documents that contradicted official statements related to what the United States was doing in Vietnam. The Nixon administration had also pursued subpoenas and investigations of reporters in and out of the courts. William Small, a CBS vice president at the time, said the whole exercise was "insulting to journalists . . . who are not ready to surrender their role in a democracy to bureaucrats and other politicians simply because they wear American flags in their lapels. It's our flag, too—it's our country, too—and if our institutions are being corrupted, it's being done by those who want the news to be bland, innocuous and devoid of any substance other than obeisance to the status quo. . . . Good things don't happen because bad news is not reported. . . . If we give only the good news, only the safe news, only the uncontroversial, then we are compounding the ignorance of our constituents." (8) Another former CBS vice-president added: "The tragedy of this kind of reaction [to the "Pentagon" program] is that CBS is actually getting attacked for doing their best. No one says a word all the time they are doing their worst with the usual run of comedies. And the fuss created over that program means that everyone from Dick Salant [president of CBS News] on down will have to spend weeks replying to all the criticism instead of getting on with making good television. The producer will be so busy explaining himself he won't have a chance to make another documentary for months." (9)

Unfortunately, from CBS's perspective, there had apparently been defects in the editing procedures of "Pentagon." As Ernie Leiser explained, "There were things that made a lot of people uncomfortable about that ["Pentagon"], not the thrust of the program itself, but there were some shoddy editing practices employed in that. I know, because one of the people who was done wrong was the chief flack at the Pentagon, Assistant Secretary of Defense Dan Hankin. When he complained to me, and . . . pointed out what he said they'd done, I looked at the transcript of the interview, and indeed they'd taken things out of context. So CBS News had standards, but . . . all along it was a struggle [to] keep people observing them." (10)

After his appearance before the subcommittee and his refusal to supply notes and outtakes, Frank Stanton was threatened by Chairman Staggers with contempt of Congress. That could have meant going to jail. Earlier, Stanton had said that he would take the issue to the Supreme Court if necessary. That, however, proved unnecessary when Congress rejected the committee's proposal to place Stanton in contempt.

The final outcome was a triumph of sorts for CBS: for the first time in modern history, the House failed to sustain the vote of one of its committees to cite for contempt. Clearly, "Pentagon" was a milestone for the television documentary. But not because of the content. Rather, it was because CBS had shown that it could not be forced to bend to the government's will. And in doing so, the network had strengthened broadcasting's cause in its battle to convince others that the First Amendment applied to it as well as to print journalism.

The early 1970s brought inevitable changes on the news side as well. Harry Reasoner's urbane features and manners had given "60 Minutes" a certain flair. He was clearly the dominant personality in the early days of that program. But then he defected, going over to ABC to become the news anchor there in 1970 because "Walter Cronkite was showing no inclination toward stepping in front of a speeding truck." Just prior to Reasoner's joining ABC, the ratings of the evening news programs showed CBS in the lead with 31, NBC with 28, and ABC trailing far behind with only 15. But less than three years later—in the spring of 1973—Reasoner had engineered something of a miracle: CBS still led with 26, NBC was next with 25, but the combination of Reasoner and Howard K. Smith showed a respectable 22. There were even some weeks in which NBC and ABC were even. Reasoner remained at ABC for eight more years, and only in 1978 did he return to CBS and "60 Minutes."

Reasoner's departure from CBS was a blessing in disguise for a couple of other correspondents. His leaving paved the way for Dan Rather to become the anchor of the Sunday night news program. Rather's salary hike was not large—he went from $43,000 to $49,000 a year—but achieving the new prestige of being the Sunday anchor eventually meant a great deal: when he renegotiated his contract four years later, his income was more than $100,000 a year. When Reasoner left "60 Minutes," Charles Kuralt was offered the chance to replace him. He seemed the most like Reasoner. But Kuralt was still quite attached to his "On the Road" series and didn't want to yield that assignment.

So in November 1970 of that year the job was offered to Morley Safer. He had been in Paris and was about to feed a satellite report to New York. Charles de Gaulle had just died. There was a call from New York for Safer. Bill Leonard, then vice president of CBS News, was on the line. Safer imagined the worst whenever a top executive phoned. The phone call must have meant that he had messed something up. He was all set to defend himself against the inevitable allegation when Leonard said kindly, "How would you like to move to New York and take Reasoner's place, be the co-editor of '60 Minutes'? By the way, the de Gaulle stuff was very good."

"Shit," Safer replied, dumbfounded, "This is the phone call I would like to get five years from now."

"We can't wait five years," Leonard barked. "Reasoner is leaving on Monday. Come to New York tomorrow."

Safer squirmed inside. "I can't come tomorrow. Tomorrow we're burying de Gaulle."

As little as he wanted to give in even an inch, Leonard knew he had no choice. "Okay, the day after. 'Bye, have a nice funeral." (11)

For Dan Rather, the job of covering the Nixon White House would be a constant source of stress and frustration. It was not easy to cover a president like Richard Nixon. Nor was it a simple matter to cover the presidency while the United States remained in the thick of the Vietnam war.

The job often led to confrontation with the president's aides. Once, in April 1971, during a meeting with John Ehrlichman and H. R. Haldeman, two senior Nixon aides, in Ehrlichman's White House office, Ehrlichman accused Rather of being wrong 90 percent of the time.

"Then," said Rather, "You have nothing to worry about; any reporter who's wrong 90 percent of the time can't last."

Haldeman found that answer irrelevant. "What concerns me is that you are sometimes wrong, but your style is very positive. You sound like you know what you're talking about; people believe you."

Chimed in Ehrlichman, "Yeah, people believe you, and they shouldn't."

"I hope they do," replied Rather, "and maybe now we are getting down to the root of it. You have trouble getting people to believe you." (12)

In the spring of 1972, Rather co-authored an article for *Harper's* magazine on Haldeman and Ehrlichman. He wrote about their mysterious and murky power base within the Nixon White House. Making that point over at CBS was difficult. Rather tried to get it across through the *Harper's* article. But CBS would not let him pursue the article, convinced that he would compromise his objectivity as a reporter at the forthcoming summer conventions. Rather backed off. In time much of what he planned to write would go into a book he co-authored with Gary Gates called *The Palace Guard.*

For the most part, in his tangling with the Nixon administration, Rather would come out ahead, but there would be moments of anguish for him and for CBS. Given the ongoing tensions between the administration and the television networks, especially CBS, whenever there was a personal confrontation between representatives of the two institutions, it was a major event. One such occurrence came in August 1973, at a Nixon press conference. Rather gained the floor and began to ask a question: "I want to state this question with due respect for your office . . . ." Nixon interrupted: "That would be unusual." Then, in March 1974 came the most explosive altercation between the two men. It happened when the president was being questioned at a meeting of the National Association of Broadcasters in Houston. Rather introduced a question by saying, "Dan Rather with CBS News, Mr. President." He was interrupted by a mixture of applause and boos. Nixon then asked the CBS man, "Are you running for something?" Which led Rather to say immediately, "No, sir, Mr. President, are you?" The moment he had blurted that out, Rather felt he had made a mistake. Nixon had made him look ridiculous, precisely what the president had hoped to accomplish. A phone call came from Richard Salant the next day. He told Rather: "Well, we may get a lot of heat on this. But I want you to know that you were the White House correspondent yesterday and you're the White House correspondent today and you'll be the White House correspondent tomorrow." (13) Rather was touched by that gesture. Some fear was expressed that the CBS affiliates would take some action against Rather. In a bold departure from normal CBS behavior, he was asked to attend a meeting of the affiliates soon thereafter. Rather attended with reluctance. Salant indicated at the meeting that Rather would have preferred not to have said what he had to the president. But given the context—the applause, the boos, the question put to him by the president ("Are you running for something?"), it was understandable, if regrettable. In the end, the affiliates let Rather off without taking action.

When Salant offered Rather a better job after Nixon quit the White House in August 1974, the White House correspondent was sensitive, wondering whether he was in fact being removed from the White House post for past deeds. Maybe the affiliates were now using their influence to get rid of Rather for the Nixon remark. Salant tried to assure Dan that such was not the case; he could even keep the White House job if he really wanted it. Word was leaked that CBS was trying to move him out of the White House. Suspicion was cast at Rather, but he insisted that he had not done the leaking. He announced that he planned to take some time off. Finally, a week after Nixon's resignation, Rather accepted the job as anchorman and correspondent on "CBS Reports." He did that only for a little over a year before he joined Morley Safer and Mike Wallace at "60 Minutes" in late 1975.

ᴐᴠᴐᴠᴐᴠᴐ

When the Watergate scandal broke, CBS had to make up its mind how quickly it would jump into the journalistic fray taking on the Nixon White House. And it would have to decide what kind of news stories were fair, and what kind were not. No simple matter. Walter Cronkite had been reading about Watergate in the newspapers, and had noted that the affair was complicated, vague, in need of some orderly reporting. He decided to tackle the subject on his evening news program. On Friday evening, October 27, 1972, he presented a 14-minute installment on the scandal. Two-thirds of the entire Cronkite newscast was devoted to Watergate. "At first," Cronkite began, "it was called the Watergate caper—five men apparently caught in the act of burglarizing and bugging Democratic headquarters in Washington. But the episode grew steadily more sinister—no longer a caper, but the Watergate affair escalating finally into charges of a high-level campaign of political sabotage and espionage apparently unparalleled in American history . . . ."

With those words, echoing forth over the CBS network, Watergate had gone from a local to a national story, from a mildly interesting piece of gossip to a national scandal. Television had the power to do that to a

---

story. And that Friday evening Walter Cronkite had used that power. The second part of the two-part report would be aired shortly.

When Dick Salant watched the first Cronkite piece on Watergate, he was taken back. Wasn't all this very old? Was it necessary for CBS to put this on the air? And, more technically, wasn't it too long? He was trying to think of any excuse why the material should not have been aired. Frank Stanton had phoned Bill Paley to tell him to make sure to watch the Cronkite newscast that evening. Paley did not like what he saw, he didn't like the length, and he didn't like the fact that the allegations had not been separated clearly enough from the known facts. "The broadcast troubled me," Paley wrote later. "It just did not seem in keeping with Cronkite's usual objectivity." (14)

A call had come in Saturday morning to Bill Paley from Charles Colson, who was the Nixon White House troubleshooter. It was an unusual moment in the relations between government and the networks. Rarely had a senior government official so blatantly attempted to interfere with network programming. Colson reportedly threatened to cancel the licenses of CBS-owned stations if the network carried the second section of the two-part Watergate report. Colson accused, threatened, argued. He told Paley that CBS would live to regret doing such a thing. He charged that CBS had offered the Watergate program as a special to advertisers who had turned it down. Colson also charged that CBS journalists were in effect, working for George McGovern, the Democratic presidential nominee at the time. Finally, Colson asserted that the White House insisted that the second segment be killed.

The CBS chairman was in a quandary. He was definitely upset with CBS News for the program, but he was equally disturbed with Colson for the phone call. After Paley asked Stanton to check on some of Colson's accusations, the CBS president came up with no evidence that CBS had put up the program for sale to an advertiser. He had also discovered that CBS had made a serious effort to get an administration figure to appear on the program in vain.

A meeting was called for the following Monday with Stanton; Salant, president of CBS News; Arthur Taylor, the new CBS president; and Jack Schneider, the president of the broadcast group. At the Monday meeting, Paley made his displeasure with the program known. There was no need to pass on the fact that Colson had phoned; Stanton had taken care of that earlier.

Paley let Salant know indirectly that he did not want Part Two of Cronkite's Watergate report aired. It was a difficult conversation. Paley invoked Stanton in saying that the CBS president backed him in feeling that Part Two should not be aired. (Later Stanton would say that he had done no such thing.) It was unthinkable for Stanton to disagree with his boss in public. Paley and Salant were clearly in a quandary. CBS had a

"DAMN TRUMAN, DAMN STALIN, DAMN EVERYBODY."

nearly iron-clad rule: no one could kill a story because of pressure. This could be the first time.

Part Two was planned for 14-minutes as well. That length carried something of an editorial statement. Cronkite planned to close the segment by noting that Watergate was indeed important and the version coming from the White House had not been very persuasive. It was not simply Walter Cronkite versus Bill Paley or even Bill Paley versus the White House. A lot was at stake. Morale in the CBS newsroom hinged on Part Two being screened. In the end, Paley could not allow the White House to dictate what CBS would do or air.

Instructions were finally sent forward that the second part could be aired. But it would be cut to just 8 minutes. As little as he liked what the Cronkite program had done in undertaking the two-part Watergate series, Paley understood what the news division was all about; he understood that even issues as delicate as Watergate were fair game for exploration by the news department. Paley would not stand in the way of CBS televising the second part. There was a principle involved. And for acting that way, he would be lauded by CBS employees years later. "You've got to remember Paley put his wallet on the line," said David Buksbaum, who is a CBS News vice president for special events. "He had station licenses. The biggest, single moneymaker in the television business. Those station licenses were on the line. Gosh, you've got to have a lot of balls to do that, and he did it. To his credit. . . . He has a sense of what CBS News ought to be." (15)

Sandy Socolow, a top producer on the Cronkite program, was ordered to trim the script. When he did, he showed it to Cronkite, who approved it. Paley was still bridling when the truncated Part Two was aired. He told Salant that never again must something like this happen. The White House was still furious with CBS. And Paley was himself agitated because his network's reputation for hard-hitting independence had been damaged when CBS's decision to cut the segment became a news story of its own.

Shortly after the two parts were run, Katherine Graham, who ran the *Washington Post,* bumped into Bill Paley at a party. Until then, she had been proud but worried about her newspaper's reporting on Watergate— and lonely. But then Walter Cronkite had gone on national television and announced to the nation that indeed what the *Post* had been reporting was important, that it deserved to be treated with seriousness. She kissed the CBS founder and said simply, "You saved us." Paley's response has not been recorded, but he could not have been pleased hearing her words. She appeared to be suggesting just how little there had been to the story before CBS got into the act—confirming his own suspicions when the great debate occurred on whether to air Part Two.

Following the 1972 presidential election, Colson spoke to Stanton and now, armed with a Nixon triumph at the ballot box, was brimming over with thoughts of revenge. "We'll break your network," he threatened. The White House, he intimated, would make sure to take away the five owned and operated stations, a major factor in CBS's wealth. The White House would place its weight behind pay television. If this kind of talk sent shudders through the brass, it had no effect whatsoever on the people who had put the Cronkite show together. They were pleased that the two parts had been aired, miffed that the second part had been cut down, but eager to get on with more such programs. Whenever they asked, however, the answer always came back a resounding "No!"

There seemed to be a definite link between the Cronkite Watergate segments and Paley's decision to scrap instant analysis, though that decision would come only on June 6, 1973. The White House had been eager to have the networks scrub this technique: it reflected a kind of arrogance to be able to comment on a presidential speech so quickly. Furthermore, an analyst could "instantly" fire a verbal assault at Nixon. Paley announced that from now on "instant analysis" would be scheduled as soon after the president spoke as practicable, but generally no later than in a week's time. Paley also declared that CBS News henceforth would not provide news analysis immediately after broadcasts presenting views opposing those expressed in presidential broadcasts. That kind of analysis would be scheduled during the normal CBS News broadcast schedule.

Few among CBS's correspondents were sympathetic with the White House pressure. Indeed, Roger Mudd went so far as to do a piece protesting the order. Not surprisingly, it never made it to the air. One of the main practitioners of instant analysis, Eric Sevareid, actually came out in favor of the CBS ban saying that he had always been a little uncomfortable with the idea. It worked well enough when there was an advance text of a speech, he noted, or when a briefing was given on its contents, but without these aids, the effect was poor journalism. That was neither fair to the correspondent or audience. (16)

With Roger Mudd writing a rough draft, Mudd and some other CBS correspondents wrote letters of protest. Eventually, the correspondents would get their way. With the White House weakened by Watergate, Paley reinstated the policy of instant analysis on November 12—just five months later. Paley explained rather unconvincingly that the reversal had to do with the proliferation of major news since June, as if important news events had not occurred before the ban. By that time, the White House was reeling from Watergate, so that Paley could take the step without incurring much wrath from the Nixon administration.

The morning hours remained a problem for CBS. The CBS morning news continued to lag after 1965 when it was switched from 10 A.M. to 7 A.M. In that latter hour it went head to head with the "Today" show and never quite made it. Still, CBS was not willing to abdicate that spot to NBC. It was the one news program Chairman Paley watched faithfully, the morning being the one time of the day that his busy schedule, social and otherwise, allowed him to be in front of a television set.

Whether it was an early morning program or any other, the network could not accept any weakness in its schedule. Once in the late 1960s, when Mike Dann, who was then in charge of programming for CBS, told Bill Paley with great glee that CBS had nine of the ten top-rated daytime shows, the chairman frowned and grumbled, "that Goddamn NBC always hangs in there for one." (17) And so CBS was always searching for the gimmick that would bring about a turnaround in the morning hours. In the spring of 1973 CBS thought it had just the gimmick. Her name was Sally Quinn.

She was the *Washington Post's* gossip columnist. CBS had enticed her to leave the *Post* and go on the CBS morning news opposite Barbara Walters on "Today." Sally had wanted to be an actress when she had graduated from Smith College as a drama major. An MGM talent scout had seen her at Smith in her senior year and wanted her to go on television. But it didn't work out. So she took a variety of research and secretarial jobs in Washington, D.C., Mexico, Europe, and New York. At one point in 1958 she became a secretarial assistant to CBS News President Richard Salant. He took her to the political conventions in Miami and Chicago. So she was not an unfamiliar face when she came to work for the network five years later.

Almost from the beginning the Sally Quinn project was a dud. She was overpromoted. She was described in the press as CBS's new "blonde bombshell," "femme fatale," and "sex symbol." Some would blame CBS or the press for her downfall. Some would blame Sally Quinn herself. Once she actually got on the air, her performances were less than sensational. In her book, *We're Going to Make You a Star,* she argued that she had not been trained properly for the role of anchorwoman. That may have been true. She is best remembered for the various gaffes she made on the air. On the morning of her debut in early August 1973, the show featured a film piece on child-labor abuse among migrant workers. And there she was ad-libbing that when her parents had made her clean her room, she thought that was child labor. On one occasion in the next few weeks, when Hughes Rudd, who was co-anchor on the show, read a story about a decompression mishap that had caused a man to be blown out of an airplane at 39,000 feet she thought it was funny and burst out laughing. To make matters worse, Quinn was not considered a good interviewer—she looked even worse in comparison with Rudd, one of the best writers in television news.

By that fall, Sally Quinn had become the laughing stock of the television industry. While the ratings had not been good before she came aboard, they dropped slightly after she and Rudd began to co-anchor. That was indeed bad news as she was supposed to be the tonic that would lift the ratings skyward. In December she asked to be relieved of her contract. A few weeks later she quit CBS News and returned to the *Washington Post.* Not one person at the network tried to dissuade her from her decision.

ຫ·ຫ·ຫ·ຫ

"60 Minutes" was fast becoming a national institution. During the 1970s it would grow into the most important program on television. The program would make huge profits for CBS, sometimes as much as $70 million a year. The money would roll in because the public loved the show. Nearly 70 percent of the mail CBS received—80,000 letters a year—would be about "60 Minutes." Advertising rates jumped: in 1975, a 30-second spot sold for between $17,000 and $27,000. A year later the figure had jumped to between $30,000 to $50,000. By 1979 each of its 6 minutes of advertising time was commanding over $200,000. The show cost about $200,000 a week to produce—less than half the cost of an hour-long prime-time entertainment show—which meant the network took home around $1 million each week. (By 1982, the news magazine was getting the highest advertising rate for a 30-second advertisement on prime time—$175,000.)

On November 26, 1978, "60 Minutes" rose to the top of the ratings. It was the only regularly scheduled news and public affairs program to have reached that elite status. By the end of that year, the show was competing for the top rating spot with another CBS program, "Dallas." Its popularity was based on its correspondents' ability to get newsmakers to say and do things that ordinarily they might not have. One such case occurred in the spring of 1971. It centered on Mike Wallace and Don Hewitt. The two men flew to Texas at that time to do a story on the opening of the Lyndon Baines Johnson Presidential Library. Vietnam was very much on Wallace's mind. Eager to cooperate, Johnson invited the two CBS men to be guests as his ranch. Proudly, the former president showed them library exhibits covering aspects of his administration. It was odd. Everything was touched upon except Vietnam. When Mike Wallace said he couldn't help notice that Vietnam had been excluded, Johnson said angrily, "Don't ask me about Vietnam. I don't want to talk about Vietnam." Hewitt and Wallace issued a soft protest, noting that it was impossible to ignore the subject on the program. But Johnson held his ground and threatened that if they brought the subject up during filming, he would send them packing.

Johnson was dealing with Mike Wallace and the CBS correspondent would not give up so easily. When he was alone with the former president, Wallace told him how much he had admired him, how he had thought long ago that he was the kind of leader the nation needed but would probably never get. Then the Kennedy assassination occurred, followed by the early days of the Johnson presidency when he had done so much for civil rights. "But then," said Wallace, "everything turned sour, Mr. President, and you know why?"

"Why?" Johnson snapped.

"Because you let the war get out of hand. Vietnam fucked you, Mr. President, and so, I'm afraid, you fucked the country. And you've got to talk about that."

It was the kind of performance that would have made great television. A network correspondent lecturing a former persident of the United States on his conduct of a war, chewing him out for leading the nation astray. It was also the kind of performance that appeared unquestionably about to lead to the early exit of Wallace and Hewitt. Wallace did some fast calculations. One of two things would happen. Johnson would melt, as unlikely as that seemed, or he would grow agitated and kick the CBS men out of the ranch without doing the program. At first Johnson looked at Wallace with disbelief; he then walked off without saying a word.

Wallace thought that was it. The next step would be to pack their bags.

Extraordinarily, the filming went on and Wallace honored Johnson's request not to talk about Vietnam when they walked through the exhibits. But then suddenly, without advance warning, Johnson observed that . . . "President Kennedy was spared that crucial action [of having Vietnam called Kennedy's war] because his period was known as Mr. McNamara's war. And then it became Mr. Johnson's war, and now they refer to it as Mr. Nixon's war in talking about getting out. I think it is very cruel to have that burden placed upon a president because he is trying to follow a course that he devotedly believes is in the best interest of this nation . . . ." Wallace was taken off guard. He had in fact gotten Johnson to talk about the war, and when he had spoken, the former president issued a brief, but eloquent statement, in effect asking to be remembered in history as a leader who had the country's interests at heart. Later Johnson would say to Wallace, "Well, Goddammit, Mike, I gave you what you wanted. I hope you're satisfied." Stunned by the experience, Wallace could only say that indeed he was. (18)

Vignettes like this one put "60 Minutes" in a special class. And, as the viewers responded by watching in larger and larger numbers, executives at CBS became increasingly astonished at what was happening. "I've waited twenty years for this," observed Richard Salant as he neared the end of his long period as president of CBS News. Prime time had been largely off limits to news programs in the past. That was for sitcoms and other light fare. Now Salant could take great satisfaction. "I always knew," he joked, "that if I survived in this job long enough, the day would come when those characters would turn to me to help them out with a ratings problem." (19)

The public became accustomed to tuning in to see what "Hewlitt's angels" were doing each week. Rather was described as sympathetic, skeptical, earnest. Reasoner possessed a dry wit. Safer had a friendly demeanor. Wallace, with his tough questions and tougher personality, gave the show some electricity. Wallace was considered something special. He was raking in money for the network, and everyone knew it. In 1980, Ed Bradley, the Philadelphia-born black correspondent who had covered the White House and Vietnam for CBS, replaced Rather when he left to take over as anchorman in place of Walter Cronkite. By 1984 Diane Sawyer would become the fifth member of the reporting staff. Harry Reasoner returned to CBS from ABC in 1979 and became the fourth correspondent (along with Mike Wallace, Dan Rather, and Morley Safer).

One of the mainstays of "60 Minutes" was a long-time behind-the-scenes writer named Andy Rooney who had been associated with CBS since 1949. Don Hewitt called him the program's Russell Baker or its Art Buchwald. He also called him a cross between Charles Kuralt and H. L. Mencken. Rooney came from Albany, New York. He had done some writing for the campus newspaper at Colgate University in Hamilton, New York, and then for the Stars and Stripes in World War II. After writing a few books about his wartime experiences, Rooney went to Hollywood when MGM bought the screen rights to "The Story of the Stars and Stripes." But nothing came of the project. He started a freelance writing career but earning $350 for a Harper's piece that took him six weeks, he decided he was not going to survive long as a magazine writer. In 1948 he began writing for Arthur Godfrey's radio and television programs. This time he earned $625 a week. Beginning with the 1979 season, he joined "60 Minutes" as a regular commentator, doing 3-minute pieces.

Rarely did "60 Minutes" take on complicated issues. Rather, it sought to examine situations that could be easily and quickly grasped by its viewers. That went along with Don Hewitt's philosophy of television. "The trick in TV," he liked to say, "is to grab the viewer by the throat." When the program did an exposé, it would try simply to focus on the issue, "to shine light in dark corners," in Hewitt's apt phrase, rather than enter into lengthy "See It Now" or "CBS Reports" shows. Added Hewitt, "If people are doing things in dark corners they shouldn't be doing, well, all we did is shine a light." (20) While not complex, the show was hard-hitting. It probed the Pentagon so often that a standing order finally came that no one was to cooperate with the program. Its interviews could be penetrating as on December 30, 1979 when Wallace interviewed John Connally.

Wallace: "Governor, did you really say more people died at Chappaquidick . . . than at Three Mile Island?"
Connally: "No, I did not."
Wallace: "You're sure?"
Connally: "I'm positive."
Wallace: "If I could show it to you on tape."
Connally: "If you [could]—you were taping something you shouldn't have been taping."

Controversy was never far from the news division. It would stalk Daniel Schorr in the mid-1970s. In the wake of the Watergate scandal, newsmen intensified their investigation into government institutions that had heretofore been largely outside the public view. The Central Intelligence Agency was one of them. Schorr, like other journalists at the time, had been looking into the question of alleged assassination plots and other possible cases of the overstepping of the CIA's power. In January 1976 the House Intelligence Committee, chaired by Otis Pike, was about to release a 340-page report on the subject. Excerpts of the report were passed on to newsmen, and a particularly generous leak came Dan Schorr's way.

On January 26, Schorr obtained a complete copy of the report, but four days later, the committee, reversing an earlier decision, voted not to make the report public. Schorr was in the remarkable position of being the only journalist with a complete copy of the report. He asked CBS to publish it—as a paperback. The network was in no mood to get involved, but before Schorr heard about the network's negative response he went ahead and provided the report to the *Village Voice,* which published it on February 16 and 23. The day after, the *Washington Post* wrote a story saying Schorr was the source of the *Village Voice* publication. The House Ethics Committee decided to investigate Schorr. He now faced the possibility of being cited for contempt of Congress unless he revealed who had supplied him with the Pike report.

Schorr's relations with CBS deteriorated. He was suspended with pay until the committee probe was over. Adding to his problems with the network, Schorr had at one stage given the impression that he was trying to blame CBS correspondent Leslie Stahl with supplying the *Village Voice* with a copy of the Pike report. Stahl was then a close acquaintance of Aaron Latham, whose byline appeared on the *Voice* story.

As for Schorr's bout with Congress, one issue was whether the House could prohibit someone from publishing a committee's official report. Meanwhile, the Ethics Committee used twelve former FBI agents to track down the culprit who had given the report to Dan Schorr. But they had no luck. Called as a witness, Schorr was directed on September 15 to tell the Committee who had given him the report. Time and time again he refused to do so. During his opening statement, Schorr told the committee that "to betray a source would for me be to betray myself, my career and my life. And to say that I refuse to do it isn't quite saying it right. I cannot do it." Schorr was skirting a citation for contempt of Congress. But, with public sympathy high for Schorr, the committee recommended no contempt charge.

When the episode was over, the question remained whether Dan Schorr would return to CBS to work. Much debate ensued among the CBS brass. Bill Paley thought it might be a good idea to bring Schorr back. Schorr, after all, was now a hero—and therefore had more value to CBS. That was the showman in Paley coming out. Schorr was not rushing to return. He was livid with CBS for suspending him when the incident arose. Since CBS had agreed to give him his full salary for the next three years despite the suspension, Schorr could afford not to return to active work. He gave it some thought, decided to quit, and began writing his memoir of the incident, *Clearing the Air.*

Here it was the 1970s, and Bill Paley was still around. He had once vowed that he would retire at age 35. He never did, of course. The broadcasting world was a lot more exciting than manufacturing cigars, and no one was going to brush him aside. That was back in the 1930s. Now, four decades, later, he had not changed his mind: he still didn't want to let go. He had, as those around him would quickly notice, a streak of stubbornness mixed with an air of self-confidence that was hard to break down. He wanted the best all the time, whether it was the best baseball team (the New York Yankees), or the best toy company (Creative Playthings), or the best textbook house (Holt, Rinehart). As Mike Dann, the programming chief of the 1960s at CBS, noted, "He was a lovable tyrant. . . . Paley loved to win. He loved everything. He was a man for all seasons. He had a *joie de vivre*. Good food. Lovely women. News. Loved everything. Sports. He liked class. He liked to buy the best. If he went after somebody or hired someone, he wanted them to be the best. That also was in the news aspect. He couldn't stand, whether it was in clothes or food or anything else, anything being second-rate. He was a very classy fellow." (21)

And it was very hard for the "classy fellow" to admit that his days were numbered. To give too much power to others was a way of acknowledging that the baton was passing. He made sure to keep those around him weak and uncertain. He and CBS would probably have been better off if he had spent the time grooming someone to take over, rather than knocking down potential candidates. But, when he looked around at those who might succeed him, he found it impossible to let one of them advance too far. This was true of a whole string of leading executives, including Frank Stanton.

Stanton had been the president of CBS since 1946. His leadership had given a stability to CBS that had been lacking at the other networks. He had been more than CBS president, he had acquired a reputation as the unofficial spokesman of the broadcasting industry. His opinions were routinely sought, his speeches frequently quoted, his testimony before Congress a major part of any debate in the broadcasting field. Given the frequent absences of Bill Paley from CBS headquarters, it was inevitable that Stanton would become the de facto head of the organization. And given the care Stanton took with making sure that every managerial instruction was carried out perfectly, it was taken for granted that he would one day want to take over the chairmanship of CBS. It was clear to many people, including Frank Stanton, but most important, it was not clear to the one man who counted—Bill Paley.

And he was not eager to turn the running of the company over to Stanton. The problem of an heir had begun in 1966 when Paley, then 65, had decided only the day before the board was to name Stanton as Chief Executive Officer not to retire but to continue as chairman, forcing Stanton out of the company. By the early 1970s, it bothered Stanton that control of the company had not yet come to him even though Paley was already getting on in age. It was, however, fairly clear to Stanton that Paley could never detach himself from CBS as long as Paley was alive. Stanton had cast his lot with CBS, refusing to leave the company when other important offers had come his way (he might have taken a senior job with either the Kennedy or Johnson administrations, had he chosen; he might also have run for the U.S. Senate). But he stayed on, hoping, assuming that one day Paley would turn things over to him formally. The switchover never came. And so on March 30, 1973—when Stanton had reached the mandatory retirement age of 65—he retired from CBS. In public, Stanton naturally insisted that he was neither surprised nor disappointed by his departure from CBS. But the testimony of his colleagues suggests that just the opposite was true. The sorrow of parting was made sweeter by the fact that Stanton still held $13 million worth of CBS stock and a retirement contract that lasted until 1987.

He was appointed Principal Officer of The American Red Cross by President Nixon in 1973. He remained there, happily, for six years.

In replacing Stanton, Paley turned not to one of his underlings but to an executive more practiced and comfortable with managing conglomerates. That seemed only natural. After all, by the 1960s and into the early 1970s, CBS had become a huge conglomerate. Selected on October 1, 1971 was an unassuming, muscular 51-year-old named Charles T. Ireland, Jr., then the senior vice president of ITT, International Telephone & Telegraph Corporation. After being thoroughly scrutinized by the network, Ireland reported that "the job they did on me far exceeded anything the CIA did in clearing me for my ITT work." Ireland was characterized by the broadcasting industry press as someone who represented a new type of business thinking that would appeal more to investors than to communications specialists. (At the same time Stanton became Vice Chairman and Chief Operating Officer of CBS.)

Ireland had very little time in the job. He died of a heart attack after eight months as CBS president. And so another search was on. The man tapped for the job was only 37 years old. Arthur R. Taylor had been executive vice president of International Paper, had boyish good looks, was moralistic and temperate, and had a missionary zeal. These were not the usual qualities of character in the broadcasting world. Taylor viewed himself as a private citizen suddenly given a trust. Before giving Taylor the job, Paley spent hours talking with him. They talked a great deal about what kinds of managerial problems needed to be tackled. During the founding years, Paley had kept a steady hand at the helm, guiding the network to higher and higher profits. But then, as it diversified, the company became too big for a single man—even a Bill Paley—to control. In those private conversations, Paley admitted to Taylor that over the years a kind of laissez-faire system had developed at CBS in which employees did pretty much what they wanted. Communications among divisions had grown poor, fiefdoms had developed, and worst of all financial controls had all but disappeared as had strategic planning. Paley said he did not want that to happen again, that he looked to Taylor to straighten this situation out. He had chosen Taylor because he wanted a strong-minded manager who was adept at accountability and could inject a new efficiency and discipline into the company.

Taylor's policies proved highly profitable. He would lead the company to seventeen straight quarters of high profit during his presidency. There was a price to be paid, however. Undertaking belt-tightening, Taylor was assailed for taking the task so seriously. He acted as if he was certain that he would succeed Bill Paley. As for Paley, he did little to dispel such notions. He would travel to Europe and the Bahamas for as much as six weeks without once calling Taylor to check in. Upon Paley's return, he would spend two or three weeks immersing himself in the one aspect of CBS that interested him—programming.

Taylor's most controversial stance was his advocacy of programming that would be free of sex and violence. The idea was designed to respond to the growing belief that violence over television was a prime inducer of violence among youngsters. Taylor was convinced that sex and violence could be done away with or muted on television without affecting ratings. He was convinced that the public agreed with his moralistic views. But he was frustrated. Paley kept talking to him about putting more "pizzazz" into CBS's shows, and when the new president asked others what Paley meant, he was told, he meant more violence. In the fall of 1974, Taylor promised in public that CBS would not schedule anything prior to 9 P.M. that was "inappropriate for general family viewing." This Family Viewing Hour—an hour of prime time—would have no references at all to sex, violence, or off-color subjects. (Taylor's idea was adopted by the other networks as well.) The Taylor-sponsored plan had some unhappy side effects for CBS. In the wake of the Family Viewing Hour scheme, the network felt compelled to move "All in the Family" from its highly successful Saturday night slot at 8 to Mondays at 9. In addition, CBS finally canceled "Gunsmoke" because of Family Viewing. Bill Paley loved the show, and only his enthusiasm kept it on the air. CBS also moved the violence-prone "Kojak" from 8:30 to 9 P.M. on Sundays. One programming executive recalled with dismay Taylor's calling him in California to protest the airing of singer Cher's belly button on a CBS show.

Arthur Taylor's most difficult assignment during his four-year presidency of CBS was in breaking the news to Clive Davis that his days at CBS were over. Davis stood accused of misusing company funds. Not much, just under $100,000 but enough to shake up the record industry. Davis's dismissal took place in the spring of 1973. It all seemed so shocking. Here was Davis, only 40 years old and presumably sitting on top of the broadcasting world as the head of CBS Records. Formerly a member of the company's outside law firm, he had been responsible for boosting CBS Records into the top record company in the world. Grossing over $300 million the year before, CBS Records was now nearly half as large as the CBS Broadcast Group. What was more, the $27 million profit CBS Records had earned that same year was nearly half the profit of the broadcast group. It was hardly a poor relative in the CBS family.

Davis had replaced Goddard Lieberson as head of CBS's domestic record operation in 1967. Attending the Monterey, California, pop-music festival that year, Davis realized that rock music was moving into the forefront of American popular music. So he began signing up future big-name performers such as Janis Joplin, Sly and the Family Stone, Santana, and Blood, Sweat & Tears. Since then, rock music, which had represented only 15 percent of CBS Records' volume, jumped up to more than 50 percent. Moreover, CBS Records' sales rose to $340 million a year in 1972.

Davis had no idea what was about to happen on that morning of May 29. He had been going through his mail and conferring with another record executive, when his intercom buzzed. It was Arthur Taylor's secretary asking if Davis could come see the CBS president right away. Excusing himself, Davis went to the 35th floor. What was about to occur was terribly ironic. So successful had Davis been that even before Arthur Taylor was appointed president, Davis had been mentioned as a suitable candidate for the job. But here was Arthur Taylor, two lawyers by his side, informing Davis that he was through at CBS. Later, Davis was in such shock he could not even remember what Taylor had said to him. The president had calmly told him that he was to return to his office, take what he wanted, and leave immediately. At the door he was greeted by two CBS security men who served a civil complaint against him and then escorted him back to his 11th floor offices.

The story of Davis's abrupt exit had its roots in the spring of 1973 when Dick Salant had made Stanhope Gould the head of a new investigative unit. Gould had produced a sharp report the year before on the Nixon administration's Soviet grain deal. Gould next turned his attention inward—to CBS Records. There he found a scandal that would shake up the record industry. As a result, CBS would charge Davis, who was then earning $350,000 a year, with allegedly misusing funds: $54,000 for redecorating his Manhattan apartment, $20,000 to throw a Bar Mitzvah reception for his son, and about $13,000 to rent a house in Beverly Hills (later he was indicted with failing to report $8,800 in income; pleading guilty, Davis received a $10,000 fine and was exonerated from other charges.). Bill Paley apparently had approved Gould's probe, startling as that might seem. The CBS boss may have felt that to do otherwise than investigate the scandal surrounding the record industry, and CBS Records' role in that scandal, would have been hypocritical. CBS did not just investigate Watergate, it investigated itself. That would show all his critics who thought CBS had been too tough on the White House. By the time Gould came up with a script in early 1974, however, the grand jury investigation into the record business had slackened, apparently because of lack of evidence. Gould was still eager for CBS to air his own probe as a two-part program to be narrated by Walter Cronkite. Salant decided instead to put it on as a one-hour special that was called "The Trouble with Rock." In an odd turn of events, the program was shown an hour before "60 Minutes" on August 11, 1974, just two days after President Nixon resigned. Inevitably, with all the news connected to the presidential resignation, few were overly excited about a two-year-old story that had to do with graft in the record business. A few weeks later Stanhope Gould left CBS.

Into the second half of the 1970s, things appeared to be going well. But not as far as Bill Paley was concerned. From the standpoint of turning a profit for the network, Arthur Taylor had been a wonderfully successful president. He brought in the cash. Paley ought to have been especially pleased at that, and he ought to have been thrilled at the respect and affection Taylor showed the news division. (For example, in the spring of 1976, Taylor publicly supported an expansion of the CBS evening news from 30 to 60 minutes, an idea championed by Richard Salant. With Paley lukewarm about the idea, and the affiliates considered likely opponents, the expansion proposal never got off the ground.)

Dismissing Arthur Taylor appeared most unthinkable that fall of 1976. CBS, after all, had $400 million in cash. Taylor had doubled corporate earnings during his four years. The company was doing well indeed with 213 television and 255 radio affiliates, plus divisions producing records, musical instruments, books, and magazines. What more could have been expected of Taylor? But Taylor, in the eyes of his colleagues, had begun to make a fatal mistake; he had started to act as if Bill Paley was no longer there, as if he were dead. And of course Paley was not dead; he was very much around, very much in charge. Taylor was notified of his dismissal on October 13, 1976. He was called into Paley's office and there given the news. So shocked was he—CBS had, after all, been doing quite all right under his leadership—that he responded by saying to Paley that he would think about the request to resign. But there would be no chance for Taylor to ponder things. Paley said that Taylor would be expected to resign that morning. When Bill Leonard asked Paley why he had fired Taylor, Paley answered simply, "because he thought he was bigger than the company." (22) Paley apparently believed that Arthur Taylor had still not proven himself a worthy successor to Frank Stanton, let alone to Paley himself. Moreover, Paley had no intention of moving out very soon. (When CBS correspondent Winston Burdett asked him in 1973 what would happen to the company after Paley left, the chairman gave a "don't worry about it" kind of look, and said he intended to hang around for another twenty-five years.)

Paley was 75 years old. Although he might have believed that he would be around for another quarter-century, the odds were that he would not be. A new generation of leaders would have to be installed to guarantee a stable transition. But, as he had proven with Frank Stanton, and

---

then with Arthur Taylor, Paley was not about to loosen the reins. "I do not like the idea of depending on others," he wrote in his memoirs in 1979. (23) It was a most revealing comment. He had taken over this peanut of a company in the 1920s when it was on the verge of bankruptcy, he had nurtured it into one of the great institutions of the country, and no one appeared capable in his eyes of becoming a new Bill Paley. Still, having let Arthur Taylor go, he would need to replace him. This time he would look inside the company.

And he found 44-year-old John Backe. He had been with General Electric in Cincinnati before becoming president of Silver Burdett, the textbook publishing subsidiary of General Learning Corporation, a joint venture of General Electric and Time, Inc. Taylor had heard about Backe, and pleaded with him to take over CBS's publishing group. Backe said no. He was happy where he was. Disappointed, Taylor said he would be pleased if Backe would at least look over CBS's publishing operations and give some free advice. Backe did more that that. He caved in, becoming president of the Publishing Group in March 1973. What particularly appealed to Paley was Backe's purchase of Fawcett, the paperback house, for just $50 million, a price that was several million dollars cheaper than what CBS would have been willing to pay.

Paley offered him Taylor's job even before the axe had been dropped on the current president. And the chairman added a sweetener: Backe would become chief executive officer the following April 1977 when Paley would step down. Dwelling on the future further, Paley imagined Backe as an appropriate successor to himself—for the time being, at any rate. At first, Backe played hard to get. But Paley wouldn't yield. After phoning him incessantly, the chairman got his way—and a new CBS president.

And so the John Backe era began. By the spring of 1977 Paley indeed had taken a preliminary step toward retiring when he stepped down as chief executive officer of CBS. The post was taken over by Backe. Paley remained chairman and as such the power behind the throne. But other outside pressures began to take their toll on him. One was the terminal illness of his wife Babe (whom he married in July 1947 after divorcing his first wife Dorothy.) The search for a cure for Babe's cancer preoccupied Paley in the late 1970s above all else. She died on July 6, 1978, one day after turning 63. Also eating away at Paley at this time was the need he felt to produce a "true" version of his and CBS's life story. David Halberstam, the former *New York Times* reporter and author of *The Best and the Brightest,* had been working on a book about the media in which CBS would play a prominent role. Paley decided to spend hours with Halberstam but was clearly disappointed that *The Powers That Be* portrayed him incorrectly, in his view. He set about to write his own autobiography, which he hoped would be ready by the spring of 1979—to provide a kind of antidote to Halberstam's book. When *As It Happened* appeared, however, the critics attacked Paley sharply for taking full credit for everything good that had happened at CBS and for concealing a lot of the truth that Halberstam had uncovered.

Paley was clearly drifting away from CBS. Unconsolable over the loss of Babe, he continued to watch pilots of programs but had little other interest in the operation of the company. Invited frequently to meetings by John Backe, he rarely showed up. Meanwhile there were important changes taking place at the top layers. Backe let John Schneider go as president of the Broadcast Group, a move that Paley had urged Ireland and Taylor but had failed to bring off. Schneider was replaced by Gene Jankowski, who had spent much of his career in sales and management at CBS. On the news side, Richard Salant finally retired in 1978 at the mandatory age of 65, after serving as president of CBS News for most of the previous sixteen years. Salant disappointed Paley immensely by jumping over to NBC to become vice chairman for news. Paley could never let go entirely. In an April 1979 interview with *People* magazine, he described in the briefest terms his role at the network: "He [Backe] already runs the network. I gave the title of chief executive officer to Mr. Backe almost two years ago. I continue on as chairman, more as elder statesman and adviser than anything else. My successor is in place." But elsewhere in the same magazine article, when he was asked if he would retire, Paley said candidly, "In a conventional sense, no." (24)

twelve

"THE COCA-COLA DAYS"

No one had really wanted Walter Cronkite to leave. But by late 1981 the veteran anchorman's retirement was in the offing: his contract would run out. It was widely held that no one would be able to step into Walter's shoes. No one could remember when his program didn't lead in the ratings race. Moreover, he remained the most trusted man in America, an informal title that bestowed on him a magic that no one could really challenge. Still, the search was on; the main contenders were Roger Mudd, Charles Kuralt, and Dan Rather.

Mudd appeared to have the inside track if only because of late he had been substituting for Cronkite whenever Walter went on vacation or went on an out-of-town assignment. Before his own retirement, Richard Salant had been a strong backer of Mudd as an eventual replacement for Cronkite. As early as 1972, Salant, then president of CBS News, had indicated his preference for Mudd should Cronkite get hit by a truck. When the remark leaked, an angry Salant made sure not to display such enthusiasm for Mudd even in private. Kuralt was popular. He had been doing well with his "On the Road" reports on the evening news; he was a host on "Sunday Morning" and was anchor on the CBS morning news.

Substituting for Cronkite in the summer of 1979, he won the admiration of many viewers who urged in letters that he be given the post after Walter retired.

But Dan Rather was the brightest star on the CBS horizon. Next to Cronkite, he was the best election night studio man around; he was a great convention floor reporter; and when he moved on to "60 Minutes," the ratings actually went higher. Still, there was uncertainty. Some suggested having Rather and Mudd serve as co-anchors. Rather thought the idea OK. But Mudd was against it, and so the notion died a quick death. Dan Rather won the job of anchorman and managing editor of the CBS evening news on February 7, 1980. He was to be paid $2.2 million a year for 10 years—$22 million in all. It was a spectacular deal, and the only reason CBS would make it at all was that ABC was bidding for Rather too, offering him a lot of money. Bill Paley was infuriated: he had great trouble believing that Dan Rather, or anyone else at CBS, could contemplate leaving CBS—just over money. CBS, after all, had money too. To leave CBS, to leave this hallowed institution, it was like abandoning one's religion, giving up one's citizenship.

Both *Time* and *Newsweek* suggested that CBS had been purely interested in which of the two men, Rather or Mudd, would be the more popular anchorman. According to *Time*, Dan Rather had scored higher than Mudd on the market researchers' Q scales. These were ratings that measured the degree of a viewer's positive response to a television personality. *Newsweek*, for its part, quoted surveys by "influential" news consultant firms which showed Rather "projecting almost as much warmth, compassion and honesty" as Walter Cronkite. Mudd, said *Newsweek*, was "perceived as somewhat cold." This was all categorically denied by the people at CBS. "It was a news decision," according to Bill Leonard, the president of CBS News. (1)

It would take thirteen months between Dan Rather's appointment in February 1980 and Walter Cronkite's actual retirement in March 1981. That was in deference to Cronkite. For Dan Rather the waiting proved nightmarish. Comparisons were made between the outgoing Cronkite and the incoming Rather. It was said that Dan had talent, had charisma, had an aggressiveness, but still he didn't read the news as well as Walter. This was a dangerous thing for CBS: it allowed the public to make an advance judgment on its multimillion-dollar property before the act even went on stage!

Beyond that, during the thirteen-month period, Rather thrust himself into some awkward situations that did little to help the transition. Traveling to Afghanistan for "60 Minutes" after the Soviet invasion, Rather found himself the object of scorn from the television critics. Tom Shales of the *Washington Post* noted that Rather's peasant dress "made him look like an extra out of Dr. Zhivago." According to Barbara Matusow's book, *The Evening Stars,* (2) Rather got himself into hot water by telling an interviewer from the *Ladies' Home Journal* that he had tried heroin as a cub reporter in Texas. The wires picked up Rather's rather astonishing admission, and immediately he was the focus of a major newspaper splash. But the most damaging incident occurred when he got into a Chicago taxicab and an argument with the driver ensued. The driver accused Dan of not paying a $12.50 fare and wouldn't let him out of the cab until he paid. Rather had to flag down a police car to extricate himself from the incident. The cabbie was eventually jailed; but Rather came out on the losing side after Mike Royko, the Chicago columnist, depicted him as the bully who had stepped on the little fellow. Royko's portrayal of Rather made national headlines.

The Walter Cronkite era ended on Friday evening, March 6, 1981. It was then that he stepped down as the anchor of the CBS evening news, turning the post over to Dan Rather. Dan began the following Monday. After the final commercial that Friday evening, Cronkite came on to say: "For almost two decades, we've been meeting like this in the evening and I'll miss that. But those who have made anything of this departure, I'm afraid have made too much." However modest he was, Cronkite was an institution, and his passage was grandly noted. Rival ABC News took out full-page newspaper advertisements thanking Cronkite for his "extraordinary contributions" to the broadcast news profession. He would be well taken care of. When he retired, Cronkite was offered a seat on the CBS board of directors, plus a salary of $1 million for seven years. After that, for the next ten years, beginning on November 4, 1988, he would get $150,000 a year for performing as a special CBS correspondent.

It was decided to change nothing substantive of the evening news program after Walter left. There was talk of changing the format, of changing the screen behind Dan Rather from a soft beige to blue-gray, a color supposedly more flattering to Dan Rather, but that was scrapped. Bill Leonard, the president of CBS News, who was due to retire in June, was asked to stay on for another year just for the sake of continuity. The program's executive producer, Sandy Socolow, was also kept on. No one was taking any chances. Whatever reason viewers had for liking Walter would, it was hoped, be applied to Dan Rather. The policy was not to shock the viewer too much: he would already be shocked enough by virtue of Walter's absence each night.

Dan Rather debuted on March 9, 1981. At first, he was hesitant as he tried out different styles of delivering the news. He tried to project warmth, and sometimes that caused him to smile in the wrong places. Behind the scenes he plunged into the job of managing editor with excitement. He would take a much more active approach to the news division than did Cronkite. Walter had remained aloof from the overall running of the news division, not getting involved in the hiring, firing, or assigning of personnel. But Dan wanted to decide who would covers wars, who would cover the Pentagon, the White House, whatever. Indeed, he gave the impression of wanting to be everywhere. He would keep in touch with correspondents personally, attend as many meetings as possible, suggesting how to handle stories. It was wonderful, all that sudden power, being in charge of so many resources, being able to direct forces, sometimes sending them in one direction, sometimes another. He let on that he wanted more original, hard-hitting pieces in the evening news. It was not enough just to tell what had happened, wire service style. Stories had to have heroes and villains. And stories had to be CBS exclusives.

As Cronkite's replacement, Dan Rather would have to prove himself to his audience. He was replacing an institution, and the viewers would not be impressed that his contract called for him to be paid $2.2 million. They would decide themselves whether they liked him. At first they indicated that they did not. That was natural. Ratings had dropped when Walter Cronkite succeeded Doug Edwards in 1962. Some viewers were switching their dials, trying out the other anchors. In anticipation of the Cronkite departure, and the likely prospect that viewers would for a while be interersted in taking a look at other newscasts, both NBC and ABC prepared special reports as well as extra advertising in order to lure the Cronkite viewers.

By the end of the first three months, the program had lost slightly more than one whole rating point (then, in 1981, 815,000 homes). The audience share also dropped from 27 to 24; Cronkite usually got a 27 (27 percent of all television sets turned on at that time). Rather asked for more resources, but CBS was being tight with funds. During one week in July, ABC's "World News Tonight" actually wound up in first place. Dan wanted an investigative unit, more producers. But he got nothing from the network. Then, in the last week of October, the ratings fell part. Rather came in second one week and third the next. That was the very first time the CBS evening news had come in last place. There was a problem, and it was decided that the problem was Dan Rather. The differences between Cronkite and Rather were already noticeable. As one news editor noted, "Cronkite came across as much warmer. His avuncular image was true to life. Rather seems much more political, a wheeler-dealer, a power-broker."

Finally, executives at the network became desperate, deciding that something had to be done. It was not simply that pride was involved: it was the network's pocketbook. CBS had to lower the price it could charge for advertising. Whereas $40,000 could be obtained for a 30-second commercial on the Cronkite program, which was $10,000 higher than either of the other two network news shows, now advertising on the Rather show fell to $30,000 for the same 30-second spot. Clearly, a crisis was at hand.

In mid-November Bill Leonard was displaced abruptly by Van Gordon Sauter, a long-time CBS newsman turned executive. He had just been head of CBS Sports. Two weeks later, Sandy Socolow was sent to London to head the bureau there. Socolow's replacement was Howard Stringer, who had previously worked with Rather as executive producer on "CBS Reports." Sauter's mandate was to make Dan Rather happy, to make him feel he had the organization behind him. That, it was hoped, would ease him up, and he would show that on the air. That, at least, was the theory. Efforts were undertaken to make Rather look more relaxed on camera.

Stringer decided to shoot Dan close up. Again, in the name of appearing relaxed, two-way conversations between Rather and correspondents in the field were introduced. Producers were urged to dress up their pieces with graphic effects. That met with a lot of resistance from newsmen who thought of themselves as heirs to Ed Murrow. Graphics, which smacked of show business, were beneath their dignity. Still, the ratings had to be brought up—so reporters were urged to look more natural on camera, not to be frightened of taking a step forward to turn and look at their subject. To the correspondents, it all seemed so unjournalistic. Rather did his part. He steered the program away from being a headline service by introducing more original reports, feature stories, and backgrounders. The CBS evening news was no longer Walter Cronkite's broadcast of record.

It was a snappier show, and it was hoped that the audience would respond. One big change was for Rather to play down Washington stories. They were considered too static, too uninteresting, too far removed at times from the real story happening out in the far reaches of America. That was where CBS's cameras and correspondents should be going— and they did. The idea was for both correspondent and camera to capture a visual image that explained to the viewer what someone involved in the story had felt like. They were to capture that special "moment." People at CBS actually talked about the "moment theory," and Dan Rather, swept up in the enthusiasm, began passing out "moment" buttons. Commentary, which had not been tried since Eric Sevareid had retired in 1976, was revived. Bill Moyers, who had worked with Howard Stringer on "CBS Reports," was put on the set with Rather two or three days a week. Dan's reading of the news improved. It was noted, with some amusement, that when Rather put on a sweater that winter (he had had a bad cold for several weeks), it encouraged the audience to warm up to him. If that worked, no one complained. For whatever reason, the ratings picked up, and CBS regained the lead. Walter Cronkite, a CBS board member now, would complain often and publicly that a lot of important stories in Washington were not being covered due to Sauter's new soft approach, but the Sauter strategy produced results: Rather gradually recovered the ratings lead and kept it for the next 200 weeks.

Later there would be a reversal of some of the Sauter-Rather philosophy. By 1985, it had been generally accepted that the Dan Rather program had taken too soft an approach to news. And so new decisions were taken. The Washington Bureau was beefed up. Writers were told to avoid any cute prose. There were to be a greater number of reports out of the nation's capital, as in the heyday of Walter Cronkite. Rather, the managing editor, sent out instructions to his troops. He wanted to see more stories with the word "today" in them.

All this probing for what was the best way to get ratings irritated the oldtimers, those veterans who remembered a time when none of these things mattered. "Television," recalled Fred Friendly in dismay, "is the vehicle for charisma. Eighty percent of what it transmits is charisma. And so they're taking Dan Rather, good guy, and they're trying to manipulate him into being something he isn't. Nobody ever said to Murrow, smile. Or don't smoke. Or do smoke. Or don't be so intense. Or be a little more intense. Ed was Ed. But now they're going to take Dan, and they're going to turn him into something that they think is television." (3) It bothered Friendly to think of how television news had changed, how easy it had been in the past to disregard these superficial concerns—ratings, appearances, and the like. Now, these things had become of crucial importance.

"In about the fifth year of Huntley-Brinkley, 1960 or so, Jack Gould, pretty good guy, wrote a pretty rough piece about Ed, saying Huntley-Brinkley were the new television and Murrow was too serious, too dour, too ponderous, etc., etc., etc. We used to get the *Times* on Thursday, the Sunday *Times*. That part. So I figured rather than have Ed read it alone, I'd show it to him. So I showed it to him. He had a reading stand he used to read on. He stood up and read it with his glasses on. He looked up, and he said, 'Fuck 'em.' He couldn't have cared less. Dan Rather does care. And I don't think any less of Dan. I think it's because Ed knew that whatever his fortunes were, they were going to be determined by what he put on the air, not by how he looked." (4)

The transition from Walter Cronkite to Dan Rather was a major passage for CBS News as it moved into the 1980s. But it had other problems seething below the surface. It was getting increasingly difficult to maintain CBS's traditional commitment to providing the best news coverage. There were all sorts of reasons.

First and foremost, the news was getting expensive. CBS's news budget had risen dramatically in the past decade and stood now at nearly $300 million. And why? Each network was spending up to $10 million a year to run its Washington bureau. The smallest bureau, however, could cost $500,000 a year. The contracts for the big stars had mushroomed. Walter Cronkite, even in retirement, was getting $1 million a year. Dan

"THE COCA-COLA DAYS"

Rather, was getting $2.2 million. CBS had spent $1.2 million on correspondent Diane Sawyer's contract. The average annual salary for an experienced network correspondent had risen to $150,000; at CBS the pay ranged from $90,000 to $600,000. A cameraman earned $43,000 before overtime; junior producers, between $45,000 and $75,000; senior network producers, from $100,000 to $150,000.

Ernest Leiser, who had been executive producer of the Cronkite program, noted that in the early days, it was accepted that news for all three networks was a loss leader: "It brought the networks respectability; it made people forget about the game-show scandals, the 'Hee-Haws,' and the other crap we put on the air, and gave us an image of seriousness, which helped keep the Feds off the backs of the networks, and of the local stations. Well, that no longer is the case, because the FCC isn't looking over your shoulder." What had happened? "What happened," Leiser continued, "is that more money was involved. Television became not just a big moneymaker, over the years, but then the money got harder to make. In 1981, network profits leveled off. And news got more and more expensive. In 1962 the CBS News budget was $50 million. In 1981, the figure was perhaps $100 million. The costs went up, and as the costs went up, as the competition for broadcasters grew more intense, the pay scale of the best broadcasters increased enormously. Nobody would have believed that Diane Sawyer would get $1.2 million a year. Cronkite got twice as much after he stopped being the anchorman as he did as anchorman. At least I believe that's true. . . . It started . . . with Barbara Walters. They fobbed that off by charging half of her salary to entertainment. And half to news. Harry Reasoner left CBS in 1970 because he felt he wasn't making enough money and that he wasn't being properly appreciated. He got what seemed an enormous amount of money, $200,000 a year.

". . . And when the revenues become important, that's when the ratings become doubly important, because the ratings are based on audience size. And there are a lot of things you do which remain losing propositions; when you do live coverage the figure hit like $1 million a day for the three networks to cover the [Ollie North] hearings. Ten years ago it would have been half that much." (5)

As ratings grew in importance, reporting and writing skills correspondingly diminished in importance and the physical appearance of the correspondent took on added significance. As Sam Roberts, a former foreign editor at CBS, recalled: "The organization of Paul White and Ed Klauber . . . insisted on real journalists. . . . If you think of the correspondents that we had who were big correspondents in the 1960s, for instance, Dan Shorr, Peter Kalischer, the Kalb brothers, not great broadcasters, but they were very good at what they did, and they knew what they were talking about. . . . I'm not sure some of those guys could make it now because the emphasis, now with the shift at CBS News, since Bill Leonard, was more of an emphasis on broadcasting ability . . . the ability to stand on the camera and be believable and perform well, have a good voice, a good delivery. . . . Take a guy like Charles Kuralt who's a superb broadcaster. Charles Kuralt is a superb writer and also a very good reporter. Although he doesn't like to report as much as he likes to write. Harry Reasoner is the same way. Mike Wallace is a great reporter and a great broadcaster. I think he would say that his writing skills aren't as good as those others. But he's still a damn good writer. But now somebody coming in the door, if they're going to make it as a star here, has got to be a broadcaster first. . . . It changed with Sauter . . . like Fred Graham. I don't think he would have been hired by Van Sauter. He did superb work for us for ten or fifteen years covering the [Supreme] Court. [But] he sounded funny. He's got this Tennessee accent . . . ." (6)

Bruno Wassertheil had been a radio reporter for CBS for most of the sixteen years from 1970 to 1986. He bemoaned the fact that the network had after he left become something less than what it was during his time. "They had their strength in the people who wanted to see a 'serious' network. . . . But in the last five years we've lost many, many of our best people like the Kalbs. The beginning of the end was when Marvin Kalb left, it was like when Leo Durocher went to the Giants. It was inconceivable. He was one of our mainstays, one of the pillars. Gradually, a lot of our best people, in television and in radio, went. Dan Schorr, Roger Mudd." Why did they leave? Adds Wassertheil: "CBS lost the touch. The men at the top lost the touch. They were businessmen, narrowminded executives. A lot of people now say it's not a fun place to work anymore. There was a lot more company loyalty in Cronkite's days. But not now, because there is a feeling that the company won't look out for you as it would then. There used to be room for a creative genius. Someone who would work on a documentary for a year, win an award, and no one would care about the cost. But now everyone has to be more productive." (7)

Bill Leonard, who had been president of CBS News from 1978 to 1982, wrote in his 1987 book, *In the Storm of the Eye,* that he had watched CBS News abandon its high standards, standards that had been set by Bill Paley and Frank Stanton. But now, "the top management appeared to have come to regard CBS News as almost more trouble than it was worth, and the management of the news division itself began to think of it as just a step on the corporate ladder."

It had been different earlier. Leonard wrote that he never heard the word duty in the boardroom or the cutting room at CBS news throughout his years, but "Men like Bill Paley and Frank Stanton had a sense that their duty extended beyond their stockholders, beyond their employees to viewers and listeners. Their conscience dictated that they had a duty to inform as well as entertain. . . . in truth, a rather extraordinary sense of obligation did run through the place, as if the privilege of being there—

stamping one forever—should be paid back with extra effort. The spirit of Ed Murrow and his fierce independence haunted the halls. There was the sense that at least this part of the company was marching to a drummer other than the laugh meter and that William S. Paley knew it, understood it and approved of it. As Bill Moyers said, 'do you come to work to escape the day or engage the day? CBS News believed the latter." (8)

Just as the news was losing ground, so too were documentaries. They had been the backbone of the news operation. They had given the network prestige and a heightened degree of seriousness. But, as money became more important in the 1980s, documentaries began to dwindle in importance. Besides "60 Minutes," CBS would do instant specials at 11:30 P.M. or in prime time, and it would do some twenty documentaries a year. But then the numbers trickled down. When Ed Joyce came in as the new president of CBS News in late 1983, he promised with great fanfare that CBS news would do twelve documentaries a year. Cynics noted that was eight less than used to be done, and only half that number were actually done, three of which had been owed to Walter Cronkite after he left the CBS evening news. As Ernest Leiser lamented, "The decline of documentaries is one of the . . . things that I find terribly discouraging, dispiriting, since I spent 30 years of my life in this business. . . . Part of [the reason is] the economics, and partly the fact that nobody is supervising the way they used to. Nobody is monitoring. The critics have become lethargic . . . and there's less concern for respectability than there used to be. . . . What has been said is that the attention span of the audience is shorter . . . that they don't really care about news. But they never cared. . . . There's another reason, alas, why documentaries have declined. There aren't any regulators who will not only call television a vast wasteland, but will do something about trying to make it less so. Intimidate, if you will, the networks. And that's wrong. It shouldn't have to be done that way. Have a government agency tell people to do what they ought to do." (9)

It was more than that, of course. It was a sense that it was just not possible anymore to report the news the way it had been in the past. Now there was news on television 24 hours a day, thanks to Ted Turner's Cable News Network. The veterans, when they looked at news in the 1980s, found it a watered-down version of what it had once been. "I think," said Fred Friendly, "that what made our profession worthy of First Amendment protection, what created the Lippmanns and the Murrows and the Klaubers . . . was much more serious news. I would defy anybody to do a serious subject in two minutes on television. It's impossible. You can't even do the who, where, why, when, in that . . . I mean, these are very tough times."

Tough times because the viewer thinks he is getting a lot of news, but he is not. Adds Friendly, "People will say, well, it looks like a news program, and it sounds like a news program, and there's a guy saying, this is your reporter, such and such . . . and now back to you, Dan. But they're not really. . . . If you listen to Murrow at Buchenwald, that's 32 minutes of him explaining to you what happened at Buchenwald. If Murrow was at Buchenwald tomorrow, he'd be told to do it in one minute and 45 seconds. That's only a slight exaggeration." (10)

New pressure on CBS News came in 1982 after "CBS Reports" had aired a documentary on the former American commander in Vietnam, General William Westmoreland. Westmoreland filed a lengthy and controversial libel suit on September 13, 1982, against CBS, Inc., for its portrayal of Westmoreland the previous January. The suit demanded $120 million in compensatory and punitive damages. CBS had at that time aired a documentary entitled "The Uncounted Enemy: A Vietnam Deception."

The documentary opened with narrator Mike Wallace saying, "Tonight we are going to present evidence of what we have come to believe was a conscious effort—indeed a conspiracy—at the highest levels of American military intelligence to suppress and alter critical intelligence on the enemy in the year leading up to the Tet offensive." The documentary charged that while commander of the U.S. forces in Vietnam, Westmoreland had joined in a conspiracy to misrepresent enemy troop strength to make it appear that his own forces were strong and were winning the war.

Several months after the broadcast CBS News President Van Gordon Sauter admitted that the documentary, which had been produced by George Crile, had violated some of the network's journalistic standards. He agreed also that the claim of conspiracy was "inappropriate." But he rejected Westmoreland's demand for 45 minutes of rebuttal time.

In May, TV Guide called the program a "smear" and accused CBS of distorting facts that could have contradicted its thesis. It also accused the network of omitting rebuttals from officers who had challenged the idea that Westmoreland had underreported enemy strength to avoid stirring up domestic protest over the war. Sauter, clearly stunned by all this, asked Burton "Bud" Benjamin, a former executive producer of the Cronkite show and at the time a senior news department executive, to hold an in-house probe. Two months later, Sauter issued a memo that said the program had indeed violated some journalistic procedures. But, he added, the network stood behind the documentary, noting that Benjamin's report had supported such a conclusion.

CBS tried in vain to keep the sixty-eight-page Benjamin report a secret. But, according to Judge Pierre N. Laval, who ruled on the matter in U.S. District Court in Manhattan, by issuing the Sauter memo, CBS had lost any Constitutional privilege to keep the Benjamin report from the public. One week after Judge Laval's ruling, CBS gave up and publicized the Benjamin report.

Nothing less than the integrity and professionalism of the newsmen who worked for CBS News in the 1980s was at stake. David Boies, who was chief attorney for CBS in the Westmoreland trial, recalled afterward just how crucial the trial was for the future of CBS News: "People who wanted to do good, aggressive reporting were concerned that somehow if CBS lost the Westmoreland case, they would say we don't want to do '60 Minutes.' We don't want to do documentaries anymore." (11)

Westmoreland, who said he would donate the money to charity if he won, told a Washington, D.C., news conference that "the issue here is not money, not vengeance." Rather, he had no other way, he said, to clear his name, his honor, and the military's honor. Also named in the suit were Sauter, Crile, Wallace, and Samuel A. Adams, a former CIA employee who had served as CBS's paid consultant for the program. In response, Sauter assured that "CBS will mount a vigorous defense of this lawsuit not only because we see this suit totally devoid of merit but because it constitutes a serious threat to independent journalism in our society."

When on September 8 CBS offered Westmoreland 15 minutes of unedited time at the start of a proposed program to reexamine the issue of enemy troop strength raised in the documentary, he refused outright. Dan M. Burt, Westmoreland's attorney, said there would have been no opportunity in the 15 minutes to undo the harm that CBS had allegedly done, unless the network was prepared to admit that it had been wrong. CBS, of course, was not willing to do that. Added Burt, "All he would have done would have been to dignify a lie."

The Westmoreland trial began in October 1984. Given the news coverage and general public interest, it was widely touted as the most important legal proceeding dealing with a former senior American official since the 1949 Alger Hiss perjury trial. The dramatic finale came on February 1985 when Westmoreland withdrew the $120 million suit against CBS. Westmoreland obviously drew the conclusion that the trial was going against him and that the verdict, if it came to one, would almost certainly be unfavorable.

On the surface, the wind-up of the Westmoreland trial appeared beneficial to CBS. As David Boies would note, "One of the things that happened in the trial is that both the people within CBS and . . . the majority of the people outside CBS came to view the litigation process as vindicating journalistic judgment. When Westmoreland quit, I think it was perceived by everybody as him simply giving up. And when the jurors were interviewed, they said overwhelmingly: we think that CBS was right. We think the broadcast was true." (12)

The threat of a corporate takeover had hung over the entire broadcast industry in the early 1980s as the large American television networks, once bastions of permanence and strength, had exhibited signs of the same malaise and vulnerability that other large corporations in America had experienced. In March 1985 Capital Cities Communications, Inc., one-fourth the size of its target, had acquired ABC for more than $3.5 billion. That takeover represented the first time that one of the three major American networks had switched hands since 1953, when Leonard H. Goldenson's United Paramount Theaters merged with a young network to create the modern ABC. (That had been a friendly merger, not like the hostile ones that were occurring in the late 1970s and early 1980s.) The major networks appeared immune to the current phenomenon of unfriendly takeovers. And with that historical record as apparent proof that the communications giants could not be overcome against their will, the top brass at CBS felt safe. But no one could be sure just how long the invulnerability of CBS would last.

CBS's problems with takeover artists began in earnest in January 1985, when a group calling itself Fairness in Media, endorsed by North Carolina Senator Jesse Helms, declared that it would try to win control of CBS to eradicate the liberal bias it accused the network of displaying. The group encouraged political conservatives to purchase CBS stock in anticipation of a proxy fight. Larry Tisch, the billionaire head of Loews, heard about the Jesse Helms ploy while playing tennis with his investment banker friend James D. Wolfensohn, a CBS board member. The idea that somebody from one of the two political extremes would try to push a mighty institution like CBS around irritated Tisch. If CBS ever required his help, Tisch told his friend, he would be glad to pitch in.

The following month, February, Ted Turner made it clear that he had designs on CBS. Turner was a financial wizard who had accomplished some remarkable things in Atlanta, Georgia: he had taken a rundown local television station and turned it into an impressive, money-earner with programming that had attracted a national audience. He had also put together Cable News Network (CNN), creating for the first time a fourth network on the American broadcasting landscape. Turner was ambitious, always seeking new worlds to conquer. At first, Turner had pondered a takeover of ABC, but then Capital Cities moved in, preempting the bid. So he focused on CBS.

There was a certain irony in all of this. For, back in the spring of 1981, CBS had conducted a negotiation with Turner about CBS purchasing CNN! At that time, Turner was still losing money. Bill Leonard, the president of CBS News, thought there might be room for CBS to undertake its own 24-hour news coverage and make it available to its affiliates, thereby stealing a march on CNN, which had already been engaged in the 24-hour news trade. Commissioning a study to probe the situation,

Leonard discovered that establishing its own round-the-clock news service would be too expensive. And so Leonard and Gene Jankowski, who was head of the CBS Broadcast Group, decided that it would be cheaper to purchase CNN if Turner could be convinced. So they went and talked with him.

A secret meeting was held in an Atlanta motel room. Present were Turner, Leonard, Jankowski, and Bob Wussler, a former president of CBS Television, who had become Turner's right-hand man. The conversation fell flat when it became apparent that Turner was not prepared to sell 51 percent of CNN, the minimum that CBS wanted. Turner was prepared to sell 49 percent or less, but that was unacceptable to Jankowski and Leonard. All Turner could say was, "You guys, you CBS guys are something. Someday I'm going to own you, you bet I am. Remember I told you so." (13) Leonard and Jankowski simply laughed. After the negotiations broke up, both sides had their own version of what had happened. Appearing before the Washington Press Club, Turner said: "CBS came down to Atlanta trying to acquire CNN. I didn't let them make an offer. I was too busy telling them I was going to bust them." Around the same time, CBS President Tom Wyman noted that "We were invited to come to Atlanta by Mr. Turner. He said he wanted to talk about some sort of collaboration. He's a factor in this business, so we said, 'Why not?' But the suggestion that we were dying to make an offer for CNN is outrageous and untrue." (14)

It was little surprise that CBS had begun to attract outsiders. There had been a widespread feeling that the major American networks had been undervalued—that, whatever difficulties they were experiencing, with solid management they could be put back on their feet. That was particularly the case at CBS. Tom Wyman had taken over the network from John Backe in June 1980 after Paley had grown weary of Backe, holding the vague, but firm, view that his current chief executive was not up to the job, that he lacked vision. CBS was then a $4 billion conglomerate and was clearly going through a decline. The overall record of the CBS conglomerate, dating back to the 1960s, was problematic. After paying too high a price to purchase the New York Yankees baseball franchise, CBS did not do well on the deal. Fawcett Books was losing millions of dollars; CBS Records demonstrated little sign of breaking out of its tailspin. The same was true of the CBS chain of stores which sold high-fidelity sound equipment. Even CBS Television, the crown jewel of the conglomerate, which now accounted for 60 percent of the company's profits, was sliding, sensitive as it was to the new competition from cable television and the independent stations. (Cable television was indeed affecting ratings: for the country's 35 million cable viewers—40 percent of the total television households—Home Box Office and its cable competitors offered programming that until recently had been the exclusive province of the three major networks. Hence CBS, as well as NBC and ABC, had slipped from a viewing share of 92 percent in 1975 to only 78 percent in 1983. Projections were that by 1990, the networks' share could drop to as little as 60 percent.)

Nothing appeared to be working for CBS. When Wyman succeeded John Backe as president and chief executive officer, he was the fifth president of the corporation in only nine years (Stanton, Ireland, Taylor, and Backe preceding Wyman); he was also the third in the past four years. Wyman, on the face of it, looked like an odd choice. By his own acknowledgment, "I haven't had any broadcast experience, or publishing or toy-business experience, and I don't know much about music." (15) Some cynics believed that Bill Paley intentionally chose someone with non-broadcasting experience in order not to pose a new rival to himself. Whatever the case, Wyman did possess good credentials as a generalist and that undoubtedly appealed to Paley. Even the fact that Wyman had been an English major at Amherst College (Amherst, Mass.) and not a Harvard M.B.A., added merit to his record. Wyman came to CBS from the Pillsbury Corporation in Minneapolis, where he had been vice chairman. Prior to that he had been president and chief executive officer of the Jolly Green Giant Corporation, which Pillsbury had acquired in 1979. He had spent ten years at the Polaroid Corporation as well, rising to the number two position in the company at the age of 42. *Time* magazine had included him in its list of America's 200 future leaders in 1974. When Paley made the offer to Wyman, he found it too good to pass up: $800,000 a year for three years plus a $1 million bonus. Some suggested spitefully that CBS had appeared to be buying a major league baseball star.

Upon taking over the weakened CBS, Wyman's strategy had been to shed the money-losing parts of the corporation and look for new profitable enterprises: thus he shut down the CBS record plant in Terre Haute, Indiana, dismissing 1,250 workers. He also sold Fawcett Books. As for the television network, that was for the time being untouchable. In fact, he beefed it up, investing $150 million to upgrade news broadcasting and daytime shows; he also moved news shows into prime-time slots. Wyman's strategy showed signs of working: prime-time ratings for the 1982–83 season rose. In March 1981 Wyman had set up the CBS Theatrical Films, but when that lost $10 million, he dropped the project quickly. He spent $58 million to buy Ideal Toys, the company that produced the famous Rubik's Cube. In the early 1980s CBS's broadcasting income more than made up for the poor performance of the records group. But in 1984 a young singer named Michael Jackson rose to spectacular fame: his hit record "Thriller" on the CBS Records label brought in $8 million alone. Wall Street appeared to appreciate what Wyman was doing. The CBS stock shot up from a low of $33 to $53. When Paley announced that he was retiring as of April 20, 1983, as chairman, Tom Wyman was appointed to succeed him. It was an announcement, like previous ones, that few took as an indication that Paley was finally stepping down from the seat of power, only that he was giving up a formal title. He adopted the title founding chairman, seemingly a meaningless post but signifying that Paley had grown disenchanted with Wyman by this time. It may have had to do with some of Wyman's diversification schemes. His acquisition of the Ideal Toy Company was not considered wise. Nor was his joint venture of Tri-Star Pictures with Home Box Office and Columbia Pictures. Moreover, his decision in 1985 to pay $362.5 million for twelve Ziff-Davis magazines was considered bad judgment: the price was too high. By the fall of 1982, Wyman's performance hardly looked impressive. CBS's sales had risen only slightly in the previous year to $4.1 billion from $4.0 billion, while profits had dropped to $162.8 million from $189.4 million in 1980.

With its stock low, and with the corporation undervalued, CBS appeared increasingly like a takeover target. Although never a serious affair, Fairness in Media's bid in early 1985 had awakened CBS's executives to the possibility that the company could come under serious threat. If Jesse Helms could not become Dan Rather's boss—as he was hoping— he did at least focus attention on CBS's stock price, which was far below the value of the corporation's assets (CBS had sales in 1984 of $4.9 billion). The Fairness in Media campaign against CBS did little to push the company into a defensive posture. Indeed, in February the CBS board chose not to introduce antitakeover measures. The board had no interest in focusing on CBS's potential vulnerability. CBS did bring a lawsuit against the Fairness in Media group in March aimed at delaying its obtaining of a list of CBS stockholders—that was a minor triumph which kept the conservative organization from turning to stockholders in time for the April 17 meeting.

The idea that Ted Turner would make a run on CBS appeared laughable to many inside and outside CBS. Who would bankroll him? How could he do it? Yet Turner had worked miracles before, and that alone was enough to give pause at CBS. Still, it looked preposterous. Turner Broadcasting, the backbone of Ted Turner's "empire," had sales in 1984 of only $300 million, a dwarf in comparison to CBS. Yet, the rumors persisted, and they had the positive effect of driving the CBS stock up to $88.50.

No one had warned Ted Turner that his challenge against CBS would be met with the stiffest resistance. No one had told the Southern broadcasting executive that CBS would be willing to do almost anything to keep a corporate raider like Turner at bay. Back in 1983, Ted Turner had acknowledged that "I'd like to get my hands on a network. I'd like to be the big guy for a while." Then again in 1984, in a speech before the National Conservative Foundation, he had said, "These networks need to be gotten into the hands of people who care about this country." But Turner apparently had no idea how stubborn CBS would be. One of its executives had expressed it aptly in saying that CBS's plan for anyone who tried to win control was "to make him sorry he ever got up in the morning." (16) Tom Wyman, when asked what one should do about prospective raiders like Turner, made it clear that he intended to act aggressively. "You ought to reflexively bite their ankle," he said without hesitation. (17)

Although others familiar with CBS thought there was no reason for Tom Wyman to do so, the CBS leader took the Turner takeover threat seriously. He began regular Wednesday strategy meetings. His colleagues were expected to report on everything heard in order to devise a defense strategy. CBS would not cave in, it would not let a Ted Turner or anyone else accumulate stock and build up enough of a stake to become a genuine takeover threat. Wyman phoned around to investment bankers asking them not to aid Turner. Wyman even threatened to rip up the contracts of CBS stars like Dan Rather and Michael Jackson. New ones would be drawn that would contain provisions calling for the contracts to be broken if management changed hands. More barriers were erected: in early April the board decided to eliminate a bylaw that had enabled holders of 10 percent of CBS's stock to call special stockholders' meetings; after the change only certain board members could call such a meeting. Also, CBS took a $1.5 billion line of credit that could be used to finance the acquisitions of companies and thus make CBS less attractive to a takeover raider like Turner. The move would be weakening. CBS was forced to raise its debt from $370 million to $1 billion; the equity in the company dropped from $1.5 billion to only $519 million.

As CBS was erecting those barriers, trouble came from an unexpected source. On April 1, just three days after it had stopped the Fairness in Media group in its tracks, CBS learned that the king of Wall Street's arbitragers, Ivan F. Boesky, had disclosed that he now owned 8.7 percent of CBS. Astonishingly, he had become the largest CBS stockholder without anyone's taking much notice. Bill Paley owned only 6.5 percent. (This was the same Ivan Boesky who would be laid low on November 14, 1986, when the Securities Exchange Commission charged him with taking at least $50 million in illegal trading profits. In a settlement, Boesky agreed to give up $50 million in illegal profits and beyond that to pay another $50 million in civil penalties, amounting to a $100 million fine). Although Boesky insisted that he had no plans to seek control of CBS—and in fact it was not his style to raid corporations—the mere fact that he, an outsider, had become CBS's largest stockholder meant that Boesky might align himself with some other force, and together they could make a bid for the corporation. This would not bode well for CBS. So CBS filed suit in U.S. district court in Manhattan against him, hoping perhaps that the legal action would force Boesky to leave

CBS alone. The arbitrager greeted the maneuver with shock: "I didn't think that was a very nice thing to do to their largest shareholder." (18) The network charged Boesky with making false and misleading statements to the Securities and Exchange Commission regarding the way he had financed his CBS stock purchases. The lawsuit caused a loss of nerve on Wall Street. CBS stock fell nearly ten points on April 10, the day after the suit was brought. On April 17, when the CBS stockholders met, Tom Wyman was in a fighting mood: "Those who seek to gain control of CBS in order to gain control of CBS News threaten its independence, its integrity—and this country."

The company Turner was trying to win over appeared to be sitting at the top of the heap with 1985 sales of $4.8 billion. But it had only a $27.4 million profit that year. Still, it had the top-rated evening news program for the last five years, and had been the leader in prime-time entertainment for twenty-five of the last thirty years. Not only that. It produced and distributed television programs, owned two radio networks, and a number of local television stations, and seven AM and eleven FM radio stations; it published books and magazines and was the world's largest producer and manufacturer of recorded music. In its size and strength, it seemed invincible. Nonetheless, Turner decided to seek control. He made his move on April 19, 1985, announcing at a news conference in Manhattan that he would indeed try to take over the network. Turner had combined clever financial maneuvering with raw nerve. CBS stockholders were asked to exchange their shares for some Turner Broadcasting System, Inc., stock and high-yield, high-risk junk bonds with a total value of $5.41 billion. Turner said the offer amounted to $175 a share, but others thought it nearer to $125. He then walked the twelve blocks to the Madison Avenue office of the law firm he had hired. Taking the walk, rather than driving, was seen as Turner's way of thumbing his nose at those who doubted he could pull off the takeover. It also appeared to demonstrate the "grass-roots" nature of the move. Why this was so, no one could explain. But Turner got a lot of publicity out of the stroll.

The news that Turner was about to raid CBS did not exactly sit well with the network's management. It was true that Turner had built up his own little television empire, but that had been done far from New York. So his success was hardly noted by the New York financial community. What was more, Turner's moralizing turned the people in New York off. He sounded all too much like the Fairness in Media people, promising, as he did, to improve the quality and objectivity of CBS's programming, insisting that he would get rid of the sleaze and stupidity and violence, as he had preached. Paley had purged Arthur Taylor for similar crimes, and here was an outsider, as upstart, trying to take the same tack. It was hardly surprising that the stalwarts at CBS would not welcome Ted with open arms. "I have yet to come across anybody at CBS News who has the slightest desire to work for Turner," observed Mike Wallace. "No one takes him seriously." (19) To this Walter Cronkite added, "CBS News has achieved the greatest credibility. It would be terrible to change all that."

No one could figure out just where Turner would get the cash, where would he raise the $4 to $5 billion it would take. Certainly not from his Turner Broadcasting. Some refused to write Turner off; yet Wall Street appeared to take his offer as some kind of bad joke. One sign was the fact that the stock went up only $3.25 after the offer—to $107—rather than shooting up sharply as stock of a targeted company routinely did. Turner had a lot going against him. Inasmuch as the CBS stock was valued at between $220 and $240, his offer was way too low. Also, he was offering CBS no cash: indeed, stockholders were in effect being asked to pay for the deal with CBS's own money, a neat trick on Turner's part. He planned to sell off parts of the company after the takeover, including all eighteen radio stations CBS owned and one of the four CBS-owned television stations. He was also thinking of selling the CBS Records Group or its publishing division.

CBS chose not to employ the increasingly popular "poison pill" defense against Turner as being too drastic. But rumors abounded that CBS was searching for a "white knight": Time, Inc., and General Electric were mentioned. Soon, however, it became manifest that CBS was not going to sell out to anyone. Three days after the offer, the CBS board of directors turned it down unanimously, calling its "grossly inadequate." The board then fought Turner in the courts, charging him with materially misstating the earnings of Turner Broadcasting in 1983 and 1984. CBS wanted to show that Turner would not be able to service the debt on the securities that Turner Broadcasting planned to issue in the merger. Tom Wyman employed another tack: he passed word that he felt Turner unfit morally to run the network.

CBS's first triumph in its anti-Turner campaign concerned its lawsuit against Ivan Boesky. Perhaps sensing that Turner's offer was going nowhere, Boesky decided to cut his holdings in CBS stock by nearly half to 4.3 percent. Between April 8 and 19, the day Turner made his offer for CBS, Boesky sold 1.3 million CBS shares, totaling $142.7 million; that gave him a profit of $16.7 million. Negotiating with the arbitrager, the CBS board agreed that it would drop its lawsuit against Boesky if he would pledge in turn not to increase his stake in the company. Boesky, of course, had good reason to come to terms with CBS. By getting the network to drop the lawsuit, he would extricate himself from a prolonged legal battle. And he could walk away, claiming that he had been exonerated. For its part, CBS was joyous that Boesky would no longer threaten to join forces with anyone, Ted Turner included, to make a serious bid for the network. Wall Street took little notice of the CBS-Boesky settlement when it was announced May 3rd: CBS's stock closed at $108.76, up only $2.

In keeping with its plan to do everything it could to defend itself, CBS enlisted support from a wide assortment of groups, some acting out of affection for the network, some out of hostility toward Turner. CBS could not have cared less; the effect was the same. Such groups as the National Organization for Women and the United Church of Christ expressed sympathy for the network. The Hispanic National Association asserted that Turner had demonstrated an insensitivity to blacks, Hispanics, women, and Jews. Some one hundred CBS affiliates offered their support as well.

During the summer the battle switched to high gear. In June 1985 CBS petitioned the FCC to halt Turner's bid. By mid-July, Turner himself had filed with the FCC, detailing his takeover plans: should he succeed, he indeed planned to break up CBS, something that many suspected for a long time. He would sell for cash all the operating parts of the corporation as a way of getting his hands on the network and its television stations: WCBS in New York, KCBS in Los Angeles, WBBM in Chicago, and KMOX in St. Louis. Just as CBS had alleged, Turner would generate $4.5 billion in debt. As a CBS vice president noted, "Had he gotten that, there was great concern that this thing would have gone, because he would have had someone giving him cash and not junk." Turner had no regrets, but CBS called it a "death spiral." No stockholder was eager to push CBS into such a spiral.

Few gave Turner a fighting chance in early summer. CBS still felt it needed something more decisive to keep Turner at bay, a true knockout blow. Although many of the defenses discussed by management would have staved off Turner, they had the disadvantage of adding to CBS's financial burdens. Still, Tom Wyman realized there was little choice. The alternative would be to invite trouble, not necessarily from Ted Turner—he could be handled—but from others, waiting to see how CBS would react to the Atlanta broadcaster. If the barriers did not go up against Ted Turner, surely they would not go up against other, more formidable foes. So the Ted Turner bid was a most serious test case for CBS and the entire financial world by now was watching.

Wyman did have some choices. He could have kept CBS intact by engineering a leveraged buyout. Or he could have improved the stock price by selling off assets and restructuring the company. But he chose not to restructure. He chose instead to put through a measure in July that would all but assure the removal of Turner from the takeover battleground. The board would offer to buy 21 percent of CBS's stock at $150 a share—or a total purchase price of $955 million. Wyman informed stock analysts in the Manhattan studio where the daytime soap opera "As the

World Turns" was once broadcasted. CBS planned to pay stockholders $40 a share in cash, plus $110 in ten-year securities that would pay 10.875 percent annual interest. CBS would pay in other ways too: its debt, $386 million in 1984, would rise to $1.4 billion. Wyman asserted that CBS would sell some $300 million in assets but would not get out of the broadcasting, records, or publishing side of the business. But in fact, CBS found itself forced to sell off its St. Louis television station, KMOX. This came at a time when others were showing interest in buying television stations. Wyman also announced a goal of cutting $20 million.

By midsummer CBS's defensive scheme was in place, making the stockholders most happy. Suddenly their shares, valued the previous March at just $82.38, had skyrocketed to $150 a share. Turner, undoubtedly dismayed, could only say, "We believe that our offer . . . is far more attractive . . . and we intend to pursue it vigorously." (20) But by early August he acknowledged that it had become "very, very difficult, if not impossible" to finalize his takeover offer, and only if he were to acquire the support of the FCC and the courts did he stand a chance. (21) But both places had disheartening news for Turner: his challenges to block the network's buyback plan went nowhere.

Sensing that its troubles were not entirely over, even with Ted Turner effectively taken off the takeover playing field, Tom Wyman had had some discussions with Laurence Tisch of Loews Corporation over the summer.

During the first six months of 1985, Bill Paley and the CBS board had relied upon James Wolfensohn who as a former partner at Salomon Brothers, was the board's expert on takeovers. CBS relied as well on its own investment banking adviser, Morgan Stanley, and on takeover attorney Joe Flom. Tisch, by now, had made it clear that if Wolfensohn and Flom were indeed searching for a "white knight," Loews would be interested.

The Brooklyn-born Tisch was the billionaire chairman of Loews, the New York—based conglomerate that owned a hotel chain, sold insurance, and manufactured Kent cigarettes as well as Bulova watches. Tisch was chairman of the New York University Board of Trustees, a leading supporter of the Metropolitan Museum of Art, and a major force behind the Federation of Jewish Philanthropies. The Tisch empire had started in 1946 when Laurence and his brother Preston, the president of the fourteen-hotel Loews chain, borrowed money from their parents to purchase the 300-room Laurel-in-the-Pines, a resort hotel in Lakewood, N.J. By 1955 they owned twelve hotels; in 1960 they obtained control of Loews Theaters. They also acquired control of CNA Insurance and Lorillard Tobacco. Their company eventually had $12.5 billion in assets. The personal fortune of the two Tisch brothers was estimated at $1.7 billion each. (22)

Laurence was the son of a clothing manufacturer who had also owned a summer camp in the Pennsylvania Pocono mountains. A sharp-witted youngster, he raced through public schools and by age 15 had entered New York University, graduating cum laude at age 19. There followed a Master's degree in industry and management from the University of Pennsylvania's Wharton School of Business. During World War II he served in the U.S. Army, deciphering enemy codes for the O.S.S. Attending Harvard Law School, he dropped out to take an early stab at money-making.

Tom Wyman met Larry Tisch at the Loews offices on May 2, 1985. Wyman asked Tisch for his advice on which Jewish and civil organizations might be prepared to urge the federal regulatory agencies to oppose Ted Turner's bid against CBS. Tisch supplied some names. But the subject of Loews investing in CBS did not come up.

Tisch's interest in CBS intensified early that summer. It was the morning of July 3. Larry Tisch was working in his New York office when the phone rang. Nearby was his Quotron machine. On the phone was Dan, one of Tisch's four sons and also managing director of the risk arbitrage department of Salomon Brothers. Dan had just noticed a Dow Jones wire service story recounting Tom Wyman's buyback proposal. Quickly, Tisch's right hand went for the Quotron. He punched up CBS. Green letters came on the screen. Lots of statistics suddenly appeared. Father and son talked, as they often did, about what to do. As they talked, a plan materialized: Dan calculated that, relying upon Salomon's trading capability, he could purchase CBS stock on behalf of Loews at an average price far below $150. Moreover, the profit would be taxed at the dividend rather than the higher capital gains rate. Dan proposed the plan to his father who readily agreed. Somewhere in the process, though, Larry Tisch changed his mind about his arbitrage strategy and rather than sell to make a quick profit, he decided to hang onto the stock. And that would set tongues wagging. Loews paid $951 million for its CBS stock at an average share price of $127.

In mid-July Tisch phoned Tom Wyman to say that Loews had acquired 5 percent of CBS. Tisch assured the CBS president that he had nothing to worry about, this was not the start of a serious takeover threat. Still, Wyman and the board were edgy. Bill Paley, for his part, was confused. He had mistakenly thought that Larry Tisch was a Tishman (the Tishmans were in real estate).

On August 7, Wyman sent a memo to CBS employees, telling them that Turner Broadcasting had just announced the withdrawal of its proposal to acquire CBS. And he added, "This episode in our company's history is now over. We have addressed all of these challenges with integrity and dignity . . . (our recapitalization plan) is a well-balanced response to our needs and responsibilities as a company . . . my sense is that as a company we have never been closer. We have been apprehensive together, we have worked together, and we may now be forgiven for savoring our independence together. Our future is obviously bright, but the achievement of our goals will require our best efforts . . . ."

It was a football coach's speech to a team that was losing 60–0 with 30 seconds to go. The CBS battle for survival would prove costly to the network. The effort to block Turner would place the company in a financial situation that would in effect create a new, downsized company, one that was no longer the robust, moneymaking machine of past decades. Instead, the network would now be fighting to stay above water, trying to bring itself back to its former, healthier position. Was it all necessary? Was the decision to take Ted Turner so seriously a wise one? Obviously, Tom Wyman thought so. But many would second-guess him later, arguing that it had been a mountain-sized mistake to inflate Ted Turner into the tycoon that he was not. As one former CBS executive noted, "They did not need to leverage the company in order to save it. The Turner thing would have fallen of its own weight. It was a proxy fight. They thought it was a tender offer. It wasn't. It was a tender offer, all with CBS's own money. It was a proxy fight, really, and if they had treated it like a proxy fight, like a political battle, rather than a financial battle, I think it would have been fine. But somebody said, 'We can't take the chance,' so they go off and borrow $4.2 billion and they leverage the company, so it's in a straightjacket."

Now, none of this mattered. What counted was the burden under which CBS now fell. To finance the 21 percent stock buyback, CBS would have to nearly double the interest it was paying to borrow money for the fourth quarter of 1985—from $22.2 million to $40.8 million. In early August came word from the CBS bosses that some 2,000 employees, or 7 percent of the work force, would be given incentives to retire early, a move that would save $7 million annually. In all, 600 of the 24,000 jobs at CBS were eliminated in 1985. In November CBS closed its toy, computer software, and theatrical film businesses. It reported its first quarterly loss—$114.1 million—since the early days of the network in the late 1920s.

Meanwhile, by the fall Wyman and Tisch had joined together on a plan, not the friendly merger they had discussed in the early part of the summer, but rather something that would fall far short of that. It envisaged keeping control in the board's hands without a hostile takeover. CBS decided to place a sizable block of its stock in friendly hands, asking Laurence Tisch to take Loews' stake to as much as 25 percent from its current 11.7 percent level. Tisch had done some clever engineering, all right. As *The Wall Street Journal* wrote, "Without spending a dime on lawyers or investment bankers, Laurence A. Tisch may have accomplished what Ted Turner and an $18 million roster of takeover advisers couldn't do: de facto control of CBS Inc." (23)

But CBS was not worred about Larry Tisch. "We want this guy," said CBS Vice President William Liley III, "we welcome this guy." (24) Tisch had already benefited from CBS's takeover woes: as the result of the 21 percent buyback, he had sold a quarter of Loews' holdings in CBS at what was described as a "nice" profit. Tisch seemed bent on noninvolvement at CBS. Finally, he would not purchase more than 25 percent of CBS stock. He was available to lend advice and expertise to the network, but that was all. Yet, despite his disavowals, in November 1985 Tisch joined the CBS board.

In the following months—through the winters of 1985 and 1986—CBS remained the object of takeover rumors. The reasons were obvious. CBS was a company in some trouble. The CBS portion of the network slice of prime-time audience had dropped from 29 percent in the 1982–83 season to 26 percent in 1985 while NBC's had grown from 24 to 27 percent on the strength of the "Bill Cosby Show" and "Family Ties." CBS had not had one prime-time hit show the previous season. Profits in the broadcast division had fallen from $409 million in 1984 to $361 million in 1985 as well. (During 1985, a group of news division people organized by Don Hewitt, and including Dan Rather, actually offered to buy CBS News and run it separately from the rest of the company, but reporting directly to the CEO. CBS declined the offer.) Nor was the network the only part of CBS affected: earnings for the publishing group had gone down from $59 million to $41 million; profits in the records division dropped from $124 million to $87 million. And, as noted, in 1985 CBS had a profit of $27.41 million on revenue of $4.8 billion.

It was no wonder that CBS remained a potential takeover victim. Meanwhile, Larry Tisch was taking a greater bite out of CBS. His own actions with regard to his CBS stock raised speculation every time he made a move. In early February 1986 Loews had raised its stake in CBS—then at 11.9 percent—to 12.3 percent. CBS's stock rose twenty points during one four-day period on the strength of rumors that Tisch might be preparing himself for a takeover of CBS. For its part, the network appeared sincerely interested in having Tisch raise his stake to the 25 percent level mentioned the previous October.

An overture came that month from Marvin Davis, the 60-year-old Denver oil man and former owner of Twentieth Century Fox Film Corporation. Davis had hoped to reestablish his prestige in Hollywood. He had bought Twentieth Century Fox in 1981 but sold it to Rupert Murdoch, the press magnate, in 1985: Davis earned a $325 million profit from the sale. He might have tried for a hostile takeover of CBS at this point but decided against it, saying that he was too old for that type of thing. He offered

Tom Wyman $150 a share for CBS. Predictably, the answer was an emphatic no. Davis returned a month later with a second, improved offer: an all-cash bid of $160 a share worth $3.75 billion. But CBS had not changed its mind even though this was an all-cash offer, the kind the stockholders might have been hoping to get from Ted Turner the previous summer. CBS's management obviously felt strong enough to rebuff Davis without worrying too much about the distress the stockholders might feel. What the Davis bids made clear was that CBS was still in the eyes of Wall Street a most desirable property, the "vanity stock of the decade," in the words of one broadcasting executive.

Not surprisingly, one week after the rejection of Marvin Davis, Loews raised its stake in CBS from 12.3 percent to 16.7 percent. This seemed to remove a takeover threat from another apparently interested duo, the reclusive Fisher brothers, Lawrence and Zachary. Loews, it was presumed, bought the entire 4.4 percent of CBS stock owned by the Fishers, paying $143.50 a share, or $149.3 million altogether. Resisting takeovers became increasingly costly for CBS. It began to sell off $300 million in assets, including two jets. Some 600 employees had accepted a special early retirement package. And the company was forced to lay off another 500 people. CBS News itself lost 74 staff members. CBS had remained independent. But if CBS was feeling particularly heroic after the battle, its generals knew better. The company was badly wounded even though Tom Wyman's goal of repelling Ted Turner had been accomplished.

Concern developed over Laurence Tisch's motives by the spring of 1986, particularly when, in an interview with USA Today, his brother Robert declared that the eventual goal of Laurence's policy "is to control CBS." Tisch aroused more suspicion when he would not disavow the report. And when asked to put into writing his oral commitment to Tom Wyman that he would not buy more than 25 percent of CBS's stock, he also refused.

Meanwhile, the company's wounds were getting worse. CBS had run up its debt to a high of $1.44 billion. By late summer 1986 Wyman had managed to bring the amount down to $780 million. But to do so, he was forced to sell off such once-valued assets, in addition to the St. Louis television station, as the CBS toy division and a 29 percent interest in the Tri-Star movie production firm. In July came more bad news as the CBS Broadcast Group announced that it was eliminating 700 more jobs, including some 90 positions in the news division. One more blow landed when the network announced the removal of the CBS morning news, effective January 1987. (The program, which cost $34 million a year to produce and was losing $12 million a year, routinely got bad ratings.)

CBS was fast becoming a different entity to many who still worked there. In his syndicated newspaper column in August, Andy Rooney thought enough was enough. Entitled, "TV News Takes Turn for the

Worse," the Rooney column lashed into CBS, assailed all the layoffs and the demise of the CBS morning news, and said these were symptoms of a growing bottom-line approach to the news. "CBS," wrote Rooney, "which used to stand for the Columbia Broadcasting System, no longer stands for anything. They're just corporate initials now. In the past year, CBS has fired 190 people from its news division. Business is bad and the company has been through a difficult battle from being bought by money operators. You live by the dollar, you die by the dollar." He closed the article by writing, "The golden days of television news are over." A spokesman for the company said there would be no official comment on the Rooney piece. There was, in truth, not much to say. If Andy Rooney, one of the network's mainstays, could use his newspaper column to blast away at CBS, the enterprise was clearly in bad straits. The Rooney article was quickly circulated through the CBS headquarters.

Matters came to a head in the fall of 1986. A board meeting had been scheduled for   September 10. But the night before an extraordinary dinner was held in a private second floor room at Manhattan's Ritz Carlton Hotel.

News stories reported that Tom Wyman had invited a number of CBS board members to the dinner, but cancelled it at the last moment, apparently to avoid a confrontation with board members. Yet, Wyman, in a conversation with the author on March 9, 1988, insisted that he had neither initiated the dinner nor cancelled it at the last moment. Under any circumstances, the five-hour dinner took place when an unidentified director decided that the board should meet informally minus Tisch and Wyman. Both were informed that the dinner was taking place. The atmosphere was tense, angry. *Newsweek* had just run a cover story on CBS's problems and mentioned that Wyman had asked James Wolfenson, the CBS board member, to approach Philip Morris and Westinghouse about buying CBS. But the network publicly denied that such an overture had been made. All board members were given a written denial from Wolfenson himself.

The board members around the dinner table generally felt that such a step was a bad idea. The goal was to keep CBS independent. Also present were two high-powered attorneys, Sam Butler, of Cravath, Swaine & Moore, and Arthur Liman, of Paul, Weiss, Rifkin, Garrison & Wharton. Board members asked the two whether the board had an obligation to seek a buyer. The answer came back in the negative. Paley insisted that Wyman should be forced to leave. He had been making that plea for the past few months and was now even more convinced. But, as the five-hour dinner wound up, it was apparent that Wyman still had the support of nine of the fourteen board members; some, however, were moving against him because of CBS's financial woes. As for Bill Paley, now nearly 85, the adrenalin was flowing; the previous six weeks had revived his interest in the company, and given him a new sense of purpose. To friends, he said that he could not go out anywhere on the Monday or Tuesday night before the critical September 10 meeting because he had to save his company. Going into the meeting, Larry Tisch could count on the votes of four board members to support whatever proposal he would make: Walter Cronkite; Marietta Tree, a New York City planner; Newton Minow, then a Chicago lawyer; and possibly Michael Bergerac, the former Chairman of Revlon.

Finally, the board met on the morning of September 10 in the CBS corporate board room. When it did, according to some news accounts, Tom Wyman, who was the only CBS executive with a board seat, shocked his thirteen fellow board members by raising the subject of CBS's corporate future. However, Wyman told the author, he had in fact disclosed to eight directors the Coke offer some weeks before and, according to Wyman, all eight had indicated interest in selling to Coke. Indeed, these members had encouraged Wyman to bring the Coke proposal to the September 10th board meeting. At that meeting, Wyman began by saying that he had a plan that would bring more money to CBS stockholders. He announced that he had been conducting secret negotiations with Coca-Cola and that it was ready to purchase CBS for a price that was substantially higher than the network's market price. He never mentioned the price Coke planned to pay. Wyman said the deal was not sewn up and he needed ten more days to find out whether Coke was indeed serious. Asking the board to authorize the continuation of negotiations, he noted that there were some hurdles to overcome before the deal could go through. For one, CBS would have to figure out how to get around federal regulations that forbade television networks from owning a company that syndicates television shows to local stations: Coca-Cola's Columbia Pictures was doing just that, enjoying a large profit by syndicating television programs. Wyman then said that if the Coke deal fell through, he knew of a second unnamed company who was also prepared to buy CBS at an attractive price. It was assumed that he meant Disney Productions. He didn't give the name.

When he stopped speaking, there was absolute silence. Larry Tisch and Bill Paley had not been informed by Wyman of the Coke offer. Tisch, with 24.9 percent (worth $780 million), was the largest CBS stockholder. Paley was second with 8.1 percent (worth $257 million). Acting together, they could make sure that the Coke offer could be scuttled and that was precisely what Tisch was intent upon doing, once he learned of Wyman's idea. Tisch went on the offensive, asking Wyman how could he contemplate selling the company given the precarious nature of its finances. Another board member thought, upon hearing the Wyman proposal, what had all the fight against Jesse Helms and Ted Turner been about? By 12 noon, Wyman had been asked to wait outside. For several hours, the board discussed the Wyman proposal. Some board members were legitimately concerned that CBS might have an obligation to put the company up for sale in light of Wyman's formal announcement at the board meeting that he had shopped the company. They sought legal opinion. Attorneys offered the comforting news that the board did not have an obligation at the moment. That would only happen once it began entertaining outside offers. Then, it would have to listen to all other offers.

Tisch was furious. He told the board that he had not become part of CBS to make money; he was not interested in selling his shares. The Wyman talk of letting someone take over CBS was the last straw, as far as he was concerned: a management change was needed; it would help turn the company around. Someone asked Tisch if he could continue to work with Wyman. He answered the question indirectly: he had no plans, he said, to take any action against Wyman if he (Wyman) remained at his job. But it was clear that Tisch had turned against the CEO. Tisch made sure to note that his stoke in CBS was not meant to stake out a position that could lead to a Loews takeover of the network. At this point, Wyman, Tisch, and Paley were asked to leave the room. Walter Cronkite was asked for his view of company morale. He reported that Wyman did not seem to appreciate the news division. His words apparently had a strong effect on the outcome. Wrapping up the nine-hour meeting, the rest of the board reached a unanimous decision. The company would not be put up for sale. Once that was conveyed to Wyman, he had no choice but to resign. Sometime after 5 P.M. he was told by two directors that he had lost the backing of the group. The board expected him to resign. And so he did. At the time he was being paid $680,000 a year. By the end of the meeting, the board was unanimous that Tisch should be named acting chief executive officer and Bill Paley named acting chairman on an "interim basis," until a search committee could come up with permanent choices. The "acting" before Paley's name was put there as a signal to all those who were concerned that Paley would never give up his leadership of the network.

The outcome of the board meeting was indeed startling. Leadership of the company had effectively passed to Larry Tisch. For the first time since the days when Bill Paley was truly in charge of the company, leadership would be in the hands of someone who had a major financial investment in the network—and was not simply an employee, hired by Paley. That could mean that for the first time in a long while CBS might stabilize.

The outcome of the meeting signified as well the return of Bill Paley, founder of CBS, to the company's helm. Because of his age—he would soon turn 85—no one expected the network's founder to play an active role in company's affairs. But his selection as acting chairman reflected the new management's awareness that the network was afflicted with more than financial distress. That it was slowly losing its original identity. Nothing suggested that as strongly as the attempted sale to Coca-Cola. As a result of the devastating Turner takeover experience, CBS would have to get used to functioning without the resources once available. Resurrecting Bill Paley was supposed to comfort the anxious that fewer resources did not automatically mean the abandonment of CBS's vaunted standards.

As Dan Rather got ready to sign off at 7:30 P.M., he was handed a piece of paper. He read it nervously, announcing the changes briefly. Meanwhile, Paley and Tisch were emerging from CBS headquarters into a mass of reporters and cameramen, who had been waiting around since the start of the board meeting. Paley said only that he was very pleased. Tisch talked of a return to the high standards of CBS. Word of Wyman's sudden resignation spread to a party on Manhattan's East Side at the Park Avenue apartment of designer Mollie Parnis who was honoring "60 Minutes" reporter-host Mike Wallace and his new bride Mary Yates. The guests included Walter Cronkite, Dan Rather, and NBC's Tom Brokaw. When another "60 Minutes" correspondent, Morley Safer, heard the news about Tom Wyman and the appointment of Bill Paley as acting chairman, he said: "It's back to the future. That's good news."

There was hope. Hope that CBS would be saved. But from what? Tisch and Paley faced the same set of problems that Wyman had. They could assure that the shopping of CBS would halt immediately. But cuts there would have to be. Tisch promised in those first few weeks that he would not sell off any of CBS's assets. It was a nice promise, but he would not live up to it. A search committee was appointed, but it was soon realized that Tisch and Paley had no intention of relinquishing their new power. Names for the job of CBS chairman, considered by some the toughest job in the media business, were mentioned in the press. Among them, N. J. Nicholas Jr., newly named president of Time, Inc.; Michael D. Eisner, chairman of Disney Productions; Douglas H. McCorkindale, vice chairman of Gannett; and Daniel B. Burke, president of Capital Cities/ABC. Most of them said they were not interested. It didn't matter. No one was interviewed for the job. Before long it was understood that Tisch and Paley would be staying on. And indeed, on January 14, 1987, the two men were elected to their posts on a permanent basis, removing the "acting" from their titles.

Wyman did not leave the job in penury. He received a settlement of more than $4.3 million and an annual payment of $400,000 for life. (25) Tisch would be paid $750,000 in 1987, and the Loews Corporation, of which Tisch was chairman and CEO, also received $262,540 for his services as acting CEO from September 1986 until February 1987. (26)

After the Tisch-Paley takeover, dismissals became routine. Among

Tisch's first actions was to accept the resignation of the increasingly un-popular Van Gordon Sauter as president of CBS News; Sauter had been criticized of late for introducing show business elements into the news and for sapping the news division of its traditional autonomy. His hiring of Phyllis George, the former Miss America, as anchor of the morning news program brought Sauter stiff criticism; George was dismissed when ratings didn't improve. Tisch also removed CBS Publishing President Pe-ter Derow and 14 of Derow's assistants. He cut 400 people in October, another 100 in November, a further 700 in December. Thus within three months he had pared 1,200 CBS jobs. Entire departments were reduced. The Corporate Public Relations staff in Manhattan was downsized from 21 to 4. The Investor-Relations Department, which dealt with stockhold-ers, lost 6 of its 8 staff members. The corporate personnel office, in charge of hiring, dropped from 120 to 50. Twenty-six pages who earned $6 an hour were fired. So were 2 doctors and 4 nurses. Corporate charity was frozen at the 1985 level of $7 million. Three executive dining rooms were shut down. A ban was placed on company-subsidized birthday par-ties for employees. Also, CBS's entire educational and professional pub-lishing operation was sold for $500 million to Harcourt Brace Jovanovich in October as was a music publishing affiliate, CBS Songs, to three entre-preneurs for $120 million. As a result of all this, morale suffered. Inevita-bly, the grumbling turned against the new management. To be fired was, in the new vernacular, to be "Tisched."

Tisch and Paley, meanwhile, were getting along fine. Tisch, for his part, was not intimidated by Paley, and that alone was unusual among those who had worked closely with the CBS founder. It was said, for exam-ple, that Tisch had been the first person who could actually cut Paley off, politely but firmly, during CBS board meetings. In others, that had been considered insubordination. Tisch, however, knew enough to keep away from the creative process, leaving that area to Paley. That, after all, was Paley's strength. It certainly was not Tisch's. As one CBS vice president noted, "Paley and Tisch complement each other, because they're two very successful businessmen, who have made it independently, who have spe-cial talents. Paley is a showman and a programmer. Tisch is a consum-mate businessman and a professional entrepreneur. Those things fit . . . Larry does not pretend to know the shows he should put on or off the air. He does have opinions, but he does not say I'm the programmer, and you listen to me . . . Paley is more involved in the programs, and Larry is the CEO, and runs this business every single day, and runs it completely." Tisch, in short, had taken over. As one news editor noted, "You don't hear Paley's name in the newsroom. You hear's Tisch's name. Of course some of the remarks about Tisch are sarcastic. Paley's role now is that of the quiet diplomat."

Tisch was clearly in charge. Again, in the words of a senior CBS executive, "[Tisch] has a significant financial stake in the company. He has a true enthusiasm for this business. He has opinions. He wants to make this thing work. He has become a part of CBS, as CBS has become a part of him. He does care about it. Now, that does not run at odds with firing people, and trying to trim down. Those exercises were necessary for where we are." Bill Paley was said to be nearly as active as he had been decades earlier. "He's at the office every day," said one senior executive. "He's thoroughly involved in the programming. Watches all the pilots. He reads scripts. He has conversations with people here every day."

On March 14 it was reported that CBS had agreed to sell its magazine group to four division executives for $650 million. Among the 21 titles are *Woman's Day, Car and Driver,* and *Stereo Review.* As part of the sale, CBS planned to drop the magazines it bought from Ziff-Davis in 1985 for $362.5 million. Criticized for overpaying for these publications, CBS, it was now agreed, had gotten a good deal. The sale was the largest of an important CBS asset since Tisch's ascendancy in the fall. This sale left the network with about $1.6 billion in cash, most of it from sales of assets.

As for the news division, Tisch had made all the right sounds when he came into power in the early fall. It appeared that if the news people did their jobs, that was all that would be expected of them. Tisch was quoted in *The New York Times* on September 5, 1986, just five days before he became CBS's acting CEO, as saying "Whether the news loses money or makes money is secondary to what we put on the air. I can't picture any point at which profit becomes the main thought in deciding on a news program." News executives would recall that statement in agony when so many were being "Tisched." The new CEO said ten days later: "The quality of the news programming—and the quality of the entertainment programming—is the most important thing. If you do the right thing, the profits will take care of themselves." Agreeing, Paley said: "We would certainly lose money if we had to, within limits, in order to keep up the standards of CBS News that used to be very strong." (27) The proof would come during the final three months of 1986. It was then that the CBS evening news, which had been number one for nearly two decades, dropped into second place. It was then that NBC's news program with Tom Brokaw earned the first quarterly victory since Huntley and Brinkley had led in 1967. NBC had a quarterly rating of 11.8; CBS, 11.6; and ABC, 10.6. That translated into 10.3 million sets tuned to Brokaw, 10.1 million to Rather, and 9.2 million to ABC's Peter Jennings. Rather, Brokaw, and Jennings were competing in only 112 of the nation's 205 television markets. Profits for the CBS Broadcast Group dropped in 1986 to $360.6 million, which was down from the record 1984 level of $408.6 million. For 1986, CBS's network profits dropped to about $80 million as compared with $200 million the year before. (ABC had a $70 million loss in

1986, and only NBC's network showed a profit, an estimated $400 million.)

The controversy between Tisch and the news division centered on the amount of money that would have to be cut. Early in 1987, despite CBS's denials that its news division had been asked to cut spending by up to $50 million, CBS News executives sadly confirmed that they had been approached on the subject. Tisch would later explain that the main reason was the enormous jump in the CBS News budget over the past nine years: from $88 million to nearly $300 million.

The picture on the entertainment side was no better. It simply generated fewer news headlines. During the 1985–86 season, CBS had moved into second place after six straight seasons at the top. Not since "Murder She Wrote" debuted in 1984 had CBS been able to produce a top-ten show.

In early March 1987 came the bleak news that CBS was laying off some 200 employees in the news division, including 20 on-air correspondents—out of a news staff of 1,200; the aim at first was to cut $30 million from the swollen budget. Among those dropped were Pentagon correspondent Chris Kelley, Capitol Hill correspondent Ike Pappas, legal correspondent Fred Graham, Boston correspondent Ned Potter, and economics contributor Jane Bryant Quinn, and the Saturday morning children's news spots "In the News" and 8 of its staffers. Also dismissed were 11 Miami-based staffers, 60 London-based ones, 10 of the 25 employees on the New York desk responsible for routing footage, and 15 of the 65 Los Angeles staffers. But the worst hit was the 65-person CBS morning news staff: 28 were let go. As a result, within the previous two years, the CBS News operation had been trimmed from 1,400 to 1,000 people.

The dismissals became known as "the slaughter on 57th Street." Tisch angered news executives when it appeared that he was trying to shift the blame for the layoffs on the CBS News President Howard Stringer. Tisch told *The New York Times* on March 9, "I never said to Howard, 'We have to cut the budget at the news division.' That's the truth. Howard called me a month ago and said, 'Larry, I've got some ideas on restructuring the news division. It'll take me about 30 days to put them together.' I said, 'Fine, Howard, I'll be happy to go over them with you.'" Stringer argued that in fact Tisch had expected large cuts from the CBS news budget. Stringer was shocked, and only after a two-hour meeting between the two men did he calm down. Tisch then issued a memo in which he said, "The management of CBS News accepted this painful and difficult assignment. I believe they carried it out superbly under Howard Stringer's leadership, and I accepted wholeheartedly their recommendations of an approximate 10 percent reduction. It was not an assignment anyone relished or that I enjoyed giving them." (28)

The cuts were painful indeed. Ike Pappas, a veteran CBS correspondent who had just lost his job, spoke to striking news writers for CBS ouside the CBS Broadcast Center in Manhattan: "I feel very poorly for the people who have to get up every morning and pretend to work for CBS News," he told the crowd. "It's not CBS News anymore." (29)

Dan Rather, Diane Sawyer, and others offered to take substantial pay decreases if that would save jobs. But the company refused. Rather offered to take a 10 to 30 percent pay cut, which came to an estimated $600,000 reduction in his $2 million–plus annual salary. Others who volunteered pay cuts and who earned more than $500,000 would have taken the same 30 percent cut.

In frustration and bitterness, Rather wrote an op-ed page article for *The New York Times* on March 10 that was titled, "From Murrow to Mediocrity?" In the article, he condemned the layoffs and worried about a "product that may inevitably fall short of the quality and vision it once possessed." He added, "Let's get one thing straight. CBS Inc. is not a chronically weak company fighting to survive. . . . 215 people lost their jobs so that the stockholders would have even more money in their pockets. More profits. That's what business is about.

". . . What we cannot accept is the notion that the bottom line counts more than meeting our responsibility to the public. Anyone who says network news cannot be profitable doesn't know what he is talking about. But anyone who says it must always make money is misguided and irresponsible. We have lost correspondents, producers, camera crews. That means we will cover less news. We will go to fewer places and witness fewer events. For the viewer, that means a product that may inevitably fall short of the quality and vision it once possessed.

"Our concern, beyond the shattered lives of valued friends and colleagues is, How do we go on? How do we cover the world? Can we provide in-depth reporting and analysis with resources so severely diminished? Can we continue to do our jobs in the finest tradition of this great organization? In the tradition of Edward R. Murrow, Walter Cronkite, Eric Sevareid, Douglas Edwards, Charles Collingwood? We are determined that our new corporate management not lead us into a tragic transformation from Murrow to mediocrity. We take our public trust very seriously. It is why we are journalists in the first place. Our new chief executive officer, Laurence Tisch, told us when he arrived that he wanted us to be the best. We want nothing more than to fulfill that mandate. Ironically, he has now made the task seem something between difficult and impossible. I have said before that I have no intention of participating in the demise of CBS. But do the owners and officers of the new CBS see news as a trust . . . or only as a business venture?"

It was an astonishing document. Just as Ed Murrow had done in October 1958 in his hard-hitting Chicago speech, here was one of CBS's most prominent figures going public with an indictment of his own house, so to speak. There were differences, to be sure. Murrow's career at CBS had been waning when he unleashed his attack against the broadcasting industry. Rather's was still at its peak. He had a great deal to lose, both financially and professionally.

Two Democratic members of a House Subcommittee on Telecommunications, Dennis Eckart of Ohio and John Bryant of Texas, called for hearings on whether the cost paring at CBS (and other networks as well) had been in the public interest. Rather signed off one newscast at that time on behalf of "your can-do CBS Evening News." The question that remained, as some pointed out, was whether CBS could do with less.

Anger was rampant. Ike Pappas, the dismissed Capitol Hill correspondent for CBS, noted that "the quality, the integrity and the standards that we had are being compromised by the accountants, the bean counters, the Tisches of the world." Added CBS correspondent Leslie Stahl, "We thought after Tisch came we could pull ourselves together. Instead, we're a ship listing, every day there's another blow." But Dan Rather was not ready to go down with the ship. "I think we're a long way from sinking. I'll fight till she sinks." But then he conceded, "It's painful; we look at one another and the less said the better and that's the way it is with pain. You can't have 300 good pros laid off and can't cut the budget by $30 million and say there will be no effect. Of course, there'll be an effect. What I really felt good about was that I knew I had the best pros in the world behind and around me. I still feel that way. We just don't have as many as we had then." (30)

No less a figure than Walter Cronkite expressed some disenchantment with the cuts in the news budget. He understood the need for them, he said, but he disagreed with the manner in which they were handled. Emerging from a meeting with the CBS board of directors, Cronkite said that "My anger is not directed at the size of cuts or the need for cuts. My disappointment is over the style of the cuts and timing of the cuts. I think the necessity of getting that fat out of the budget is definitely there, and I only quarrel over the tactics."

Within CBS News, the staff believed that the cuts would affect their ability to cover the news. "Knowing that the company has always stood for excellence in journalistic pursuits," observed one senior editor in the summer of 1987, "means that we still have pride whether we are number one or number three in the ratings. We want the best product, the best photos from Korea. We want to break the story." But he noted sadly, "There is less of a commitment to news in part because news is too expensive. In the past, there would be cheering in the newsroom if we were first to have photos of a big story. But that takes money. The cutbacks stifle creativity and imagination. Before we didn't think that much about the cost of a story, now we go to a committee which asks, Is it worth it? Before no one thought of spending $8,000 for a picture that would appear on the screen for only eight seconds. Now they do."

The editor recalled one incident in which he phoned a correspondent to ask how much a story was going to cost. "Fuck you" came the correspondent's reply. "I'm not going to tell you. You can find out how much the airline tickets cost yourself and figure it out." The editor replied that he simply wanted to know whether "we are talking about a $10,000 story or a $2,000 one. It makes a difference in our decision." In earlier days, questions like that would have never been asked.

It was not that CBS News had forgotten what its purpose was. As Bill Leonard had noted, a commitment to the news pervaded the newsroom. So when the summer of 1987 rolled around, and the major witnesses in the Irangate hearings before Congress were scheduled, it was unthinkable that CBS would not cover their testimony live. Even as pressures had mounted to keep news costs low, CBS would deliver. There would be no repetition of the Fred Friendly experience of 1966. No reruns of "I Love Lucy." As David Buksbaum, the CBS News vice president in charge of special events, noted, explaining why CBS carried the hearings focusing on Lt. Col. Oliver North, "We thought that ought to be part of what CBS News does. We have a philosophy. . . . We all feel a sense of responsibility. That sounds almost sophomoric but we really do sense the responsibility." When he was told that it did not sound sophomoric, that indeed that was what CBS is all about, he added sourly, "That's what it was all about." (31)

Howard Stringer, the president of CBS News, was proud of what CBS had done that summer. In a memo he had sent around on July 13, he patted everyone on the back. "This riveting drama [the North hearings] has had a healthy impact on all of us at CBS News. For much of this year, there has been the distraction, confusion and pain of other issues. But last week we were totally immersed in journalism, covering a major news story with potentially profound impact on the nation . . . of course, we watch the ratings. And, of course, we would prefer to be number one. But this issue has grown out of proportion. We are not primarily in the ratings business . . . by those standards, CBS News has always been the leader, and watching Dan [Rather] and the entire CBS News team handle the Iran-Contra hearings makes clear that we still are. This is a professional judgment, confirmed by the view of the American people. A recent poll of 1,000 TV viewers showed that Dan Rather was rated as the best anchor by a wide margin . . . there is a consensus that something is wrong with the ratings system; its accuracy has been called into question. But it should be equally clear that nothing in these numbers indicates that something is wrong with the [CBS] Evening News."

In September 1987, "60 Minutes" was going strong, 20 years old. The program had just tied "Bonanza" as the third longest-running show in the top ten, the first time that feat had been recorded by a news show. One newspaper reported that "60 Minutes" had generated $1 billion in profits since its inception, 800 broadcasts earlier. (32) Reports persisted that Diane Sawyer would leave "60 Minutes" to become a co-anchor on the "CBS Evening News" with Dan Rather.

Unquestionably, the star of that show was having his troubles. Dan Rather had spent the summer mired in third place in the ratings race. However, in trial runs of the new "people meter" rating system, which debuted in September, Rather wound up in first place.

That same month, he was involved in a bizarre incident which added to his controversial image. On September 11, Rather angrily walked off the set of the CBS Evening News, leaving the network with a blank screen. Rather had been in Miami to cover the arrival of Pope John Paul II. He grew disturbed upon learning that the network's coverage of the U.S. Open Tennis Tournament might be put on during his 6:30 P.M. newscast. Rather told CBS News President Howard Stringer that, if that should happen, CBS Sports should fill the remaining time until the second, final edition of Rather's news program began at 7 P.M.

With the Steffi Graf–Lori McNeill semifinal match still being shown during the 6:30 P.M. time slot, Rather unclipped his microphone, and left the set to call Stringer. But Rather was caught unaware that the match was coming to an end. When it did, the network switched from New York to Miami for Rather's program. It took six minutes for the 100 CBS affiliates that run the 6:30 P.M. news to fill the time before Rather could be found and rushed back to his desk.

Why had Rather left his desk? Some perversely argued that he had done so intentionally to underscore his fury that the tennis match would eat up some precious news time. But, he has denied this, scotching reports that he had to be urged to return. "I would never even think of deliberately allowing the network to go to black," he insisted. Larry Tisch could not find it in him to criticize Rather, saying it was "human nature" for Dan Rather to be upset.

CBS board member Walter Cronkite was less charitable. When asked by the Daily Texan, the University of Texas's student newspaper, what he would have done, Cronkite said, "I can answer that in five words: I would have fired him." Those remarks, said CBS News spokesman, Tom Goodman, "do not reflect the position of CBS News and we disagree with them." Later, Cronkite changed his position, noting "I don't know what I would have done" to Dan Rather and praising the anchorperson for contributing so much to CBS.

In one more effort to improve its ratings on the entertainment side, CBS switched leaders of its entertainment division during the fall. On October 30, B. Donald Grant resigned as president of that division, after heading it for seven years. During that period he had failed to lift CBS's rating. Replacing him was a 38-year-old named Earle H. "Kim" LeMasters, who had been a programming vice president for CBS. LeMasters, who had worked for CBS since 1976, has been credited with bringing "Dallas," "Magnum, P.I.," and "The Dukes of Hazzard" to CBS. In the current 1987 fall season, "Beauty and the Beast" was a LeMasters project. In the fall of 1987, CBS, spurred on by LeMasters, decided to replace eight of its twenty-two hours of weekly prime-time programs.

Later that fall came the stunning news that CBS would scale down its operations dramatically in order to repair its faltering financial situation. On November 18 Larry Tisch did what he had said he would never do. He sold the CBS Records Group, the world's largest record company—to Sony for $2 billion. This was the equivalent of amputating a major limb. CBS Records, which Bill Paley had built up into the giant of the industry, and was still home to such recording stars as Michael Jackson, Bruce Springsteen, and Barbra Streisand, accounted for 37 percent of CBS's total operating profit and 31 percent of its revenue.

It was a decision that had not been easy for Tisch to make partly because the records operation had been such a major part of the CBS family. CBS Records had an operating profit of $162.1 million on revenue of $1.49 billion in 1986. Profits at the CBS Records Group were expected to approach $200 million in 1987. It had $141 million in operating profit on revenues of $1.2 billion in the first nine months of 1987.

But in recent years the record division had been subject to sharp profit swings, and fears were raised within the CBS leadership that the company could not afford to retain such a volatile entity any longer. The sale was part of Tisch's "back to broadcasting" program, stripping away assets that had nothing to do with CBS's original efforts in broadcasting. Apart from its significant implications for the network, the sale had national importance: it marked the largest Japanese purchase of an American company.

A year earlier, in November 1986, Sony had offered $1.25 billion for CBS Records, but CBS said no. But when the higher offer came, it was too good to be rejected. Sony happened to be a most suitable acquirer of CBS Records: for 20 years CBS and Sony had been partners in a Japanese label, CBS/Sony. With the cash, Tisch was expected to buy television stations or to pay down debt. The selling of CBS Records, which would take effect in early January 1988, would represent the final step in the scaling down of CBS: once a sprawling conglomerate involving records, magazines and book publishing, CBS was left with only its core television and radio operations. The radical change had come about only in the previous year when CBS had shed its magazine, music and book publishing divisions. The news of the record group sale sent CBS's stock up $8.625 to close at $176 on the New York Stock Exchange.

Why had Sony been so interested in CBS? One theory had it that

Sony may have purchased CBS to soften CBS's opposition to digital audio tape recorders (DAT). As the leading maker of these recorders, Sony had been confronting opposition from, among others, CBS Records. Sony's DAT threatened to take sales away from CBS Records for the reason that music issued in a DAT format permitted a consumer to make virtually perfect copies of compact discs and most record labels.

Changes were being made that fall within the television network as well. On November 30 CBS brought the news division back to the morning programming schedule as "This Morning," co-anchored by Kathleen Sullivan and Harry Smith, premiered at 7 A.M.. It replaced "The Morning Program," hosted by actress Mariette Hartley, which had been in third place from the beginning of its 10-month stint. The new format on "This Morning" was designed to emulate the successful formats of rival "Today" and "Good Morning America."

Kathleen Sullivan had for five years been an anchorperson on "World News This Morning," "Worlds News Saturday," and "The Health Show," and was considered one of the rising stars at ABC. She subbed for Joan Lunden on "Good Morning America" during the summer of 1987, and was therefore considered to be her likely replacement in August 1988 when Lunden's contract expired. Harry Smith had been a CBS corespondent in Dallas.

It was not lost on people that Larry Tisch had discarded in the year before much of what had made CBS a veritable empire of the communications industry. It was all terribly ironic. When Ted Turner had asserted that he planned to strip CBS down to its barest assets, he was assailed as a destroyer of sacred icons. But Tisch had turned what had seemed like a gross act of disrespect into a legitimate, indeed shrewd business technique. Tisch was trying to keep CBS among the giants of the industry— and to do so, paradoxically, he had to slim CBS down much as a boxer would do to get into fighting shape. To be sure, CBS was still very much a heavyweight in the communications industry. It had come a long way from that "mere shoestring," a description that seemed so terribly apt in its early days when survival was indeed a burning issue. And here it was in the fall of 1987, its revenues the previous nine months reaching $3.25 billion. If it seemed to be faltering, it was not sputtering, and certainly not in any danger of demise.

Precisely why the company had faltered in the mid-1980s was, of course, a subject open to dispute. The most likely explanation for CBS's difficulties was the mishandling of the Ted Turner takeover threat. Taking him seriously had, according to some, caused CBS to shoot itself in the foot, to do itself damage that was needless. Yet, if one wanted to search more deeply for the roots of CBS's problems, one had to look no further, said others, than founder Bill Paley himself. His unwillingness to turn over the leadership of the company to anyone else left CBS without decisive management for the better part of the last two decades. Management CBS had, but not the kind which had the capability of making far-reaching decisions, or any decisions for that matter which ran counter to the wishes and convictions of Bill Paley.

To a large extent, the Paley problem, if one could call it that, seemed to be passing, seemed to be no longer a stumbling block during Larry Tisch's period of leadership. Whether it was a product of Paley's age or Tisch's leadership abilities—or perhaps a combination of both—by the fall of 1987, the company had begun to act as if the post-Paley era had already taken hold.

And so sixty years later, there was still the pride and still the pursuit of excellence, and still the conviction that CBS could only be CBS if it outperformed all others. There were gloomy faces, for example, when in December 1987, NBC's Tom Brokaw had obtained a coveted exclusive interview with the Soviet leader Mikhail Gorbachev—and CBS's Dan Rather had not. But mixed with the gloom was a tinge of pride within the CBS News Division that it had been Dan Rather's tough question at a Gorbachev news conference some time before, that had lost the network the interview. CBS may have lost out on the interview, but it had been doing its job.

As it entered 1988, CBS remained a major newsmaker. First there was CBS Sports' headline-grabbing dismissal of Jimmy "the Greek" Snyder for comments he made during an interview on January 15. The 69 year-old analyst-oddsmaker had been asked by a local television reporter, Ed Hotaling, for his thoughts on the progress blacks had made in sports. The setting for the interview was Duke Zeibert's restaurant in Washington, D. C. The occasion: Martin Luther King's birthday. After noting that blacks dominated most major sports, Jimmy added, "If they take over coaching like everybody wants them to, there's not going to be anything left for the white people." He then suggested that blacks owed their athletic superiority to the white man's genetic breeding during the slavery era. "The slave owner," said Snyder, "would breed his big black to his big woman, so that he could have a big black kid, you see." CBS Sports fired Jimmy from his estimated $500,000 a year job on the network's "The NFL Today." Quickly apologizing, Snyder won some unexpected support from important black personalities. "The man apologized," said Democratic presidential candidate Jesse Jackson. "That's all a human can do." (33)

Ten days later, on January 25, came Dan Rather's controversial interview with Vice President George Bush, who at the time was running for the Presidency. After the heated exchange between the two men, some asked whether Rather would feel compelled to apologize. A few even demanded the anchorman's resignation. What caused all the fuss?

Rather opened his CBS program that evening with a six-minute report on Bush's role in the Iran-Contra affair. Until then, the Vice President had appeared evasive when asked why he had supported the secret sale of arms to Iran. As the live, nine-minute interview got under way, Bush assailed Rather for allegedly duping him into believing that he was to be merely the subject of a "political profile" and would not be grilled exclusively on the Iran-Contra matter—and for appearing to suggest that Bush had misstated the truth previously in answer to Iran-Contra questions. But Rather persisted, leading Bush to say, "There's nothing new here. I thought this was a news program. You've impugned my integrity by suggesting . . . that I didn't tell the truth . . . "

Rather: "One third of Republicans in this poll . . . believe you're hiding something."

Bush: "I am hiding something. You know what I'm hiding? What I told the President—that's the only thing. I've answered every question put before me. Now, if you have a question, what is it?"

Rather: "I do have one. You said if you had known that this was an arms for hostages swap, you would have opposed it."

Bush: "I went along because I heard about Mr. (William) Buckley (a CIA officer) being tortured to death. So if I erred, I erred on the side of trying to get those hostages out of there."

At one stage, Rather asserted that "Bush had made us hypocrites in the face of the world. How could you sign on to such a policy?" It was an accusation that would haunt Rather later. Bush's reply: "I signed on to it, for the same reason that the President signed on to it. When a CIA agent is being tortured to death, maybe you err on the side of human life. But everybody has admitted mistakes. I've admitted mistakes. And you want to dwell on them."

Toward the end of the interview, Bush insisted that "It's not fair to judge my whole career by a rehash on Iran. How would you like it if I judge your career by those seven minutes when you walked off the set? Would you like that?" Referring to Rather's exit from the set in Miami the previous September, Bush managed to catch the anchorman off guard. Still, Rather replied, "Mr. Vice President . . . your qualifications for president and what kind of leadership you'd bring the country . . . is much more important than what you just referred to."

Rather asked Bush, "Are you willing to go to a news conference, before the Iowa caucuses, and answer questions from all comers?"

Bush: "I've been answering questions, I've been to 86 news conferences since March . . . "

Rather, cutting the Vice President off in mid-sentence, said: "I gather the answer is no. Thank you very much for being with us, Mr. Vice President."

After the interview, CBS affiliates around the nation were flooded with calls, most complaining that Dan Rather had been disrespectful. Bush's people were ecstatic. They felt that their man had, thanks to Rather's aggressive tone and Bush's answers, had laid to rest once and for all the Vice President's image of being a wimp. Campaigning in Wyoming the following day, Bush said the interview was "kind of like combat" but he added that he had no hard feelings about it. "I don't want to have a big running fight with Dan Rather or anybody else," he said.

But CBS people were livid, convinced that Bush had baited a trap for Dan Rather. Appearing on the ABC *Nightline* program, CBS New Producer Richard Cohen said the day after the Rather-Bush confrontation that Bush had had a game strategy all along for the interview: "George Bush sat there before the interview and when he heard Iran-Contra he muttered audibly, 'If I hear Iran-Contra, he's going to hear Miami.' This was all planned."

Rather took the defensive after the interview. He won support from his immediate boss, CBS News President Howard Stringer, who said, "That's what Dan Rather does for a living. That's what a great reporter does for a living." But the anchorman came in for heavy criticism from his own colleges for going beyond the bounds of aggressive journalism. As ABC's White House correspondent, Sam Donaldson said: "Rather went too far. He had a legitimate reason to try to press Bush. But in the give and take of these things I don't think we can get to a situation where we make—on our own authority—accusations." (34)

Insisting that he had not been rude to the Vice President, Rather offered an unusual "personal word" on the next day's "CBS Evening News." He acknowledged that viewers might have been made "uncomfortable" and said that the abrupt ending to the interview wasn't "done as gracefully" as he had intended. "However," he went on, "it may seem at any given time, the intention of even persistent questioning in a spirited interview is to do an honest, honorable job. The fact that more attention is sometimes given to the heat than the light is regrettable, but it goes with the territory."

The Rather-Bush exchange was treated as a mixture of open warfare and lively theater. Rather's strident tones and his seeming disrespect for the Vice President fed ammunition to media critics who have long believed that television newsmen were too arrogant. Yet, the Rather interview appeared likely to serve as one of the major highlights of the Presidential campaign, a moment when the Republican front-runner was put to his most severe public test. And that, as Dan Rather said repeatedly after the interview, was what journalism was all about. It was, in many ways, what CBS was all about as well. Certainly as far as Rather and CBS were concerned, the interview underlined what the anchorman had articulately suggested in that *New York Times* article when he had written that working for CBS in the 1980s meant striving to reach the heights of an Ed Murrow, and not making due with mediocrity.

In an ironic footnote to the Rather-Bush incident, Frank Stanton recalled that Richard Salant, at the time President of CBS News, as early as 1976, had issued a policy statement banning live interviews over The CBS Evening News Program. That policy statement included the following: "All interviews, unless on a live broadcast or an interview broadcast pretaped to time, are subject to editing, and no CBS News Employee should represent to an interview subject that the interview will be carried in full and be unedited."

It may have been the case that CBS has subsequently changed that policy. However, there was no indication immediately after the controvercial interview with Bush that the network had indeed altered its policy.

BIBLIOGRAPHY

Andrews, Bart, and Ahrgus Juilliard, *Holy Mackerel!: The Amos 'n' Andy Story.* New York: E. P. Dutton, 1986.

Barnouw, Erik, *The Sponsor: Notes on a Modern Potentate.* Oxford, England: Oxford University Press, 1978.

Barnouw, Erik, *Tube of Plenty: The Evolution of American Television.* New York: Oxford University Press, 1975.

Barnouw, Erik, *The Image Empire: A History of Broadcasting in the United States,* Volume 3 *From 1953.* New York: Oxford University Press, 1970.

Barnouw, Erik, *The Golden Web: A History of Broadcasting in the United States.* Volume 2, *1933 to 1953.* New York: Oxford University Press, 1968.

Barnouw, Erik, *A Tower in Babel: A History of Broadcasting in the United States,* Volume 1, *To 1933.* New York: Oxford University Press, 1966.

Barrett, Marvin, ed., *Moments of Truth?* New York: Thomas Y. Crowell, 1975.

Bedell, Sally, *Up the Tube: Prime-Time TV and the Silverman Years.* New York: Viking Press, 1981.

Bergreen, Laurence, *Look Now, Pay Later, The Rise of Network Broadcasting.* Garden City, N.Y.: Doubleday & Co., 1980.

Bilby, Kenneth, *The General: David Sarnoff and the Rise of the Communications Industry.* New York: Harper & Row, 1986.

Bliss, Edward, Jr., ed., *In Search of Light: The Broadcasts of Edward R. Murrow, 1938–1961.* New York: Alfred A. Knopf, 1967.

Blythe, Cheryl, and Susan Sackett, *Say Goodnight, Gracie!: The Story of Burns & Allen.* New York: E. P. Dutton, 1986.

Brewin, Bob, and Sydney Shaw, *Vietnam on Trial: Westmoreland Vs. CBS.* New York: Atheneum, 1987.

Brown, Les, *Television: The Business Behind the Box.* New York: Harcourt Brace Jovanovich, 1971.

Castleman, Harry, and Walter J. Podrazik, *Four Decades of American Television.* New York: McGraw-Hill, 1982.

Comstock, George, *Television in America.* Beverly Hills, Calif.: Sage, 1980.

Diamond, Edwin, *Sign off: The Last Days of Television.* Cambridge, Mass.: The M.I.T. Press, 1982.

Diamond, Edwin, *Good News, Bad News.* Cambridge, Mass.: The M.I.T. Press, 1978.

Diamond, Edwin, *The Tin Kazoo.* Cambridge, Mass.: The M.I.T. Press, 1975.

Emery, Edwin, and Michael Emery, *The Press and America: An Interpretative History of the Mass Media.* Englewood Cliffs, N.J.: Prentice Hall, 1954.

Epstein, Edward Jay, *News from Nowhere: Television and the News.* New York: Random House, 1973.

Friendly, Fred, *Due to Circumstances Beyond Our Control . . . .* New York: Random House, 1967.

Gates, Gary Paul, *Air Time: The Inside Story of CBS News.* New York: Harper & Row, 1978.

Gelfman, Judith S., *Women in Television News.* New York: Columbia University Press, 1974.

Gitlin, Todd, *Inside Prime Time.* New York: Pantheon, 1983.

Goldman, Albert, *Elvis.* New York: McGraw-Hill, 1981.

Goldmark, Peter C., and Lee Edson, *Maverick Inventor: My Turbulent Years at CBS.* New York: Saturday Review Press/E. P. Dutton, 1973.

Green, Timothy, *The Universal Eye: The World of Television.* New York: Stein and Day, 1972.

Halberstam, David, *The Powers That Be.* New York: Alfred A. Knopf, 1979.

Harris, Michael David, *Always on Sunday: Ed Sullivan: An Inside View.* New York: Meredith Press, 1968.

Hewitt, Don, *Minute by Minute . . . .* New York: Random House, 1985.

Johnston, Moira, *Takeover: The New Wall Street Warriors: The Men, The Money, The Impact.* New York: A Belvedere Book, Arbor House, 1986.

Kendrick, Alexander, *Prime Time: The Life of Edward R. Murrow.* Boston: Little Brown, 1969.

Leonard, Bill, *In the Storm of the Eye: A Lifetime at CBS.* New York: G. P. Putnam, 1987.

Lichty, Lawrence W., and Malachi G. Topping. *American Broadcasting: A Source Book on the History of Radio and Television.* New York: Hastings House, 1975.

MacNeil, Robert, *The Influence of Television on American Politics.* New York: Harper & Row, 1968.

Madsen, Axel, *60 Minutes: The Power & the Politics of America's Most Popular TV News Show.* New York: Dodd, Mead, 1984.

Manchester, William, *The Glory and the Dream: A Narrative History of America, 1932–1972.* Boston: Little, Brown, 1974.

Matusow, Barbara, *The Evening Stars: The Making of the Network News Anchor.* Boston: Houghton Mifflin, 1983.

Mayer, Martin, *Making News.* Garden City, N.Y.: Doubleday & Co., 1987.

McCabe, Peter, *Bad News at Black Rock: The Sell-Out of CBS News.* New York: Arbor House, 1987.

Metz, Robert, *CBS: Reflections in a Bloodshot Eye.* Chicago: Playboy Press, 1975.

Mickelson, Sig, *The Electric Mirror: Politics in an Age of Television.* New York: Dodd, Mead, 1972.

Morella, Joe, and Edward Z. Epstein, *Forever Lucy: The Life of Lucille Ball.* Secaucus, N.J.: Lyle Stuart, 1986.

O'Connor, John E., ed., *American History, American Television: Interpreting the Video Past.* New York: Frederick Ungar, 1983.

Paley, William S., *As It Happened: A Memoir.* Garden City, N.Y.: Doubleday & Co., 1979.

Paper, Lewis J., *Empire: William S. Paley and the Making of CBS.* New York: St. Martin's Press, 1987.

Quinn, Sally, *We're Going to Make You a Star.* New York: Simon & Schuster, 1975.

Rather, Dan, with Mickey Herskowitz, *The Camera Never Blinks: Adventures of a TV Journalist.* New York: William Morrow, 1977.

Read, William H., *America's Mass Media Merchants.* Baltimore: The Johns Hopkins University Press, 1976.

Reasoner, Harry, *Before the Colors Fade.* New York: Alfred A. Knopf, 1981.

Reel, A. Frank, *The Networks: How They Stole the Show.* New York: Scribners, 1979.

Rivers, William L., *The Other Government: Power & the Washington Media.* New York: Universe Books, 1982.

Schoenbrun, David, *America Inside Out.* New York: McGraw-Hill, 1984.

Schorr, Daniel, *Clearing the Air.* Boston: Houghton Mifflin, 1977.

Sevareid, Eric, *Not So Wild a Dream.* New York: Atheneum, 1976.

Shayon, Robert Lewis, ed., *Walter Cronkite, Television and the News, The Eighth Art: Twenty-three Views of Television Today.* New York: Holt, Rinehart and Winston, 1962.

Shirer, William L., *The Nightmare Years, 1930–1940, A Memoir of a Life and the Times.* Boston: Little, Brown, 1984.

Shurkin, Joel, *Engines of the Mind.* New York: W. W. Norton, 1984.

Smith, R. Franklin, *Edward R. Murrow: The War Years.* Kalamazoo, Michigan: New Issues Press, 1978.

Steel, Ronald, *Walter Lippmann and the American Century.* Boston: Little, Brown, an Atlantic Monthly Press Book, 1980.

Stoler, Peter, *The War Against the Press: Politics, Pressure and Intimidation in the 80's.* New York: Dodd, Mead, 1986.

Tebbel, John, *The Media in America.* New York: Thomas Y. Crowell, 1974.

Thomas, Dana L., *The Media Moguls: From Joseph Pulitzer to William S. Paley: Their Lives and Boisterous Times.* New York: G. P. Putnam, 1981.

Thomas, Lowell, *Good Evening Everybody: From Cripple Creek to Samarkand.* New York: William Morrow, 1976.

Wallace, Mike, and Gary Paul Gates, *Close Encounters.* New York: William Morrow, 1984.

Westin, Av, *Newswatch: How TV Decides the News.* New York: Simon & Schuster, 1982.

Yellin, David G., *Special: Fred Freed and the Television Documentary.* New York: Macmillan, 1972.

FOOTNOTES

CHAPTER 1

1. William S. Paley, *As It Happened: A Memoir* (Garden City, N.Y.: Doubleday & Co., 1979), p. 32.
2. Columbia University Oral History Project, interview with Arthur Judson, p. 7.
3. *Radio Broadcast*, December 1927, pp. 140–141.
4. Quoted in Laurence Bergreen, *Look Now, Pay Later: The Rise of Network Broadcasting* (Garden City, N.Y.: Doubleday & Co., 1980), p. 49.
5. Paley, *As It Happened*, p.34.
6. Ibid., pp. 36–37.
7. *Fortune*, June 1935.
8. Peter C. Goldmark, and Lee Edson, *Maverick Investor: My Turbulent Years at CBS* (New York: Saturday Review Press/E. P. Dutton, 1973), p. 4.
9. Paley, *As It Happened*, p. 43.
10. Ibid., p. 53.
11. The Paley-Lee encounter is described in detail in Paley, *As It Happened*, pp. 49–52.
12. Ibid., pp. 18–19.

CHAPTER 2

1. William S. Paley, *As It Happened: A Memoir* (Garden City, N.Y.: Doubleday & Co., 1979), p. 331.
2. Ibid., p. 66.
3. Ibid., p. 66.
4. William L. Shirer, *The Nightmare Years, 1930–1940, A Memoir of a Life and the Times* (Boston: Little, Brown, 1984), p. 414.
5. Quoted in A. M. Sperber, *Murrow: His Life and Times* (New York: Freundlich Books, 1986), p. 85.
6. Lowell Thomas, *Good Evening Everybody: From Cripple Creek to Samarkand* (New York: William Morrow, 1976), p. 307.
7. Ibid., p. 308.
8. Erik Barnouw, *A Tower in Babel: A History of Broadcasting in the United States,* Volume 1, *To 1933* (New York: Oxford University Press, 1966), p. 248.
9. William Manchester, *The Glory and the Dream: A Narrative History of America, 1932–1972* (Boston: Little, Brown, 1974), Bantam paperback edition, p. 972.
10. This story was recounted to the author in an interview with Ernest Leiser, August 10, 1987.
11. Columbia University Oral History Project, interview with H. V. Kaltenborn, p. 169.
12. Martin Mayer, *Making News* (Garden City, N.Y.: Doubleday & Co., 1987), pp. 111–112.
13. Quoted in Alexander Kendrick, *Prime Time: The Life of Edward R. Murrow* (Boston: Little, Brown, 1969), p. 161.
14. Paley, *As It Happened,* p. 2.
15. Ibid.

CHAPTER 3

1. Columbia University Oral History project, interview with H. V. Kaltenborn, pp. 191–192.
2. Ibid.
3. Ibid., p. 193.
4. Ibid., pp. 193–94.
5. Ibid., p. 194.
6. Alexander Kendrick, *Prime Time: The Life of Edward R. Murrow* (Boston: Little, Brown, 1969), p. 138.
7. Ibid., p. 139.
8. Quoted in David Halberstam, *The Powers That Be* (New York: Alfred A. Knopf, 1979), Dell paperback edition, pp. 64–65.
9. William L. Shirer, *The Nightmare Years, 1930–1940, A Memoir of a Life and the Times* (Boston: Little, Brown, 1984), p. 284.
10. Quoted in A. M. Sperber, *Murrow: His Life and Times* (New York: Freundlich books, 1986), p. 115.

11. William S. Paley, *As It Happened: A Memoir* (Garden City, N.Y.: Doubleday & Co., 1979), p. 131.
12. Shirer, *The Nightmare Years,* p. 304.

CHAPTER 4

1. Columbia University Oral History project, interview with H. V. Kaltenborn, p. 201.
2. Ibid., p. 202.
3. Alexander Kendrick, *Prime Time: The Life of Edward R. Murrow* (Boston: Little, Brown, 1969), pp. 165.
4. William S. Paley, *As It Happened: A Memoir* (Garden City, N.Y.: Doubleday & Co., 1979), pp. 134–135.
5. Columbia University Oral History project, interview with Howard Barlow, p. 133.
6. Quoted on ABC's "One World" television program, July 23, 1987.
7. Martin Mayer, *Making News,* (Garden City, N.Y.: Doubleday & Co., 1978), pp. 109–10.
8. *Time,* November 7, 1938.
9. Quoted on "One World," July 23, 1987.
10. Quoted in Laurence Bergreen, *Look Now, Pay Later: The Rise of Network Broadcasting* (Garden City, N.Y.: Doubleday & Co., 1980), p. 89.

CHAPTER 5

1. Quoted in William S. Paley, *As It Happened: A Memoir* (Garden City, N.Y.: Doubleday & Co., 1979), p. 136.
2. Alexander Kendrick, *Prime Time: The Life of Edward R. Murrow* (Boston: Little Brown, 1969), p. 189.
3. William L. Shirer, *The Nightmare Years, 1930–1940, A Memoir of a Life and the Times* (Boston: Little, Brown, 1984), p. 457.
4. Eric Sevareid, *Not So Wild a Dream* (New York: Atheneum, 1976), p. 11.
5. Shirer, *The Nightmare Years,* p. 539.
6. Ibid., p. 595.
7. Kendrick, *Prime Time,* p. 174.
8. Quoted in a profile of Larry LeSueur, *Current Biography Yearbook,* Ed. Charles Moritz, H. W. Wilson Co., New York, 1943.
9. Kendrick, *Prime Time,* p. 238.
10. Quoted in A. M. Sperber, *Murrow: His Life and Times* (New York: Freundlich Books, 1986), p. 207.
11. Goldmark, Peter C., and Lee Edson, *Maverick Inventor: My Turbulent Years at CBS* (New York: Saturday Review Press/E. P. Dutton, 1973), p. 55.
12. Paley, *As It Happened,* p.162.
13. Kendrick, *Prime Time,* p. 266.

CHAPTER 6

1. Quoted in David Schoenbrun, *America Inside Out* (New York: McGraw-Hill, 1984), paperback edition, p. 165.
2. William S. Paley, *As It Happened: A Memoir* (Garden City, N.Y.: Doubleday & Co., 1979), p. 173.
3. Ibid., p. 173.
4. Schoenbrun, *America Inside Out*, p. 207.
5. Interview with Av Westin, July 8, 1987.
6. Ibid.
7. Anectode recounted in A. M. Sperber, *Murrow: His Life and Times* (New York: Freundlich Books, 1986), p. 302.
8. Quoted in ibid., p. 311.
9. Ibid.
10. Paley, *As It Happened*, pp. 174–75.
11. Ibid., p. 195.
12. Ibid., p. 200.
13. Ibid., p. 201.
14. Ibid., p. 200.
15. William Manchester, *The Glory and the Dream: A Narrative History of America, 1932–1972* (Boston: Little, Brown, 1974), Bantam paperback edition, p. 973.
16. Goldmark, Peter C., and Lee Edson, *Maverick Inventor: My Turbulent Years at CBS,* (New York: Saturday Review Press/E. P. Dutton, 1973), p. 142.
17. Interview with Douglas Edwards, August 5, 1987.
18. Ibid.
19. Ibid.
20. Kendrick, *Prime Time*, p. 318.
21. *The New York Times,* July 18, 1948.
22. Gary Paul Gates, *Air Time: The Inside Story of CBS News* (New York: Harper & Row, 1978), p. 55.
23. Interview with Douglas Edwards, August 5, 1987.
24. Ibid.
25. Michael David Harris, *Always on Sunday: Ed Sullivan: An Inside View* (New York: Meredith Press, 1968), p. 159.
26. Ibid., p. 84.
27. Interview with Fred Friendly, August 12, 1987.
28. Ibid.
29. Ibid.
30. Ibid.
31. David G. Yellin, *Special: Fred Freed and the Television Documentary* (New York: Macmillan, 1972), p. 19.
32. Interview with Fred Friendly, August 12, 1987.

CHAPTER 7

1. David Halberstam, *The Powers That Be* (New York: Alfred A. Knopf, 1979), Dell paperback edition, pp. 196.

2. Alexander Kendrick, *Prime Time: The Life of Edward R. Murrow* (Boston: Little, Brown, 1969), p. 321.
3. Bill Leonard, *In the Storm of the Eye: A Lifetime at CBS* (New York: G. P. Putnam, 1987), p. 70.
4. William S. Paley, *As It Happened: A Memoir* (Garden City, N.Y.: Doubleday & Co., 1979), p. 281.
5. Interview with Frank Stanton, July 20, 1987.
6. David Schoenbrun, *America Inside Out* (New York: McGraw-Hill, 1984), paperback edition, pp. 266–67.
7. Kendrick, *Prime Time,* p. 328.
8. Ibid., p. 327.
9. Columbia University Oral History project, interview with Fred Friendly, p.17.
10. William Manchester, *The Glory and the Dream: A Narrative History of America, 1932–1972* (Boston: Little, Brown, 1974), Bantam paperback edition, p. 585.
11. Crosby's letter is quoted in Paley, *As It Happened,* p. 231.
12. Paley, *As It Happened,* p. 232.
13. Joe Morella and Edward Z. Epstein, *Forever Lucy: The Life of Lucille Ball* (Secaucus, N.J.: Lyle Stuart, 1986), p. 111.
14. Ibid., p. 116
15. Erik Barnouw, *The Image Empire: A History of Broadcasting in the United States,* Volume 3, *From 1953* (New York: Oxford University Press, 1966), p. 23.
16. Interview with Michael Dann, July 15, 1987.
17. Ibid.
18. David G. Yellin, *Special: Fred Freed and the Television Documentary* (New York: Macmillan, 1972), p. 26.
19. *Time,* September 30, 1957.
20. Kendrick, *Prime Time,* p. 335.
21. Interview with Daniel Schorr, February 18, 1987.
22. Interview with Fred Friendly, August 12, 1987.
23. John E. O'Connor, ed., *American History, American Television: Interpreting the Video Past* (New York: Frederick Ungar, 1983), p. 7.
24. Kendrick, *Prime Time,* p. 337.
25. Columbia University Oral History project, interview with Fred Friendly, p. 9.
26. Ibid., p. 10.
27. Sig Mickelson, *The Electric Mirror: Politics in an Age of Television* (New York: Dodd, Mead, 1972), p. 98.
28. *Time,* October 14, 1966.
29. Ibid.
30. Recounted in Joel Shurkin, *Engines of the Mind* (New York: W. W. Norton, 1984), pp. 250–53.
31. This anectode appears in Gary Paul Gates, *Air Time: The Inside Story of CBS News* (New York: Harper & Row, 1978), pp. 68–69.
32. Interview with Daniel Schorr, February 18, 1987.

CHAPTER 8

1. Interview with Fred Friendly, August 18, 1987.
2. Fred Friendly, *Due to Circumstances Beyond Our Control . . .* (New York: Vintage Books, 1967), p. 10.

3. Ibid.
4. Erik Barnouw, *The Image Empire: A History of Broadcasting in the United States,* Volume 3, *From 1953* (New York: Oxford University Press, 1966), p. 51.
5. Interview with Fred Friendly, August 18, 1987.
6. William S. Paley, *As It Happened: A Memoir* (Garden City, N.Y.: Doubleday & Co., 1979), p. 284.
7. David Halberstam, *The Powers That Be* (New York: Alfred A. Knopf, 1979), Dell paperback editions, p. 210.
8. Friendly, *Due to Circumstances Beyond Our Control,* p. 36.
9. These reactions to the Murrow broadcast are quoted in A. H. Sperber, *Murrow: His Life and Times* (New York: Freundlich Books, 1986), p. 419.
10. Columbia University Oral History project, interview with Fred Friendly, p. 43.
11. Interview with Fred Friendly, August 12, 1987.
12. Interview with Ernest Leiser, August 10, 1987.
13. Interview with Daniel Schorr, February 18, 1987.
14. Ibid.
15. Daniel Schorr, *Clearing the Air* (Boston: Houghton Mifflin, 1977), p. 5.
16. Harry Reasoner, *Before the Colors Fade* (New York: Alfred A. Knopf, 1981), p. 12.
17. Ibid., p. 24.
18. Ibid., p. 39.
19. Ibid., p. 40.
20. *Time,* September 30, 1957.
21. The material about the secret CBS campaign comes from Sperber, *Murrow: His Life and Times,* pp. 54–55.

CHAPTER 9

1. Interview with George Schweitzer, July 27, 1987.
2. Interview with Michael Dann, July 15, 1987.
3. David Halberstam, *The Powers That Be* (New York: Alfred A. Knopf, 1979), Dell paperback edition, pp. 354–55.
4. William S. Paley, *As It Happened: A Memoir* (Garden City, N.Y.: Doubleday & Co., 1979), p. 251.
5. Quoted in Lawrence Bergreen, *Look Now, Pay Later: The Rise of Network Broadcasting* (Garden City, N.Y.: Doubleday & Co., 1986), p. 215.
6. Erik Barnouw, *Tube of Plenty: The Evolution of American Television* (New York: Oxford University Press, 1975), p. 307.
7. Quoted in Fred Friendly, *Due to Circumstances Beyond Our Control . . .* (New York: Vintage Books, 1967), p. xi–xii.
8. Quoted in Bergreen, *Look Now, Pay Later,* p. 215.
9. Interview with Daniel Schorr, February 18, 1987.
10. Interview with Frank Stanton, July 20, 1987.
11. The story of the Lippmann interviews is told in Ronald Steel, *Walter Lippmann and the American Century* (Boston: Little, Brown, 1980), pp. 516–17.
12. Interview with Ernest Leiser, August 10, 1987.

13. Interview with Burton "Bud" Benjamin, July 20, 1987.
14. Walter Cronkite, "Television and the News," in Robert Lewis Shayon, ed., *The Eighth Art: Twenty-three Views of Television Today* (New York: Holt, Rinehart, and Winston, 1962), p. 238.
15. Barbara Matusow, *The Evening Stars: The Making of the Network News Anchor* (Boston: Houghton Mifflin, 1983), p. 111.
16. *Time*, September 10, 1973.
17. A copy of this memo was given to the author by Ernest Leiser.
18. This account is taken from David Schoenbrun, *America Inside Out* (New York: McGraw-Hill, 1984), paperback edition, pp. 347–60.
19. This anecdote is recounted in Dan Rather, with Mickey Herskowitz, *The Camera Never Blinks: Adventures of a TV Journalist* (New York: William Morrow, 1977), Ballantine Books paperback edition, p. 65.
20. Rather's activities during the Kennedy assassination are recounted in his *The Camera Never Blinks*, pp. 117–38.
21. Interview with Fred Friendly, August 12, 1987.
22. Interview with Frank Stanton, July 20, 1987.
23. Ibid.
24. Ibid.
25. Ibid.

CHAPTER 10

1. Quoted in William S. Paley, *As It Happened: A Memoir* (Garden City, N.Y.: Doubleday & Co., 1979), p. 343.
2. Ibid., p. 338.
3. Harry Reasoner, *Before the Colors Fade* (New York: Alfred A. Knopf, 1981), p. 132.
4. Bill Leonard, In *The Storm of the Eye: A Lifetime at CBS* (New York: G. P. Putnam, 1987), p.102.
5. *Time*, March 13, 1964.
6. Daniel Schorr, *Clearing the Air* (Boston: Houghton Mifflin, 1977), p. 9.
7. Ibid., pp. 10–11.
8. *Time*, October 14, 1966.
9. Columbia University Oral History project, interview with Fred Friendly, pp. 29–30.
10. Ibid.
11. Fred Friendly, *Due to Circumstances Beyond Our Control . . .* (New York: Vintage Books, 1967), p. 244.
12. Interview with Fred Friendly, August 18, 1987.
13. Interview with Frank Stanton, July 20, 1987.
14. Gary Paul Gates, *Air Time: The Inside Story of CBS News* (New York: Harper & Row, 1978), p. 176.
15. Interview with Sam Roberts, July 22, 1987.
16. John E. O'Connor, ed., *American History, American Television: Interpreting the Video Past* (New York: Frederick Ungar, 1983), p. 179.

17. The Wallace incident is recounted in Mike Wallace and Gary Paul Gates, *Close Encounters* (New York: William Morrow, 1984) Berkley Books paperback edition, pp. 119–20.
18. Don Hewitt, *Minute by Minute* . . . (New York: Random House, 1985), pp. 25–26.
19. Wallace and Gates, *Close Encounters,* p.107.
20. Hewitt, *Minute by Minute* . . . , p. 31.
21. Interview with Burton "Bud" Benjamin, July 20, 1987.
22. Interview with Robert "Shad" Northshield, August 11, 1987.
23. *Playboy,* March 1985.
24. Ibid.
25. Interview with Burton "Bud" Benjamin, July 20, 1987.

CHAPTER 11

1. Interview with Mike Dann, July 27, 1987.
2. Les Brown, *Television: The Business Behind the Box* (New York: Harcourt Brace Jovanovich, 1971), p. 56.
3. Interview with Norman Lear, May 6, 1987.
4. Todd Gitlin, *Inside Prime Time* (New York: Pantheon, 1983), p. 217.
5. Ibid., p. 217.
6. John E. O'Connor, ed., *American History, American Television: Interpreting the Video Past* (New York: Frederick Unger, 1983), p. 262.
7. Interview with Ernest Leiser, August 10, 1987.
8. John Tebbel, *The Media in America* (New York: Thomas Y. Crowell, 1974), p. 390.
9. Timothy Green, *The Universal Eye: The World of Television* (New York: Stein and Day, 1972), p. 33.
10. Interview with Ernest Leiser, August 10, 1987.
11. The Leonard-Safer conversation is quoted in Don Hewitt, *Minute by Minute* . . . (New York: Random House, 1985), p. 43.
12. This exchange is quoted in Dan Rather, with Mickey Herskowitz, *The Camera Never Blinks: Adventures of a TV Journalist* (New York: William Morrow, 1977), Ballantine Books paperback edition, pp. 248–49.
13. David Halberstam, *The Powers That Be* (New York: Alfred A. Knopf, 1979), Dell paperback edition, p. 977.
14. William S. Paley, *As It Happened: A Memoir* (Garden City, N.Y.: Doubleday & Co., 1979), p. 318.
15. Interview with David Buksbaum, August 7, 1987.
16. As noted in Gary Paul Gates, *Air Time: The Inside Story of CBS News* (New York: Harper & Row, 1978), p. 314.
17. Interview with Mike Dann, July 15,1987.
18. The Wallace-Hewitt visit to Johnson's ranch is recounted in Mike Wallace and Gary Paul Gates, *Close Encounters* (New York: William Morrow, 1984), pp. 152–56.
19. Gates, *Air Time,* p. 414.

20. Erik Barnouw, *The Sponsor: Notes on a Modern Potentate* (Oxford, England: Oxford University Press, 1978), p.137.
21. Interview with Mike Dann, July 15, 1987.
22. Quoted in Bill Leonard, *In the Storm of the Eye: A Lifetime at CBS* (New York: G. P. Putnam's Sons, 1987), p. 28.
23. Paley, *As It Happened,* p. 2.
24. *People* magazine, April 9, 1979.

CHAPTER 12

1. Edwin Diamond, *Sign off: The Last Days of Television* (Cambridge, Mass.: The M.I.T. Press, 1982), p. 67.
2. Quoted in Barbara Matusow, *The Evening Stars: The Making of the Network News Anchor* (Boston: Houghton Mifflin, 1983), p. 256.
3. Interview with Fred Friendly, August 18, 1987.
4. Ibid.
5. Interview with Ernest Leiser, August 10, 1987.
6. Interview with Sam Roberts, July 22, 1987.
7. Interview with Bruno Wassertheil, February 4, 1987.
8. Bill Leonard, *In the Storm of the Eye: A Lifetime at CBS* (New York: G. P. Putnam's Sons, 1987), p. 231.
9. Interview with Ernest Leiser, August 10, 1987.
10. Interview with Fred Friendly, August 18, 1987.
11. Interview with David Boies, August 12, 1987.
12. Ibid.
13. Leonard, *In the Storm of the Eye,* p. 222.
14. *The New York Times,* October 16, 1981.
15. Quoted in *Current Biography,* 1983.
16. Quoted in *The Wall Street Journal,* April 12, 1985.
17. Ibid.
18. Moira Johnston, *Takeover: The New Wall Street Warriors: The Men, The Money, The Impact* (New York: A Belvedere Book, Arbor House, 1986), p. 126.
19. *Time,* April 29, 1985.
20. *Time,* July 15, 1985.
21. *Fortune,* August 5, 1985.
22. *Time,* October 28, 1985.
23. *The Wall Street Journal,* October 2, 1985.
24. *Time,* October 28, 1985.
25. According to a CBS proxy statement quoted in *The New York Times,* April 7, 1987.
26. Ibid.
27. *The New York Times,* September 15, 1986.
28. *USA Today,* March 11, 1987.
29. *Time,* March 23, 1987.
30. *USA Today,* March 11, 1987.
31. Interview with David Buksbaum, August 7, 1987.
32. *USA Today,* September 18, 1987.
33. *People* magazine, February 1, 1988.
34. *USA Today,* January 27, 1988.

INDEX

Fromson, Murray, 231
"Frontier Justice," 187
Fulbright, J. William, 262
"Funny Face," 258

G

Gallop, George, 171
Garland, Judy, 240
Garment, Len, 246
Gates, Gary, 237
Gavin, Lt. Gen. James, 233
Gelbert, Larry, 259
"General Electric Theater," 179
George Phyllis, 312
Gershwin, George, 27, 36
"Get Smart," 252
Gibbons, Floyd, 32–34
Gleason Jackie, 130, 147, 150, 200, 227, 256
"The Glen Campbell Goodtime Hour," 200, 254
Godfrey, Arthur, 114, 122, 131, 144, 148–51, 200
Goebels, Joseph, 60
"The Goldbergs," 16, 136
Golden, Marc, 255
"Golden Hour of the Little Flower," 43–44
Goldmark, Peter, 13, 36–38, 96–97, 118–20, 152
Goldwater, Barry, 230–31
"Gomer Pyle, U.S.M.C.," 197, 227, 255
"Good Times," 255
Goodman, Benny, 132
Goodman, Tom, 319
Goodson, Mark, 206
Gorbachev, Mikhail, 322
Gosden, Freeman, 16, 115, 144
Gould, Jack, 157, 174, 192, 290
Gould, Stanhope, 280–81
Goulet, Robert, 132

Graham, Billy, 171
Graham, Fred, 292, 315
Graham, Katherine, 269
Grandin, Thomas, 83–84, 100
Grant, B. Donald, 319
"Green Acres," 200, 255
Greene, Hugh C., 203
Griffith, Andy, 227
Gude, Jap, 55, 133, 142
"Gunsmoke," 198, 227, 254, 279

H

Hagerty, Jim, 206
Halberstam, David, 196, 283
Haldeman, H. R., 266
Hammerstein, Oscar, 130
Hankin, Dan, 264
Hard, William, 34
Hartley, Mariette, 321
"Harvest of Shame," 202–3
"Have Gun—Will Travel," 187
Hayes, Arthur Hull, 122
"He and She," 227
"The Health Show," 321
"Hear It Now," 153
"Hee Haw," 200, 254, 255, 257
Heifetz, Jascha, 25
Helms, Jesse, 296, 299, 310
Henning, Paul, 227
Hewitt, Don, 127–28, 159, 164–66, 211, 244–48, 272, 274–75, 307
Hicks, James, 139
Hilgemeier, Ed, 186
Hill, George Washington, 25
Hitler, Adolf, 33, 35, 61, 65–66, 69–71, 80, 86–88, 134
Hobson, Laura Z., 174
Hodge, Herbert, 57
"Hogan's Heroes," 255
Hollenbeck, Don, 113, 173

O

O'Connor, Carroll, 256
"Old Gold Program," 27
"Omnibus," 244
"On a Note of Triumph," 105
"On the Road with Charles Kuralt," 237, 265, 285
Oppenheimer, J. Robert, 176-78
Ormandy, Eugene, 220
Overend, Bill, 209

P

Paar, Jack, 131
Paley, Blanche, 2, 8
Paley, Goldie, 2
Paley, Jacob, 3-5
Paley, Samuel, 2-5
Paley, William S., 23-34, 37, 42, 44-47, 51, 61-65, 74, 85, 89-90, 93, 101-3, 107-20, 130, 135, 137, 144-46, 149-52, 158, 171-79, 188-90, 195-200, 204-8, 210-11, 223-29, 235, 254, 259, 268-71, 276-83, 286, 292-93, 297-301, 304, 309-13, 320-22
   early involvement in CBS, 10-22
   marital history, 46
   purchase of CBS, 11
   reaction to "All in the Family," 257
   Smothers Brothers Show and, 242
   Watergate scandal and, 268-70
Pappas, Ike, 315, 317
Parnis, Molly, 312
Paulsen, Pat, 240
Peabody Award, 105, 126, 142, 202

"Person to Person," 169-70, 174-75, 189, 191-92
"Personal Closeup," 214
Peters Roberta, 132
"Petticoat Junction," 197, 227
Phillip, Carl, 76-77
Pierpoint, Robert, 156
Pike, Otis, 275
Pinza, Ezio, 25
"Playhouse 90," 199-200
"The Plot to Overthrow Christmas," 81
Polk, George, 111-12
Pons, Lily, 25
Popular Library, Inc., acquisition of, 226
Potter, Ned, 315
Power, Ron, 210
Prentiss, Paula, 227
Presley, Elvis, 121, 131
Program analysis system, 51

Q

Quinn, Jane Bryant, 315
Quinn, Lt. Gen. William, 230
Quinn, Sally, 231, 271-72
Quiz show rigging scandal, 186-88

R

Radio
   alleged Communist influence, 136
   early advertising, 4
   extensive use of, 106-7
   first broadcast, 3
   initial problems in, 7-10
Radio Corporation of America (RCA), 6-7, 15, 26, 97, 120, 151